CAREER OPPORTUNITIES IN EDUCATION AND RELATED SERVICES

Second Edition

SUSAN ECHAORE-MCDAVID

Checkmark Books®
An imprint of Infobase Publishing

To two wonderful friends —
Kathy Ferguson Siudzinski,
who planted the seed in my head
(many years ago when we were teenagers)
that maybe I could write for a living,
and
Winifred Ho Roderman,
who took the chance and taught me
how to make it come true!

Career Opportunities in Education and Related Services, Second Edition

Copyright © 2006, 2001 by Susan Echaore-McDavid

Checkmark Books
An imprint of Infobase Publishing
132 West 31st Street
New York NY 10001

For Library of Congress Cataloging-in-Publication Data, please contact the publisher.

ISBN 0-8160-6155-6

Checkmark Books are available at special discounts when purchased in bulk quantities for businesses, associations, institutions, or sales promotions. Please call our Special Sales Department in New York at (212) 967-8800 or (800) 322-8755.

You can find Facts On File on the World Wide Web at http://www.factsonfile.com

Cover design by Nora Wertz

Printed in the United States of America

VB Hermitage 10 9 8 7 6 5 4 3 2 1

This book is printed on acid-free paper.

CONTENTS

ACKNOWLEDGMENTS

I would like to thank the following people and organizations who helped me learn about the various occupations for this second edition of *Career Opportunities in Education and Related Services:* Karen E. Breseman, Association Administrator, International Association of Campus Law Enforcement Administrators; Herb Fong, Grounds Manager, Stanford University; Carol Ann Hanshaw, Hanshaw Ink & Image; Jim Loter; Connie McReynolds, Ph.D., CRC, Licensed Psychologist; The National Rehabilitation Counseling Association; Kevin O'Donnell, Superintendent of Grounds for Villanova University; The Professional Grounds Management Society; Donna Reiman; Priscilla A. Stevens, Director of Public Safety, University of Wisconsin River Falls, President, International Association of Campus Law Enforcement Administrators 2005–06; and Larry Yant, Sports Deputy Editor, *San Francisco Chronicle.*

I would also like to express my thanks to the editorial and production crew at Facts On File, especially Sarah Fogarty and Vanessa Nittoli. Most of all, my deepest appreciation to James Chambers, who is the kind of editor every author ought to have. Last, but not least, thank you, dear Richard A. McDavid, for being you!

And once again, I want to acknowledge the following people and organizations who helped me learn about the many occupations in this book while I was writing the first edition.

DiAnn K. Adams, Career Technician, Indian Trails Career Cooperative/Twin Lakes High School, Monticello, Indiana; Dory Adams; Joan Adams, St. James School, Montgomery, Alabama; Lori Arkin-Diem, Manager of Education and Community Programs, Animal Services, American Humane Association; Andrea Babbitt; Dana Barchak, Rapid City, South Dakota; Tim Bedley, Temecula Valley Unified School District; Laura Black, St. Mary Elementary School, Winchester, Massachusetts; Michelle Y. Blassengale, M.M.E.; L. Gaye Botts, Driver/Safety Trainer; Ursula Boyle, The Little Red Schoolhouse, Medford, Massachusetts; Tamora K. Brewer, Assistant Principal, Tzouanakis Intermediate School, Greencastle, Indiana; Janis Brock; Elyse Brown; Willeen W. Buchholz, Counseling Coordinator, West Irondequoit Central School District, Rochester, New York; Christina Burkart, Coquitlam District 43, Coquitlam, B.C., Canada; Gene Cain, Resource Teacher, Strategic Planning, The School Board of Broward County, Florida; David W. Carlson, President, DynoTech Software; Shelley Chambers.

Helen Chance, Statesboro, Georgia; Ken R. Churches, Director and Farm Advisor, Calaveras County, California; Stan Clark, President, Association of College Administration Professionals; Coalition of National Health Education Organizations; Sharon Conley, National Association of School Nurses; Valerie Cornelius, Ashtabula, Ohio; Tina Daberkow, Member Service Coordinator, American Association of School Administrators; James J. D'Anza; Jill Davis, Pre-K Teacher, Allen Bowden School, Tulsa, Oklahoma; Karen DeBord, Ph.D., Associate Professor and State Specialist, Child Development, North Carolina State University; Valerie Dehombreux, Cradleboard Elementary, Whiteriver, Arizona; Sheryl Dickstein, Ph.D., Director of Humane Education, ASPCA; Mrs. Sandra Di Ponio, Muir Middle School, Milford, Michigan; Laura Dowling; Peggy Drechsler, Area Specialized Dairy Agent, North Carolina Cooperative Extension Service; Tom Drummond, Child and Family Education Division, North Seattle Community College; Bess Emanuel, Director Credential Liaison, Center for Career Development in Early Care and Education, Wheelock College, Boston, Massachusetts; Lisa A. Estee; Maureen E. Farr, Snips and Snails Preschool, Port Jervis, New York; Paula Ferland, M.Ed., College of Education Faculty, East Tennessee State University; Zelandia Fero; Karen E. Finkel, Executive Director, National School Transportation Association.

Ken Fox; Charmiane Freeman; Susan Galletti, Associate Executive Director, National Association of Secondary School Principals; Linda Gallipoli; Natalie Gamboa; Bev Garcia, Educational Technology Specialist, Cornell College; Mrs. Mary J. Gasch, Nerinx Hall High School, Webster Groves, Missouri; Phoebe Gillespie, Ph.D., Recruitment/Retention Outreach Manager, National Clearinghouse for Professions in Special Education, Council for Exceptional Children; Terry Gilman, M.Ed., K-8 School Counselor, Lynden Christian School, Lynden, Washington; Teresa Glenn, Larinburg, North Carolina; Margaret W. Goldsborough, Director of Public Information and Resource Development, National Association of Independent Schools; Nancy Golubic, Market Street School, Boardman, Ohio; Jim Goske; Jodi Gullicksrud, Eleva-Strum School District, Wisconsin; Diane L. Harney, Administrative Assistant, National Office, American Art Therapy Association, Inc.; Wayne Hashiguchi, Principal, Denny Middle School, Seattle, Washington; Scott Hawbaker, Executive Assistant, National Association of County Agricultural Agents.

Patricia Herbel, Elementary Principal, St. Leo's Elementary School, Minot, North Dakota; Darrel Hess, Chairperson, Earth Sciences Department, City College of San Francisco, San Francisco, California; Stacey Hild, Elementary Music Teacher, North Carolina; Deanna Homer, Language Lab Supervisor, Oklahoma State University; Gen Hooper; Deborah House, Career Guidance Technician, Fayetteville Technical Community College, North Carolina; Carrie Howren; Teresa Ilgunas, Technology Coordinator, Jefferson School, Lennox School District; Alice Iverson; Jerry Jerman, Director of Marketing and Communication, College of Continuing Education, The University of Oklahoma; Denise Jessup; Jeff Johnson, District Technology Coordinator, Greendale School District, Greendale, Wisconsin; Karl Johnson, Technology Coordinator, Tipton Community Schools, Tipton, Iowa; Melanie Johnson, Recruitment and Career Development Representative, American Speech-Language-Hearing Association; Sandra Kangas, Director, Child & Adult Nutrition Services—DECA, Pierre, South Dakota; Nancy J. Keane, Rundlett Middle School; Terry L. Keeneth, ANR Educator (Gibson County), Purdue University; Rachel Kramer, Assistant Executive Director, Programs and Convention, Music Teachers National Association; Kirsten Lincoln; Amy Lindsay, Information Services Assistant, MENC: The National Association for Music Education; Mary-Jo MacRae-Smith, Technology Mentor, New Brunswick Department of Education, New Brunswick, Canada.

Ina Lynn McClain, State 4-H Youth Development Specialist, Columbia, Missouri; Tharon McDavid; Linda M. McGuire, Technology Coordinator, Au Sable Valley Central School; Jonanne Haynes Manogue, M.S., Department of Kinesiology, University of Wisconsin-Madison; Ron Markley, Trainer/Director, Camelot K-9 Academy, Loma, Colorado; Dianne Martinez; Eloisa Maria Martinez, Information Specialist and Administrative Assistant, Lamaze International; Brian Meegan, High School Principal and College Counselor, Bilkent University Prep School, Ankara, Turkey; Joseph Metzler, Assistant Contract Manager, Ryder Student Transportation Inc.; Carol Mezzacappa, Director, Young Dancers In Repertory and Dance Consort; Pam Michael, MBA, RD, Director, Networks Team, American Dietetic Association; Lori J. Moore, First-grade Teacher; Lawrence D. Newell, Ed.D., NREMT-P, Educational Consultant, National Safety Council; New York State Coalition for Health Education; Bonnie J. Nichols; Larry Olsen, Professor, Towson University, Towson, Maryland.

Colleen Pace, President, American Association of Riding Schools; Randy Palmer, North Mankato, Minnesota; Jim Pennington; Nancy Perry, Executive Director, American School Counselor Association; Dorothy Peselli; Beth Powell, Director, Public Policy and Legislation, American Mental Health Counselors Association; Doug Prouty, Contra Costa County Office of Education, California; Donna Ransdell, Ramona Unified School District, California; Sue Rarus, Manager, Information Services, MENC: The National Association for Music Education; Claudia Readwright; Becky Reed; Kathleen Remington, Masters of Education, Adjunct Faculty, Salt Lake Community College; Donna Richert, Our Lady Immaculate Catholic School; Winifred Ho Roderman; June Roman, Special Education Team Leader/Life Skills Teacher, Georgetown Middle School Georgetown, Kentucky; Bonnie Rubinstein; Allen Russell, Physical Educator, Columbine Elementary School, Grand Junction, Colorado.

Michele Schindler, M.Ed., N.C.C., Harborview Elementary Counselor, Juneau, Alaska; School Social Work Association of America; Viviane Scnhupbach; Bonni Schwiderson, Marquette, Michigan; Susan J. Scollay, Ph.D., Associate Professor and Director of Graduate Studies, Department of Administration and Supervision, University of Kentucky; Rhonda Shafer, 4-H Youth Specialist, University of Missouri Outreach and Extension; Elisa M. Simon, M.Ed., Secondary School Counselor, Lampeter-Strasburg High School, Lampeter, Pennsylvania; Kathy Ferguson Siudzinski; Sheryl Skufca, Library/Media Specialist; Julian A. Spain, Kubasaki High School, Department of Defense Dependents Schools—Pacific, Okinawa, Japan; Jenine Stanley, President, Guide Dog Users Inc.; Glenn Sterley; Laurie Thomas, Seventh Grade Teacher, Valley Jr. High, Carlsbad, California; Dana Topousis, Peace Corps Public Affairs Specialist; Ted Tull, Administrative Director, National Association for State Directors for Pupil Transportation Services.

Marilynn Vandor; Jennifer Vega, Secondary Technology Specialist/Curriculum Integrator, Malverne Union Free School District, Malverne, New York; Lawrence Vincent, Michigan Certified Teacher, Engadine, Michigan; Deborah Walsh; Elizabeth Warson, ATR-BC, LPC; Jim Watson, accredited NAPWDA Master Trainer and Mentor, Police K-9 Unit-Retired (Ohio); Virginia Webb, Coordinator, On Site Services, National Food Services Management Institute, University of Mississippi; Mary Jo Weisenburger, Grade 8; Jennifer Johnson, Eighth-Grade Mathematics, Waluga Junior High School, Lake Oswego, Oregon; Fred Wesson, Director, American International School of Bucharest; Rosemary West, past president of the Educational Software Cooperative; Riley Whitsett, Teacher/Coordinator Marketing Education; Barbara A. Wilmer, Programs Division, National Association of Elementary School Principals; Nancy Wise; Tom Woods, Corrections Educator; Kimberlee Woodward, Substitute Teacher, Michigan; and Marc Zimmerman.

Thank you!

HOW TO USE THIS BOOK

In *Career Opportunities in Education and Related Services,* you will learn about 103 occupations in school and nonschool settings. They include teachers, administrators, counselors, student service specialists, librarians, technology specialists, curriculum developers, support staff, and others.

For each profession, you'll learn what the job is like. You'll learn what basic requirements are needed to enter the profession. You'll also learn what the salary, job market, and advancement prospects are like for a profession. Perhaps after reading some, or all, of the professions in this book, you'll find one that is right for you.

Sources of Information

The information presented in *Career Opportunities in Education and Related Services* comes from a variety of sources. They include:

- Web sites of schools, colleges, universities, professional associations, federal agencies, libraries, and other organizations and businesses
- personal webpages of various professionals
- interviews with professionals and professional organizations
- questionnaires answered by professional individuals and organizations
- books about the different professions
- professional textbooks, handbooks, and manuals
- newspapers, magazines, and professional journals
- brochures, pamphlets, and other written materials from professional associations and firms, federal agencies, and other organizations

How This Book is Organized

Career Opportunities in Education and Related Services is designed to be easy to use and read. The 103 jobs are divided into 19 sections. A section may have three to 10 job profiles, and the profiles are between two and three pages long. Each profile follows the same format so that you can read the job profiles or sections in any order that you prefer.

Sections one through 10 discuss many familiar and not-so-familiar teacher, administrator, specialist, and support staff professions found in educational institutions, from preschools to universities. Sections 11 through 19 describe various types of educators and education-related professions that are found both in traditional school settings as well as in nontraditional settings such as companies, government agencies, libraries, parks, and outdoor settings.

The Job Profiles

The job profiles give you basic information about 103 occupations. Each job profile starts with *Career Profile,* a summary of a job's major duties, salary, job outlook, and promotion possibilities. It also sums up general requirements needed for a job, as well as special skills and personality traits that these professionals usually possess. The *Career Ladder* section is a visual presentation of a typical career path, showing what positions lead to and stem from the job being profiled.

The rest of the job profile is a narrative description that is divided into the following parts:

- The "Position Description" details a job's major responsibilities and duties and provides information about working conditions.
- "Salaries" presents a general idea of the wages that workers may earn. Most salary information comes from the U.S. Bureau of Labor Statistics.
- "Employment Prospects" describes potential employers and the job outlook for an occupation.
- "Advancement Prospects" discusses promotional career prospects and suggestions for alternative career paths.
- "Education and Tranining" describes the type of diploma or degree that is needed to enter a profession. The section also discusses any training programs that may need to be completed.
- "Special Requirements" details any license, certification, or registration that may be required for a profession.
- "Experience, Special Skills, and Personality Traits" discusses the minimum experience requirements that are needed for a job. It also describes some employability skills that employers desire in candidates. In addition, this section mentions some personality traits that successful professionals have in common.
- "Unions and Associations" gives the names of some national organizations that professionals might join.
- "Tips for Entry" presents advice for finding jobs; suggestions for improving employability; and ways to find out more information on the Internet.

The Appendixes

At the end of the book are five appendixes that provide additional information about the various occupations profiled in *Career Opportunities in Education and Related Services.*

In Appendix I, you can learn about resources on the Internet where you can find information about academic or training programs for some of the occupations in this book. In Appendix II, you can read about what is needed to teach in public schools, and in Appendix III, you will find a listing of state educational offices that grant licensure for teachers, administrators, and teaching specialists. Contact information for professional associations and unions described in the profiles can be found in Appendix IV, and a listing of resources on the World Wide Web for many of the occupations is available in Appendix V. Furthermore, a bibliography and index are included at the back of the book.

The Constantly Changing World Wide Web

Resources on the Internet are provided throughout the book so that you can learn more on your own about occupations that interest you. All the Web sites were accessible as the book was being written. Keep in mind that Web site owners sometimes change their URL or remove their sites completely. Most Web sites are continually being updated, therefore, a webpage to which you have been referred may no longer be available. If you come across a URL that no longer works, you may still be able to find the new Web address by entering the name of the organization, individual, Web site, or webpage into a search engine.

This Book Is Yours

Career Opportunities in Education and Related Services is your reference book. Use it to read about jobs you have often wondered about. Use it to learn about educational professions that you never knew existed. Use it to start your search for the career of your dreams.

Good luck!

INTRODUCTION

Do you want a career in education? Are you puzzled about which profession to enter? Maybe you would like to be a teacher. Maybe not. Actually, the education industry offers a wide range of career opportunities—teaching as well as nonteaching professions. Most opportunities are found in public and private schools, two-year colleges, four-year colleges, and universities. Many opportunities are also found in businesses, corporations, government agencies, community agencies, nonprofit organizations, hospitals, museums, zoos, parks, fitness facilities, dance studios, resorts, recreational facilities, and many other settings outside of educational institutions.

Let's first look at some of the types of teaching professions that are available. In educational institutions, various instructors teach a wide variety of academic, vocational, and other subjects. They teach students of different ages and different grades from prekindergartners to doctoral candidates. Many teachers are specialists who provide instruction to students with special learning, reading, and language needs. Some of these teachers are special education teachers, reading specialists, bilingual teachers, ESL (English as a second language) teachers, and adult education teachers.

Teachers in nonschool settings provide a wide range of instructional services for their employers. In nonschool settings, teachers generally go by titles such as trainers, educators, instructors, or guides. They may work with employees, customers, clients, patients, or the general public on an individual basis or in groups. Some may work with animals and their handlers. Some teaching professionals in nonschool settings are corporate trainers, technical trainers, health educators, recreational leaders, personal trainers, environmental educators, dance instructors, tour guides, riding instructors, and guide dog trainers.

Now let's look at the different types of nonteaching professions. In both school and nonschool settings, educational administrators are needed to plan, coordinate, organize, manage, and oversee educational programs, departments, divisions, or institutions so that they run efficiently and effectively each day. Educational administrators may be supervisors, coordinators, directors, managers, or chief executive officers.

Educational specialists and support staff are other types of nonteaching professions. In both school and nonschool settings, they provide various types of services to assist educators, administrators, and students or clientele. They may assist with teaching, perform administrative support duties, provide counseling services, develop curriculum or instructional materials, maintain educational resources, develop technol-

ogy resources, and so on. School psychologists, school nurses, educational technology specialists, instructional designers, academic librarians, educational diagnosticians, college career counselors, teacher aides, and bus drivers are some professions that you would find in educational institutions. Among those in nonschool settings are public librarians, employment counselors, textbook editors, educational software developers, nutritionists, and training developers.

Opportunities are also available for experienced educators, administrators, and specialists who wish to become self-employed or business owners. Teachers, for example, may become private tutors or teach private classes. Some other professionals who might choose to become self-employed are music teachers, flight instructors, personal trainers, dog trainers, textbook editors, educational software developers, childbirth educators, employment counselors, reading specialists, or art therapists. The success of freelancers and business owners depends on their ambition, business know-how, the local demand for their particular educational services, and other factors.

As you can see, there are many options in the education industry. The next step is to start learning about some of the various professions to find ones that interest you. In *Career Opportunities in Education and Related Services,* you will learn about occupations in school and nonschool settings.

What's New in the Second Edition
Several new job profiles and a new appendix, "How to Become a Public School Teacher," have been added to the second edition of *Career Opportunities in Education and Related Services.* In addition, all the original profiles have been updated with information about salaries, employment prospects, job requirements, and job duties. Furthermore, contact information and Web site addresses have been updated in the appendixes.

Job Outlook
In 2002, the educational services industry was the second-largest industry in the nation, according to the U.S. Bureau of Labor Statistics (BLS), an agency within the U.S. Department of Labor. This industry employed about 12.7 million workers, including salaried employees and self-employed workers, mostly in the public sector. Almost half of all workers in this industry are teachers.

The BLS predicts that the employment growth for wage and salary employees in the education services industry should increase by 20 percent through the 2002–12 period. According to the BLS, 47 percent of employees in this industry are over the age of 45 years. Consequently, many opportunities for teachers, administrators, support staff, and other employees should be available in the years to come as those older employees retire.

Job growth varies with the different occupations. For example, the BLS reports that employment through 2012 is expected to grow:

- over 36 percent for postsecondary teachers, self-enrichment instructors, fitness trainers, and aerobics instructors
- between 21 and 35 percent for preschool teachers, kindergarten teachers, special education teachers, coaches, adult education teachers, teacher assistants, school administrators, education administrators in higher education, instructional coordinators, librarians, rehabilitation counselors, health educators, occupational therapists, speech-language pathologists, and training specialists and managers
- between 10 and 20 percent for elementary school teachers, secondary school teachers, school counselors, vocational counselors, school psychologists, school social workers, child care workers, computer support specialists, school bus drivers, and janitors

Many job openings will also be created as workers advance to higher positions, transfer to other occupations, retire, or leave the work force for various reasons. Keep in mind that employers may create new jobs as their needs grow as long as funding is available. Usually, when employers are faced with tight budgets, they hire fewer employees and sometimes lay off workers.

The Changing World of Education

You should know that the education industry is constantly creating new jobs to meet the needs of society. For example, in the 1970s, these professions were rare or did not exist at all in education: bilingual teacher, computer teacher, instructional technology specialist, special education technology specialist, school occupational therapist, art therapist, environmental educator, aerobics instructor, or childbirth educator. Today, all these professions are in demand.

Another thing to keep in mind about many professions is that roles may change with time. For example, school counselors today are found at all school levels and provide personal counseling as well as academic and vocational counseling. In decades past, school counselors mostly worked in high schools, providing academic and vocational counseling. Sometimes a role change is reflected by a profession's job title. An example of a relatively recent title change is that of the school librarian. In most schools, this position is called a school library-media specialist because this profession manages both print and technology resources in a combination library and multimedia center.

A Note about Private Schools

In this book, you will learn that many of the teaching, administrative, specialist, and support staff positions in public K–12 schools are also found in private K–12 schools. Private schools include day schools, boarding schools, and military academies, as well as parochial schools (those that are affiliated with a religious denomination, such as Roman Catholic, Lutheran, or Seventh-Day Adventist). Private schools may be coeducational, girls-only, or boys-only. They may be of any size or any configuration of grade levels.

Although the term *private school* is used throughout *Career Opportunities in Education and Related Services,* you should be aware that some private schools are also known as independent schools. Independent schools are not part of or connected to any other organization. Independent schools have their own boards of trustees, and develop their own sources of funding.

Start Exploring Your Options

Career Opportunities in Education and Related Services provides you with basic general information about 103 professions in education. When you come across occupations that interest you, take the time to learn more about them. You might read books that explore a profession in more depth. You might check out magazines and journals that professionals read for their work. If possible, talk with professionals about their jobs. Perhaps they might let you observe them at work.

In addition, use the Internet to continue your research. Check out personal Web sites of professionals. Many discuss their jobs and provide links to other Web sites that have information about their professions. Also, visit Web sites for the types of workplaces (schools, hospitals, libraries, parks, fitness centers, and so forth) in which you are interested. You can get an idea of what it may be like to work in such a setting.

Furthermore, get hands-on experience in different educational settings to help you decide what occupation—and career—may be right for you. For example, you might volunteer to tutor younger children at your school. If you participate in recreational programs, scouting, or Sunday school, offer to help lead activities from time to time. You can also volunteer or obtain part-time or summer work with a child care center, school, library, or educational program in a park, zoo, museum, community agency, health care center, or another place that interests you.

As you explore various occupations, you will discover careers you may or may not like. You will also be gaining valuable knowledge and experience. In addition, you will be building a network of contacts who may be able to help you find jobs as well as advise you with your career.

May you have the best of luck in the pursuit of your career goals and dreams!

PRE-K–12 TEACHERS

EARLY CHILDHOOD TEACHER

CAREER PROFILE

Duties: Nurture and educate infants and young children; create activities that develop social, physical, and intellectual growth; perform other duties as required

Alternate Title(s): Preschool Teacher, Prekindergarten Teacher, Child Care Teacher

Salary Range: $15,000 to $37,000

Employment Prospects: Excellent

Advancement Prospects: Good

Prerequisites:

Education or Training—Associate's or bachelor's degree

Experience—One or more years of working in a child care setting

Special Skills and Personality Traits—Teamwork, interpersonal, communication, organizational, and management skills; be trustworthy, tactful, open-minded, patient, gentle, energetic, flexible, persevering, and creative

Special Requirements—A teaching license or professional certification may be required

CAREER LADDER

```
┌─────────────────────────────────────┐
│  Early Childhood Program Director or │
│       Elementary School Teacher      │
└─────────────────────────────────────┘

┌─────────────────────────────────────┐
│        Early Childhood Teacher       │
└─────────────────────────────────────┘

┌─────────────────────────────────────┐
│       Assistant Teacher or Intern    │
└─────────────────────────────────────┘
```

Position Description

Early Childhood Teachers work in child care centers, home daycare programs, preschools, nursery schools, Head Start programs, and prekindergarten programs. Their primary responsibility is to nurture and educate infants and young children during the hours that the children's parents need to be at work or school. The number of hours that children are under the supervision of an Early Childhood Teacher varies according to the needs of their families. For example, one child might stay at a child care center for three hours twice a week while another child might stay for 10 hours five days a week.

Different Early Childhood Teachers work with different age groups from newborn infants to five-year-olds. State regulations limit the number of infants and children for which each teacher may be responsible. In some states, infant teachers may supervise six to eight babies while teachers of toddlers and preschoolers may supervise 10 to 20 children.

Many Early Childhood Teachers work with children who receive special instruction and related services for their physical, emotional, or learning disabilities. With these children, teachers must follow specific goals and objectives outlined on children's Individualized Education Programs (IEPs) that are developed by teachers and specialists such as school psychologists, special education teachers, and school nurses. Early Childhood Teachers may consult special education teachers and other specialists for advice on implementing the IEPs.

Early Childhood Teachers establish a relationship with each child and help each child develop socially, physically, emotionally, intellectually, aesthetically, and morally. They are able to encourage children to explore and be creative, yet guide them with gentle firmness and discipline. For infants, toddlers, and preschoolers, learning is done through play, questioning, observation, exploration, and discovery. Thus, teachers provide experiences and activities that help children use their powerful imagination and curiosity. Teachers develop a curriculum that introduces infants and young children to literacy, numbers, science, social studies, art, music, health, nutrition, technology, and other areas that affect their lives and the world around them. They try to work with all children every day in large groups, small groups, and on an individual basis.

Early Childhood Teachers make sure all activities, materials, and toys are developmentally age-appropriate for the children they work with. In addition, they plan activities that help children develop fine motor skills (such as holding crayons, drawing circles, and buttoning their jackets) and gross motor skills (such as running, hopping, jumping, walking, and skipping). Early Childhood Teachers also help children develop healthy and proper habits for eating, washing hands, putting toys away, and so on. In addition, they teach children social skills to get along with others.

Teachers create a daily routine so that children have an idea of what to expect. They plan different types of activities throughout the day—story time, outside play time, large group activities (such as singing or performing finger puppet plays), small group activities, independent activities, meals and naps.

Most Early Childhood Teachers create learning centers to develop different skills, to explore different subject areas, and to develop imagination. Simple, yet challenging, activities are developed for each learning center. Children can quickly get into the activities with few directions. Teachers change the activities daily or weekly, basing them on weekly themes, such as rain, autumn leaves, trains, or Chinese New Year.

As one of their major duties, Early Childhood Teachers observe the children, assessing and evaluating each child's development. They adapt instruction, each child's materials, or space to accommodate needs. When necessary, they discipline children according to school policies. Early Childhood Teachers also are ready to respond to any emergency situation.

Because parents are children's primary teachers, Early Childhood Teachers keep in constant communication with parents. They consult with parents about their children's needs as well as discuss their children's growth and development in general. Teachers try to make contact with parents daily, by either talking with them or sending them notes, to let them know what happened with their children that day.

Early Childhood Teachers also perform various nonteaching duties. For example, they attend and participate in faculty meetings, perform administrative tasks (such as taking attendance), and train and supervise aides and volunteers.

Early Childhood Teachers work part time or full time. Those employed by child care centers usually work year-round while many employed by preschools and public school programs normally work a 10-month schedule.

Salaries

Earnings for Early Childhood Teachers vary, depending on such factors as their education, credentials, experience, employer, and geographical location. According to the November 2004 *Occupational Employment Statistics* (OES)

survey, by the U.S. Bureau of Labor Statistics (BLS), the estimated annual salary for most preschool teachers ranged between $14,540 and $37,470.

Employment Prospects

Early Childhood Teachers work for public and private early childhood care and education programs. Many teachers are employed by programs run by public schools, higher education institutions, churches, and hospitals. Some work in child care services that businesses, corporations, government agencies, and other organizations offer to their employees or customers. According to the November 2004 OES survey, by the BLS, about 350,000 preschool teachers were employed in the United States.

The job outlook is favorable for Early Childhood Teachers. The turnover is high due to the low pay and demanding working conditions. Replacements are also needed for teachers who retire or advance to higher positions. Additional positions will be created by existing and new programs to meet the growing needs for services in their communities. Furthermore the need for teachers may increase in states that decide to make preschool mandatory for four-year-olds.

Advancement Prospects

Early Childhood Teachers can advance to head teacher, teacher/assistant director, and program director positions. Generally, continuing education units are needed to advance further. Many teachers pursue advancement by earning bachelor's or master's degrees and teaching credentials to obtain better paying positions in public or private schools. Some Early Childhood Teachers start their own early childhood programs. Some other career options are becoming university professors, researchers, or consultants in early childhood care and education.

Education and Training

Applicants for public school positions must possess a bachelor's degree in any field. Some employers prefer applicants to possess a master's degree in early childhood education, or show they are pursuing this degree. Applicants must also have completed a teacher education program in either early childhood education or elementary education that fulfills the requirements for the appropriate state teaching license.

The requirements in private and community-based settings vary from possession of a high school or general equivalency diploma to completion of a minimum number of units in early childhood education, to having an associate's or bachelor's degree. Some employers require that applicants successfully complete their own teacher training program.

Throughout their careers, Early Childhood Teachers enroll in courses, workshops, and seminars to increase their knowledge and update their skills, as well as to renew their professional licensure or certification.

Special Requirements

In most private settings, applicants are required to possess a professional certificate granted by either the prospective employer or by a recognized professional organization. Many private and community-based early childhood programs require applicants to possess the Child Development Associate (CDA) certificate. This voluntary credential may be obtained through community colleges, community agencies, or professional associations. Some child care employers prefer their teachers to possess the Certified Childcare Professional (CCP) credential from the National Child Care Association.

Applicants for public school positions must usually be state licensed teachers with a credential in either early education or elementary education. Requirements for teaching licenses vary from state to state. For specific information, contact the state board of education for the state where you wish to work. See Appendix III for a list of state boards.

Experience, Skills, and Personality Traits

Most employers require that applicants have at least one year of work experience as a child care aide or teaching assistant in a child care or preschool setting. They should also have a broad knowledge of the subjects—math, science, social studies, music, art, health, and so on—that they will be introducing to children.

Along with teaching skills, Early Childhood Teachers need strong teamwork, interpersonal, and communication skills to interact well with children, parents, and other staff members. They also need good organizational and management skills to complete all their duties and tasks each day. Being trustworthy, tactful, open-minded, patient, gentle, energetic, flexible, persevering, and creative are some personality traits that successful Early Childhood Teachers have in common.

Unions and Associations

Many Early Childhood Teachers belong to professional associations to take advantage of networking opportunities, education programs, and other professional services and resources. Some national societies that many teachers join are the National Head Start Association, the National Association for the Education of Young Children, the National Child Care Association, and the Council for Exceptional Children. See Appendix IV for contact information for these organizations.

Tips for Entry

1. Get practical experience working with infants, toddlers, and preschoolers before entering the early childhood field.

2. Many early childhood programs advertise job openings in neighborhood newspapers. Look in the classified job ads under "teacher." You might also call or visit programs directly and talk with the program director about vacancies.

3. To enhance their employability and advancement prospects, many teachers obtain the CDA certificate. For further information, contact the Council for Professional Recognition, 2460 16th Street, NW, Washington, DC 20009. You may also visit its Web site at http://www.cdacouncil.org.

4. You can learn more about early childhood education on the Internet. You might start by visiting these Web sites: National Association for the Education of Young Children, http://www.naeyc.org; Zero to Three (by the National Center for Infants, Toddlers and Families), http://www.zerotothree.org; National Child Care Association, http://www.nccanet.org; and Preschool Education.Com, http://www.preschooleducation.com.

KINDERGARTEN TEACHER

CAREER PROFILE

Duties: Teach simple academic concepts and skills to five- and six-year-olds; create daily lesson plans; perform other duties as required

Alternate Title(s): None

Salary Range: $28,000 to $68,000

Employment Prospects: Good

Advancement Prospects: Good

Prerequisites:

Education or Training—Bachelor's degree; for licensed teachers, completion of an accredited teacher education program

Experience—Student teaching, internship, or other teaching experience

Special Skills and Personality Traits—Communication, teamwork, interpersonal, organizational, and management skills; be patient, creative, flexible, enthusiastic, and energetic

Special Requirements—Teaching credential or other certification

CAREER LADDER

```
┌─────────────────────────────┐
│  Mentor Teacher or          │
│  administrative position    │
└─────────────────────────────┘

┌─────────────────────────────┐
│  Kindergarten Teacher       │
└─────────────────────────────┘

┌───────────────────────────────────┐
│ Student Teacher or Substitute Teacher │
└───────────────────────────────────┘
```

Position Description

In both public and private schools, kindergarten is part of the elementary school level. (Kindergarten is usually abbreviated as *K,* as in K through grade 3.) For many five- and six-year-olds, kindergarten is their first school experience. Thus, a Kindergarten Teacher's first teaching goal is to help children become comfortable and accustomed to a formal classroom setting. Unlike in the other elementary grades, kindergartners learn mostly through concrete experiences, hands-on activities, and play.

Kindergarten Teachers may have anywhere from 15 to 30 students in their class. They are responsible for teaching all academic subjects, art, music, and physical education. (In some schools, specialists teach the latter three subjects.) For their special education students (children with learning, emotional, or physical disabilities), Kindergarten Teachers follow certain instructional goals and objectives that are outlined on students' Individualized Education Programs (IEPs). Kindergarten Teachers may be also involved in pro-

viding assessments of special education students, as well as helping develop IEPs.

Kindergarten Teachers develop their curriculum based on school guidelines. They create daily lesson plans that describe what concepts and skills would be taught on a particular day and how the teacher plans to instruct the students. Many Kindergarten Teachers set up several learning centers to involve students in activities that teach basic concepts and skills in math, reading, writing, science, and other subjects.

To help students feel secure, Kindergarten Teachers establish a daily routine so that students know what activities follow each other. Teachers designate blocks of time for different activities—reading, writing, math, science, art, physical education, health and so on. Each activity usually lasts 10 to 15 minutes because of children's short attention spans. Teachers will also alternate activities to accommodate children's need to move about from time to time. In addition, teachers plan activities for the whole class, for small groups, and for the individual student.

Kindergarten Teachers also complete other duties. They assess each student's development and keep parents informed of their child's progress. They take attendance and do other administrative tasks. They may supervise hallways, lunchrooms, and other school areas during recess and lunch times. They may also supervise and direct teacher aides, student teachers, and parent volunteers. Furthermore, they participate in faculty meetings and school committees.

Kindergarten Teachers teach half-day sessions (between 2.5 and 3.5 hours) or full-day sessions (6 hours). However, they put in many more hours to complete all their tasks— making lesson plans, contacting parents, attending meetings, and so on. Most Kindergarten Teachers have a 10-month work schedule, from September to June; some have a year-round work schedule.

In most public school systems, teachers receive tenure after completing three to five years of continuous teaching service. With tenure, teachers cannot be fired without just cause.

Salaries

Salaries for Kindergarten Teachers vary, depending on such factors as their credentials, education, experience, employer, and geographical location. The U.S. Bureau of Labor Statistics (BLS) reports in its November 2004 *Occupational Employment Statistics* (OES) survey that the estimated annual salary for most Kindergarten Teachers ranged between $27,570 and $67,730.

Employment Prospects

The BLS reports in its November 2004 OES survey that an estimated 164,800 Kindergarten Teachers were employed in the United States. Most job openings become available as teachers retire, transfer to other schools, or advance to higher positions.

Teaching jobs are expected to be favorable through 2012 due to the large number of teachers becoming eligible for retirement. However, opportunities vary by region and communities. Opportunities are particularly stronger in inner cities and rural areas as well in fast-growing states in the South and West, where schools are expected to have the largest increases in enrollment. Opportunities may also increase in states that decide to reduce class size and/or implement all-day kindergarten.

Advancement Prospects

Kindergarten Teachers have several ways to advance their careers. Experienced teachers can become mentor teachers, providing guidance to beginning teachers. With additional education and endorsements, elementary school teachers in public schools can teach special subjects (such as art and physical education) or teach in special areas (such as bilingual education and special education). They can also become counselors, educational technologists, or other school-related professionals.

School administration is also another career path. In private schools, teachers can become school heads, deans of students, or other administrators. In public schools, teachers can become school principals and central office administrators with additional education and credentials.

Kindergarten Teachers might also enter other areas of education. For example, they may become adult education instructors, corporate trainers, or educational software developers.

Education and Training

Kindergarten Teachers usually have a bachelor's degree in a liberal arts field. To become licensed teachers, they must complete an accredited teacher education program that includes courses in child development, teaching pedagogy, and instruction of subject matter, as well as a supervised field practicum.

In many schools, beginning teachers are assigned to mentor teachers, who advise them on lesson plans, class management, and so on. Many schools require teachers to attend in-service workshops throughout the year.

Special Requirements

In public schools, Kindergarten Teachers must hold an early childhood education or elementary education teaching credential. The type of license and licensing requirements vary from state to state. For specific information, contact the state board of education for the state in which you wish to teach. (See Appendix III for a list of state boards.) In addition, Kindergarten Teachers may need to complete continuing education units and, eventually, a master's degree, for licensure renewal.

All private schools have their own requirements for teacher certification. Some schools require that Kindergarten Teachers have a state teaching license. Some private schools, such as Montessori schools, require internal teaching certifications. Other schools may require certification from a certain school accreditation group, professional association, or other recognized organization.

Experience, Skills, and Personality Traits

Both public and private schools hire candidates who have experience teaching young children, which may have been gained through their work as student teachers, interns, substitute teachers, or teacher aides.

Kindergarten Teachers need excellent communication, teamwork, and interpersonal skills to work with students, school staff, and parents. To juggle their many responsibilities, they also need strong organizational and management skills. Being patient, creative, flexible, enthusiastic, and energetic are some personality traits that successful Kindergarten Teachers share.

Unions and Associations

Many Kindergarten Teachers belong to professional associations that provide networking opportunities and other professional services and resources. For example, many join the National Association for the Education of Young Children, which serves early childhood educators. Most public school teachers belong to a union, such as the National Education Association or the American Federation of Teachers, that negotiates teaching contracts with their employers. See Appendix IV for contact information for the above organizations.

Tips for Entry

1. Find out if you would like working with large groups of five- and six-year-olds for several hours each day. Gain experience by volunteering or working in kindergarten classes, Sunday school, after-school programs, or recreational programs.
2. Use the placement center at your college or university when you're job hunting. There, you can learn about job postings and educator job fairs, as well as get help writing resumes and interviewing for jobs.
3. To find private and independent schools with kindergarten programs, look in city telephone books. Many books have a listing such as this in the yellow pages: "Schools—Academic—Pre-School and Kindergarten."
4. The Internet is a valuable resource for learning more about teaching kindergartners. To start searching for pertinent Web sites, use the keyword *kindergarten* in a search engine.

ELEMENTARY SCHOOL TEACHER

CAREER PROFILE

Duties: Provide instruction of academic and most nonacademic subjects; create daily lesson plans: perform duties as required

Alternate Title(s): A title that reflects a grade level, such as First Grade Teacher

Salary Range: $30,000 to $69,000

Employment Prospects: Good

Advancement Prospects: Good

Prerequisites:

Education or Training—Bachelor's degree; for licensed teachers, completion of an accredited teacher education program

Experience—Student teaching, internship, or other teaching experience

Special Skills and Traits—Communication, teamwork, interpersonal, organizational, and management skills; be flexible, creative, enthusiastic, energetic, and patient

Special Requirements—A teaching credential or other certification

CAREER LADDER

```
┌─────────────────────────────┐
│   Mentor Teacher or         │
│   administrative position   │
└─────────────────────────────┘

┌─────────────────────────────┐
│   Elementary School Teacher │
└─────────────────────────────┘

┌─────────────────────────────────┐
│ Student Teacher or Substitute Teacher │
└─────────────────────────────────┘
```

Position Description

Elementary school is where the academic careers of most students begin. They learn to read, write, and do basic math operations, and begin to learn fundamental facts and concepts about the world around them. The typical age range of elementary school students is six to 12 years old. Most public and private elementary schools are made up of first through fifth grades. Some schools go up to sixth grade, and others go up to eighth grade. (Kindergarten is usually part of elementary schools.)

Starting at first grade, Elementary School Teachers are responsible for providing instruction of the academic subjects—math, language arts, science, and social studies—usually to 20 to 30 students. (In private schools, teachers generally have smaller classes.) They may also teach art, music, physical education, and computer skills, but in some schools, many of those subjects are taught by teaching specialists. Elementary School Teachers also help students develop learning skills (such as study skills and problem-solving skills) as well as social skills—such as how to behave and how to get along with each other.

As part of planning for their classes, Elementary School Teachers make schedules to determine when each subject is to be taught during the week, as well as the order of subjects during the school day. They confer with music teachers, physical education teachers, and other teaching specialists to schedule when the specialists should teach the class during the week. Elementary School Teachers also decide when students with special reading, language, or learning needs should be scheduled to receive individual tutoring, therapy, or other special services.

Elementary School Teachers are knowledgeable in the different subjects they teach. They follow school curriculum guidelines to develop the units of study for each subject. Some Elementary School Teachers have multi-age classes, in which students from two grades are combined. Teachers then must follow the curriculum guidelines for both grades.

Elementary School Teachers are responsible for creating daily lesson plans, which are usually filed with the school principal's office. The lesson for each subject is outlined—the lesson's content, purpose, and learning objectives; how the lesson is taught; and what exercises and activities are used to reinforce learning.

Because students have different abilities, skill levels, learning styles, and maturity levels, Elementary School Teachers use a variety of teaching methods and strategies. They also use films, tapes, computers, and other audiovisual aids to help with their instruction. In addition, they decorate their classrooms and create bulletin board displays to reflect the seasons, holidays, and unit themes to reinforce and motivate learning.

Elementary School Teachers are also responsible for monitoring their students' academic progress. They review students' assignments and give students feedback on their work. They also administer quizzes and tests to check students' comprehension of new learning. At the end of each quarter or semester, they evaluate each student's academic performance and assign a grade as well as comment on the development of his or her learning skills and social skills.

From time to time, Elementary School Teachers may have special education students—children with learning, emotional, and physical disabilities—as members of their classes. For each special education student, Elementary School Teachers follow instructional goals and objectives that are outlined in a student's Individualized Education Program (IEP). If help is needed to implement IEPs, they consult special education teachers. In some schools, general education and special education teachers work together to provide instruction to all students in class. Furthermore, Elementary School Teachers may be involved in providing assessments of special education students and helping to develop IEPs.

Elementary School Teachers perform many other tasks; for example, they:

- gather teaching and student materials
- create student exercises and activities
- confer with parents about their children's development and academic progress
- take daily attendance
- perform monitoring duties during class breaks
- sponsor extracurricular activities such as clubs, sports, and after-school tutoring sessions
- attend school functions and events
- participate in faculty meetings and on school committees
- supervise teacher aides, interns, or school volunteers

Typically, Elementary School Teachers work long hours each day, sometimes as many as 10 to 12 hours, to complete all their tasks—planning lessons, contacting parents, grading papers, attending school functions, and so on. Most Elementary School Teachers have a 10-month work schedule, usually from September to June.

Before the beginning of a school term, Elementary School Teachers may be reassigned to teach another grade level or teach in another school. In most public school systems, teachers receive tenure after completing three to five years of continuous teaching service. With tenure, teachers cannot be fired without just cause.

Salaries

Salaries for Elementary School Teachers vary, depending on such factors as their education, credentials, experience, employer, and geographical location. According to the U.S. Bureau of Labor Statistics (BLS), in its November 2004 *Occupational Employment Statistics* (OES) survey, the estimated annual salary for most Elementary School Teachers ranged between $29,370 and $68,930.

Employment Prospects

The BLS reports in its November 2004 OES study that an estimated 1,431,380 Elementary School Teachers were employed in public and private schools in the United States.

Teaching opportunities are expected to remain favorable through 2012, according to the BLS, partly due to the large number of teachers becoming eligible for retirement. However, opportunities vary by region and communities. Opportunities are particularly stronger in inner cities and rural areas as well in fast-growing states in the South and West, where schools are expected to have the largest increases in enrollment.

Advancement Prospects

Several different career paths are available for Elementary School Teachers. Experienced teachers can become mentor teachers who provide guidance to beginning teachers. With additional education and endorsements, Elementary School Teachers can teach special subjects (such as art and physical education) or teach in special areas (such as bilingual education and special education). They can also become counselors, librarians, or other school-related professionals.

School administration is another career path open to Elementary School Teachers. In private schools, teachers can work their way up to become department heads, school heads, or other administrators. In public schools, teachers need additional education and credentials to become school principals and district administrators (such as curriculum specialists, program directors, and superintendents).

Elementary School Teachers can pursue careers in other areas of education. For example, they can become community college instructors, university professors, corporate trainers, textbook editors, or educational software developers.

Education and Training

Elementary School Teachers must have at least a bachelor's degree, usually in liberal arts, to teach in public and private schools. Many Elementary School Teachers have master's degrees. To become licensed teachers, Elementary School Teachers complete an accredited teacher education program that includes course work in pedagogy and instruction of subject matter, as well as a supervised field practicum.

In many schools, beginning teachers are assigned to mentor teachers who advise them with lesson plans, class management, and so on. Many schools require teachers to attend in-service workshops throughout the year.

Special Requirements

To teach in public schools, Elementary School Teachers must hold a valid elementary education credential. The type of license and licensure requirements vary from state to state. For specific information, contact the state board of education for the state in which you wish to teach. (See Appendix III for a list of state boards.) In addition, they may need to complete continuing education units and, eventually, attain a master's degree for licensure renewal.

Many private schools require certification from a state board of education, school accreditation group, professional association, or other recognized organization. Some schools, such as Waldorf schools, require internal teaching certifications, which are obtained after completing their training programs.

Experience, Skills, and Personality Traits

Employers look for candidates who have previous teaching experience with young children as a student teacher, intern, substitute teacher, and so on. Additionally, most private schools look for candidates who have a strong background in extracurricular activities, such as sports or drama.

Elementary School Teachers need strong communication, interpersonal, and teamwork skills as they must work well with students, staff, and parents. In addition, teachers need adequate organizational and management skills to handle the many tasks that they must complete each day.

Being flexible, creative, enthusiastic, energetic, and patient are some of the personality traits that successful Elementary School Teachers share. In addition, they have a deep compassion for young children, as well as a strong desire to help them succeed in the learning process.

Unions and Associations

Most public school teachers belong to a union, such as the National Education Association or the American Federation of Teachers, that negotiates teaching contracts with their employers.

Many Elementary School Teachers belong to professional associations to take advantage of networking opportunities and other professional resources and services. For example, many teachers are members of the National Association for the Education of Young Children and the Council for Exceptional Children.

See Appendix IV for contact information for the above organizations.

Tips for Entry

1. Get lots of (volunteer or paid) experience working with groups of young children. As a middle school or high school student, you might babysit, tutor, read stories in library read-aloud programs, be a classroom aide, assist in after-school child care programs, coach children's sports, or work in recreational programs.

2. Be sure the elementary school level is the right level for you before enrolling in a teacher education program. Talk with Elementary School Teachers in different grades. Also visit several classes while they are in session.

3. As a student teacher or intern, develop a teaching portfolio to bring to job fairs and interviews. In it, keep copies of your resume, professional letters of reference, samples of your lesson plans, and photographs of your classes that show bulletin boards, learning centers, student work, and so on.

4. To learn more about private and independent schools, contact the National Association of Independent Schools, http://www.nais.org, or the Council for American Private Education, http://www.capenet.org.

5. You can learn more about elementary schools on the Internet. Use the keyword *elementary school* in a search engine to get a list of Web sites to read.

MIDDLE SCHOOL TEACHER

CAREER PROFILE

Duties: Provide instruction for one or more subjects at the intermediate, middle, or junior high level; create lesson plans; perform other duties as required

Alternate Title(s): Junior High Teacher, Intermediate School Teacher; a title that reflects a subject area, such as Science Teacher, or a grade level, such as Seventh Grade Teacher

Salary Range: $30,000 to $70,000

Employment Prospects: Good

Advancement Prospects: Good

Prerequisites:

Education or Training—Bachelor's degree; for licensed teachers, completion of an accredited teacher education program

Experience—Student teaching, internship, or other teaching experience

Special Skills and Personality Traits—Communication, teamwork, interpersonal, organizational, and management skills; be creative, flexible, fair, patient, and tolerant

Special Requirements—A teaching credential or other certification

CAREER LADDER

```
┌─────────────────────────────────┐
│      Mentor Teacher or          │
│    administrative position      │
└─────────────────────────────────┘

┌─────────────────────────────────┐
│      Middle School Teacher      │
└─────────────────────────────────┘

┌─────────────────────────────────┐
│ Student Teacher or Substitute Teacher │
└─────────────────────────────────┘
```

Position Description

Middle School Teachers are involved in the education of children ranging in age from 10 to 14 years in public and private schools. They instruct young adolescents who are adjusting to physical, emotional, and social changes as they grow into adulthood.

Middle school is the level between elementary school and high school. Teachers are usually employed in one of two middle-level models—the middle school or the junior high school. Most middle schools comprise sixth through eighth grades; some middle schools also include fifth grade. Junior high schools, on the other hand, comprise either seventh and eighth grades or seventh through ninth grades. Junior high students may range from ages 12 to 15.

In the middle schools, teams of two to four teachers are assigned to teach a group of students (for example, 80 students) at the same grade level. The team is responsible for the instruction of the core academic subjects—math, science, social studies, and language arts. Each teacher is responsible for teaching one or more subjects. For example, in a three-member team, one teacher might teach math and science, another might teach language arts, and the third might teach social studies. Class periods are typically combined in blocks of two to four hours.

The exploratory classes—such as art, music, physical education, foreign language, and health—are taught by specialists. Students might receive instruction in these subjects once or twice a week, or daily, within a grading period.

Unlike middle schools, junior high schools are modeled after the high school model. The school day is divided into several class periods and students move from class to class. They receive daily instruction in the core subjects—language arts, social studies, math, and science. Other subjects such as music, art, physical education, health, foreign languages, technology, and industrial arts are either taught daily or once or twice a week within a grading period. Traditionally, class periods are usually 50 to 55 minutes long. Some junior high schools have flexible block schedules in which periods are two to four hours long. Classes are then scheduled for alternate days.

Like high school teachers, junior high teachers are specialists in their subject matter—English, social studies, mathematics, science, art, music, physical education, foreign language, and so on. They are assigned courses to teach for different grade levels. For example, a junior high social studies teacher might teach world history to ninth graders, government to eighth graders, and history and geography to seventh graders. Junior high teachers generally have between 20 and 35 students in each class. (Teachers in private schools normally have smaller class sizes.)

Many Middle School Teachers have special education students—children with learning, emotional, and physical disabilities—included in their classes. With special education students, teachers must follow instructional goals and objectives that are outlined in their students' Individualized Education Programs (IEPs). When needed, Middle School Teachers consult with special education teachers for assistance in implementing IEPs. In some schools, Middle School Teachers are involved in providing assessments of special education students, as well as in helping develop IEPs.

Whether teaching in a middle school or a junior high school, teachers perform similar routine duties. They take attendance, collect assignments, review the previous day's work, present the day's lesson, and make class assignments. Instruction is done through various methods, including lecture, group discussion, demonstration, and modeling. Teachers might use films, videotapes, and other audiovisual media to help reinforce instruction. Some teachers also supplement learning by having students work with computer programs or access the Internet during class time. Teachers who have longer class periods can provide additional reinforcement and enrichment activities to help students learn new concepts and skills.

Middle School Teachers generally follow curriculum guidelines to develop their courses. Junior high teachers develop a course syllabus that outlines the topics and sequence of topics to be taught for each course, while the core subject teachers in middle schools usually work together to plan the units of study for the academic subjects. They may organize the units in themes, such as the environment or myths and legends, to help students understand the connection between core subjects. In addition to teaching subject matter, all Middle School Teachers help students acquire basic learning skills, such as problem-solving skills, critical thinking skills, and using resources to find answers.

Middle School Teachers are responsible for creating daily lesson plans for each of their classes. They prepare for each lesson by studying the topic, gathering materials, creating exercises and activities, setting up experiments or demonstrations, and so on. Middle School Teachers also are responsible for monitoring their students' academic progress. Along with reviewing their students' class work, homework, and projects, they give quizzes and tests to check their students' comprehension. At the end of each grading period, Middle School Teachers evaluate each student's work and assign a grade for his or her academic performance.

Middle School Teachers perform many nonteaching duties. They contact parents to discuss their children's academic performance and behavior. Teachers also complete daily administrative tasks such as taking student attendance and making school announcements. Middle School Teachers may be assigned teacher aides or student teachers, whom they train and supervise. In addition, Middle School Teachers participate in faculty meetings and sit on school committees. In some schools, Middle School Teachers may have lunchroom, bus, or other monitoring duties. Teachers may be assigned to help supervise school games, dances, and other school functions. Furthermore, Middle School Teachers act as counselors and mentors—directly and indirectly—to their students.

Middle School Teachers work long hours, often completing their many tasks at home in the evenings and on weekends. Most Middle School Teachers have a 10-month work schedule, and usually work from September to June.

Before the beginning of a school term, teachers may be reassigned to teach at another grade level or in another school. In most public school systems, teachers receive tenure after completing three to five years of continuous teaching service. With tenure, teachers cannot be fired from their jobs without just cause.

Salaries

Salaries for Middle School Teachers vary, depending on such factors as their education, experience, employer, and geographical location. According to the November 2004 *Occupational Employment Statistics* (OES) survey, by the U.S. Bureau of Labor Statistics (BLS), the estimated annual salary for most Middle School Teachers ranged between $30,190 and $69,960.

Middle School Teachers may receive additional compensation for coaching, being a class adviser, or sponsoring extracurricular activities.

Employment Prospects

The BLS reports in its November 2004 OES survey that an estimated 626,110 Middle School Teachers were employed in the United States.

According to the BLS, teaching opportunities are expected to be favorable through 2012, partly due to the large number of teachers becoming eligible for retirement. Opportunities are particularly stronger in inner cities and rural areas as well as in fast-growing states in the South and West, where schools are expected to have a large increase in student enrollment. Middle School Teachers with endorsements in science, mathematics, special education, bilingual education, or English as a second language (ESL) are in demand nationwide.

When a school administration changes its junior high schools to middle schools, or middle schools to K–8 elementary schools, teachers' jobs are generally not affected. Teachers may continue teaching in the new school, or be reassigned to teach another grade level.

Advancement Prospects

In public schools, Middle School Teachers can pursue several career paths. Experienced teachers can become mentor teachers who advise beginning teachers. Licensed teachers can obtain additional endorsements to coach, teach in special areas such as bilingual education, or teach special subjects such as music and technology. With further education and licensure, Middle School Teachers can become counselors, librarians, school psychologists, or other school-related professionals.

School administration is also a path open to Middle School Teachers. In private schools, teachers can work their way up to positions such as school heads, division heads, or dean of students. With additional education and licensure, public school teachers can become school principals and district administrators.

Furthermore, Middle School Teachers can pursue careers in other areas of education. For example, they can become college professors, technical trainers, or educational software developers.

Education and Training

Minimally, Middle School Teachers need a bachelor's degree in a discipline related to the subjects that they are hired to teach. Along with their degree, teachers in the middle-school model also have the required course work to teach in one or more core subjects. Many teachers in both public and private schools possess a master's degree.

To become state licensed teachers, applicants must complete an accredited teacher education program. The program includes course work in pedagogy and instruction of subject matter, as well as a supervised field practicum.

Special Requirements

To teach in public schools, Middle School Teachers must hold a valid teaching credential. The type of credential differs from state to state. In some states, Middle School Teachers hold an elementary education credential; while in other states, they hold a secondary education credential. In a few states, they hold a middle-grades credential. Junior high teachers must usually hold a secondary education credential with an endorsement in each subject area that they teach. Licensure requirements vary from state to state. (For specific information, contact the state board of education for the state in which you wish to teach. See Appendix III for a list of state boards.) In addition, Middle School Teachers may need to complete continuing education units and, eventually, attain a master's degree for licensure renewal.

In private schools, teachers may be required to possess state licensure or professional certification from a recognized organization. Some schools grant internal teaching certifications to candidates who complete their training programs.

Experience, Skills, and Personality Traits

Entry-level Middle School Teachers usually have previous experience teaching young adolescents as student teachers, interns, substitute teachers, teacher's aides and so on. In addition, teachers in private schools generally have a strong background in sports, drama, community service, or other extracurricular activities.

To work with students, staff, and parents, Middle School Teachers need adequate communication, teamwork, and interpersonal skills. Additionally, they need strong organizational and management skills to complete their many different tasks each day.

Successful Middle School Teachers have several personality traits in common, such as being creative, flexible, fair, patient, and tolerant. Additionally, they are passionate about teaching young adolescents and are in tune with the physical, emotional, and social changes that their students are going through.

Unions and Associations

Public school teachers usually belong to a union, such as the American Federation of Teachers or the National Education Association, that negotiates teaching contracts with their employers.

Many Middle School Teachers join various professional associations to take advantage of teaching resources, networking opportunities, and other professional resources and services. They may belong to societies that serve their general interests, such as the National Middle School Association. Many also join organizations that serve specific disciplines, such as the National Science Teachers Association, the National Council of Teachers of English, or the National Council of Teachers of Mathematics. For contact information, see Appendix IV.

Tips for Entry

1. Get lots of (volunteer or paid) experience working with groups of young adolescents in recreational programs, church youth groups, scouting, or other youth organizations.

2. Contact public and private schools where you wish to teach to learn about job vacancies. Submit an application even if jobs are not currently available. Call back from time to time to learn the status of your application.

3. An alternative path for teacher licensure is available for those who would prefer to obtain their credential by teaching full time in a classroom under the supervision of certified educators. To learn more, contact your state board of education or a school district office.

4. Use the Internet to learn more about teaching at the middle school level. You might start by visiting these Web sites: National Middle School Association, http://www.nmsa.org, and Middle Web, http://www.middleweb.com. To find other relevant Web sites, use any of these keywords in a search engine: *middle school, middle level schools, junior high school,* or *intermediate school.*

HIGH SCHOOL TEACHER

CAREER PROFILE

Duties: Provide instruction for several courses in one or more subject areas; create lesson plans; perform other duties as required

Alternate Title(s): A title that reflects the area of specialization, such as English Teacher

Salary Range: $31,000 to $72,000

Employment Prospects: Good

Advancement Prospects: Good

Prerequisites:

Education or Training—Bachelor's degree; completion of an accredited teacher education program

Experience—Student teaching, internship, or other teaching experience

Special Skills and Personality Traits—Communication, interpersonal, teamwork, organizational, and management skills; be patient, tolerant, flexible, creative, fair

Special Requirements—A teaching credential or other certification

CAREER LADDER

Mentor Teacher or Department Head

High School Teacher

Student Teacher or Substitute Teacher

Position Description

High school is the last level of compulsory education in the United States. Most public and private high schools are made up of ninth through 12th grades; some high schools include only 10th to 12th grades. In high school, teachers and other staff prepare adolescent students (most between the ages of 14 and 18) to become responsible, participating adults in society, as well as provide students with essential knowledge and skills to become lifelong learners.

High School Teachers are specialists in their subject matter and may be part of one or more high school departments, such as social studies, physical education, or industrial arts. They teach courses in different grades. For example, a high school science teacher might teach general science to ninth graders, biology to 10th graders, and anatomy to 11th and 12th graders.

Most High School Teachers provide instruction for classes in English, social studies, mathematics, science, fine arts, foreign language, physical education, and other subjects that are required for high school graduation and for future enrollment in colleges and universities. Many High

School Teachers also teach courses in business, culinary arts, building and construction, auto services, agriculture, or other vocational areas that can prepare students for enrollment in apprenticeship programs and technical and vocational schools as well as for obtaining employment after high school graduation.

Typically, High School Teachers have six or seven classes with as few as 15 or as many as 35 students in a class. (The class load for teachers is usually smaller in private schools.) Most High School Teachers instruct between 120 and 180 students each school day.

For each course, High School Teachers develop a course syllabus that outlines the topics to be taught within a quarter, semester, or year. In addition, they create daily lesson plans for each course, and prepare the lessons for each class. Lesson preparation may involve studying a topic, gathering teaching materials, creating student materials, or setting up demonstrations or experiments. (In most public high schools, teachers get a free period for preparing lessons.)

Within a class period, High School Teachers complete attendance tasks; collect homework; review the previous day's lesson; present the new lesson through lecture, demonstration, and modeling; check students' understanding of concepts and skills with written and oral exercises, quizzes, or tests; and assign classwork, homework, and projects. To help reinforce instruction, High School Teachers may use films, slides, videotapes, and other audiovisual equipment. Many teachers also supplement instruction by having students work with computer programs as well as access the Internet during class time.

In many high schools, flexible block schedules are used in which periods are two to four hours long. Classes are then scheduled for alternate days. With flexible block schedules, High School Teachers can plan more complex lessons with hands-on activities and independent research work. In addition, teachers have the chance to work with students who may need more individual attention.

High School Teachers are responsible for monitoring students' academic progress. They maintain a record book of students' test scores and grades for class assignments. At the end of each grading period, teachers evaluate each student's work and assign a grade for his or her academic performance.

Some High School Teachers are assigned to teach inclusive classrooms that include special education students, or children with behavioral disorders, learning disabilities, or visual, hearing, or physical impairments. With special education students, High School Teachers follow instructional goals and objectives that are outlined in students' Individualized Education Programs (IEPs). High School Teachers may also be involved in providing assessments of special education students, as well as helping develop IEPs. In some schools, general education and special education teachers collaborate in creating lesson plans and providing instruction to all students in inclusive classrooms.

High School Teachers have many other duties. They might:

- confer with students and their parents about students' work and behavior
- be assigned to a group of students to meet with and advise each day
- sponsor extracurricular activities (such as clubs, student government, or school publications) or coach athletic teams
- supervise school dances, games, concerts, plays, or other school functions
- participate in department and faculty meetings and on school committees
- supervise teacher aides, interns, or school volunteers

Most High School Teachers work beyond the regular school day and often complete their tasks (making lesson plans, calling parents, grading papers, etc.) at home during evenings and on weekends. Most High School Teachers have a 10-month work schedule, from September to June.

High School Teachers in most public schools receive tenure after completing three to five years of continuous teaching service. With tenure, teachers cannot be fired without just cause.

Salaries

Salaries for High School Teachers vary, depending on such factors as their education, credentials, experience, employer, and geographical location. They may earn extra compensation for coaching and sponsoring extracurricular activities. The U.S. Bureau of Labor Statistics (BLS) reports in its November 2004 *Occupational Employment Statistics* (OES) survey that the estimated annual salary for most High School Teachers ranged between $30,540 and $72,110.

Employment Prospects

More than 1 million High School Teachers were employed in private and public schools in the United States in 2004, according to the BLS's November 2004 OES survey.

The BLS reports that teaching opportunities are expected to be favorable through 2012, partly due to the large number of teachers becoming eligible for retirement. Teachers in the areas of mathematics, science, bilingual education, foreign languages, and vocational education are especially in demand. However, opportunities vary by region and communities. Opportunities are particularly stronger in inner cities and rural areas as well as in fast-growing states in the South and West, where schools are expected to have large increases in enrollment.

Advancement Prospects

High School Teachers can pursue a number of career paths. Experienced teachers can become mentor teachers and department heads. With additional education and credentials, licensed High School Teachers can teach in special areas such as bilingual education and special education. They can also become guidance counselors, school librarians, educational technologists, or other school-related professionals.

High School Teachers can also advance to administrative positions. In private schools, teachers can work their way up to be school heads, deans of students, or other administrators. With advanced education and licensure, public school teachers can become principals and district administrators.

Furthermore, teachers can pursue careers in other areas of education. For example, they can become correction instructors, corporate trainers, textbook editors, or educational consultants.

Education and Training

In general, High School Teachers need at least a bachelor's degree in the primary subject that they are teaching. Many

High School Teachers in both public and private schools have master's degrees in their subjects. All state-licensed teachers must complete an accredited teacher education program that includes pedagogy, instruction of subject matter, and a supervised field practicum.

In many schools, beginning teachers are assigned to mentor teachers who advise them with lesson plans and classroom management. In addition, many High School Teachers are required to attend mandatory in-service workshops throughout the year.

Special Requirements

High School Teachers in public schools are required to hold a secondary education credential with an endorsement in each subject area that they teach. Licensure requirements vary from state to state. For specific information, contact the state board of education for the state in which you wish to teach. (See Appendix III for a list of state boards.) In addition, High School Teachers may need to complete continuing education units and, eventually, a master's degree for licensure renewal.

Many private schools require certification from a state board of education, school accreditation group, professional association, or other recognized organization. Some schools, such as Waldorf schools, require internal teaching certifications, which are obtained after completing their training programs.

Experience, Skills, and Personality Traits

Employers typically choose candidates who have previous teaching experience with adolescents as student teachers, interns, substitute teachers, and so on. Along with teaching experience, private schools desire candidates with a strong background in sports, drama, community service, or other extracurricular activities.

High School Teachers should have strong communication, teamwork, and interpersonal skills to work well with students, parents, and school staff. In addition, they should have adequate organizational and management skills to complete the various duties that are required of High School Teachers each day.

Successful High School Teachers generally have a fine sense of humor and share several personality traits, such as being patient, tolerant, flexible, creative, and fair. Additionally, they have a talent and passion for teaching adolescents, willing to reach out and listen to their students' questions and concerns.

Unions and Associations

Most public school teachers belong to a union, such as the American Federation of Teachers or the National Education Association, that negotiates teaching contracts with their employers.

Many High School Teachers (in both public and private schools) join professional associations to take advantage of networking opportunities and other professional resources and services. Many of them belong to national societies that serve their particular disciplines, such as the following:

- American Council on the Teaching of Foreign Languages
- National Art Education Association
- National Council for the Social Studies
- National Council of Teachers of English
- National Council of Teachers of Mathematics
- National Science Teachers Association

See Appendix IV for contact information for the above organizations.

Tips for Entry

1. Volunteer or obtain jobs in settings that provide you with experiences to work with groups of teenagers.
2. Subscribe to professional teaching magazines, such as *Education Week,* to learn about nationwide job opportunities and to keep up with current educational events and issues.
3. Develop a teaching philosophy—your teaching mission, goals, objectives, and so on. Being clear in your mind about your purpose for teaching can give you more confidence in job interviews as well as in the classroom.
4. To find out what it would be like to work at a particular private school, you might work first as a substitute teacher.
5. You can get an idea of what different high schools are like on the Internet. Use the keyword *high school* in a search engine to get a list of Web sites to read.

SUBSTITUTE TEACHER

CAREER PROFILE

Duties: To fill in for an absent teacher and teach his or her daily lesson plans and perform his or her nonteaching duties; perform other duties as required

Alternate Title(s): None

Salary Range: $50 to $100 or more per day

Employment Prospects: Excellent

Advancement Prospects: Poor, if not planning to obtain permanent teaching jobs

Prerequisites:

Education or Training—A bachelor's degree; for licensed teachers, completion of an accredited teacher education program

Experience—Student teaching, internship, or other teaching experience

Special Skills and Personality Traits—Communication, interpersonal, self-management, and class-management skills; be firm, decisive, flexible, creative, and resourceful

Special Requirements—A teaching credential or substitute teacher's certificate

CAREER LADDER

```
┌─────────────────────────────────────┐
│              Teacher                 │
└─────────────────────────────────────┘

┌─────────────────────────────────────┐
│         Substitute Teacher           │
└─────────────────────────────────────┘

┌─────────────────────────────────────┐
│  Student Teacher or Former Teacher   │
└─────────────────────────────────────┘
```

Position Description

Occasionally, teachers are absent from their classes for various reasons—illness, personal business, mandatory attendance at professional development workshops, and so on. Substitute Teachers are then contacted to fill in for the absent teachers to teach their daily lesson plans, as well as complete their nonteaching duties, such as monitoring students during recesses and supervising club meetings. They sometimes accept assignments in subjects in which they are not formally trained. An assignment may be short-term—for several hours or one or more days—or long-term—for several weeks or months.

Substitute Teachers are responsible for working the absent teachers' schedule. Typically, they are requested to report to school 15 to 30 minutes earlier so that they can become familiar with the school as well as the absent teacher's routine. Upon reporting to the school office, Substitute Teachers receive classroom keys. They check the absent teachers' mailbox for daily lesson plans, notes from the absent teacher, and any school announcements that are to be made in class. Substitute Teachers also familiarize

themselves with the school's rules, the day's schedule, procedures for fire drills, and other matters.

Substitute Teachers go over the absent teacher's lesson plans before students arrive in class. Most teachers provide Substitute Teachers with the materials needed to teach the day's lessons or give instructions for preparing instructional materials. If a teacher has not left any lesson plans, or if a Substitute Teacher wants to alter the lesson plans, the Substitute Teacher must first talk with the principal or the appropriate school official. (Some Substitute Teachers carry emergency lesson plans with them so that they are ready for any class should a teacher forget to leave lesson plans.)

From time to time, a teacher's lesson plan does not fill out the class period. Substitute Teachers might then assign exercises or activities to supplement a lesson; for example, a Substitute Teacher might pick out vocabulary words from the day's lesson and have students use the words in sentences. Many Substitute Teachers bring in crossword puzzles, word games, and other activities for students to do if they finish their work early.

Substitute Teachers are responsible for maintaining class order and have the authority to discipline students according to school policies and procedures. If misbehaving students become uncontrollable, Substitute Teachers may send them to the principal's office or request help from the principal or other administrator.

At the end of the school day, Substitute Teachers usually leave the absent teachers a brief summary of the day's activities, including lesson results and student behavior.

Work days for Substitute Teachers are flexible. They can choose how many days and which days of the week they wish to work.

Salaries

Substitute Teachers are paid a per diem, or daily rate, that ranges from $50 to $100 or more per day, depending on the school or school district. Those with teaching credentials usually receive a higher per diem rate. Substitute Teachers may receive an increase in the daily rate after working the same assignment for a maximum number of days. In some school districts, long-term Substitute Teachers may receive a regular teacher's per diem rate.

Employment Prospects

Substitute Teachers are hired by private and public schools for all grade levels—prekindergarten to high school. Many Substitute Teachers work for one or more private schools and/or public school districts.

Job opportunities are readily available nationwide. In the late 1990s, many schools reported a shortage of qualified Substitute Teachers. This trend should continue as an increasing number of Substitute Teachers find permanent positions due to the need for replacing a large force of retiring teachers and the creation of additional positions to handle increasing student enrollment.

Advancement Prospects

Many individuals make substitute teaching their career because of the freedom and flexibility of choosing when and where to work, as well as the opportunity to teach different classes and different grade levels. For many Substitute Teachers, receiving choice assignments is an advancement. For many educators, substitute teaching is the stepping-stone for starting their careers.

Education and Training

Most private and public schools require that Substitute Teachers have a bachelor's degree in any field. Some schools accept applicants with a high school or general equivalency diploma if they also have a minimum number of college units.

More and more school districts provide an orientation session for Substitute Teachers, covering topics such as school policies, procedures, and rules; substitute teacher responsibilities; and classroom management strategies.

Special Requirements

Licensure requirements for Substitute Teachers differ among the states, public school districts, and private schools. Generally, Substitute Teachers are required to hold a valid teaching credential or a local Substitute Teacher Certificate. Some employers require only proof that Substitute Teachers have completed an accredited teacher preparation program. For specific information about becoming a Substitute Teacher in public schools, contact the school districts in which you would like to work or the state board of education. See Appendix III for a list of state boards.

Experience, Skills, and Personality Traits

Substitute Teachers should have previous teaching experience, particularly with the age groups in the grade levels to which they will be assigned. Many public school districts require that Substitute Teachers have one or more years of classroom teaching experience.

Along with teaching skills, Substitute Teachers need strong communication skills, interpersonal skills, self-management skills (getting to class on time, self-motivation, etc.), and class-management skills. Successful Substitute Teachers share several personality traits, such as being firm, decisive, flexible, creative, and resourceful.

Unions and Associations

Many Substitute Teachers join professional associations to take advantage of networking opportunities, teaching resources, and other professional resources and services. Many belong to societies, such as the National Substitute Teachers Alliance, that serve the particular interests of Substitute Teachers. Some also join professional associations that serve their particular disciplines, such as the International Reading Association or the National Council for the Social Studies. See Appendix IV for contact information for the above organizations.

Tips for Entry

1. When you first start as a Substitute Teacher, accept most, if not all, assignments that are offered you. If you turn down too many assignments, you may not be called as often as you want.
2. If you like substituting at a specific school, ask the principal if you can be placed on a priority substitute list.
3. Many resources are available on the Internet for Substitute Teachers. To start a search of pertinent Web sites, use either of these keywords in a search engine: *substitute teacher* or *substitute teaching*.

PRE-K–12 TEACHING SPECIALISTS

MUSIC TEACHER

CAREER PROFILE

Duties: Provide general music, choral, or instrumental instruction; create lesson plans; perform other duties as required

Alternate Title(s): Music Specialist, Band Teacher, Orchestra Teacher, Choral Teacher, Band Director, Choral Director, Orchestra Director

Salary Range: $19,000 to $70,000

Employment Prospects: Good

Advancement Prospects: Good

Prerequisites:

Education or Training—Bachelor's or master's degree; for licensed teachers, completion of an accredited teacher education program

Experience—Student teaching, internship, or other teaching experience

Special Skills and Personality Traits—Performance, interpersonal, teamwork, communication, organizational, and management skills; be patient, creative, flexible, enthusiastic, and energetic

Special Requirements—A teaching credential or other certification

CAREER LADDER

```
┌─────────────────────────────────────────┐
│   Mentor Teacher or Department Head       │
└─────────────────────────────────────────┘

┌─────────────────────────────────────────┐
│            Music Teacher                  │
└─────────────────────────────────────────┘

┌─────────────────────────────────────────┐
│   Student Teacher or Substitute Teacher   │
└─────────────────────────────────────────┘
```

Position Description

Most public and private schools have a music program as part of their school curriculum for all grade levels, prekindergarten to 12th grade. As specialists in their discipline, Music Teachers introduce schoolchildren to the joy and beauty of music, and teach them basic vocal and instrumental skills.

In elementary and middle-level schools, students usually receive music instruction once or twice a week. Music Teachers at these school levels have the challenge of teaching classes in different schools. For example, a Music Teacher right teach five classes at three different schools in one day. At the high school level, music classes are electives and are usually taught daily by Music Teachers.

Music Teachers provide different instruction at the different grade levels. In prekindergarten, kindergarten, and elementary grades, Music Teachers guide children in activities such as singing, clapping, moving, dancing and playing percussion instruments. They also begin teaching music history and music patterns (such as beat, rhythm, and tempo). In some schools, Music Teachers begin teaching fifth and sixth graders how to play individual instruments.

In the middle-level grades, Music Teachers provide instruction in general music (basic music theory and music appreciation), choral singing, and instruments for band or orchestra. The choir and instrumental classes usually participate in annual school music concerts performed before their communities.

In high school, Music Teachers teach band, choir, and orchestra classes, which are elective classes. As part of their instruction, Music Teachers direct the student bands, orchestras, and choral groups in public performances throughout the year. For example, a band might play at school football games or an orchestra might perform the musical score for a high school play. In many communities, the high school music department is the only source for performance art.

In some high schools, music departments participate in regional, state, or national musical competitions. Music Teachers are responsible for preparing students for the competitions, as well as for supervising and managing students while traveling to and from competitions and during the competitions. In addition, Music Teachers organize the trips—obtaining permission slips; making arrangements for transportation; finding chaperones; and so on. Music Teachers may also be involved in raising funds for transportation, uniforms, meals, and other needs for the music competitions and other music activities.

Like all schoolteachers, Music Teachers carry out their school policies, goals, and objectives. Depending on the school, Music Teachers may be responsible for creating their own curriculum based on school guidelines or other standards. Additionally, they create and prepare daily lesson plans; assess and evaluate students' work; and confer with students and their parents about students' work and behavior. If special education students are part of their classes, Music Teachers modify lessons to fit the students' abilities. A special education teacher is usually available to help Music Teachers with instructional strategies.

Music Teachers—at all school levels—have other duties that may include:

- performing administrative tasks such as taking attendance
- supervising detention or study hall
- acting as a corridor, lunch room, or playground monitor during class breaks
- sponsoring extracurricular activities
- supervising and directing teacher aides, student teachers, and volunteers
- supervising attendance at school functions
- participating in faculty meetings and on school committees

Their work hours often extend into the evenings and on weekends to complete their tasks—grading papers, attending meetings, conferring with parents, fund-raising, and so on. Most Music Teachers have a 10-month work schedule, usually from September to June.

Most public schools give teachers tenure after completing three to five years of continuous teaching service. With tenure, teachers cannot be fired without just cause.

Salaries

Salaries for Music Teachers vary, depending on such factors as their education, credentials, experience, employer, and geographical location. According to MENC: The National Association for Music Education, the estimated annual salary for school music educators ranges from $19,000 to $70,000.

Employment Prospects

Music Teachers are employed in both private and public school settings. Job opportunities are expected to be good for the next few years as many schools will need to find replacements for veteran Music Teachers who are reaching retirement age. In general, teaching jobs are more available in rural areas and inner cities, as well as in states in the South and West that are experiencing rapid growth.

Advancement Prospects

Music Teachers have several advancement opportunities in schools. Along with becoming mentor teachers, they can become music directors and department heads. They can also pursue administrative positions. Private school teachers can work their way up to positions such as school heads and development directors. With additional education and licensure, public school teachers can become principals, instructional supervisors of music, or program directors.

In addition, Music Teachers can pursue other areas or interests in music. For example, they can become conservatory educators, music librarians, church choir directors, music therapists, music arrangers, or private music teachers.

Education and Training

A bachelor's or master's degree in music education is needed to teach in public or private schools. Those applying for teaching licensure must complete an accredited teacher education program that includes course work in pedagogy and instruction of subject matter, as well as a supervised field practicum.

In many schools, beginning teachers are assigned to mentor teachers who advise them with lesson plans, classroom management, and so on. Music Teachers may be required to attend in-service training throughout the year.

Special Requirements

To teach in public schools, Music Teachers must hold a valid teaching credential in music education. Some states require an endorsement for each music specialty (such as choral or band) that a Music Teacher plans to teach. Licensure requirements vary from state to state. For specific information, contact the state board of education for the state in which you wish to teach. See Appendix III for a list of state boards.

Many private schools require certification from a state board of education, school accreditation group, professional association, or other recognized organization. Some schools, such as Montessori schools, require internal teaching certifications, which are obtained after completing their training programs.

Experience, Skills, and Personality Traits

Employers typically hire Music Teachers who have student teaching or other teaching experience with the age groups whom they would be teaching. Employers look for candidates who have musical talent and skills, as well as performance skills.

Music Teachers must be able to work well with people—students, school staff, parents, and the public—thus they need teamwork, communication, and interpersonal skills. In addition, they need organizational and management skills to accomplish the many different tasks that must be done each day.

Some personality traits that successful Music Teachers share are being patient, creative, flexible, enthusiastic, and energetic.

Unions and Associations

Music Teachers join professional associations that provide teaching resources, education programs, networking opportunities, and other professional services and resources. Some organizations are specifically for music teachers, such as MENC: The National Association for Music Education and the American String Teachers Association. Most Music Teachers in public schools belong to a union, such as the National Education Association or the American Federation of Teachers, that negotiates teaching contracts with employ-ers. For contact information for these organizations, see Appendix IV.

Tips for Entry

1. Get experience performing music with a group, such as church chorus or a community band. Also gain experience working with the age groups that you wish to teach.

2. Many music educators recommend that high school students prepare themselves for the hard work of being a college music major. They suggest that students regularly practice their music reading, music notation, aural skills, and other basic music skills. In addition to being skilled in voice or an instrument, students should possess fundamental piano keyboard skills.

3. You may be able to find job listings at Web sites of schools, professional associations, and state departments of education.

4. On the Internet, you can learn more about teaching music in schools. You might start by visiting the Web site for MENC: The National Association for Music Education. Its URL is http://www.menc.org.

PHYSICAL EDUCATION TEACHER

CAREER PROFILE

Duties: Provide physical fitness and physical activity instruction; create daily lesson plans; may coach competitive sports; perform other duties as required

Alternate Title(s): Physical Education Specialist

Salary Range: $33,000 to $57,000

Employment Prospects: Fair

Advancement Prospects: Good

Prerequisites:

Education or Training—Bachelor's degree; for licensed teachers, completion of an accredited teacher education program

Experience—Student teaching, internship, or other teaching experience

Special Skills and Personality Traits—Interpersonal, teamwork, communication, organizational, and management skills; be self-disciplined, firm, fair, observant, flexible, and creative

Special Requirements—A teaching credential or other certification

CAREER LADDER

Mentor Teacher or Department Head

Physical Education Teacher

Student Teacher or Substitute Teacher

Position Description

Physical Education Teachers are specialists who help students develop lifetime habits of including physical activity into their daily lives.

Physical education instruction is different at each school level. In elementary school, Physical Education Teachers instruct students once or twice a week, usually for 30 minutes. (Many Physical Education Teachers in public schools travel from school to school to teach classes.) In the primary grades, they develop students' gross motor skills—running, jumping, skipping, and so on—and abilities to play cooperative games. Beginning ball activities and working with apparatus, such as jump ropes, are introduced. Beginning sports skills are introduced in the upper elementary grades.

In most middle-level schools, physical education classes are taught every day. Physical Education Teachers teach several periods each day. Instruction includes physical fitness, dance, formal sports skills, and recreational games. In some middle schools and junior high school, Physical Education Teachers are responsible for teaching health classes.

In high school, Physical Education Teachers also teach several periods of physical education. Some of the activities they teach are physical fitness, dance, weight training, swimming, gymnastics, individual sports, dual sports, and team sports.

At all grade levels, Physical Education Teachers are responsible for planning safe physical activities. They make sure instruction is developmentally appropriate for all students within their classes. If special education students are part of their classes, Physical Education Teachers modify instruction to fit their abilities. (A special education teacher is usually available to help Physical Education Teachers with instructional strategies.) Furthermore, Physical Education Teachers help students develop sports skills such as communication, responsibility, teamwork, and sportsmanship.

As part of their teaching duties, Physical Education Teachers create and prepare daily lesson plans. They assign students class projects, and give quizzes or tests to check students' understanding of new concepts and skills. Physical Education Teachers monitor students' progress, and evaluate their performance at the end of each grading period. Teachers also meet with students and parents to discuss students' work and behavior.

Physical Education Teachers also perform nonteaching duties. They do administrative tasks, such as taking attendance and reading aloud school announcements. They may monitor hallways, lunchrooms, and other parts of the campus during recesses and lunchtimes. Most teachers attend school games, dances, and other functions to help supervise attendance. They may sponsor extracurricular activities, such as clubs, student government, and school publications. They may also supervise and direct teacher aides, student teachers, and volunteer aides. In addition, they participate in faculty meetings and serve on school committees.

Some Physical Education Teachers coach girls' and boys' teams that participate in school athletic leagues. Football, basketball, baseball, volleyball, tennis, soccer, swimming, golf, wrestling, field hockey, and track and field are some of the sports that different Physical Education Teachers coach.

As part of their coaching duties, Physical Education Teachers guide and supervise teams in practice and prepare students for competitions. The coaches are responsible for managing and supervising teams as they travel to and from games and during games. Coaches may also organize competitions that take place in their schools—contacting league officials, referees, and scorekeepers; writing press releases; and making sure the grounds, such as baseball diamonds and football fields, are maintained and ready for play. In addition, Physical Education Teachers, in the role of coaches, may be involved in fund-raising for uniforms, equipment, travel expenses, and other needs for the teams.

Physical Education Teachers work long hours, often into the evenings and on weekends to complete all their tasks. Most Physical Education Teachers have a 10-month work schedule, usually from September to June.

Most public schools give teachers tenure after completing three to five years of continuous teaching service. With tenure, teachers cannot be fired without just cause.

Salaries

Salaries for Physical Education Teachers vary, depending on such factors as their education, credentials, experience, employer, and geographical location. According to the 2003–04 salary survey by the American Federation of Teachers, the average annual salary for teachers in public school ranged from $33,236 (in South Dakota) to $56,516 (in Connecticut).

In many schools, Physical Education Teachers receive extra compensation for each sport they coach. They may also receive additional pay for other extracurricular activities they sponsor.

Employment Prospects

Physical Education Teachers are employed in both private and public school settings. Most job openings will become available as Physical Education Teachers retire, advance to higher positions, or transfer to other occupations.

Opportunities are generally better in inner cities and rural areas as well as in fast-growing states in the South and West, where schools are expected to have large increases in enrollment.

Advancement Prospects

Physical Education Teachers can pursue several career paths. Experienced teachers can become mentor teachers and department heads, as well as head coaches and athletic directors. With additional education and endorsement, Physical Education Teachers can become Adapted Physical Education Teachers, specialists who instruct special education students with physical, emotional, or mental disabilities. They can also become school counselors, educational technologists, or other school-related professionals.

Additionally, they can pursue administrative positions. Private school teachers can work their way up to become school heads and other administrators. With additional education and licensure, public school teachers can become principals, instructional supervisors, program directors, or other school administrators.

Physical Education Teachers can also pursue other areas in their field. For example, they may become university professors recreation center directors, professional coaches, athletic trainers, or educational consultants.

Education and Training

Most Physical Education Teachers hold either a bachelor's or master's degree in physical education. Those applying for teaching licensure must complete an accredited teacher education program that includes pedagogy, instruction of subject matter, and a supervised field practicum.

In many schools, beginning teachers are assigned to mentor teachers who advise them with lesson plans, classroom management, and so on. Many schools require teachers to attend in-service workshops throughout the year.

Special Requirements

Physical Education Teachers in public schools must hold a valid teaching credential. The type of license and licensure requirements vary from state to state. Those wishing to coach may need to obtain a coaching endorsement for each sport they plan to coach. For specific information, contact the state board of education for the state in which you wish to teach. See Appendix III for a list of state boards.

Many private schools require certification from a state board of education, school accreditation group, professional association, or other recognized organization. Some schools, such as Waldorf schools, require internal teaching certifications, which are obtained after completing their training programs.

Experience, Skills, and Personality Traits

Most employers choose candidates who have previous experience teaching physical fitness and sports to children. For example, applicants may have gained work experience as student teachers, coaches, and recreational leaders. Many employers prefer Physical Education Teachers who have coaching experiences in competitive sports.

Physical Education Teachers should have strong interpersonal, teamwork, and communication skills as they must be able to work well with students, school staff, and parents. In addition, teachers need organizational and management skills to complete the various tasks they must handle each day.

Successful Physical Education Teachers have several personality traits in common, such as being self-disciplined, firm, fair, observant, flexible, and creative. In addition, they are passionate about teaching children to appreciate lifelong physical fitness, sportsmanship, and the many different physical activities.

Unions and Associations

Physical Education Teachers join professional associations that provide teaching resources, education programs, net-work opportunities, and other professional services and resources. Some organizations, such as the National Association for Sport and Physical Education, specifically serve Physical Education Teachers. Typically, Physical Education Teachers in public schools belong to a union, such as the American Federation of Teachers, that negotiates teaching contracts with their employers. For contact information for these organizations, see Appendix IV.

Tips for Entry

1. As a middle school, junior high, or high school student, you can begin getting valuable experience working with children. Volunteer (or apply for a part-time job) in a summer camp, recreation program, or children's sports league, such as baseball or soccer.
2. As an adult, find work in private gyms as an aerobics instructor or fitness trainer.
3. Learn more about a prospective employer before going to a job interview.
4. On the Internet you can learn more about teaching physical education in schools. To find relevant Web sites, use the keyword *physical education* in a search engine.

READING SPECIALIST

CAREER PROFILE

Duties: Develop, implement, and evaluate school-wide reading programs; perform assessments; provide resources and consulting services to teachers and other school staff; perform other duties as required

Alternate Title(s): Reading Supervisor

Salary Range: $33,000 to $57,000

Employment Prospects: Fair

Advancement Prospects: Fair

Prerequisites:

Education or Training—Master's degree; for licensed teachers, completion of an accredited reading specialist credential program

Experience—Two or more years of classroom teaching; some administrative experience

Special Skills and Personality Traits—Interpersonal, teamwork, communication, supervisory, and program management skills; be patient, flexible, creative, hardworking

Special Requirements—Teaching credential with a reading specialist endorsement

CAREER LADDER

```
┌─────────────────────────────────┐
│   Lead Reading Specialist or     │
│      Reading Coordinator         │
└─────────────────────────────────┘

┌─────────────────────────────────┐
│       Reading Specialist         │
└─────────────────────────────────┘

┌─────────────────────────────────┐
│           Teacher                │
└─────────────────────────────────┘
```

Position Description

Reading Specialists coordinate various developmental, remedial, early intervention, and other reading programs in public and private schools. They help students at all grade levels, from kindergarten to 12th grade, develop and build their reading skills, which is important to their success in school and everyday life.

Responsibilities for Reading Specialists vary from school to school. Most Reading Specialists assist administrators in the development of reading programs that follow state educational guidelines or frameworks and align with national and other professional standards. Many Reading Specialists perform reading assessments to determine students' reading abilities when requested by parents, teachers, administrators, or other school personnel. Some Reading Specialists are responsible for coordinating the administration of all formal standardized testing in a school.

Most Reading Specialists act as resources for teachers, parents, and administrators. They distribute useful information, materials, and current research that may help teachers with their instruction. They may provide parents with reading lists and tips about how to get their children to read more at home. Many Reading Specialists plan and conduct in-service training, presenting new reading methods and techniques for improving students' reading skills in academic and nonacademic subjects.

Reading Specialists also provide consulting services to individual teachers. They may provide guidance to teachers in specific grade levels or in certain schools in a school system. In small schools or school systems, Reading Specialists provide guidance to teachers at all grade levels. Reading Specialists might discuss various reading and classroom teaching strategies that may help students with reading problems in a teacher's classroom. In addition, specialists might model instructional techniques for teachers. Some Reading Specialists also provide intervention services, working with students individually or in small groups.

In addition, Reading Specialists promote reading in the schools and the community. For example, they may encourage teachers to allow for time in class to read; or they motivate students by providing them with nonfiction and fiction books that match their individual interests. Many Reading Specialists organize school-wide reading contests, reading book clubs, author days, book fairs, and other programs and events to encourage students to read.

Reading Specialists sometimes work into the evenings and on weekends to attend meetings, confer with parents, complete paperwork, or to perform other tasks. Most Reading Specialists have a 10-month work schedule, usually from September to June.

Salaries

Salaries for Reading Specialists vary, depending on such factors as their education, credentials, experience, employer, and geographical location. They normally receive a salary based on their school's teacher salary schedule. According to the 2003–04 salary survey by the American Federation of Teachers, the average annual salary for teachers in public school ranged from $33,236 (in South Dakota) to $56,516 (in Connecticut).

Employment Prospects

Reading Specialists are hired by public and private schools. Most job opportunities become available as Reading Specialists retire, resign, or advance to other positions. Schools may create additional positions when school funding is available.

Advancement Prospects

Promotions are limited to a few supervisory and administrative positions. With additional education and licensure, Reading Specialists can pursue other school administrative positions such as becoming principals, curriculum specialists, school program directors, or assistant superintendents. Additionally, they can pursue careers in other areas of education; for example, they might become university professors, reading consultants, educational software developers, or private reading program directors.

Education and Training

Reading Specialists have a master's degree in education or reading education. To obtain a reading specialist credential, teachers must complete a reading specialist program from an accredited reading education program. The program includes courses on the reading process, instructional strategies, diagnosis in reading, reading in the content areas, and so on. It also includes a supervised field practicum.

Special Requirements

In public schools, Reading Specialists must hold a valid teaching credential in addition to a reading specialist endorsement. Licensure requirements for a reading specialist credential vary from state to state. For specific information, contact the state board of education for the state in which you wish to work. See Appendix III for a list of state boards.

All private schools have their own requirements for teacher certification. They may require that Reading Specialists possess state licensure or professional certification from a recognized organization. Some private schools require an internal teaching certification.

Experience, Skills, and Personality Traits

Reading Specialists should have previous classroom teaching experience. To obtain licensure, individuals need two or more years of classroom teaching, depending on the state where they live. In addition, they should have some administrative experience.

Reading Specialists need interpersonal, teamwork, communication, supervisory, and program management skills in order to perform their responsibilities effectively. Successful Reading Specialists share several personality traits, such as being patient, flexible, creative, and hardworking. They have a passion for reading and the desire to help children find the joy, and competency, in reading for themselves.

Unions and Associations

Many Reading Specialists join professional associations, such as the International Reading Association, to take advantage of networking opportunities, education programs, and other professional services and resources. Specialists in public schools may belong to a union, such as the National Education Association, that negotiates contracts with employers. See Appendix IV for contact information for the above organizations.

Tips for Entry

1. To learn more about the profession, talk with Reading Specialists. If possible, help out on book fairs and other promotional programs that the Reading Specialist in your school may organize.

2. Contact schools directly about job vacancies and selection processes.

3. You can learn more about reading issues on the Internet. One place to start is at the International Reading Association Web site at http://www.reading.org.

SPECIAL EDUCATION TEACHER

CAREER PROFILE

Duties: Provide instruction to students with disabilities; prepare lesson plans, provide consulting services to general education teachers; participate in Individualized Education Program (IEP) meetings; perform other duties as required

Alternate Title(s): Special Education Resource Teacher; Visually Impaired Teacher and other titles that reflect an area of specialization

Salary Range: $30,000 to $75,000

Employment Prospects: Excellent

Advancement Prospects: Good

Prerequisites:

    Education or Training—Bachelor's or master's degree; for state licensure, completion of an accredited special education teacher education program

    Experience—Student teaching, internship, or other teaching experience with children with disabilities

    Special Skills and Personality Traits—Interpersonal, teamwork, communication, organizational, behavior management, and report-writing skills; be patient, honest, creative, flexible, and firm

    Special Requirements—A teacher's credential with a special education endorsement

CAREER LADDER

Mentor Teacher or Department Head

Special Education Teacher

Teacher, Substitute Teacher, or Student Teacher

Position Description

Public and private school are mandated by the Individuals with Disabilities Education Act (IDEA), a federal law, to provide special education programs and related services to children with disabilities from newborn to age 21. The law ensures that all special education students receive the same instruction and assessment that regular students receive in general education classrooms. Special education programs serve children with autism, traumatic brain injury, mental retardation, specific learning disabilities, visual impairment, hearing impairment, speech or language impairment, orthopedic impairment, serious emotional disturbance, and multiple disabilities. Gifted and talented children are also served by special education programs.

Special Education Teachers, who are trained in one or more specialties, provide instruction in academic subjects as well as other skills that students need to succeed in school and in life. They help students develop behavioral management skills—getting along with others, being comfortable in social situations, practicing socially acceptable behavior, and so on. Many also help students learn study skills. Some Special Education Teachers help students develop life skills for an independent life. For example, they might teach students how to read bus schedules or balance checkbooks. Some teachers help students prepare for life after high school by teaching them job search skills and providing career counseling.

When planning instruction, Special Education Teachers follow instructional goals and objectives and evaluation procedures that are outlined on students' Individualized Education Programs (IEPs). Special Education Teachers may be involved in providing assessments and evaluations of special education students, as well as developing IEPs.

Special Education Teachers teach in a variety of settings. Some teach in self-contained classrooms, providing instruction for all subjects to a small group of special education students. The students usually have different abilities, skill levels, and learning styles, so teachers must modify instruction to fit each student's needs. To help with instruction, teachers may use specialized equipment such as audiotapes, educational software programs, and computers with synthesized speech.

Many special education students are mainstreamed into general education classrooms to receive instruction alongside regular students for one or more subjects. Some special education students receive instruction for all subjects in general education classrooms. These classrooms are often referred to as inclusive classrooms. In some inclusive classrooms, general education teachers and Special Education Teachers work collaboratively to prepare lesson plans and provide instruction to all the students. Special Education Teachers use their expertise to adapt the lessons and materials to the skill levels and abilities of the special education students.

Many Special Education Teachers work in resource rooms, providing support services to special education students in general education classrooms. They work with special education students in resource rooms for a few hours each day on specific subjects, such as math or reading. The teachers individualize instruction to fit the students' abilities and learning styles so that they can best learn their lessons. For example, a learning disabled student learns best aurally, so the Special Education Resource Teacher helps the student read his math assignments aloud.

Some Special Education Teachers travel from school to school to provide instructional support to special education students. Most traveling, or itinerant, Special Education Teachers work with visually, hearing, and physically impaired students.

As part of their duties, resource and itinerant Special Education Teachers also provide consulting services to general education teachers. They help general education teachers modify their teaching methods and instructional materials to fit the needs of their special education students.

Some Special Education Teachers are also case managers, overseeing the IEP for each student on their caseload. As case managers, they make sure IEPs are being implemented and followed by general education teachers, special education teachers, and specialists such as school social workers and speech-language pathologists. Case managers also schedule and coordinate meetings; maintain individual IEP files; and act as liaison between schools and parents.

Depending on the school, Special Education Teachers may perform other tasks, such as monitoring duties, study hall supervision, and extracurricular activity supervision. They also participate in faculty meetings and on school committees.

Special Education Teachers work long hours each day, often completing tasks at home in the evenings and on weekends. Most work 10-month schedules, from September to June. Public schools may offer tenure to teachers after they have completed three to five years of continuous service. With tenure, teachers cannot be fired from their jobs without just cause.

Salaries

Salaries for Special Education Teachers vary, depending on such factors as their education, experience, employer, and geographical location. The U.S. Bureau of Labor Statistics (BLS) reports, in its November 2004 *Occupational Employment Statistics* (OES) survey, that most Special Education Teachers at the different school levels received an estimated salary that fell between the following ranges:

- $30,410 and $69,820 in preschool, kindergarten, and elementary schools
- $30,700 and $75,390 in middle schools
- $31,350 and $74,240 in secondary schools

Employment Prospects

According to the BLS's November 2004 OES survey, about 440,000 Special Education Teachers were employed in public and private schools. The BLS also reports that employment of these teachers is expected to increase by 36 percent or more through 2012. The need for additional teachers is due to the continuing growth of special education students and by legislation requiring higher standards for graduation. In addition, opportunities are created to replace teachers who retire, return to teaching in general education, or transfer to other occupations.

Job opportunities are strongest in inner cities and rural areas, as well as in some states in the West and South that are growing rapidly and thus seeing an increase in student enrollment. There is also an increasing demand for Special Education Teachers who are bilingual as well as for those who specialize in early childhood education.

Advancement Prospects

Special Education Teachers can advance to any number of professions. They may become special education work study coordinators, program supervisors, or directors. They may also become educational diagnosticians, adapted physical education teachers, or special education technology specialists. In addition, they may become school psychologists, social workers, speech pathologists, creative arts therapists, or other professionals who provide related services to special education students.

Special Education Teachers also can pursue school administrative positions. In private schools, teachers can become school heads, deans of students, and other administrators.

With additional education and licensure, teachers in public schools can become principals and district administrators such as curriculum specialists and assistant superintendents.

Education and Training

Special Education Teachers must have a bachelor's or master's degree in the discipline for which they receive their teaching credential. Many Special Education Teachers also have a master's degree in special education.

Licensed teachers have completed a teacher education program leading to special education licensure in addition to the general teacher education training program for the teaching credential. The special education teacher program includes a supervised field practicum and course work in the different disabilities, pedagogy, assessment and testing strategies, behavior management techniques, and laws regarding special education.

Beginning teachers may be assigned to mentor teachers who advise them with lesson plans, classroom management, and so on. Many Special Education Teachers enroll in continuing education programs to keep up with new teaching methods, changes in laws, and other developments in their field.

Special Requirements

In public schools, Special Education Teachers must hold a valid teaching credential in elementary, middle-level, or secondary education with a special education endorsement in each specialty—learning disabled, severely handicapped, visually impaired, and so on—in which they wish to teach. The type of special education licensure and requirements vary from state to state. For specific information, contact the state board of education for the state in which you wish to teach. See Appendix III for a list of state boards.

Private schools may require Special Education Teachers to possess state licensure or professional certification granted by a recognized organization. Some schools require internal teaching certifications.

Experience, Skills, and Personality Traits

Schools typically hire entry-level teachers who have previous experience working with children with disabilities. For example, they may have been student teachers, teacher aides, peer tutors, counselors, or volunteers in special education settings.

Interpersonal, teamwork, and communication skills are necessary for Special Education Teachers. They must be able to work well with their students as well as with teachers, administrators, school-related professionals, and parents. Furthermore, Special Education Teachers should develop strong organizational, behavior management, and report-writing skills. Being patient, honest, creative, flexible, and firm are some of the personality traits that successful Special Education Teachers share.

Unions and Associations

Special Education Teachers join professional associations that provide teaching resources, continuing education programs, network opportunities, and so on. Some organizations specifically serve special needs teachers, such as the Council for Exceptional Children and the Learning Disabilities Association of America. Teachers in public schools belong to a union, such as the American Federation of Teachers or the National Education Association, that negotiates teaching contracts with employers. See Appendix IV for contact information for these organizations.

Tips for Entry

1. Gain experience working with children with different disabilities, as well as with the different ages (infants to age 21) in a variety of settings—school, residential facility, juvenile detention center, psychiatric setting, and so on. You might also volunteer with community programs that serve children with disabilities, such as Special Olympics, United Cerebral Palsy Association, or The Arc of the United States.

2. Many school districts offer alternative credentials for Special Education Teachers. Contact a district central school office to find out what may be available.

3. Use the job interview to get more specific information about a position. After the interviewers have asked their questions, ask yours. Find out what the class load is like, what the school's philosophy on special education is, what kind of support special education teachers receive, and so on.

4. Use the Internet to learn more about working in special education. You might start by visiting these Web sites: Council for Exceptional Children, http://www.cec sped.org, and National Clearinghouse for Professions in Special Education, http://www.special-ed-careers.org.

BILINGUAL TEACHER

CAREER PROFILE

Duties: Provide instruction of academic subjects in English and a second language; create daily lesson plans; perform other duties as required

Alternate Title(s): Bilingual Education Teacher

Salary Range: $33,000 to $57,000

Employment Prospects: Excellent

Advancement Prospects: Good

Prerequisites:

 Education or Training—Bachelor's or master's degree; for licensed teachers, completion of an accredited teacher education program

 Experience—Student teaching, internship, or other teaching experience in bilingual or ESL settings

 Special Skills and Personality Traits—Literate in a second language; communication, interpersonal, teamwork, organizational, and management skills; be patient, flexible, creative, and sensitive

 Special Requirements—Teaching credential with a bilingual education teaching endorsement

CAREER LADDER

```
┌──────────────────────────────────────┐
│  Mentor Teacher or Department Head     │
└──────────────────────────────────────┘

┌──────────────────────────────────────┐
│          Bilingual Teacher             │
└──────────────────────────────────────┘

┌──────────────────────────────────────┐
│     Teacher or Student Teacher         │
└──────────────────────────────────────┘
```

Position Description

Bilingual Teachers instruct students who are only minimally able to speak, read, write, or understand English. Some schoolchildren have no English language skills at all. Thus, these limited-English-proficient (LEP) students have two goals in school—to learn English and to learn the subjects that are being taught at their grade level. (Research shows that it generally takes between five to seven years to develop enough English language skills to understand academic instruction.)

Bilingual Teachers provide instruction of academic subjects in two languages—English and the native language of the LEP students in the class, which may be Spanish, Russian, Korean, Chinese, Vietnamese, Tagalog, and so on.

Bilingual programs are mostly used in kindergarten, elementary grades, and middle-level grades. There are different types of bilingual programs, but almost all bilingual programs have an English as a second language (ESL) component in which LEP students receive instruction for a few hours a day to learn English language skills.

One type of bilingual program is the transitional bilingual program in which Bilingual Teachers teach subjects in English, and use the native language only to help students understand instruction. Another type is the developmental bilingual program. In this program, Bilingual Teachers provide instruction in both languages so that children can become literate in both English and their native language. Classes in transitional and developmental bilingual programs are usually made up of LEP students who all speak the same native language.

Still another type of program is the two-way immersion bilingual program, in which Bilingual Teachers use both English and a second language to teach the academic subjects. Classes in this program are made up of LEP students and native English-speaking students. (Two-way immersion programs are popular with many English-speaking parents who want their children to learn valuable second language skills and fluency as well as be exposed to a cross-cultural learning environment.)

Bilingual Teachers are responsible for preparing lesson plans in two languages. They often create their own student materials because of the lack of published materials. In addition, Bilingual Teachers continually assess and monitor their students' performance and behavior. In some schools, Bilingual Teachers work collaboratively in preparing lesson plans and providing instruction to students.

Bilingual Teachers also perform many nonteaching duties. They complete administrative tasks, such as taking attendance and reading school announcements. Many may have monitoring duties during class breaks; they may also help supervise attendance at school functions. Some Bilingual Teachers supervise and direct bilingual aides, tutors, and school volunteers who may be assigned to help them in class. In addition, Bilingual Teachers participate in faculty meetings and on school committees. Some teachers also coach after-school sports or sponsor extracurricular activities, such as school clubs, computer labs, or tutoring programs.

Some Bilingual Teachers are resource teachers for one or more schools or school districts, working with LEP students from general education classrooms. Many Bilingual Teachers also provide consulting services to general education teachers who have LEP students in their classrooms. In addition, some Bilingual Teachers are in charge of administering and coordinating language assessment tests.

Bilingual Teachers work long hours, often into the evenings and on weekends to complete all their tasks. Most have a 10-month work schedule, usually from September to June.

Most public schools give teachers tenure after completing three to five years of continuous teaching service. With tenure, teachers cannot be fired without just cause.

Salaries

Salaries for Bilingual Teachers vary, depending on such factors as their education, credentials, experience, employer, and geographical location. In some schools, teachers receive extra compensation for coaching or sponsoring extracurricular activities. According to the 2003–04 salary survey by the American Federation of Teachers, the average annual salary for teachers in public school ranged from $33,236 (in South Dakota) to $56,516 (in Connecticut).

Employment Prospects

Bilingual Teachers are employed by public and private schools. The U.S. Bureau of Labor Statistics reports that the job outlook for school teachers in general is favorable through 2012, partly due to the large number of teachers becoming eligible for retirement. The population of non-English-speaking students has been increasing in the United States, thus creating a need for qualified Bilingual Teachers, particularly in Florida, Texas, and California. The primary demand is for Bilingual Teachers who are literate in Span-

ish; but many schools also need teachers literate in other foreign languages.

Advancement Prospects

Bilingual Teachers have several advancement opportunities. They may become mentor teachers, department heads, or program coordinators. They can pursue administrative positions, becoming assistant principals, principals, and administrators in the central school office. Furthermore, they can pursue their careers in other settings. For instance, they might become educational researchers, university professors, textbook editors, or bilingual education consultants.

Education and Training

Because Bilingual Teachers teach academic subjects, they should have at least a bachelor's degree in their discipline. For example, to teach bilingual classes in elementary grades, a Bilingual Teacher might have a bachelor's degree in liberal studies. In some schools, a master's degree in education or another related field is required.

Licensed Bilingual Teachers have completed an accredited teacher education program as well as a bilingual education program. The bilingual education program includes a supervised field practicum and courses in second language acquisition theory and pedagogy that focuses on integration of language.

In some schools, new Bilingual Teachers may be assigned to mentor teachers who advise them on teaching strategies, classroom management, and other matters. Many schools require Bilingual Teachers to attend in-service workshops throughout the year.

Special Requirements

Bilingual Teachers in public schools must hold a teaching credential in elementary, middle level, or secondary education along with a bilingual education endorsement. For information about requirements, contact the state board of education for the state in which you wish to teach. See Appendix III for a list of state boards.

Many private schools require certification from a state board of education, school accreditation group, professional association, or other recognized organization. Some schools require internal teaching certifications, which are obtained after completing their training programs.

Experience, Skills, and Personality Traits

In general, Bilingual Teachers should have previous teaching experience in bilingual or ESL settings. They should be sufficiently proficient in a second language in order to assess a student's language proficiency in both the native language and English.

Because Bilingual Teachers must work well with students, parents, and school staff, they should have adequate communication, interpersonal, and teamwork skills. In addition, organizational and management skills are also needed to complete the many, different tasks that must be done each day.

Successful Bilingual Teachers share several personality traits, among them patience, flexibility, and creativity. They are sensitive to the needs and changes that take place in children as they learn a second language in a new culture.

Unions and Associations

Bilingual Teachers join professional associations that provide teaching resources, education programs, networking opportunities, and other professional services and resources. Some organizations specifically serve bilingual educators, such as the National Association for Bilingual Education and TESOL, Inc. Most public school teachers belong to a union, such as the National Education Association, that negotiates teaching contracts with employers. See Appendix IV for contact information for the above groups.

Tips for Entry

1. Keep up your second language proficiency. You should be literate in reading, writing, and speaking skills in your second language.
2. Many school districts offer alternative certification programs to encourage bilingual aides and individuals literate in Spanish or other languages in demand to become Bilingual Teachers. To learn what may be available in your area, contact the state board of education or a school office.
3. Start applying for jobs early. Many schools accept applications as early as December or January.
4. Learn more about bilingual education on the Internet. You might start by visiting the National Association for Bilingual Education Web site at http://www.nabe.org.

ESL (ENGLISH AS A SECOND LANGUAGE) TEACHER

CAREER PROFILE

Duties: Teach English as a second language to limited-English-proficient (LEP) students; provide consulting services to mainstream ESL teachers; perform other duties as required

Alternate Title(s): None

Salary Range: $33,000 to $57,000

Employment Prospects: Excellent

Advancement Prospects: Good

Prerequisites:

Education or Training—Bachelor's or master's degree; for licensed teachers, completion of an accredited teacher education program

Experience—Student teaching or other teaching experience in ESL settings

Special Skills and Personality Traits—Communication, interpersonal, teamwork, organizational, and management skills; be patient, flexible, creative, respectful

Special Requirements—Teaching credential with an ESL teaching endorsement

CAREER LADDER

```
┌─────────────────────────────────────┐
│  Mentor Teacher or Department Head   │
└─────────────────────────────────────┘

┌─────────────────────────────────────┐
│             ESL Teacher              │
└─────────────────────────────────────┘

┌─────────────────────────────────────┐
│     Teacher or Student Teacher       │
└─────────────────────────────────────┘
```

Position Description

English as a Second Language (ESL) Teachers are specialists in English-language acquisition. They help limited-English-proficiency (LEP) students—those with little or no English language skills. These students are usually recent immigrants to the United States whose primary language may be Spanish, Korean, Chinese, Polish, Russian, Arabic, Tagalog, or another language.

ESL Teachers work in ESL programs in elementary schools, middle schools, and high schools. In most programs, LEP students are pulled out from their general education or bilingual classrooms for a few hours each day to receive instruction in English language skills—listening, speaking, reading, and writing skills. ESL Teachers provide all instruction in English although classes are typically made up of students who have different native languages. ESL Teachers may or may not know a second language; however, they are aware of the transitions that immigrants

and refugees experience as they learn a new language and culture. Many teachers have aides who are fluent in native languages to help LEP students.

Like all other schoolteachers, ESL Teachers create and prepare daily lesson plans. Many teachers create their own student materials—worksheets, word games, and so on—because of the lack of published materials. In addition, they assess students' skill levels and monitor their progress.

In many schools, advanced ESL students are placed in mainstream ESL content-area classes, such as U.S. history, general science, and math, which are taught by general education teachers. Some ESL Teachers are responsible for conducting in-service workshops and providing consulting services to mainstream ESL teachers. They may also advise mainstream ESL teachers on how to alter their teaching strategies and modify instructional materials, as well as discuss the cultural differences among their ESL students.

Most ESL Teachers have nonteaching duties, such as taking daily attendance, performing monitoring duties during class breaks, conferring with parents, participating in faculty and school committee meetings, and supervising at school functions. Many ESL Teachers also sponsor extracurricular activities, such as clubs and after-school tutoring programs.

Most ESL Teachers have 10-month work schedules, usually working from September to June. Public school teachers may earn tenure after they have completed three to five years of continuous teaching service. With tenure, teachers cannot be fired without just cause.

Salaries

Salaries for ESL Teachers vary, depending on such factors as their education, credentials, experience, employer, and geographical location. According to the 2003–04 salary survey by the American Federation of Teachers, the average annual salary for teachers in public school ranged from $33,236 (in South Dakota) to $56,516 (in Connecticut).

In some schools, ESL Teachers may receive extra compensation for coaching after-school sports or sponsoring extracurricular activities.

Employment Prospects

ESL Teachers work in both public and private schools where jobs are readily available at all grade levels. The U.S. Bureau of Labor Statistics reports that the job outlook for school teachers in general is favorable through 2012, partly due to the large number of teachers becoming eligible for retirement. The population of non-English-speaking students has been increasing throughout the United States, thus creating a need for qualified ESL Teachers. According to the TESOL, Inc. Web site, the demand is particularly strong in areas with large immigrant and refugee populations, such as in California, Florida, Illinois, New York, and Texas.

Advancement Prospects

ESL Teachers can advance their careers in any number of ways. They may become mentor teachers, department heads, and program coordinators. They may also pursue administrative positions by becoming principals or central office administrators. Additionally, they can pursue careers in other areas of education; for instance, they can become university professors, English language development researchers, textbook editors, or private ESL program administrators.

Education and Training

ESL Teachers need either a bachelor's or master's degree, depending on state licensure or school requirements.

Licensed ESL Teachers have completed an accredited teacher education program as well as an ESL education program. The ESL education program includes a supervised field practicum and course work in second language acquisition, teaching methods, testing and evaluation, and materials development.

In some schools, beginning ESL Teachers are assigned to mentor teachers who advise them about teaching strategies, behavior management, and so on. Many ESL Teachers are required to attend in-service workshops throughout the year.

Special Requirements

To teach in public schools, ESL Teachers must hold a teaching license in elementary, middle level, or secondary education along with an ESL teaching endorsement. For information about current requirements, contact the state board of education for the state in which you wish to teach. See Appendix III for a list of state boards.

Private schools may require certification from a state board of education, school accreditation group, professional association, or other recognized organization. Some schools require internal teaching certifications. Other schools require no certification at all.

Experience, Skills, and Personality Traits

In general, employers choose candidates who have practical experience teaching LEP students. For example, applicants may have gained their experience as student teachers or volunteer tutors. Employers also prefer candidates who have knowledge of other cultures and have learned a second language, regardless of proficiency.

ESL Teachers must have strong communication, interpersonal, teamwork, organizational, and management skills, which teachers need to complete their many different duties each day. Successful ESL Teachers share several personality traits, such as being patient, flexible, creative, and respectful. They also enjoy and appreciate working with people from different cultures.

Unions and Associations

Many ESL Teachers belong to TESOL, Inc. (Teachers of English to Speakers of Other Languages, Inc.), a professional association that offers networking opportunities, teacher resources, continuing education programs, and other services.

Most ESL Teachers in public schools belong to a union, such as the American Federation of Teachers or the National Education Association, that negotiates teaching contracts with employers.

For contact information for the above organizations, see Appendix IV.

Tips for Entry

1. Gain experience working with people of other cultures. For example, you might volunteer as a tutor in an ESL program.

2. Broaden your experience of other cultures. You might learn another language, read books or watch films about different cultures, attend ethnic festivals, eat at ethnic restaurants, or visit other countries.

3. Contact schools directly about job vacancies and selection processes.

4. You can learn more about teaching ESL in schools on the Internet. You might start by visiting the TESOL, Inc. Web site at http://www.tesol.org.

POSTSECONDARY EDUCATORS

PROFESSOR

CAREER PROFILE

Duties: Teach undergraduate or graduate courses within an academic unit; conduct scholarly research; perform other duties as required

Alternate Title(s): Instructor, Assistant Professor, Associate Professor, Full Professor

Salary Range: $40,000 to $92,000

Employment Prospects: Good

Advancement Prospects: Fair

Prerequisites:

    Education or Training—A doctoral degree

    Experience—Previous teaching experience

    Special Skills and Personality Traits—Communication, presentation, interpersonal, teamwork, social, organizational, and management skills; be independent, intelligent, analytical, inquiring, self-motivated, and confident

    Special Requirements—Occupational licensure and professional certification may be required

CAREER LADDER

```
┌─────────────────────────────────┐
│        (Full) Professor         │
└─────────────────────────────────┘


┌─────────────────────────────────┐
│       Associate Professor       │
└─────────────────────────────────┘


┌─────────────────────────────────┐
│       Assistant Professor       │
└─────────────────────────────────┘
```

Position Description

Professors in four-year colleges and universities prepare students for careers that require bachelor's, master's, or doctoral degrees—for example, lawyers, architects, teachers, accountants, FBI agents, business managers, medical doctors, veterinarians, engineers, and journalists. Many Professors are also responsible for conducting scholarly research in their fields that can lead to important discoveries and inventions that benefit society.

Professors belong to specific academic units which comprise departments or divisions. For example, a college might have a department of social science with history, geography, economics, anthropology, and political science as some of its academic units. Each term, Professors are assigned to teach several undergraduate or graduate courses within a prescribed curriculum.

For each of their courses, they develop a course syllabus that outlines the topics and sequence of topics to be taught as well as bibliographies for outside reading assignments. They are also responsible for preparing lectures and laboratory experiments. Depending on the course, Professors may lecture to hundreds of students in large halls, instruct small groups in

classrooms or laboratories, or lead discussions in seminars made up of 10 or fewer students. Some Professors teach online courses or courses on cable or closed-circuit television.

Their teaching responsibilities include assigning papers and administering exams. They grade papers and exams and return them to their students with positive and critical comments. At the end of each term, Professors evaluate their students' academic performances with a letter grade. At large universities, teaching assistants and graders are usually available to help Professors with administering exams, grading papers and exams, leading discussion sections, and supervising laboratory experiments.

Professors are required to hold regularly scheduled office hours, usually three to six hours a week, for meeting with students and advising them in course and career matters. Many Professors are responsible for supervising students with their research projects. For example, they may provide guidance to undergraduate students with independent study projects, graduate students with their theses, or doctorate candidates with their dissertations. Some Professors also supervise postdoctoral students who are managing their own research projects.

At universities and many four-year colleges, Professors are expected to conduct academic research and to write up the results of their research for publication in scholarly journals, books, and electronic media. For many Professors, their research is usually a continuation of the work begun during their doctoral program. Some research projects are conducted in collaboration with colleagues or students.

Part of the research process includes the writing of grant proposals to obtain funds from private corporations, government agencies, and other funding sources. The money pays for equipment and supplies, travel to research sites, overhead costs, financial support for themselves and research assistants, and so on. Some Professors support their own research projects during unpaid summer terms.

Along with teaching and research, Professors are required to participate in faculty meetings where they discuss and handle departmental matters, such as curriculum, equipment purchases, and hiring. Professors are also expected to serve on academic and administrative advisory committees which deal with institutional policies. Additionally, Professors perform community service, such as providing consultation services to community agencies, nonprofit organizations, corporations, government agencies, and other institutions. Many Professors serve on committees, panels, or commissions established by government agencies.

Due to the flexible nature of their profession, Professors can participate in various nonacademic activities. For example, they might:

- conduct seminars or workshops for professional associations
- go on lecture tours
- act in an editorial capacity to a professional journal
- participate in a musical, dramatic, or other artistic performance
- practice a profession, such as law, on a part-time basis
- testify as an expert witness in a court of law

Professors are responsible for keeping up with developments in their field through independent study, networking with colleagues, and participating in professional conferences and workshops.

The number of hours that Professors divide among teaching, research, and other duties varies according to their situation and the type of institution where they work. Generally, undergraduate faculty teach 12 to 15 hours per week while graduate faculty usually teach 10 hours or less. University Professors typically spend more time conducting research than Professors in liberal arts colleges.

Professors may be appointed to part-time or full-time positions. Many full-time Professors are tenured—that is, they are assured of a job at an institution until they retire or resign. With tenure, they cannot be fired without just cause and due process.

Salaries

Salaries vary, and depend on factors such as a Professor's rank, his or her field, the type of institution, and the geographical location. Full Professors typically earn the highest salaries. According to a 2004–05 survey by the American Association of University Professors, the average salaries for instructor, assistant, associate, and full Professor ranged from $39,899 to $ 91,548.

Many Professors make additional earnings from research projects, publications, consulting work, lecture tours, teaching courses for college extension programs or professional associations, and so on.

Employment Prospects

Professors are hired by private and public four-year colleges and universities for either tenure track or nontenure track positions. Opportunities for postsecondary instructors, in general, are expected to increase by 21 to 35 percent through 2012, according to the U.S. Bureau of Labor Statistics. An expected increase in student enrollment as well as a large number of Professors becoming eligible for retirement should create a demand for additional positions. In addition, opportunities become available as Professors advance to higher positions or transfer to other institutions.

Fewer tenure-track positions are becoming available each year. Due to tight budgets, colleges and universities have been hiring more part-time faculty or offering prospective full-time faculty limited contracts of one to five years which may be renewed. The competition is high for both tenure and nontenure track positions at any college.

Advancement Prospects

Professors advance through the academic ranks as instructor, assistant professor, associate professor, and full professor. Full Professors can advance administratively up the ladder to department chair, faculty dean, provost, and eventually college or university president.

Appointments and promotions are based on Professors' records of teaching, research, publication, and community service. Receiving promotions is separate from being given tenure.

Tenure-track positions start at either the instructor or assistant professor level, with tenure attained at the associate professor rank. Usually after six years, an assistant professor's record is reviewed by the tenured faculty in his or her academic unit and then voted on to decide whether to recommend the candidate for tenure. The school's board of trustees makes the final decision to grant tenure to a Professor. With tenure, Professors have prestige, professional freedom, and job security for the rest of their academic career. Job satisfaction is extremely high, and few tenured Professors leave the profession.

Tenured or nontenured Professors who wish to leave the academic world can pursue employment in government agencies, businesses, companies, nonprofit institutions, and professional organizations. They can also become consultants in their fields.

Education and Training

Professors must hold doctoral degrees in their field of specialization. In general, their academic career includes at least four years of undergraduate work for a bachelor's degree, then one to two years of graduate study for a master's degree. This is followed by four to six years in a doctoral program which includes a dissertation on original research that they complete in their major field of study. Upon completion of their doctorate, some students complete an additional two or more years in postdoctoral research and study.

Special Requirements

Professors in disciplines such as law, medicine, psychology, or engineering need appropriate occupational licenses and professional certifications.

Experience, Skills, and Personality Traits

Depending on the institution's mission, candidates may need to demonstrate that they have a strong teaching or research background. For example, smaller liberal arts colleges emphasize teaching over research.

Professors should have excellent communication and presentation skills as well as interpersonal and teamwork skills to establish rapport with students and colleagues. They should also have adequate social skills as Professors commonly attend various college functions. Furthermore, they need strong organizational and management skills.

Successful Professors share several personality traits such as being independent, intelligent, analytical, inquiring, self-motivated, and confident.

Unions and Associations

Professors join different professional associations to take advantage of networking opportunities, professional development, and other services and resources. Along with belonging to societies that serve their disciplines, Professors join the National Association of Scholars.

Many also join the American Association of University Professors, in which some chapters in public institutions negotiate salaries and benefits for their members. Professors in public institutions are also eligible to join the higher education divisions of the National Education Association and the American Federation of Teachers.

See Appendix IV for contact information for the above organizations.

Tips for Entry

1. Experts recommend that doctoral candidates gain teaching experience before they earn their doctoral degrees. For example, they might teach courses at their institution, community colleges, or college extension programs.
2. When applying for a position, read the job announcement carefully. Also learn something about the school—whether it is more research-oriented or more teaching-oriented, and so on. Then tailor your resume and cover letter to fit the position. For example, if you know the school is more interested in teaching, then you would want to emphasize your teaching strengths and experiences.
3. Check out Web sites for professional associations. Many of them post job listings. Also visit the following Web sites for job announcements: The Chronicle of Higher Education, http://chronicle.com, and Higher EducationJob.com, http://www.higheredjobs.com.
4. Learn more about higher education on the Internet. You might start by visiting these Web sites: National Association of Scholars, http://www.nas.org, and Higher Education Resource Hub, http://www.higher ed.org. Also visit the U.S. Department of Education Office of Postsecondary Education Web site. First go to http://www.ed.gov. Click on the link for *Offices,* then click on the link for the *Office of Postsecondary Education.*

LECTURER

CAREER PROFILE

Duties: Teach undergraduate or graduate courses on a temporary basis in four-year colleges and universities; advise students; perform other duties as required

Alternate Title(s): Visiting Lecturer, Adjunct Lecturer, Senior Lecturer

Salary Range: $44,000 to $47,000

Employment Prospects: Good

Advancement Prospects: Fair

Prerequisites:

Education or Training—A master's or doctoral degree

Experience—Previous teaching experience

Special Skills and Personality Traits—Communication, interpersonal, teamwork, organizational, and management skills; be independent, analytical, intellectual, flexible, and creative

Special Requirements—Occupational licensure and professional certification may be required

CAREER LADDER

```
┌─────────────────────────────┐
│      Senior Lecturer        │
└─────────────────────────────┘

┌─────────────────────────────┐
│          Lecturer           │
└─────────────────────────────┘

┌─────────────────────────────┐
│      Doctoral Candidate     │
└─────────────────────────────┘
```

Position Description

Lecturers in four-year colleges and universities are temporary faculty members who have been appointed to teach courses for one or more departments (such as history, physical science, elementary education, or theater arts). They usually are not required to conduct research or publish creative work because of their heavy teaching loads.

Lecturers teach one to four undergraduate or graduate classes per term. The courses are usually basic requirement classes and can be for any academic unit in a department. For example, a Lecturer in a Classics Department might teach beginning Latin, classical Greek, and Roman religion. Their teaching load may be reduced if they are performing extensive program development for a department, or are helping students in a production such as a play or concert.

For each course they teach, Lecturers develop a syllabus that outlines the topics to be taught. Lecturers also prepare for their classes—studying the topic, writing lecture notes, gathering materials for lab demonstrations, choosing appropriate assignments within assigned texts, compiling bibliographies for outside reading assignments, and so on.

Their instruction may involve presentations to small groups of students in classrooms or to hundreds of students in large lecture halls. Lecturers may also supervise students in laboratory or field experiments. Many Lecturers use computer technology as teaching aids in their instruction.

Lecturers are also responsible for administering and grading student papers and examinations. They evaluate students' work in a timely manner, giving students critical feedback. At the end of each school term, Lecturers evaluate students' overall performance with a letter grade and report the grades to the appropriate office.

As part of their duties, Lecturers keep regular office hours each week to advise students on academic and career matters. Lecturers may be responsible for directing students in independent studies or supervising students, such as teacher education majors in practicum field experiences. Some Lecturers act as advisers to student organizations.

Some Lecturers are given the additional duty of assisting program coordinators within their departments. For example, they might help in the development and evaluation of courses; collect program data; help with student recruitment; prepare student advisement materials; or design professional development activities for teaching assistants or part-time faculty.

Lecturers are responsible for keeping up with developments in their discipline as well as in teaching methodologies, the use of technology in instruction, and so on. Professional development may be acquired by independent study, networking with colleagues, and participating in professional workshops and conferences.

Lecturers may be appointed to part-time or full-time positions, which are nontenure track. They normally receive limited term contracts for one to three years or longer, which may be renewed.

Many part-time Lecturers also hold down other jobs. They might teach courses in community colleges or college extension programs as well as teach classes, seminars, or workshops for professional associations. Some Lecturers find part-time employment in government, business, private industry, nonprofit, and community organizations as consultants, researchers, program developers, writers, or other occupations.

Salaries

According to a 2004–05 survey by the American Association of University Professors, the average annual salary for Lecturers in four-year colleges and universities ranged from $44,181 in baccalaureate institutions to $47,285 in doctoral institutions.

Employment Prospects

Along with teaching in four-year colleges and universities, Lecturers are hired by community colleges as well as by college and university extension programs.

Job prospects are currently favorable for part-time positions as well as for limited term contracts for full-time positions. However, the competition is high for most faculty positions.

Advancement Prospects

Generally, the position of Lecturer is a stepping-stone to academic positions as instructor, assistant professor, associate professor, and so on up to college president.

With experience and advanced degrees, Lecturers may be appointed to the rank of senior lecturer, which confers a status of superior performance as well as higher pay.

Education and Training

Lecturers in universities and four-year colleges should have doctoral degrees. Many institutions hire Lecturers with master's degrees if they have qualifying professional work experience.

Special Requirements

Lecturers who are in professions (such as nursing and occupational therapy) must hold appropriate licensure and professional certification.

Experience, Skills, and Personality Traits

Lecturers should have previous teaching experience, for example, as a teaching assistant, at the four-year college or university level. Employers look for candidates who are able to teach introductory courses within their discipline.

To work effectively with students, colleagues, and others, Lecturers should have adequate communication, interpersonal, and teamwork skills. In addition, they should have effective organizational and management skills to complete their duties each day. Successful Lecturers share several personality traits such as being independent, analytical, intellectual, flexible, and creative.

Unions and Associations

Lecturers join different professional associations to take advantage of networking opportunities, professional development, professional resources, and other services. Along with belonging to societies that serve their specific disciplines, Lecturers might join the National Association of Scholars or the American Association of University Professors. For contact information, see Appendix IV.

Tips for Entry

1. Many colleges and universities have a pool of qualified Lecturers whom they contact at any time to fill temporary positions. Contact the colleges and universities where you would like to work and find out if they have such a pool for which you can apply.
2. College and university extension programs are constantly looking for new courses to offer. If you have an idea for a course, talk with the appropriate staff member at an extension program.
3. The Internet can provide you with sources to keep up with developing issues and trends in higher education. On the Internet, you can also find community bulletin boards and mailing lists (also known as *listservs*) that can be used to network with colleagues across the nation. To begin a search of relevant Web sites, enter the keyword *higher education* in a search engine.

COMMUNITY COLLEGE INSTRUCTOR

CAREER PROFILE

Duties: Teach general education, developmental, or vocational courses in a two-year college; perform other duties as required

Alternate Title(s): Professor; also known by the subject taught (such as History Instructor or Cosmetology Instructor)

Salary Range: $40,000 to $66,000

Employment Prospects: Good

Advancement Prospects: Fair

Prerequisites:

    Education or Training—A master's degree or equivalent

    Experience—Previous teaching experience in community college settings preferred

    Special Skills and Personality Traits—Communication, interpersonal, teamwork, organizational, and management skills; be independent, analytical, intellectual, versatile, adaptable, curious, and creative

    Special Requirements—Teaching credential, occupational license, and/or professional certification may be required

CAREER LADDER

```
┌─────────────────────────────────────┐
│   Tenured Instructor or Professor    │
└─────────────────────────────────────┘

┌─────────────────────────────────────┐
│  Instructor or Assistant Professor   │
└─────────────────────────────────────┘

┌─────────────────────────────────────┐
│         Part-time Instructor         │
└─────────────────────────────────────┘
```

Position Description

Community College Instructors work at two-year colleges that serve the educational needs of the local communities as well as provide training for the local professions, businesses, industry, and government agencies. In some community colleges, the faculty are given the title *professor;* and are ranked academically from instructor, assistant professor, associate professor, and full professor. Some public and private two-year colleges are known as junior colleges or technical colleges.

Students at community colleges can be any age and often come from different ethnic and socioeconomic backgrounds. They may go to school part time or full time to fulfill different educational goals—for example, to learn a specific vocation, earn credits to transfer to a four-year college, pass a high school equivalency diploma examination, improve work skills, or learn about a subject for fun.

Most Community College Instructors teach in programs that lead to associate degrees or occupational certificates.

Many instructors teach general education courses in liberal arts and sciences programs, which prepare students to transfer to four-year institutions. (General education courses in community colleges usually fulfill lower undergraduate requirements in four-year institutions.) Some instructors also teach developmental courses in reading, writing, or math to help students improve their skills to succeed at college-level work.

Many Community College Instructors teach courses for vocational (or occupational) and technical programs such as dental hygiene, nursing, police science, business services, telecommunications, culinary arts, cosmetology, automotive services, and hospitality services.

Some institutions offer community service programs in which instructors integrate academic instruction with volunteer service in the community. For example, an English instructor might require students in an American literature class to tutor participants in an adult literacy program. Community College Instructors might also teach in continuing education programs that offer noncredit courses to members of the general public who wish to gain new knowledge or improve skills.

Community College Instructors are part of a department or division that corresponds to their subject or field (such as computer science, geography, horticulture, or early childhood education). For each term, they are assigned courses, as part of a prescribed curriculum, by the department chair or division dean. For example, a math instructor might teach basic arithmetic, finite mathematics, geometry, and applied mathematics for the spring semester. Instructors have flexible hours that may include teaching courses every day or every other day as well as teaching classes at night or on weekends. Depending on the course, an instructor's class load may range from 25 to 75 or more students.

For each of their courses, instructors are responsible for developing a syllabus that outlines the topics and sequence of topics to be taught. They develop and use multiple teaching methods to motivate students to engage in their own learning as well as to help them develop critical thinking skills. Instructors may use lectures, laboratory work, self-paced formats, computer-assisted instruction, multimedia demonstrations, individualized instruction, and so on. Some instructors teach on-line courses or courses on cable or closed-circuit television.

As in any teaching profession, Community College Instructors perform administrative tasks such as keeping attendance records. They grade students' papers, lab work, and exams, and give students critical feedback about their work. At the end of a term, instructors evaluate students' overall performance and assign letter grades. In addition, Instructors maintain scheduled office hours to advise students on academic matters.

Instructors also participate in faculty meetings and work with colleagues to develop and evaluate courses, programs, and services. Many instructors serve on school committees that handle academic or administrative issues for the institution. Some instructors become student club advisers or work with community organizations.

Community College Instructors are also responsible for keeping up with developments in their disciplines as well as in teaching methodologies and educational issues. Their professional development may be pursued through independent study, networking with colleagues, and participating in professional workshops and conferences. Though teaching is the main emphasis at two-year colleges, instructors are encouraged to conduct scholarly research projects and have their results published in scholarly journals, books, and electronic media.

Full-time faculty generally teach five courses, which is equivalent to 15 teaching hours; however, most instructors typically work between 40 to 50 hours a week—teaching courses, holding office hours, preparing for classes, grading papers and exams, participating in staff and committee meetings, and so on. Most two-year institutions have a tenure track for full-time instructors. (With tenure, instructors cannot be fired without just cause and due process.)

Part-time, or adjunct, instructors teach between one to three courses, usually in the evenings and on weekends. They have limited administrative and student advising duties. Many part-time instructors teach at more than one community college in different parts of a city, county, or region. Some also teach courses for extension programs in community colleges, colleges, or universities.

Salaries

Salaries vary, and depend on factors such as an instructor's experience and education as well as the type, size, and location of the two-year college. According to a 2004–05 survey by the American Association of University Professors, full-time faculty in two-year colleges receive average salaries that range from $40,295 to $66,215.

Adjunct instructors usually earn a fee for each course they teach. An informal search on the Internet has found adjunct instructors earning as little as $400 per course to more than $5,000 per course.

Employment Prospects

Private and public two-year colleges, technical colleges, junior colleges, and community colleges hire instructors for part-time or full-time positions.

Competition is keen, particularly for full-time tenure track positions. Most opportunities are for part-time positions or for nontenured full-time positions. The U.S. Bureau of Labor Statistics predicts that employment for postsecondary instructors, including Community College Instructors, should increase by 21 to 35 percent through 2012. This would be partly due to growing student enrollment as well as a large number of instructors reaching retirement age. In general, the best prospects for Community College Instructors are in fields expected to have the strongest job growth, such as nursing, health specialties, biological sciences, business, and computer science.

Advancement Prospects

Many Community College Instructors realize advancement through full-time positions, tenure, and pay raises. Instructors interested in administrative and management careers may become department chairs, program coordinators, assistant deans, and deans. (Having a doctoral degree enhances, but does not guarantee, an individual's chances for obtaining top administrative positions.)

Community College Instructors have the option to move to other careers in education, becoming corporate trainers, adult education teachers, university lecturers, or researchers. They can also pursue careers in their chosen fields, working for the government, private industries, community organizations, or other institutions.

Education and Training

For academic subjects, Community College Instructors need master's degrees in their subjects, or in related fields with a minimum number of units in each of the subjects they would teach. Employers sometimes hire instructors who have a bachelor's degree, if they have qualified professional work experience.

Educational requirements for instructors in vocational or occupational certificate programs vary from college to college. Vocational instructors have master's degrees in their subject, or associate's or bachelor's degrees along with qualified professional work experience.

Some colleges or individual departments assign mentors to new instructors to advise them with instruction.

Special Requirements

Community College Instructors who teach in vocational and technical programs must hold valid professional licenses and certifications. In some states, instructors may require additional teaching licensure or certification by their professional licensing board or board of education. Contact the occupational licensing board or board of education in the state where you would like to teach for more information. See Appendix III for a list of state boards.

Experience, Skills, and Personality Traits

Community colleges prefer instructors who have previous teaching experience, particularly at the community college level. Additionally, employers look for candidates who have an excellent background in their discipline and are willing to teach a wide variety of courses. Strong candidates also demonstrate that they are sensitive and respectful of the diversity of the student body that is often found in community colleges.

Community College Instructors should have strong communication, interpersonal, and teamwork skills to work well with students, colleagues, and administrators. They should also have effective organizational and management skills to complete their duties each day.

Successful Community College Instructors share several personality traits such as being independent, analytical, intellectual, versatile, adaptable, curious, and creative. They have a strong desire to pursue knowledge in their field as well as to teach and share the knowledge with their students.

Unions and Associations

Community College Instructors join different professional associations to take advantage of networking opportunities, professional development, and other professional resources and services. Along with belonging to organizations that serve their specific fields, they join groups such as the American Association for Adult and Continuing Education and the National Association of Scholars. They may also join the American Association of University Professors, in which some chapters in public institutions negotiate contracts with administrators. Community College Instructors in public institutions are also eligible to join these two teacher unions: the National Education Association and the American Federation of Teachers.

See Appendix IV for contact information for the above organizations.

Tips for Entry

1. As a student, join professional associations and network with professionals. Contact them when you are ready to do a job search for leads to current or upcoming vacancies on their campuses.
2. Get experience in community college settings by applying for part-time or temporary lecturer positions.
3. Send your resume to department chairs at all the two-year colleges where you would like to work. Call each department chair a few days after sending your resume and introduce yourself.
4. If no jobs are currently available, keep calling back from time to time. It is common for colleges to hire new instructors at the last minute for part-time instructors who have suddenly left for full-time positions.
5. The Internet is a valuable tool for doing a job search. Many two-year colleges have Web sites which include job listings for current vacancies so check the sites of colleges where you would like to work. To find a Web site for a particular college, enter its name in a search engine.

VOCATIONAL INSTRUCTOR

CAREER PROFILE

Duties: Provide instruction for courses in a vocation or trade; create lesson plans; perform other duties as required

Alternate Title(s): Career and Technical Education Teacher; a title, such as Paralegal Instructor or Welding Instructor, that reflects the vocation or trade being taught

Salary Range: $24,000 to $71,000

Employment Prospects: Good

Advancement Prospects: Fair

Prerequisites:

Education or Training—Associate's, bachelor's, or master's degree; for licensed teachers, completion of an accredited teacher education program

Experience—Generally three to six years of work experience; some teaching experience

Special Skills and Personality Traits—Communication, interpersonal, teamwork, organizational, and management skills; be patient, inspiring, flexible, creative, and resourceful

Special Requirements—A teaching credential and occupational license or professional certification may be required

CAREER LADDER

```
┌─────────────────────────────┐
│   Department Chair or        │
│   Program Coordinator        │
└─────────────────────────────┘

┌─────────────────────────────┐
│   Vocational Instructor      │
└─────────────────────────────┘

┌─────────────────────────────┐
│   Professional in one's field │
└─────────────────────────────┘
```

Position Description

Vocational Instructors are experienced professionals who teach in postsecondary vocational education programs, which are also known as career and technical education programs. These programs prepare students for entry-level positions in business, skilled trades, health, agriculture, marketing, technology, protective services, education, and other fields. Occupations include avionics maintenance technician, chef, computer repair technician, cosmetologist, court reporter, dental hygienist, electrician, emergency medical technician, graphic artist, home health care aide, landscape designer, paralegal, preschool teacher, veterinary technician, vocational nurse, and many others. Most occupational programs are between six months to two years long, and generally lead to an associate degree and/or professional certification.

Vocational Instructors are responsible for developing a course outline (or syllabus) and lesson plans for each class

they teach. Instruction usually includes lectures and demonstrations. Many instructors create a classroom environment that simulates an actual work site so that students can get hands-on experience. Students use professional equipment and tools as well as perform exercises and activities that are similar to the real-life work tasks. For example, students in automotive technology classes might do car tune-ups using electronic equipment like those found in professional auto shops.

As students must meet basic levels of proficiency for entry-level positions, instructors monitor students' progress and give them critical feedback. They assign additional practice exercises for students who need extra help. Vocational Instructors also administer quizzes and exams to students to check their comprehension of knowledge and skills. In addition, they maintain records of students' progress throughout the course. Vocational Instructors may be required to evaluate the overall performance of their students with letter grades at the end of school terms.

Many Vocational Instructors teach job search skills—how to find a job, complete a job application, and so on. They also teach employability skills that help students keep jobs, such as critical thinking, problem solving, leadership, safety, and self-management skills. Some Vocational Instructors are responsible for supervising student interns at actual work sites.

Vocational Instructors are also responsible for keeping up with developments in their profession as well as in vocational education. For example, they might enroll in continuing education courses sponsored by professional associations or college extension programs, read professional journals and books, or network with colleagues. Some instructors return to the field and work for a period of time.

In addition, Vocational Instructors participate in faculty meetings to discuss curriculum, vocational education trends, professional development, and other relevant matters. Many instructors also participate on school committees.

Vocational Instructors work part time or full time. Instructors in public institutions usually have a nine- or 10-month work schedule while instructors in private vocational and technical schools teach year-round. Full-time instructors in public institutions may be eligible for tenure; with tenure, they cannot be fired without just cause.

Salaries

Salaries for Vocational Instructors vary, depending on such factors as their experience, education, employer, and geographical location. According to the November 2004 *Occupational Employment Statistics* (OES) survey by the U.S. Bureau of Labor Statistics (BLS), the estimated annual salary for most postsecondary Vocational Instructors ranged between $24,100 and $70,580.

Employment Prospects

Vocational Teachers are employed by public and private school systems, community colleges, college and university extension programs, private vocational and technical schools, job training centers, community agencies, labor unions, correctional facilities, and professional associations. According to the BLS's November 2004 OES survey, about 108,540 Vocational Instructors were employed in postsecondary institutions in the United States.

Employment for postsecondary instructors, including Vocational Instructors, should increase by 21 to 35 percent through 2012, according to the BLS. Many job openings are expected to be created to meet the demands of increasing student enrollment as well as the large number of instructors becoming eligible for retirement.

Advancement Prospects

Many Vocational Instructors realize advancement through pay raises and full-time positions. Instructors interested in administrative positions can become department chairs, program coordinators, assistant deans, and deans. Advanced degrees may be required to obtain top administrative positions.

Education and Training

Education requirements vary from school to school. Many public and private institutions prefer that Vocational Instructors have master's degrees in their fields. If a master's degree is not offered or required in a field, schools accept a bachelor's or associate's degree with a minimum number of years of professional experience.

To become licensed teachers, Vocational Instructors complete an accredited teacher education program that includes course work in pedagogy and instruction, as well as a supervised field practicum.

Special Requirements

Vocational Instructors in public institutions may be required to hold a vocational education credential with an endorsement in each subject that they teach. Type of licensure and licensing requirements vary from state to state. To learn about the requirements for the state where you wish to teach, contact the state board of education. See Appendix III for a list of state boards.

Private schools may require instructor certification from a state board of education, professional association, or other recognized organization.

Vocational Instructors may be required to have current occupational licenses and professional certification. Some professions require instructor certification from their state occupational license board. (For more information, contact your state occupational license board.)

Experience, Skills, and Personality Traits

In general, Vocational Instructors should have three to six years of work experience with at least one year of journey-level experience or its equivalent. Additionally, they should have previous teaching experience or knowledge of vocational instruction.

Vocational Instructors need communication, interpersonal, and teamwork skills to work well with students, colleagues, and others. Organizational and management skills are also needed to handle a variety of duties each day.

Successful Vocational Instructors are patient, inspiring, flexible, creative, and resourceful. They enjoy teaching others about their trade or vocation.

Unions and Associations

Vocational Instructors join different professional associations to take advantage of networking opportunities, professional development, and other professional resources and services. Along with belonging to organizations that serve their specific professions, they join groups for vocational educators, such as the Association for Career and Technical Education, the National Association of Industrial and Technical Teacher Educators, SkillsUSA-VICA, and the American Society for Training and Development.

Vocational Instructors in community colleges are eligible to join the National Educational Association or the American Federation of Teachers.

See Appendix IV for contact information for the above organizations.

Tips for Entry

1. Talk with Vocational Instructors in different settings to get an idea if this profession might be for you. If possible, observe their classes. Or get hands-on experience by volunteering as a classroom aide.

2. Apply directly to public and private schools where you would like to work. Contact them on a regular basis to let them know you are still interested in a position.

3. Learn more about vocational education on the Internet. You might start by visiting the Association for Career and Technical Education Web site at http://www.acteonline.org. In addition, visit the U.S. Department of Education Office of Vocational and Adult Education Web site. First go to http://www.ed.gov. Click on the link *Offices,* then click on the link for *Office of Vocational and Adult Education.*

ADULT EDUCATION INSTRUCTOR

CAREER PROFILE

Duties: Provide instruction for literacy, ESL, or other adult education program; develop curriculum, lessons, and instructional materials; perform other duties as required

Alternate Title(s): Adult Basic Education Teacher, GED Instructor, ESL Instructor

Salary Range: $23,000 to $71,000

Employment Prospects: Good

Advancement Prospects: Fair

Prerequisites:

Education or Training—A bachelor's or master's degree

Experience—Previous teaching experience in adult education settings

Special Skills and Personality Traits—Communication, interpersonal, teamwork, organizational, and management skills; be patient, understanding, trustworthy, supportive, flexible, creative, and resourceful

Special Requirements—Teaching credential or other certification may be required

CAREER LADDER

Lead Teacher or Program Coordinator

Adult Education Teacher

Student Teacher

Position Description

Adult Education Instructors teach courses that help men and women achieve specific educational goals, such as to learn English for the U.S. naturalization test, earn a high school diploma, improve their job skills, or learn how to read. These instructors work in adult education programs run by schools, community colleges, community centers, churches, and other organizations.

Adult Education Instructors are involved in various types of adult education and literacy programs, which address the different needs of students. The following are some programs in which Adult Education Instructors work:

- adult basic education (ABE) programs provide instruction in basic reading, writing, and math skills to students who have low-level skills or no skills at all.
- adult secondary education programs prepare students who have dropped out of school to take an examination for a high school equivalency diploma, such as the General

Education Development (GED) test. Instructors provide instruction in the academic areas in which students will be tested.
- English as a Second Language (ESL) programs teach English-language skills—speaking, listening, reading, and writing—to adults who have limited English-language proficiency.
- workplace literacy programs provide literacy and basic skills training to adults so that they can keep their jobs, advance to other positions, or gain new employment. Many of these programs are in the workplace.
- family literacy programs help parents of children in early childhood education programs gain literacy and basic skills.

Depending on the program, Adult Education Instructors might follow a prescribed curriculum, work with colleagues to develop a curriculum, or be responsible for creating the curriculum for their courses. All instructors, however, are responsible for planning and preparing lesson plans for their classes. Many instructors create original instructional materials because of lack of program funds to buy materials. Some instructors write grant proposals, ask publishers for donations, or organize students in fund-raising activities to obtain materials for their classes.

Instructors use various teaching methods, including class work, small group work, and one-on-one coaching. They modify instruction to fit students' interests as well as their skill levels and learning styles so that they can succeed in achieving their educational goals. Instructors assign exercises and activities that reinforce and enhance students' knowledge and skills. They review students' work, giving them positive reinforcement on their performance as well as ways to improve their work. Instructors also check students' comprehension with quizzes and tests. Many Adult Education Instructors use computers and audiovisual equipment to augment their instruction.

In addition to their instructional duties, Adult Education Instructors participate in faculty meetings to discuss program development, budgets, fund-raising, teaching methods, and so on. Instructors also stay current with developments in their profession through independent study, continuing education courses, and networking with colleagues.

Adult Education Instructors work part time or full time. Their schedules vary, and may include teaching classes at night and on weekends.

Salaries

Salaries for Adult Education Instructors vary, depending on such factors as their experience, education, employer, and geographical location. According to the November 2004 *Occupational Employment Statistics* survey, by the U.S. Bureau of Labor Statistics (BLS), the estimated annual salary for most Adult Education Instructors ranged between $22,540 and $70,850.

Employment Prospects

Adult Education Instructors are employed by public schools, community colleges, extension programs in colleges and universities, community centers, senior centers, libraries, community-based agencies, labor unions, religious organizations, correctional facilities, and senior centers.

The BLS reports that job growth for Adult Education Instructors is expected to increase by 21 to 35 percent through 2012. Most opportunities will become available as instructors retire or transfer to other occupations. However, the ability for employers to create additional positions or retain current positions depends on the availability of funding.

Advancement Prospects

Advancement is limited to the positions of lead Adult Education Instructors and program coordinators. In educational institutions, instructors can advance to higher administrative positions, which may require advanced degrees and several years of experience.

Being an Adult Education Instructor has been a stepping-stone for many teachers, principals, university professors, counselors, textbook editors, educational technologists, and other educators.

Education and Training

Requirements vary with the different employers but, in general, Adult Education Instructors should have bachelor's degrees in any field as long as they have qualifying work experience. Many employers prefer instructors with master's degrees in adult education.

Licensed instructors would have completed an accredited teacher education program, which includes course work in pedagogy, instruction for adult learners, as well as a supervised field practicum.

Special Requirements

Adult Education Instructors who teach academic subjects in schools and state-supported postsecondary institutions may be required to hold an adult education teaching credential. The type of licensure and licensing requirements vary from state to state. To find out the requirements for the state where you wish to teach, contact the state board of education. See Appendix III for a list of state boards.

Noneducational institutions may require English literacy instructors to hold appropriate teaching credentials or professional certification such as the Teaching English as a Foreign Language (TEFL) certificate.

Experience, Skills, and Personality Traits

Employers choose candidates who have previous teaching experience in the type of adult education programs for which they are applying. In addition, candidates must be knowledgeable in the subject matter they would be teaching. Furthermore, candidates must show that they are sensitive and respectful of the particular needs of adult learners.

To perform their work effectively, Adult Education Instructors should have strong communication, interpersonal, and teamwork skills as well as adequate organizational and management skills.

Being patient, understanding, trustworthy, supportive, flexible, creative, and resourceful are some of the personality traits that successful Adult Education Instructors share.

Unions and Associations

Many Adult Education Instructors join professional associations to take advantage of networking with colleagues, and other professional resources and services. Along with local and state organizations, they might join national societies such as the American Association for Adult and Continuing Education and TESOL, Inc. For contact information, see Appendix IV.

Tips for Entry

1. Get experience working in different adult education programs and settings. For example, you might volunteer as a tutor in a community center ESL program, public library adult literacy program, community college ABE class, or workplace literacy program at a job site.

2. To find out about job vacancies and requirements, contact public schools, community colleges, community-based agencies, and state employment offices.

3. You can learn more about adult education issues, trends, and programs on the Internet. Here are some Web sites you should visit: Literacy.org, http://www.literacy.org; the National Institute for Literacy, http://www.nifl.gov; and American Association for Adult and Continuing Education, http://www.aaace.org. Also check out the U.S. Department of Education Office of Vocational and Adult Education Web site. First go to http://www.ed.gov. Click on the link *Offices,* then click on the link for *Office of Vocational and Adult Education.*

CONTINUING EDUCATION INSTRUCTOR

CAREER PROFILE

Duties: Teach noncredit courses in a wide variety of subjects, such as computer programming, cooking, physical fitness, history, humanities, crafts, gardening, and so on; develop course outline and lesson plans; perform other duties as required

Alternate Title(s): Self-Enrichment Instructor; a title, such as Quilting Teacher, that reflects the subject being taught

Salary Range: $17,000 to $62,000

Employment Prospects: Good

Advancement Prospects: Poor

Prerequisites:

Education or Training—Bachelor's degree or equivalent

Experience—Professional experience; previous teaching experience desired

Special Skills and Personality Traits—Communication, interpersonal, teamwork, organizational, and management skills; be patient, inspiring, flexible, creative, and resourceful

Special Requirements—Occupational license and professional certification as required by profession

CAREER LADDER

```
┌─────────────────────────────────────┐
│        Program Coordinator           │
└─────────────────────────────────────┘

┌─────────────────────────────────────┐
│   Continuing Education Instructor    │
└─────────────────────────────────────┘

┌─────────────────────────────────────┐
│      Professional in one's field     │
└─────────────────────────────────────┘
```

Position Description

Continuing Education Instructors teach courses in which adults enroll for pleasure or self-enrichment. These instructors usually work on a contractual basis for continuing education programs, which are sponsored by academic institutions, community centers, private learning centers, professional associations, museums, and other institutions. Continuing education programs offer a variety of classes which vary from one institution to the next. For example, an adult school might offer classes about local history, amateur astronomy, the Internet, computer applications for carpenters, planning a wedding, line dancing, yoga, landscape design, organic pest control, sign language, or Italian.

Some continuing education programs offer certificate programs for vocations (such as a paralegal or a technical trainer specialist) or for particular skills (such as driving a forklift or performing CPR). Some programs specialize in courses for a specific profession, such as a rescue technician or an EFL (English as a Foreign Language) teacher.

Continuing education classes are taught by instructors who are experts in the subject matter, which may be related to their profession or personal interest. For example, a Continuing Education Instructor teaches a class on writing children's picture books and a beginning knitting class. Professionally, she is an author of children's books, and knitting is one of her longtime hobbies. In college and university extension programs, many credit courses are taught by professors and instructors who are part of the regular faculty on the campuses.

Continuing Education Instructors are responsible for developing the content of their courses. For each course, they define the objectives—what students will learn from the class—and what type of assessment they will use to determine that students are meeting the course objectives. Instructors also outline the topics that will be covered at class meetings. In addition, instructors decide what supplies and instructional materials they will need for the class.

Instructors are also responsible for creating lesson plans, which involves developing class exercises and activities that provide students with hands-on experience. Preparation also includes studying the topic to be taught, developing student handouts, gathering instructional materials and equipment needed for the class, and so on.

Continuing Education Instructors use instructional methods appropriate to the subject matter, such as lectures, demonstrations, modeling, group work, and individual instruction. Many instructors use computers and audiovisual equipment to augment their instruction.

Depending on the nature of the course, instructors might hold classes once or twice a week throughout a term. Classes generally run from one to four hours. Some classes are short-term; for example, an instructor might teach a one-day class for making holiday centerpieces. Most instructors teach in the evenings or on Saturdays.

Most Continuing Education Instructors teach one or two classes each term. Many instructors write proposals for courses they would like to teach, and send them to continuing education programs. A program accepts new courses that fit the needs of the community it serves.

Many Continuing Education Instructors have other full-time or part-time jobs. Some instructors teach classes for other continuing education programs.

Salaries

Salaries for Continuing Education Instructors vary, depending on such factors as their education, experience, employer, and geographical location. According to the November 2004 *Occupational Employment Statistics* survey by the U.S. Bureau of Labor Statistics (BLS), the estimated annual salary for most self-enrichment instructors ranged between $16,890 and $62,100.

Employment Prospects

Job opportunities continue to be favorable for Continuing Education Instructors because of the increasing number of adults who enroll in courses for self-enrichment. The BLS reports that self-enrichment instructors are expected to be among the fastest growing occupations in the U.S. through 2012. The federal agency predicts a 40 percent increase of self-enrichment instructors during this period.

Advancement Prospects

Continuing Education Instructors realize advancement through higher pay, and teaching additional classes due to popular demand. Instructors interested in administrative positions can advance to full-time positions, such as program coordinators and directors.

Most Continuing Education Instructors have a career in other fields. For many instructors, teaching continuing education classes is part of their overall career development.

Education and Training

Educational requirements vary, and depend on the type of course being taught. Employers generally require that Continuing Education Instructors have a bachelor's degree. However, years of experience in the subject matter may be substituted for educational training.

Special Requirements

Continuing Education Instructors do not need teaching licenses. However, they may need professional licenses or certification to teach vocational subjects or particular skills. For example, an instructor who teaches first-aid courses must be certified to teach first aid.

Experience, Skills, and Personality Traits

Continuing Education Instructors should have extensive experience with the subject matter they are teaching. Employers prefer that instructors have some teaching experience.

To work well with students, Continuing Education Instructors should have adequate communication, interpersonal, and teamwork skills. Organizational and management skills are also needed to handle teaching duties effectively. Being patient, inspiring, flexible, creative, and resourceful are some personality traits that successful Continuing Education Instructors share.

Unions and Associations

Continuing Education Instructors join different professional associations to take advantage of networking opportunities, professional development, and other professional resources and services. Along with belonging to organizations that serve their specific professions, they might join the American Association for Adult and Continuing Education, a national society that serves adult and continuing education instructors. For contact information, see Appendix IV.

Tips for Entry

1. Get teaching experience by volunteering to teach workshops or classes at senior centers, community centers, recreation centers, museums, or other organizations.
2. Look through catalogs of the different continuing education programs in your city or area to find out what classes are available. Contact the continuing education programs directly to learn about job vacancies as well as requirements for instructors and submitting course proposals.
3. Learn more about different continuing education programs on the Internet. To get a list of Web sites, enter the keyword *continuing education* in a search engine.

EXTENSION AGENT

CAREER PROFILE

Duties: Develop, implement, and evaluate educational programs; perform duties as required

Alternate Title(s): County Agent, Farm Adviser Extension Educator; a title such as Agriculture Agent that reflects a specialization

Salary Range: $22,000 to $68,000

Employment Prospects: Fair

Advancement Prospects: Good

Prerequisites:

Education/Training—Bachelor's or master's degree

Experience—Previous work experience with the Cooperative Extension System

Special Skills and Personality Traits—Teaching, public relations, program management, computer, communication, writing, leadership, interpersonal, and teamwork skills; be calm, independent, responsible, hardworking, creative, and resourceful

CAREER LADDER

```
+-----------------------------------+
|        Lead Extension Agent       |
+-----------------------------------+

+-----------------------------------+
|          Extension Agent          |
+-----------------------------------+

+-----------------------------------+
| Assistant or Associate Extension Agent |
+-----------------------------------+
```

Position Description

Extension Agents provide nonformal educational programs to rural, suburban, and urban communities in the areas of agriculture, natural resources, community and economic development, family and consumer science, and 4-H youth development. They work out of county and regional offices that are part of the Cooperative Extension System (CES). This is a federal education system in partnership with state land-grant universities and the Cooperative State Research, Education, and Extension Service (CSREES), an agency within the U.S. Department of Agriculture (USDA).

Extension Agents may be assigned to work in one or more program areas, depending on the size of their office. It is their job to develop, implement, and evaluate various educational programs that meet the needs of the communities they serve. For example, an Extension Agent in the area of family and consumer science might coordinate programs in child development, parent education, nutrition, and family resource management. The agents base their programs on results of research conducted by the USDA and land-grant university scientists.

Extension Agents may design educational programs alone, with other staff members, and as part of a team of agents from several county offices. They also obtain input from individuals, agencies, and organizations within the community. Extension specialists and educators at the land-grant universities act as resources for the agents.

Most Extension Agents oversee several educational programs at the same time. They complete various tasks for each program, such as:

- coordinating program activities
- developing brochures, information sheets, and other educational materials for consumers
- writing and distributing press releases
- writing grant proposals
- conducting workshops, classes, or demonstrations
- planning meetings or conferences
- providing consultation services
- recruiting, training, and supervising volunteers
- networking with community organizations
- answering consumer questions in person, over the phone, by e-mail, and by letters
- completing paperwork

Extension Agents typically work more than 40 hours a week. Their work involves traveling to meetings and activities within the counties they serve.

Salaries

Salaries for Extension Agents vary, depending on such factors as their education, experience, duties, and geographical location. According to the November 2004 *Occupational Employment Statistics* survey, by the U.S. Bureau of Labor Statistics (BLS), the estimated annual salary for most farm and home management advisers—including Extension Agents—ranged between $22,240 and $68,350.

Employment Prospects

Extension Agents are employed in every state, the District of Columbia, and the United States territories; however, not all counties may have a county extension office. Most job opportunities become available to replace agents who retire, resign, or advance to higher positions. Additional opportunities are created according to an extension office's needs as well as available funding.

Advancement Prospects

Extension Agents can advance to supervisory and administrative positions, eventually becoming unit leaders or county extension directors. Many agents prefer to pursue advancement by earning higher wages and receiving assignments of their choice. Some agents realize advancement by obtaining positions in larger county offices. Extension Agents can also become specialists and administrators at the state and federal levels.

Education and Training

Minimally, applicants must possess a bachelor's degree in a field related to the program area in which they would be working. For example, applicants should have a degree in agriculture or a related field if they would be working in agriculture. Some employers prefer to hire applicants with a master's degree.

Experience, Skills, and Personality Traits

Employers hire Extension Agents who have previous experience working with the CES. This may include work as volunteers and college internships in addition to participating in the 4-H program as children. Candidates should also have practical experience in agriculture, nutrition, and other subjects that are part of the program area for which they are applying.

To complete their work effectively, Extension Agents need skills in teaching, public relations, program management, computer use, communication, and writing. They also need leadership, interpersonal, and teamwork skills. Successful Extension Agents share several personality traits such as being calm, independent, responsible, hardworking, creative, and resourceful.

Unions and Associations

Extension Agents join professional associations to take advantage of networking opportunities and other professional resources and services. Some organizations for the different Extension Agents are the National Association of County Agricultural Agents, the National Association of Extension 4-H Agents, and the National Extension Association of Family and Consumer Sciences.

Many agents join societies that are related to their discipline, such as the American Farm Bureau, the American Dairy Science Association, or the American Association of Family and Consumer Sciences. Many also join Epsilon Sigma Phi, a fraternal organization for all cooperative extension professionals.

See Appendix IV for contact information for the above organizations.

Tips for Entry

1. Join a 4-H Club, if you are in middle school or high school.
2. As a student, volunteer or get a part-time or summer job at your local extension office.
3. Talk with Extension Agents to learn more about their profession. To find a county extension office, look under the county government listings in the white pages of any telephone book. Look for either "County Extension Office" or "Cooperative Extension Service."
4. To learn about job openings, contact county extension offices directly. To find out about opportunities nationwide, visit the National Job Bank Web site (by the *Journal of Extension*) at http://jobs.joe.org.
5. Use the Internet to learn more about Extension Agents. To find a list of relevant Web sites, enter *cooperative extension office* in a search engine.

CORRECTIONAL INSTRUCTOR

CAREER PROFILE

Duties: Provide instruction to incarcerated inmates as part of a specific educational program; perform other duties as required

Alternate Title(s): A title, such as Vocational Instructor, that reflects an educational program

Salary Range: $23,000 to $71,000

Employment Prospects: Good

Advancement Prospects: Fair

Prerequisites:

Education/Training—Bachelor's degree; for licensed teachers, completion of an accredited teacher education program

Experience—Previous experience teaching in an adult education program; vocational instructors must have professional work experience

Special Skills and Personality Traits—Communication, interpersonal, teamwork, organizational, and management skills; be caring, calm, honest, patient, tolerant, creative, and resourceful

Special Requirements—A teaching credential

CAREER LADDER

```
┌─────────────────────────────────┐
│        Lead Instructor          │
└─────────────────────────────────┘

┌─────────────────────────────────┐
│     Correctional Instructor     │
└─────────────────────────────────┘

┌─────────────────────────────────┐
│ Student Teacher, Schoolteacher, │
│  Adult Education Instructor, or │
│      Vocational Instructor      │
└─────────────────────────────────┘
```

Position Description

Correctional Instructors are employed by jails, prisons, and other correctional facilities to teach juvenile and adult inmates as part of their rehabilitative treatment plans. Studies show that effective educational programs can help inmates obtain adequate academic, vocational, and life skills as well as gain self-esteem to become successful members of society.

Correctional facilities provide different types of educational programs which are taught by different Correctional Instructors. Some instructors teach basic reading, writing, and math skills to inmates. Some instructors help inmates prepare for examinations which lead to a high school equivalency diploma. Other instructors teach academic subjects as part of an associate's or bachelor's degree program.

Many Correctional Instructors are known as vocational instructors. They teach inmates basic knowledge and skills for trades or vocations, such as printing, welding, baking, or automotive repair.

Some Correctional Instructors teach English as a Second Language (ESL) classes to inmates who have limited English-language proficiency. Others are special education teachers, providing direct instruction or consultation services to general education instructors. (Federal law mandates that persons under 22 years old who have disabilities—physical impairments, learning disabilities, or behavioral disorders—are eligible for special education programs and related services.)

As separate classes or as part of another course, many Correctional Instructors teach inmates employability skills that can help them find and keep jobs upon release. Some instructors teach classes in life skills—critical thinking and problem-solving skills as well as everyday skills such as balancing a checkbook, comparison shopping, and reading and following directions.

Correctional Instructors develop curriculum and instruction that meets the particular abilities and interests of each student. Their teaching responsibilities include:

- preparing a course outline for each subject they teach
- performing an assessment of each student's abilities and interests, which may include administering diagnostic and standardized tests
- preparing lesson plans and student exercises and activities
- choosing appropriate teaching materials to use with individual inmates
- providing instruction on an individual basis or in small groups
- monitoring each student's academic progress and behavior, and keeping attendance and performance records
- correcting papers and tests, and returning them to students with positive remarks about their performance and ways to improve their work
- completing a final evaluation report on each student at the end of a course
- providing guidance counseling as needed

Instructors are responsible for supervising inmates at all times. They monitor students' activities in their classroom, shop, or other assigned area. Instructors may be asked to track students as they move from an assigned area and to notify correctional officers of student movement. When students break any rules of conduct, instructors write disciplinary reports and direct them to the appropriate staff member. Instructors also maintain an inventory of equipment, tools, and supplies.

Correctional Instructors work with counselors, therapists, and other educational staff members to develop, monitor, and evaluate effective treatment plans for their students. For example, a Correctional Instructor might develop reading lessons that incorporate anger management skills.

Furthermore, Correctional Instructors are responsible for understanding and following all administrative rules, policies, and procedures at the correctional facilities where they work.

Correctional Instructors work part time or full time on a year-round schedule.

Salaries

Salaries for Correctional Instructors vary, depending on such factors as their experience, education, employer, and geographical location. According to the November 2004 *Occupational Employment Statistics* survey, by the U.S. Bureau of Labor Statistics, the estimated annual salary for most adult education instructions ranged between $22,540 and $70,850, and for postsecondary vocational instructors, between $24,100 and $70,580.

Employment Prospects

Correctional Instructors work in juvenile and adult correctional facilities at the local, state, and federal levels. Some instructors are employed by private prisons.

Qualified Correctional Instructors are always in demand, especially for temporary part-time positions. Most opportunities become available as individuals retire, resign, or advance to other positions. Additional jobs are created from time to time when funding is available.

Advancement Prospects

Advancement opportunities are typically limited to lead teachers and program coordinators. Instructors in correctional education systems that are organized like school districts can advance to administrative positions such as principals and central office administrators.

Correctional Instructors might follow other career paths in correctional education. For example, they can become researchers, curriculum developers, program developers, or program administrators in correctional education departments, correctional education advocacy groups, and other organizations.

Education and Training

Employers require that Correctional Instructors hold a bachelor's degree. Most Correctional Instructors have bachelor's degrees in disciplines that relate to the subject matter they teach. Correctional Instructors who teach vocational subjects may not be required to have a bachelor's degree if they fulfill the experience requirement.

Most licensed Correctional Instructors complete an accredited teacher education program leading to licensure. The program includes course work in pedagogy, instruction of subject matter, as well as a supervised field practicum.

Special Requirements

In most states, Correctional Instructors who teach literacy, life skills, and academic subjects must hold appropriate teaching credentials in elementary education, secondary education, adult education, or special education. Correctional Instructors who teach vocational courses must hold a vocational credential with endorsements in the subjects being taught. For specific information, contact the state board of education for the state in which you wish to teach. See Appendix III for a list of state boards.

Experience, Skills, and Personality Traits

In general, employers hire teachers for literacy and academic subjects who have previous experience teaching adults in remedial or special education programs, alternative high schools, adult schools, or job skills training programs. Correctional Instructors who teach vocational subjects must have professional work experience.

Because their job involves working with inmates and other correctional staff members, Correctional Instructors need excellent communication, interpersonal, and teamwork skills. Additionally, they need strong organizational and management skills.

Successful Correctional Instructors share several personality traits such as being caring, calm, honest, patient, tolerant, creative, and resourceful. They also have a good sense of humor. Furthermore, they are passionate about helping incarcerated inmates succeed in their educational goals.

Unions and Associations

Correctional Instructors belong to various professional associations to take advantage of networking opportunities, education programs, and other professional services and resources. Some of the different societies that they may join include the following:

- Correctional Education Association
- American Association for Adult and Continuing Education
- Council for Learning Disabilities
- Association for Career and Technical Education
- International Reading Association

- American Jail Association
- American Correctional Association

See Appendix IV for contact information for these organizations.

Tips for Entry

1. Get experience working with inmates in juvenile and adult correctional facilities by volunteering as a teacher or tutor.
2. Many Correctional Instructors recommend learning about emotional and behavioral disabilities as well as special education methodologies.
3. To learn about vacancies and qualifications, contact the correctional facilities where you would like to work.
4. Learn more about correctional education on the Internet. You might start by visiting these Web sites: National Institute for Correctional Education, http://www.iup.edu/nice, and Correctional Education Association, http://www.ceanational.org.

OVERSEAS TEACHERS

OVERSEAS TEACHER

CAREER PROFILE

Duties: Provide instruction for assigned subjects at a designated grade level (K–12); create daily lesson plans; perform other duties as required

Alternate Title(s): None

Salary Range: $20,000 to $85,000

Employment Prospects: Good

Advancement Prospects: Good

Prerequisites:

Education/Training—Bachelor's degree

Experience—One to three years of classroom teaching experience

Special Skills and Personality Traits—Communication, teamwork, interpersonal, organizational, and management skills; be flexible, creative, enthusiastic, energetic, patient, and adventurous

Special Requirements—A teaching credential

CAREER LADDER

```
┌─────────────────────────────────────────┐
│  Department Chair, or a teaching         │
│  position in an overseas school of choice│
└─────────────────────────────────────────┘

┌─────────────────────────────────────────┐
│         Overseas Schoolteacher           │
└─────────────────────────────────────────┘

┌─────────────────────────────────────────┐
│           Classroom Teacher              │
└─────────────────────────────────────────┘
```

Position Description

Many American teachers are employed by overseas schools that are specifically for children and dependents of Americans who live and work in foreign countries. The schools may be any combination of grade levels, from kindergarten through 12th grade. The student bodies in some schools are composed solely of American children, while other schools also enroll children from the host nation as well as from other countries.

Some Overseas Teachers work for American-sponsored schools that receive assistance from the U.S. Department of State in the form of grants or other resources. Other teachers work for independent international schools that have been established by individuals, private companies, churches, and other organizations.

An American-sponsored or international school is usually governed by its own board of directors. Along with American teachers and administrators, a school's staff also includes citizens from the local areas and other nations. The school staff develops its own American-based curriculum according to the school's educational philosophy and the host country's laws and regulations. Most schools are academically based and prepare students for entry into American colleges and universities.

American teachers also work in Department of Defense Dependent (DoDD) schools that are operated by the U.S. Department of Defense. These Overseas Teachers instruct the dependents of military and civilian personnel in the Department of Defense who are based overseas.

The DoDD schools make up a worldwide school system with school levels from prekindergarten to community college. The DoDD school system follows the same structure and curriculum as the U.S. public school systems. The schools provide college preparatory programs as well as vocational career programs. They also provide special needs programs such as special education programs and ESL (English as a Second Language) programs.

Overseas Teachers are assigned to provide instruction for one or more subjects, and may be assigned to teach one or more grade levels. English is the primary language for instruction in all American overseas schools. In some schools, the local language is also used for instruction. Class loads are typically smaller in American overseas schools than in U.S. public schools.

Like all teachers, overseas instructors are responsible for developing a course outline for each subject they teach, as well as creating and preparing daily lesson plans. Teachers may also help in the development of a school's overall curriculum.

Overseas Teachers monitor and evaluate students' progress as well as confer with students and parents about students' work and behavior. They also perform administrative tasks, such as taking attendance and making school announcements. Most teachers sponsor extracurricular activities—coaching sports, advising clubs, directing school plays, and so on. In addition, Overseas Teachers participate in faculty meetings and serve on school committees. Furthermore, they perform other duties as requested, such as supervising children during class breaks.

Overseas Teachers usually receive a renewable one-year or two-year contract.

Salaries

Salaries for Overseas Teachers vary, depending on such factors as their education, experience, credentials, and employer. According to the Teaching Jobs Overseas Web site (http://www.joyjobs.com), the annual salary for Overseas Teachers, as of December 2005, ranged from $20,000 to $85,000. For the 2004–05 school year, DoDD teachers earned an annual salary that ranged between $34,070 and $69,545.

Many teachers receive a benefits package that may include health insurance, retirement benefits, a housing allowance, and round-trip transportation to and from the United States.

Employment Prospects

Most positions become available as teachers resign or advance to other positions. Job prospects are more favorable for experienced teachers as well as for those who are willing to work in more than one location.

Advancement Prospects

Teaching in American overseas schools is part of an educator's overall career development. Many Overseas Teachers return to the United States and pursue teaching and administrative positions in private and public schools, colleges, and universities. For teachers who make a lifelong career in overseas teaching, advancement is usually realized through higher earnings and assignments in preferred overseas schools. Overseas Teachers can also pursue such administrative positions as department chair, principal, or director of development. Additional education and school administrative licensure may be required.

Education and Training

Employers require that Overseas Teachers have a bachelor's degree in their discipline. Many licensed teachers have a master's degree in their subject or in education.

Special Requirements

DoDD schools and most overseas schools require Overseas Teachers to have a valid teaching credential in elementary, middle, or secondary education with the proper endorsement for each subject they shall be teaching.

DoDD teachers are required to be U.S. citizens.

Experience, Skills, and Personality Traits

Most employers require Overseas Teachers to have two to three years of classroom teaching experience. Many prefer candidates who can teach several subjects as well as several grade levels. DoDD schools require at least one year of teaching experience which may be fulfilled by the student teacher requirement for credential programs.

Like all classroom teachers, Overseas Teachers need adequate communication, interpersonal, teamwork, organizational, and management skills to fulfill their duties effectively each day. Successful Overseas Teachers share several personality traits, such as being flexible, creative, enthusiastic, energetic, patient, and adventurous.

Unions and Associations

Many Overseas Teachers join professional associations to take advantage of networking opportunities and other professional resources and services. One organization specifically for Overseas Teachers is the Association for the Advancement of International Education. Overseas Teachers might also join societies that serve their particular disciplines, such as the International Reading Association or the National Council of Teachers of Mathematics. See Appendix IV for contact information.

Tips for Entry

1. In early fall, write to schools at which you would like to work. Send your resume and a brief letter of interest. You might also attach a photograph of yourself.
2. Recruitment fairs for Overseas Teachers are held throughout the United States. Ask a college career counselor for help in learning when one will take place in your area.
3. Be sure to bring several copies of your resume when you go to a recruitment fair.
4. Use the Internet to learn more about teaching in American overseas schools. Here are some Web sites you might visit: Department of Defense Education Activity, http://www.doedea.edu; Office of Overseas Schools (U.S. Department of State), http://www.state.gov/m/a/os; Council of International Schools, http://www.cois.org; and International Schools Services, http://www.iss.edu.

EFL (ENGLISH AS A FOREIGN LANGUAGE) TEACHER, OVERSEAS

CAREER PROFILE

Duties: Teach English to nonnative speakers; prepare lesson plans; perform duties as required

Alternate Title(s): None

Salary Range: Salaries are competitive with local teaching salaries

Employment Prospects: Excellent

Advancement Prospects: Fair

Prerequisites:

Education or Training—Bachelor's degree in any field, or a master's degree in TESOL (Teaching English to Speakers of Other Languages) or related field

Experience—One to two years of teaching experience

Special Skills and Personality Traits—Teaching, technology, communication, interpersonal, organizational, and management skills; be outgoing, flexible, open-minded, creative, resourceful, hardworking, dedicated

Special Requirements—TEFL or CELTA certification may be required

CAREER LADDER

```
┌─────────────────────────────────┐
│        Lead EFL Teacher         │
└─────────────────────────────────┘

┌─────────────────────────────────┐
│          EFL Teacher            │
└─────────────────────────────────┘

┌─────────────────────────────────┐
│  TEFL (Teaching English as a    │
│  Foreign Language) Student       │
└─────────────────────────────────┘
```

Position Description

Throughout the world, English is taught as a foreign language in many schools and higher education institutions as well as commercial language schools and other private programs. Local citizens wish to learn English for specific reasons. For example, a businessman may plan to do business with American companies, while a high school student needs to pass English language requirements on local university entrance examinations.

In many schools overseas, English is taught by EFL (English as a Foreign Language) Teachers who are native speakers. They are trained in the particular methodologies for foreign language teaching. Depending on the school, EFL Teachers may teach all or some English language skills—speaking, listening, reading, and writing skills. Some EFL Teachers only provide conversational English instruction so that students may have intensive speaking and listening practice.

Most EFL Teachers teach several classes each day to preschool children, elementary students, high school students, university students, business professionals, company employees, or private citizens. Each class may have 15 to 45 students.

EFL Teachers are responsible for assessing students' abilities, and providing instruction that matches their skill levels. In addition, EFL Teachers develop lessons that are age-appropriate and fit students' purposes for studying English. Like all teachers, EFL Teachers monitor their students' progress, and develop additional exercises and activities for students who need extra help. They also administer quizzes and tests to check their progress.

Their other duties include performing daily administrative tasks, such as taking attendance, that their employers may require. They also participate in faculty meetings and attend school functions, such as school parties and graduation ceremonies.

Instructional support for EFL Teachers varies from program to program. For example, some programs provide instructors with a course syllabus and all necessary teaching materials so that teachers can focus on providing instruction. Some programs require that teachers develop the curriculum, course syllabus, and instructional materials.

Work schedules vary from teacher to teacher, and, depending on their contract, may be obligated to teach 15 to 40 hours a week. They might work early morning, late afternoon, and evening hours. Many teachers also work on Saturdays.

EFL Teachers typically sign a renewable one- or two-year employment contract.

Salaries

Salaries for EFL Teachers vary, depending on such factors as their education, experience, credentials, employer, and geographical location. Formal surveys of earnings for overseas EFL Teachers are unavailable. In general they earn lower salaries than in the United States; however, their salaries are competitive with the local salaries—and sometimes higher than the local standards. Some teachers earn additional money by offering private tutoring services.

Employment Prospects

Overseas EFL Teachers work for commercial language schools, colleges and universities, elementary and secondary schools, and private companies who have language programs for their employees.

Because English is recognized as the common language for world trade and international relations, opportunities are readily available in most foreign countries.

Advancement Prospects

Being an EFL Teacher overseas is usually part of an educator's overall career development. After a few years of teaching overseas, most EFL Teachers return home and continue careers in education or other fields.

Some EFL Teachers make a full career out of teaching overseas, and realize advancement through better employment contracts as well as by working in different parts of the world. Some EFL Teachers start their own private language schools overseas.

In a commercial language school, EFL Teachers can become recruiters, trainers, and administrators. They may be based in the United States or abroad.

Education and Training

Most employers require that applicants have a bachelor's degree in any field. In many countries, a bachelor's degree is required to obtain a work permit. Employers require a master's in TESOL (Teaching English to Speakers of Other Languages), applied linguistics, English with an emphasis in TESOL, or other related field.

Many employers require applicants to have completed training in second language acquisition, pedagogy, materials development, curriculum design, and so on, which is fulfilled by completing an appropriate graduate or professional certification program.

Special Requirements

Many employers prefer to hire applicants who possess professional certification, which is usually obtained on a voluntary basis. Two certificates that are recognized by most employers worldwide are the Teaching English as a Foreign Language (TEFL) certificate and the Certificate in English Language Teaching to Adults (CELTA). To find TEFL or CELTA programs in your area, contact colleges, universities, or private language schools.

Overseas EFL Teachers must possess a U.S. passport along with the proper visa and work permit to work in a foreign country.

Experience, Skills, and Personality Traits

Many employers require applicants to have one to two years of teaching experience, preferably teaching English language skills to nonnative speakers. Proficiency in the native language of the foreign country is not necessary.

Along with teaching skills, applicants should be able to use audiovisual equipment and computers. In addition, EFL Teachers need communication, interpersonal, organizational, and management skills to perform their duties effectively. Successful EFL Teachers share several personality traits such as being outgoing, flexible, open-minded, creative, resourceful, hardworking, and dedicated.

Unions and Associations

Many EFL Teachers join professional associations to take advantage of networking opportunities and other professional resources and services. One such organization is TESOL, Inc. For contact information, see Appendix IV.

Tips for Entry

1. Gain practical experience teaching English to nonnative speakers. For example, you might tutor students in an ESL (English as a Second Language) program in a school, community college, or community agency.
2. Learn about the country where you wish to work—its history, political situation, culture, climate, work permits, and so on. One valuable source for general information is a country's embassy or consulate office.
3. Get references on a prospective employer from current and previous employees before signing a contract. Also review an employment contract carefully before signing it. Make sure the terms—salary, benefits, work conditions, living conditions, and so on—clearly state what you agree to.
4. Use the Internet to learn more about being an EFL Teacher. You might start by visiting these Web sites: TESOL, Inc., http://www.tesol.org, and Dave's ESL Cafe, http://www.eslcafe.com.

PEACE CORPS VOLUNTEER

CAREER PROFILE

Duties: Provide volunteer service in a foreign country; perform duties as required by assignment; help with other community projects as needed

Alternate Title(s): None

Salary Range: None

Employment Prospects: Not applicable

Advancement Prospects: Not applicable

Prerequisites:

Education or Training—Bachelor's degree; three months of preservice training

Experience—Varies, depending on the assignment

Special Skills and Personality Traits—Skills vary, depending on the assignment; be mature, patient, flexible, adaptable, creative, resourceful, and dedicated

CAREER LADDER

```
┌─────────────────────────────┐
│      career of choice       │
└─────────────────────────────┘

┌─────────────────────────────┐
│    Peace Corps Volunteer    │
└─────────────────────────────┘

┌─────────────────────────────┐
│           Trainee           │
└─────────────────────────────┘
```

Position Description

The Peace Corps is a United States federal agency that sends American volunteers to developing nations in Africa, Europe, the Mediterranean, Asia, the Pacific Islands, Central America, and South America. Peace Corps Volunteers commit to a two-year term of service to help communities in one of six areas—education, health and HIV/AIDS, business, information technology, agriculture, or the environment.

Education volunteers teach English in university settings, or teach English, math, or science to students in middle and secondary schools. Some Peace Corps Volunteers train teachers in university teacher-training programs or inservice training programs in local schools. Volunteers might instruct teachers in special education methodologies; secondary education teachers in English language acquisition; or primary education teachers in health, language arts, environment, childhood development, or other relevant subjects.

Peace Corps Volunteers in the area of health and HIV/AIDS help communities improve basic health care by focusing on prevention and education. Volunteers might train local teachers, community leaders, and community groups in public health topics such as maternal and child health, basic nutrition, AIDS, and hygiene related to water and sanitation conditions. Volunteers also assist local health clinics and other local organizations to identify health education needs, develop health programs, raise money for health care materials, and so on.

Business volunteers are assigned to a wide variety of projects in schools, universities, technical institutes, government agencies, cooperatives, business centers, environmental organizations, social service agencies, and other organizations. Many advise private and public businesses, cooperatives, and nongovernmental organizations. Some assist cities and regional governments with planning and implementing economic development strategies. Some conduct community workshops or teach classes in business planning, finance management, business courses, English, and other subjects.

Volunteers specializing in information technology help developing countries use computers and technology to reduce poverty. For example, they help health clinics, community groups, and government agencies identify ways to use information technology and assist in designing systems and programs to achieve those objectives. They also build computer labs in schools and communities, and train students, teachers, and others how to use computers and software.

Many agriculture volunteers are assigned to work with local farmers to help them increase food production and their income, as well as promote environmental conservation. Volunteers with a background in agricultural production, farm management, or agribusiness teach farmers and extension agents in formal training institutions, or work with small farmers, cooperatives, nongovernmental organizations, and agribusinesses.

Environment volunteers are assigned to help communities promote environmental education and awareness in natural conservation, such as sustainable use of forest resources or sanitation management in urban areas. Some volunteers work on forestry projects to conserve natural resources, such as soil conservation, watershed management, or flood control. Others provide technical assistance and training on natural resource conservation to personnel in natural parks and reserves.

Former volunteers may reenroll in the Peace Corps through its Crisis Corps program. They receive short-term assignments, from three to six months, to help countries address critical needs.

Salaries

Peace Corps Volunteers do not receive a salary, but they do receive a monthly stipend for food, housing, transportation, and incidentals. They also receive medical and dental benefits. Upon completion of their service, Volunteers receive a readjustment allowance, which was $6,075 in 2005.

Employment Prospects

As of December 2005, about 7,800 Peace Corps Volunteers were serving in 71 countries. From time to time, Congress increases or decreases the number of volunteer positions based on needs and availability of funding.

Applicants must be U.S. citizens who are at least 18 years old. They must pass an intense selection process, which includes an interview with a recruiter, medical examination, and legal clearance. This process takes between six and 12 months.

Advancement Prospects

Upon completion of their service, Peace Corps Volunteers have valuable work—and life—experience to build upon as they pursue their chosen careers in education, business, law, social work, technology, or other field.

Former volunteers have noncompetitive eligibility status for federal government jobs. They may be appointed to positions without competing with the general public. However, they only have one year after returning home to take advantage of their status. Former volunteers may also apply for staff positions (such as recruiters and program administrators) within the Peace Corps, but employment is limited to a total of five years.

Education and Training

The Peace Corps prefers that volunteers have bachelor's degrees. But the education requirement may be waived if candidates have qualifying work experience.

All Peace Corps Volunteers receive three months of intensive training in their host countries before beginning their tour of duty. Training consists of instruction in the local language and culture as well as any technical skills volunteers may need for their assignments.

Experience, Skills, and Personality Traits

Requirements vary and depend on the type of assignments for which applicants apply. In general, applicants must have experience or knowledge in the area, such as information technology or HIV/AIDS education prevention, in which they would be working.

To be effective at their work, Peace Corps Volunteers should have excellent communication, interpersonal, and teamwork skills. They also need strong self-management skills, including the ability to work independently, handle stressful situations, and prioritize multiple tasks.

Successful Peace Corps Volunteers share several personality traits such as being mature, patient, flexible, adaptable, creative, resourceful, and dedicated. In addition, they are sensitive to and respectful of different peoples and their culture and traditions.

Unions and Associations

Peace Corps Volunteers may join professional associations that serve the particular interests of their fields. These organizations can provide networking opportunities, professional resources, and other valuable services.

Tips for Entry

1. You can learn more about the Peace Corps through its Web site at http://www.peacecorps.gov.
2. Talk with a Peace Corps recruiter to learn more about becoming a volunteer. To find a local recruiter, call (800) 424–8580.
3. Check out Web sites by former Peace Corps Volunteers. You might start by visiting these sites: National Peace Corps Association, http://rpcv.org, and Peace Corps Online, http://peacecorpsonline.org.

SCHOOL ADMINISTRATORS

EARLY CHILDHOOD PROGRAM DIRECTOR

CAREER PROFILE

Duties: Administer daily operations; develop policies and procedures; supervise staff; oversee curriculum development; perform other duties as required

Alternate Title(s): Child Care Center Director, Preschool Director, Nursery School Director

Salary Range: $22,000 to $69,000

Employment Prospects: Good

Advancement Prospects: Good

Prerequisites:

Education or Training—Associate's or bachelor's degree

Experience—Previous experience as early childhood head teacher or assistant director; business experience desirable

Special Skills and Personality Traits—Leadership, communication, human relations, office management, and conflict management skills; be fair, honest, confident, organized, and innovative

Special Requirements—Child Development Associate certificate or other certification

CAREER LADDER

```
┌─────────────────────────────────────┐
│   Director of a larger program or    │
│   Early Childhood Program Owner      │
└─────────────────────────────────────┘

┌─────────────────────────────────────┐
│   Early Childhood Program Director   │
└─────────────────────────────────────┘

┌─────────────────────────────────────┐
│   Assistant Director or Head Teacher │
└─────────────────────────────────────┘
```

Position Description

Early Childhood Program Directors are responsible for administering private and public child care centers, preschools, nursery schools, and prekindergarten programs. The size and type of program differs for every program director. For example, a program director might run a large child care center that enrolls newborn babies to five-year-olds, which operates 12 hours a day. Another director might run a small preschool program that enrolls only three- and four-year-olds for half-day sessions.

The primary goal of all Early Childhood Program Directors is to ensure that their programs provide quality early childhood care and education services to all children and their families. Program directors must juggle many different responsibilities each day. They develop and implement policies and procedures that ensure a safe and healthy environment. For example, they might develop emergency evacuation plans or monitor procedures for dropping off and picking up children. They also make sure that programs are in compliance with government licensing regulations, as well as health and safety laws and regulations.

Early Childhood Program Directors coordinate all program activities—such as staff training workshops, new con-

struction plans, or parent volunteer programs—and plan future events, such as parent open houses. Some program directors plan fund-raisers and write proposals for grants. Furthermore, they complete administrative tasks that include preparing budgets, contacting vendors and suppliers, making school purchases, and writing business correspondence.

Another major responsibility is putting together a quality staff. Program directors are in charge of recruiting, hiring, training, and firing teachers and child care workers. The directors check references of potential candidates, making sure they are knowledgeable in child development and have training in early childhood care and education. In addition, program directors develop regular in-service training so that staff may learn about new teaching skills and developments in early childhood care and education.

Early Childhood Program Directors also oversee a program's curriculum, which must reflect the educational philosophy that is established by the owners, board of trustees, or higher-level administrators. With the teaching staff, program directors design a curriculum that provides for the social, emotional, intellectual, physical, aesthetic, and moral development of children. Together, the director and staff plan a daily schedule that balances child-directed and teacher-directed activities; small, large, and individual activities; and outdoor and indoor activities. Daily lesson plans, however, are the responsibility of the teaching staff, with program directors providing guidance. In some programs, the program directors also perform teaching duties.

Program directors maintain relationships with parents. Usually, the program directors are the first persons that parents meet when looking for a child care or preschool program. They give site tours, answer parents' questions, and discuss parents' needs and requirements for their children. Most program directors create and distribute school newsletters and bulletins to update parents with current activities and early childhood news.

Program directors have other duties that are performed as required. For example, they may act as substitute teachers for absent staff members. They may give presentations at local conferences or professional development workshops. Or, they may handle program recruitment duties, such as placing advertisements and notices in newspapers.

Early Childhood Program Directors often work more than 40 hours each week. Many work on a year-round schedule while others work a 10- or 11-month schedule.

Salaries

Earnings for Early Childhood Program Directors vary, depending on such factors as their education, credentials, experience, employer, and geographical location. According to the November 2004 *Occupational Employment Statistics* survey by the U.S. Bureau of Labor Statistics (BLS), the estimated annual salary for most preschool and child care center administrators ranged between $22,330 and $68,810.

Employment Prospects

The BLS reports that employment for preschool and child care center administrators should grow substantially through 2012 because of the continued increase of enrollment in formal child care programs. In addition, opportunities will become available as program directors retire, return to school, or transfer to other jobs.

Advancement Prospects

For many Early Childhood Program Directors, advancement is realized by higher wages or being hired by larger or more prestigious programs. Many also become owners of their own early childhood programs.

Program directors might also further their careers as university professors, software developers, researchers, and consultants in early childhood care and education.

Education and Training

Many employers prefer to hire candidates with at least an associate's or bachelor's degree in early childhood education (ECE). Some employers will hire candidates who have a minimum number of ECE units as long as they have sev-

eral years of administrative experience overseeing early childhood care and education programs.

Special Requirements

Most employers prefer to hire candidates who have the Child Development Associate (CDA) certificate, a professional credential in the early childhood field. This is a voluntary certification, which may be obtained through community colleges, community agencies, or professional associations. Some child care centers require that their program directors have the Certified Childcare Professional (CCP) certificate or the National Administrator Credential (NAC) granted by the National Child Care Association.

In some states, program directors are required to possess an early childhood program administrative credential. To find out about requirements in your state, contact the state board of education. See Appendix III for a list of state boards.

Experience, Skills, and Personality Traits

In general, employers choose candidates who have at least one year of experience as a teacher or assistant director in early childhood programs. Candidates should have some business experience or basic business skills, such as bookkeeping, operating office machines, and writing business correspondence.

To perform their job well, Early Childhood Program Directors need excellent leadership, communication, and human relations skills. They should also have strong office management and conflict management skills. Being fair, honest, confident, organized, and innovative are some personality traits that successful directors share.

Unions and Associations

Many Early Childhood Program Directors belong to professional associations to take advantage of networking opportunities, education programs, and other professional resources and services. Two national groups that directors may join are the National Association for the Education of Young Children and the National Child Care Association. See Appendix IV for contact information for these groups.

Tips for Entry

1. To enhance your employability, enroll in business courses, such as bookkeeping and business writing. Also learn how to use word processing and spreadsheet software.
2. Check out job listings at professional association Web sites as well as job bank Web sites, such as the America's Job Bank Web site at http://www.ajb.dni.us.
3. Subscribe to professional magazines or on-line services to keep up with current issues and trends in early childhood education.
4. Learn more about early childhood education on the Internet. You might start by visiting the ECE Web Guide at http://www.ecewebguide.com. To find other Web sites, enter the keyword *early childhood education* in a search engine.

ASSISTANT PRINCIPAL

Duties: Assist in the daily management of school; be responsible for designated administrative programs; perform duties as required

Alternate Title(s): Vice Principal, Assistant Administrator, Assistant Headmaster

Salary Range: $50,000 to $108,000

Employment Prospects: Good

Advancement Prospects: Fair

Prerequisites:

Education or Training—Master's degree

Experience—Classroom teaching; supervisory or administrative experience preferred

Special Skills and Personality Traits—Communication, interpersonal, teamwork, organizational and self-management skills; be self-motivated, energetic, creative, patient, flexible, honest, and calm

Special Requirements—School administrator credential with a principal endorsement

```
┌─────────────────────────┐
│       Principal         │
└─────────────────────────┘

┌─────────────────────────┐
│   Assistant Principal   │
└─────────────────────────┘

┌─────────────────────────┐
│     Schoolteacher       │
└─────────────────────────┘
```

Position Description

Assistant Principals provide support to principals in elementary, middle, junior high, and high schools, by assisting with site management and instructional leadership. They help enforce school policies and standards as well as local, state, and federal laws and regulations. When principals are absent, Assistant Principals carry out the leadership duties and make administrative decisions accordingly. (In private schools, Assistant Principals are known as *assistant headmasters.*)

Their responsibilities and duties vary from school to school. For example, they may assist principals with:

- developing, implementing, and evaluating instructional programs and activities
- recruiting, supervising, and evaluating school staff
- managing student discipline
- reporting and monitoring student attendance
- planning staff development programs
- creating emergency preparedness plans
- writing student and faculty handbooks

- preparing school budgets
- performing hall and lunchroom monitor duty
- performing public relations tasks, such as contacting local media about school events

Usually, Assistant Principals are assigned to coordinate one or more administrative areas, such as student discipline, student attendance, instructional supervision for certain grades, school security, or training for new teachers. Large schools often have two or more Assistant Principals, each of whom is responsible for certain administrative areas. For example, a high school might have two Assistant Principals, one in charge of school attendance and student discipline and the other responsible for student activities.

Assistant Principals also contribute to the development of student extracurricular activities. They assist in scheduling activities, finding sponsors, fund-raising, coordinating field trips, and so on. Many Assistant Principals supervise student government councils, coordinate peer mediation activities, and coach sports. In addition, they supervise school games, dances, concerts, and other activities.

Assistant Principals participate in faculty meetings and on school committees. On occasion, they attend district meetings or conferences sponsored by professional associations, educational agencies, or other organizations as their school's representatives. They also contribute to maintaining positive community relations. They become active members of school parent groups as well as network with community leaders, business leaders, social service agencies, and community groups.

Most Assistant Principals work more than 40 hours a week, including many nights and weekends.

Salaries

Salaries for Assistant Principals vary, depending on such factors as their education, experience, job duties, employer, and geographical location. The U.S. Bureau of Labor Statistics (BLS) reports, in its November 2004 *Occupational Employment Statistics* survey, that the estimated annual salary for most school administrators ranged between $49,700 and $107,960.

Employment Prospects

The BLS reports that employment of educational administrators, in general, is expected to increase by 21 to 35 percent through 2012. Opportunities for Assistant Principals should be favorable through this period due to the large number of administrators becoming eligible for retirement and fewer teachers seeking administrator jobs.

Advancement Prospects

Assistant Principals can advance to principal or headmaster positions. In public schools, they can seek administrator positions in the school district central office, rising up through the ranks to the superintendent position.

Assistant Principals can also pursue other careers in education. For example, they might become counselors, librarians, corporate trainers, or educational researchers.

Education and Training

Assistant Principals in public schools need a master's degree in educational administration or a related field. In most private schools, Assistant Principals need a bachelor's degree in any field; however, many have master's degrees.

To obtain state licensure, Assistant Principals must have completed an educational administration program from an accredited university. They have completed courses such as educational leadership, school law, school finances, curriculum and instruction, as well as completed a supervised internship.

Special Requirements

In public schools, Assistant Principals must hold a valid school administration credential with a principal endorsement. Licensure requirements vary from state to state. For specific information, contact the state board of education in the state where you wish to work. See Appendix III for a list of state boards.

Many private schools require state licensure or professional certification from school accreditation organizations, professional associations, or other recognized organizations.

Experience, Skills, and Personality Traits

Employers generally choose candidates who have previous classroom teaching experience. Most prefer that candidates have some school administrative or supervisory experience. In addition, candidates are able to demonstrate that they have successful instructional and leadership experience at the appropriate school level.

Assistant Principals need effective communication, interpersonal, and teamwork skills in order to work with teachers, students, parents, and others. In addition, Assistant Principals need strong organizational and self-management skills—the ability to handle stress, prioritize tasks, meet deadlines, and so on. Being self-motivated, energetic, creative, patient, flexible, honest, and calm are a few personality traits that successful Assistant Principals share.

Unions and Associations

Many Assistant Principals are members of professional associations that serve school administrators, such as the National Association of Elementary School Principals and the National Association of Secondary School Principals. By joining, they can take advantage of networking opportunities and other professional resources and services. Some Assistant Principals belong to the American Federation of School Administrators, a union for school administrators. See Appendix IV for contact information for these organizations.

Tips for Entry

1. As a teenager, you can begin gaining supervisory and administrative experience. Participate in school clubs, student government, and other extracurricular activities, and take advantage of opportunities to lead, plan, organize, and coordinate activities.
2. Talk with Assistant Principals as well as principals. Learn from them what experiences and skills you should obtain.
3. To learn more about school administration on the Internet, visit the Clearinghouse on Educational Policy and Management Web site at http://eric.uoregon.edu.

PRINCIPAL

CAREER PROFILE

Duties: Provide educational leadership and site management for an elementary, middle, junior high, or high school; perform duties as required

Alternate Title(s): Headmaster, in private schools

Salary Range: $50,000 to $108,000

Employment Prospects: Good

Advancement Prospects: Fair

Prerequisites:

Education or Training—Master's degree; for licensed principals, completion of an educational administration program

Experience—Several years of classroom teaching experience; supervisory and administrative experience preferred

Special Skills and Personality Traits—Communication, public speaking, interpersonal, team-building, conflict management, time management skills; be self-motivated, energetic, organized, creative, flexible, patient, honest, trustworthy, and courageous

Special Requirements—School administrator credential with a principal endorsement

CAREER LADDER

```
┌─────────────────────────────────────┐
│  Assistant Superintendent or other   │
│  higher-level School Administrator    │
└─────────────────────────────────────┘

┌─────────────────────────────────────┐
│             Principal                 │
└─────────────────────────────────────┘

┌─────────────────────────────────────┐
│  Assistant Principal or Schoolteacher │
└─────────────────────────────────────┘
```

Position Description

Principals are the head administrators of elementary, middle, junior high, and high schools. Their job is to ensure that schools provide the best education to students of all backgrounds and abilities. They are responsible for several administrative areas, including curriculum and instruction, staff supervision and evaluation, support services, staff development, student discipline, business services, and community relations. In public schools, Principals are under the supervision of superintendents, who administer school districts. In private schools, Principals (who are usually called *Headmasters*) are directed by higher-level administrators or boards of trustees.

As building, or school, managers, Principals are responsible for administering the different student services (such as food service and transportation) and administrative programs (such as security and information systems) that are essential to the daily operation of their schools. Usually, they delegate responsibilities to other staff members who work under their direction. For example, a Principal would authorize the cafeteria manager to take charge of the school's breakfast and lunch programs, or the assistant principal to oversee the security program.

As instructional leaders, Principals coordinate the curriculum programs for the different grade levels at their schools. They also oversee special programs (such as special education, bilingual education, and reading programs) that help students who have special learning, reading, and language needs. Working collaboratively with teachers, Principals develop and implement new instructional programs and activities that may help students succeed in their learning. In addition, Principals review textbooks, supplementary materials, and supplies to determine whether they are appropriate for the subject matter and for students. In small rural schools, Principals might teach one or more grades.

A major responsibility of Principals is providing support and guidance to all staff members. As the educational leader, Principals model behavior that they expect from their staff. Their staff includes certificated personnel—such as teachers, counselors, coaches, librarians, and assistant principals. It also includes classified staff—teacher aides, secretaries, clerks, custodians, food service workers, campus monitors, and others. Principals might also supervise school nurses, speech language pathologists, school psychiatrists, and other pupil services personnel.

Principals are responsible for providing in-service training for all staff members. In addition, they resolve conflicts among the staff when necessary. Performing staff evaluations is also another duty that they perform. Furthermore, Principals make recommendations to their superintendents (or boards of trustees) regarding staff promotions, demotions, transfers, contract renewals, and terminations.

Another duty is coordinating the various extracurricular activity programs that are available for students—such as interscholastic sports, student government councils, service clubs, and school publications. Many Principals also create student reward programs such as a student of the month program to recognize positive behavior and growth.

Principals are also responsible for maintaining student discipline. During breaks, lunch periods, and between class periods, many Principals get out to the hallways, cafeteria, and grounds where they can be visible and accessible to the students. Along with monitoring student behavior, Principals take the opportunity to get to know as many students as possible. When students misbehave, Principals are responsible for disciplining them. They might also meet with parents to discuss their children's behavior. With serious misconduct, Principals may recommend that a student be suspended from school.

Their jobs require completing many different tasks each day. Their duties include, but are not limited to:

- handling problems and crises as they arise
- monitoring all programs to make sure they follow school policies as well as local, state, and federal laws and regulations
- coordinating the schedules for classes, in-service workshops, extracurricular activities, student assemblies, school functions, and so on
- conducting assessments of the different instructional, business services, and noninstructional programs
- administering and preparing school budgets
- preparing reports, writing correspondence, and completing paperwork
- maintaining accurate records and files of students, staff, instructional programs, support services, school activities, and so forth
- planning emergency preparedness programs and conducting fire, safety, and other emergency drills
- recruiting and selecting school staff members
- investigating complaints and concerns brought forth by parents, students, staff, and the general public

- coordinating or participating in school fund-raising activities
- attending student games, assemblies, dances, and other school functions

In public schools, Principals are required to attend school district meetings and functions. They serve on district committees and work collaboratively with district personnel and staff from other schools.

As representatives of their schools, Principals maintain positive community relations. Using the local media, Principals keep parents and the general public up-to-date with the schedules of school events and student performances. They also inform the community of pertinent issues such as school discipline policies, new instructional programs, and teacher salary negotiations. Most Principals are active members of school parent groups. They also network with community leaders, business leaders, social service agencies, and community groups, as well as serve on community committees, task forces, or boards.

Principals work very long hours each day. They often work evenings and weekends to complete reports, attend school functions, appear at community events, conduct professional workshops, and so on.

Salaries

Salaries for Principals vary, and depend on factors such as their education, experience, employer, and geographical location. Typically, salaries are higher in public schools than in private schools. The U.S. Bureau of Labor Statistics (BLS) reports, in its November 2004 *Occupational Employment Statistics* survey, that the estimated annual salary for most administrators at the elementary and secondary school levels ranged between $49,700 and $107,960. According to a 2003–04 salary survey by the Educational Research Service, the average annual salary for elementary school Principals in public schools is $75,144; for middle school Principals, $80,060, and for high school Principals, $86,160.

Some school districts award Principals with bonuses for achieving certain goals, serving on special committees, or other accomplishments.

Employment Prospects

Most job vacancies become available as Principals retire or advance to other positions. The BLS reports that employment of educational administrators, in general, is expected to increase by 21 to 35 percent through 2012. Opportunities for Principals should be favorable through this period due to the large number of administrators becoming eligible for retirement and the fewer number of teachers seeking administrator jobs.

Advancement Prospects

Principals can become assistant superintendents or other higher-level school administrators, and, eventually, school superintendents. Many Principals prefer being building administrators; they realize advancement through pay increases, professional recognition, and obtaining positions in larger school systems.

Principals can also pursue other paths in education. For example, they can become educational administrators or consultants with state and federal educational agencies, nonprofit organizations, or educational consulting firms.

Education and Training

Principals in public schools need a master's degree in educational administration or related field. Private schools require that Principals have at least a bachelor's degree; however, many have either a master's or doctoral degree.

Licensed Principals have completed an educational administrator program from an accredited university. They have completed courses such as educational leadership, school law, school finances, curriculum and instruction, as well as a supervised internship.

Some school districts have mentor programs for new principals in which they receive formal or informal training for a certain period of time. Furthermore, Principals pursue their own professional development; for example, they attend professional workshops and seminars on topics such as conflict resolution, team building, instructional leadership, and curriculum planning and development.

Special Requirements

In public schools, Principals must hold a school administration credential with a Principal endorsement. Licensure requirements vary from state to state. For specific information, contact the state board of education for the state where you wish to work. See Appendix III for a list of state boards.

Private schools may require Principals, or headmasters, to hold state licensure or professional certification from school accreditation organizations, professional associations, or other recognized organizations.

Experience, Skills, and Personality Traits

In general, Principals must have previous classroom teaching experience and some supervisory and administrative experience. In public schools, candidates are usually required to have three to five years of full-time classroom teaching

experience. Schools may waive this requirement if candidates have teaching experience along with administrative or supervisory experience.

Along with leadership, supervisory, and administrative skills. Principals need strong communication, public speaking, interpersonal, team-building, conflict management, and time management skills to do their work effectively.

Successful Principals share several personality traits, such as being self-motivated, energetic, organized, creative, flexible, patient, honest, trustworthy, and courageous. In addition, they have a strong commitment to education and are able to inspire staff, parents, and others to participate in the development of quality educational programs.

Unions and Associations

Principals join various professional associations to take advantage of professional services and resources such as education programs and networking opportunities. Some national societies include:

- National Association of Elementary School Principals
- National Association of Secondary School Principals
- National Middle School Association
- Association for Supervision and Curriculum Development
- Phi Delta Kappa
- American Federation of School Administrators

For contact information, see Appendix IV.

Tips for Entry

1. Take advantage of workshops and seminars for aspiring Principals. The National Association for Elementary School Principals and the National Association for Secondary School Principals are two organizations that offer these types of programs from time to time.
2. Contact schools or district central offices directly to learn about job vacancies and requirements.
3. On the Internet, you can learn more about the Principal profession. You might start by visiting these Web sites: National Association of Elementary School Principals, http://www.naesp.org, and National Association of Secondary School Principals, http://www.principals.org.

INSTRUCTIONAL SUPERVISOR

CAREER PROFILE

Duties: Provide guidance and support to teachers in particular subject areas or educational services; perform teacher evaluations; plan professional development programs; perform other duties as required

Alternate Title(s): Instructional Specialist

Salary Range: $28,000 to $83,000

Employment Prospects: Fair

Advancement Prospects: Limited

Prerequisites:

Education or Training—Master's degree

Experience—Three to five years of classroom teaching experience; some supervisory experience

Special Skills and Personality Traits—Leadership, interpersonal, teamwork, communication, organizational, and management skills; be confident, steadfast, decisive, innovative, and creative

Special Requirements—Teaching credential, school administrator credential with an instructional supervision endorsement

CAREER LADDER

```
+-------------------------------------+
|   Lead Instructional                |
|   Supervisor or Curriculum and      |
|   Instruction Coordinator           |
+-------------------------------------+

+-------------------------------------+
|   Instructional Supervisor          |
+-------------------------------------+

+-------------------------------------+
|   Schoolteacher                     |
+-------------------------------------+
```

Position Description

In public schools, Instructional Supervisors are administrators at the school district central office level. They are specialists in subject areas, such as mathematics, social studies, science, foreign language, music, physical education, and vocational education. Some are specialists in educational services, such as special education, bilingual education, and guidance services. Their jobs are to coordinate the curriculum for their specialty in their school district. For example, in a K–12 school district, a math Instructional Supervisor is responsible for coordinating the mathematics curriculum from kindergarten to 12th grade. She or he is able to assist all K–12 teachers who teach arithmetic, remedial math, algebra, geometry, calculus, or other math courses.

Instructional Supervisors fill several roles. As instructional leaders, they provide guidance and support to teachers in the classroom. They also evaluate teachers' performance by observing them in the classroom. In written or oral reports, Instructional Supervisors give teachers feedback on their performance and recommend ways to improve their instruction.

Instructional Supervisors are also resources and consultants. They can provide teachers with information, references, and resources on specific topics in their specialty. They can discuss different teaching techniques and teaching methods that teachers might try in their classroom. In addition, they can recommend supplementary materials and instructional aids that would be helpful for instruction.

Being an administrator is another role that Instructional Supervisors fulfill. They perform administrative duties that include, but are not limited to:

- evaluating curriculum programs
- distributing information about content, teaching methods, and other subjects to teachers and administrators
- planning professional development programs
- conducting in-service workshops
- coordinating or conducting research for experimental educational programs
- enforcing school district policies as well as state and federal laws and regulations

Instructional Supervisors are also responsible for keeping up with developments in the content, curriculum, and teaching methods of their particular specialties. They enroll in continuing education programs and participate in professional conferences. In addition, they network with colleagues and read professional journals, reports, and books.

Instructional Supervisors spend much of their time at the different schools where they are assigned. They have a 40-hour work schedule, but sometimes work additional hours to complete their many different tasks.

Salaries

Salaries for Instructional Supervisors vary, depending on such factors as their education, experience, job duties, employer, and geographical location. The U.S. Bureau of Labor Statistics reports in its November 2004 *Occupational Employment Statistics* survey that the estimated annual salary for most instructional coordinators ranged between $27,830 and $82,690.

Employment Prospects

Most job opportunities become available as Instructional Supervisors retire, resign, or advance to higher positions. School districts may create additional positions to fill needs as long as funding is available.

Advancement Prospects

Instructional Supervisors can advance to higher administrative positions such as coordinators and directors of curriculum and instruction, assistant superintendents, and superintendents.

Instructional Supervisors can also pursue other career paths. For example, they can become curriculum developers and program directors in state and federal education agencies; editors, authors, and software developers in educational publishing companies; or curriculum and instruction consultants for private educational firms.

Education and Training

Instructional Supervisors must have either a bachelor's or master's degree in their disciplines. They also require a master's degree in education administration with an emphasis in instructional supervision from an accredited university. They have completed courses such as human relations, curriculum development, research, and advanced pedagogy courses, as well as a supervised field practicum.

Special Requirements

Instructional Supervisors must hold a teacher's license in addition to a school administrator credential with an instructional supervisor endorsement. Licensure requirements vary from state to state. For specific information, contact the state board of education in the state where you wish to work. See Appendix III for a list of state boards.

Experience, Skills, and Personality Traits

In general, applicants need three to five years of teaching experience in their subject area. Many schools also require that they have previous supervisory experience or knowledge of management principles and practices.

Instructional Supervisors need strong leadership, interpersonal, teamwork, and communication skills, as they must meet with teachers, administrators, parents, and others every day. In addition, they need adequate organizational and management skills to perform their work effectively. Successful Instructional Supervisors share several personality traits, such as being confident, steadfast, decisive, innovative, and creative.

Unions and Associations

Instructional Supervisors join various professional organizations to take advantage of services such as research, education programs, professional certification, job listings, and networking opportunities. Many join organizations that serve their particular subject area, such as the International Reading Association, the National Business Education Association, the National Council for the Social Studies, or the Council for Exceptional Children.

Many Instructional Supervisors also join school administrator organizations such as the Association for Supervision and Curriculum Development and the American Association of School Administrators.

For contact information for the above organizations, see Appendix IV.

Tips for Entry

1. As a teacher, you might obtain experience by participating on school committees that review textbooks or becoming a teacher consultant to educational publishers.
2. Job titles, as well as job descriptions, vary from employer to employer. When applying for a position, obtain the current job description.
3. To learn more about curriculum and instruction development on the Internet, visit the Web site for the Association for Supervision and Curriculum Development. Its URL is http://www.ascd.org.

PROGRAM DIRECTOR

CAREER PROFILE

Duties: Manage an instructional, noninstructional, or business service program that serves all schools in a system; perform duties as required

Alternate Title(s): A title that reflects a program area, such as Director of Curriculum or Human Resources Director

Salary Range: $50,000 to $108,000

Employment Prospects: Good

Advancement Prospects: Good

Prerequisites:

Education or Training—Bachelor's or master's degree; completion of an educational administration program

Experience—Qualifying work experience

Special Skills and Personality Traits—Leadership, supervisory, management, interpersonal, team-building, and communication skills; be energetic, self-motivated, organized, decisive, flexible, and creative

Special Requirements—School administrator or school business officer licensure

CAREER LADDER

Assistant Superintendent

Program Director

Program Coordinator or Specialist

Position Description

Program Directors are responsible for the various programs and departments in public and private schools that are needed to fulfill the educational missions and goals established by the governing school boards. In public schools, Program Directors work under the direction of superintendents or assistant superintendents in school district central offices. In most private schools, Program Directors are supervised by school headmasters.

Some Program Directors manage instructional programs and support services such as curriculum, elementary education, secondary education, vocational education, special education, technology, pupil personnel services, guidance, assessment and evaluation, or professional development. They plan, organize, and coordinate educational programs and activities that are implemented at the building, or school, level. Program Directors also act as leaders, consultants, and advisers to teachers, educational specialists, and building administrators.

Other Program Directors manage noninstructional programs that support the administrative services in schools. These include programs in transportation, food service,

security, custodial services, athletics, and so on. Still other Program Directors are in charge of business service programs that are essential to the day-to-day operations, such as human resources, fiscal services, purchasing, or risk management. Private schools also have Program Directors that manage programs for school admissions, financial aid, and development (or fund-raising activities).

The different Program Directors have duties that are specific to their area. However, all perform general duties that include, but are not limited to:

- developing departmental plans, establishing program goals, and setting deadlines
- implementing programs and activities
- preparing and administering program budgets
- conducting program reviews and evaluations
- supervising and evaluating program staff members
- enforcing district policies and regulations as well as federal, state, and local laws and regulations

In addition, Program Directors contribute to positive community relations for their schools or school districts.

They network with community leaders, business leaders, social service agencies, community groups, and so on. Many serve on community boards, task forces, and committees as well as attend community functions.

Program Directors typically work more than 40 hours a week. They often work evenings and weekends to complete tasks, attend meetings, appear at school and community events, participate in professional conferences, and so forth.

Salaries

Salaries for Program Directors vary, depending on such factors as their education, experience, employer, and geographical location. According to the November 2004 *Occupational Employment Statistics* survey, by the U.S. Bureau of Labor Statistics, the estimated annual salary for most school administrators ranged between $49,700 and $107,960.

Employment Prospects

Most job opportunities become available as Program Directors retire, resign, or advance to higher positions. On occasion, school districts create new administrative positions to fill particular needs if funds are available.

Advancement Prospects

Many Program Directors realize advancement through higher pay and more complex assignments. Some administrators pursue director positions with larger school districts while others seek such positions as assistant superintendent or superintendent.

Education and Training

Education requirements vary from school to school, as well as depend on the type of position. Directors of instructional programs need at least a master's degree in educational administration or other related field. Directors of noninstructional programs and school business officers need either a bachelor's or master's degree related to their specialty. Schools sometimes accept qualifying work experience to substitute for some or all education requirements.

Licensed Program Directors have completed an approved educational administrator program (or other related program) from an accredited institution that leads to the appropriate licensure endorsement.

Special Requirements

In public schools, Program Directors must hold a valid educational administrator credential with an endorsement for either a program director or school business officer. Types of licensure and requirements vary from state to state. To find out the requirements for the state where you wish to work, contact the state board of education. (See Appendix III for a list of state boards.) Private schools may require state licensure or professional certification from a school accreditation organization, professional association, or other recognized organization.

Experience, Skills, and Personality Traits

Experience requirements vary for the various positions. Applicants for public school positions usually need years of experience at both the building and district levels. Applicants for school business positions may not need prior experience in educational settings, as long as they have qualifying work experience in their specialty.

To do their jobs effectively, Program Directors need leadership, supervisory, management, interpersonal, team-building, and communication skills. Being energetic, self-motivated, organized, decisive, flexible, and creative are some personality traits that successful Program Directors have in common.

Unions and Associations

Program Directors join various professional associations to take advantage of networking opportunities and other professional resources and services. Many belong to societies such as the American Association of School Administrators that serve the general interests of all school administrators. They also join organizations that serve their particular areas, such as the Association for Supervision and Curriculum Development, the Council for Exceptional Children, the National Middle School Association, the Association of School Business Officials International, the American Association of School Personnel Administrators, or the School Nutrition Association. See Appendix IV for contact information for the above groups.

Tips for Entry

1. Job descriptions for Program Directors differ and vary from school to school, so be sure to get detailed job descriptions from the human resources offices.
2. To enhance your qualifications, you may want to obtain certification from a professional association or other organization that is recognized in your profession.
3. Use the Internet to research information about school districts where you would like to work. To find a particular school district, enter its name in a search engine.

ASSISTANT SUPERINTENDENT

CAREER PROFILE

Duties: Provide administrative support to the chief executive officer of a school system; perform duties as required

Alternate Title(s): Associate Superintendent, Deputy Superintendent

Salary Range: $50,000 to $108,000

Employment Prospects: Fair

Advancement Prospects: Fair

Prerequisites:

   Education or Training—An advanced degree; completion of an educational administration program

   Experience—Classroom teacher, principal, and central office administrator experience

   Special Skills and Personality Traits—Management, supervisory, communication, interpersonal, and teamwork skills; be patient, flexible, loyal, honest, analytical, creative, resourceful, and compassionate

   Special Requirements—School administrator credential with superintendent endorsement

CAREER LADDER

```
┌─────────────────────────────────────┐
│   Associate Superintendent or        │
│   Superintendent of Schools          │
└─────────────────────────────────────┘

┌─────────────────────────────────────┐
│   Assistant Superintendent           │
└─────────────────────────────────────┘

┌─────────────────────────────────────┐
│   School Principal or a              │
│   central office Program Director     │
└─────────────────────────────────────┘
```

Position Description

Assistant Superintendents contribute to the overall instructional leadership and administrative management of public school districts. Under the direction of superintendents (the chief executive officers), Assistant Superintendents have the authority to make administrative decisions that best execute the policies and standards established by the superintendents and the school boards of education.

Generally, Assistant Superintendents are assigned specific areas of responsibility, depending on the needs of the school districts. Some of these areas include curriculum and instruction, support services (such as pupil services and health services), noninstructional services (such as security and transportation), and business services.

In some school districts, Assistant Superintendents manage instructional and administrative responsibilities for assigned schools. In K–12 (kindergarten through 12th grade) school districts, Assistant Superintendents might be assigned to oversee all elementary schools or all secondary schools. Some large K–12 districts divide their schools into

geographical areas; thus, they are assigned as area Assistant Superintendents.

The duties of Assistant Superintendents vary, according to the administrative areas for which they are responsible. Some duties, however, are the same regardless of the administrative area. For example, Assistant Superintendents:

- coordinate and prepare budgets for programs and activities that are under their authority
- recruit, select, supervise, and evaluate staff members
- assist in the development, implementation, and evaluation of programs and activities
- advise department and program managers with personnel, budgets, and other administrative matters
- interpret and enforce district policies as well as federal, state, and local laws and regulations
- represent their school district at meetings with educational agencies and professional organizations

In addition, Assistant Superintendents contribute to maintaining community relations for the superintendent's office. Like other central office administrators, Assistant Superintendents network with community leaders, business leaders, social service agencies, community groups, and so on. They also serve on community boards, task forces, and committees as well as attend community functions.

Many school districts have two or more Assistant Superintendents, each of whom is assigned to different areas. Some districts have several levels of assistants—Assistant Superintendent, associate superintendent, and deputy superintendent.

Assistant Superintendents work more than 40 hours a week, including evenings and weekends.

Salaries

Salaries for Assistant Superintendents vary, depending on such factors as their education, experience, job duties, employer, and geographical location. According to the November 2004 *Occupational Employment Statistics* survey, by the U.S. Bureau of Labor Statistics (BLS), the estimated annual salary for most school administrators ranged between $49,700 and $107,960.

Employment Prospects

Most job opportunities become available as Assistant Superintendents retire, resign, or advance to higher positions. From time to time, a school district may create a new Assistant Superintendent position to fill a need if funding is available.

Advancement Prospects

With additional education and training, Assistant Superintendents can become school superintendents. Most work their way up through the ranks from assistant to associate superintendent to deputy superintendent to, finally, superintendent. Some Assistant Superintendents make this administrative level their ultimate career goal; they realize advancement through pay increases, achievements, and receiving assignments of their choice.

Education and Training

Most employers require that Assistant Superintendents have a master's degree in educational administration. Some districts require an education specialist's or doctoral degree.

In addition, Assistant Superintendents must have completed an educational administrator program at an accredited college or university. They have completed courses such as school administration, school law, curriculum development, school finance, federal programs, and student behavior management. They have also completed a one-year internship.

Assistant Superintendents usually receive in-service training. Many also participate in professional conferences and workshops to improve skills and keep up with current developments in education and educational administration.

Special Requirements

Assistant Superintendents must hold a valid school administrator credential with a superintendent endorsement for the state in which they work. Licensure requirements vary from state to state. For specific information, contact the state board of education for the state where you wish to work. See Appendix III for a list of state boards.

Private schools may require state licensure or professional certification from a school accreditation organization, professional association, or other recognized organization.

Experience, Skills, and Personality Traits

School boards look for candidates with extensive experience in classroom teaching, building (or school) administration, and central office administration. They also have experience in curriculum and staff development, as well as with school budgeting and financial management.

To handle their job effectively, Assistant Superintendents must have strong management, supervisory, communication, interpersonal, teamwork, and social skills. Successful Assistant superintendents share several personality traits, such as being patient, flexible, loyal, honest, analytical, creative, resourceful, and compassionate.

Unions and Associations

Assistant Superintendents belong to various professional associations to take advantage of networking opportunities and other professional resources and services. Two national societies that many join are the American Association of School Administrators and the Association for Supervision and Curriculum Development. See Appendix IV for contact information for these organizations.

Tips for Entry

1. Many school districts have a residency requirement, in which Assistant Superintendents (and superintendents) must live within the boundaries of the school districts or the city where they work.
2. Most Assistant Superintendents continue their own professional development through education programs sponsored by professional associations.
3. The Internet can help you learn more about school districts for which you would like to work. To find a Web site for a particular school district, enter its name in a search engine.

SUPERINTENDENT

CAREER PROFILE

Duties: Provide leadership to all schools within a school system; oversee the administration of all instructional programs, support services, and business services; maintain community relations; perform duties as required

Alternate Title(s): President, in private schools

Salary Range: $50,000 to $108,000+

Employment Prospects: Good

Advancement Prospects: Fair

Prerequisites:

Education or Training—An advanced degree; completion of an educational administration program

Experience—Classroom teacher, principal, and central office administrator experience

Special Skills and Personality Traits—Management, supervisory, executive, communication, interpersonal, team-building, and social skills; be patient, flexible, honest, trustworthy, compassionate, analytical, creative, courageous, and energetic

Special Requirements—School administrator credential with superintendent endorsement

CAREER LADDER

```
┌─────────────────────────────┐
│   Superintendent of a       │
│   larger school system      │
└─────────────────────────────┘


┌─────────────────────────────┐
│      Superintendent         │
└─────────────────────────────┘


┌─────────────────────────────┐
│  Assistant, Associate, or   │
│  Deputy Superintendent      │
└─────────────────────────────┘
```

Position Description

In the United States, public schools are organized into school districts that are administered by Superintendents. They are responsible for providing instructional leadership and management of all schools within their districts. (In private schools consisting of several school levels, the top position is termed the *president*.)

School districts differ in size and composition. Thus, a Superintendent might manage a suburban K–8 school district that is made up of three elementary schools and one middle school; another Superintendent might manage a metropolitan K–12 school district that has over 25 elementary, middle, junior high, and high schools.

Superintendents are selected by school boards that are composed of elected citizens of the communities that the school districts serve. The school boards establish the missions and goals for the schools. Working within the parameters of state laws and regulations and community values, the school boards establish policies and standards regarding curriculum, transportation, building maintenance, staff development, student services, labor relations, and so forth. Superintendents ensure that the policies and standards are realized and followed by every school in their districts. They are held accountable for all successes and failures of schools under their jurisdiction.

As Superintendents are the experts in education, they advise school boards on the best ways to handle matters regarding the school district and school administration. Additionally, Superintendents keep school boards informed on what is happening in the schools.

Working from the school district central office, Superintendents oversee four major areas:

- curriculum and instruction—for example, core curriculum, reading, special education, bilingual education, and vocational education
- support services—such as pupil services, curriculum development, and instructional supervision

- noninstructional services—food service, security, transportation, and building operations, for instance
- business services—for example, human resources, payroll, and purchasing

Because of the complexity of their jobs, Superintendents delegate areas of responsibility to their subordinate administrators. For example: a Superintendent delegates the responsibility of human resources and financial services to an assistant superintendent. The assistant oversees the different programs (such as personnel, payroll, and purchasing) within those areas. The size and makeup of a Superintendent's staff varies, depending on the types and number of programs, the district budget, the size of the district, and so forth.

Superintendents handle many different duties and tasks each day, which they perform with assistance from their administrative support staff as well as subordinate administrators. One major duty is coordinating school board meetings. They schedule meetings as often as the school board desires, inform members and the general public of the time and place for board meetings, and prepare meeting agendas. In addition, they prepare reports of all school business that they will present at the meetings. Most Superintendents communicate with the individual board members before each meeting.

Some other major duties of Superintendents are:

- overseeing the development, implementation, and evaluation of instructional programs and support services in the schools
- preparing monthly financial reports and annual budgets for the school district
- developing plans for the maintenance, improvement, or expansion of buildings and site facilities as needed
- managing human resources—hiring and firing staff for all schools, negotiating contracts, resolving personnel complaints, staff development, and so on
- supervising all school principals
- preparing accurate records and reports for compliance with federal, state, and county educational agencies
- performing fund-raising activities

Superintendents are also responsible for maintaining community relations. As advocates for the children and staff of their schools, Superintendents keep the community aware of what is happening in the schools through correspondence, local media, and presentations to local community organizations. Superintendents also network with community leaders, business leaders, social service agencies, community groups, and so on. In addition, they participate in community events, and serve on boards, task forces, and committees of local agencies and organizations.

As part of their jobs, Superintendents join professional associations to keep up with current educational issues,

trends, and developments as well as to network with colleagues. Representing their school districts, they participate in conferences, seminars, and workshops sponsored by professional associations, state and federal educational agencies, universities and colleges, as well as private industries.

Superintendents work on a 12-month schedule. They put in long hours each day to complete their duties. Many evenings and weekends are filled with meetings, school functions, community events, and other work-related activities.

Superintendents do not receive tenure. They are appointed to renewable, term-limit contracts, usually for three to four years.

Salaries

Salaries for Superintendents vary, depending on such factors as their experience, employer, and geographical location. The U.S. Bureau of Labor Statistics (BLS) reports, in its November 2004 *Occupational Employment Statistics* survey, that the estimated annual salary for most school administrators ranged between $49,700 and $107,960. According to a 2003 survey by the Council of Great City Schools, the salary for Superintendents of the 64 largest U.S. urban public school systems ranged from $120,000 to $325,500.

Superintendents may also receive additional compensation in such forms as expense accounts, a housing allowance, the use of an automobile, and membership dues for professional organizations.

Employment Prospects

The BLS reports that employment of educational administrators, in general, is expected to increase by 21 to 35 percent through 2012. However, most job opportunities for Superintendents generally become available as individuals retire, resign, or transfer to other institutions.

Advancement Prospects

School Superintendents realize advancement through higher pay, professional recognition, and appointments to larger school districts.

Superintendents can also follow other career paths in state and federal education agencies, professional associations, and other educational organizations. For example, they might become program administrators, specialists, or consultants.

Education and Training

Most public school districts require that Superintendents have a master's degree in educational administration. Some districts require that Superintendents have either an education specialist's or a doctoral degree. In addition, school Superintendents must have completed an educational administrator program at an accredited university. They have completed courses such as educational leadership, school administration, school law, curriculum development, school finance, school board relations, and special services, in addition to a one-year internship. The internship requirement may be waived if candidates have qualifying administrative experience.

Most Superintendents continue their own professional development through continuing education and professional development sponsored by professional organizations, such as the American Association of School Administrators.

Special Requirements

Superintendents must hold a valid school administrator credential with a superintendent endorsement for the state in which they work. Licensure requirements vary from state to state. For information, contact the state board of education for the state where you wish to work. See Appendix III for a list of state boards.

Private schools may require state licensure or professional certification from school accreditation organizations, professional associations, or other recognized organizations.

Experience, Skills, and Personality Traits

School boards look for candidates with extensive experience in classroom teaching, building (or school) administration, and central office administration. They have experience in curriculum, staff development, and school fiscal management. In addition, they have experience working at the school levels that the school district covers, and are knowledgeable of the educational programs and services that are provided in the schools.

To handle their job effectively, Superintendents must have superior management, supervisory, and executive skills. They also need excellent communication, interpersonal, team-building, and social skills.

Successful Superintendents share several personality traits, such as being patient, flexible, honest, trustworthy, compassionate, analytical, creative, courageous, and energetic. They are able to motivate and inspire their staff, parents, school board, and the community, earning their trust and loyalty. Furthermore, Superintendents are passionate about providing quality education to students of all backgrounds and abilities.

Unions and Associations

Superintendents join various professional associations to take advantage of networking opportunities and other professional services and resources. Some national societies that they might join are:

- American Association of School Administrators
- Association for Supervision and Curriculum Development
- Urban Superintendents Association of America
- National Association of Elementary School Principals
- National Middle School Association
- National Association of Secondary School Principals

For contact information for the above organizations, see Appendix IV.

Tips for Entry

1. Many Superintendents recommend that individuals prepare for the profession by holding a variety of teaching and administrative positions in schools.
2. For nationwide job listings, check out professional association Web sites, such as the National School Boards Association Web site at http://www.nsba.org.
3. Use the Internet to learn more about Superintendents. You might start by visiting the American Association of School Administrators Web site at http://www.aasa.org.

HIGHER EDUCATION
ADMINISTRATORS

DIRECTOR OF ADMISSIONS

Duties: Oversee the process of admissions and enrollment of new students; supervise and evaluate staff; perform other duties as required

Alternate Title(s): None

Salary Range: $39,000 to $128,000

Employment Prospects: Good

Advancement Prospects: Fair

Prerequisites:

Education or Training—Master's degree

Experience—Five or more years of work experience in admissions, preferably in higher education settings

Special Skills and Personality Traits—Leadership, supervisory, management, communication, interpersonal, team-building, conflict resolution, and computer skills; be independent, self-motivated, ethical, creative, dedicated, energetic, and organized

```
┌──────────────────────────────┐
│   Vice President of          │
│   Enrollment Management       │
└──────────────────────────────┘

┌──────────────────────────────┐
│   Director of Admissions      │
└──────────────────────────────┘

┌──────────────────────────────┐
│   Assistant Director of Admissions │
└──────────────────────────────┘
```

Position Description

The admissions office is usually the first college or university office that most students contact. This office is part of the enrollment management department, which oversees all recruitment, admission, enrollment, and student records programs for an institution. From an admissions office, prospective students can obtain general information about an institution as well as learn how to apply for admission. Applications for entry to an institution are sent to the admissions office where they are processed and a selection of new students is made.

The Director of Admissions is responsible for the administration of the admissions office. He or she develops and implements admissions policies and procedures that are consistent with an institution's mission, enrollment goals, and administrative policies. At universities and colleges, undergraduate and graduate admissions may be handled separately by different Directors of Admissions.

Most colleges and universities have three entrance terms—fall, spring, and summer. For each entrance term, directors oversee the processing of admissions applications, which includes financial aid applications and campus housing applications. They direct a staff of admissions counselors

who review the applications and select new students based on factors such as their completion of basic high school requirements, school grades, standardized test scores, extracurricular activities, academic interests, application essays, and personal recommendations. All applicants are sent a letter from the Office of Admissions informing them whether or not they have been accepted to their institution.

Many Directors of Admissions are also responsible for the recruitment of new students. In some institutions, directors coordinate or assist with the recruitment of student athletes. Along with their staff, other enrollment management teams, campus committees, and other college personnel, Directors of Admissions develop and implement strategic recruitment and marketing plans to attract a diverse population of prospective students—incoming freshmen, transfer students, graduate students, adult students, students of different ethnic and cultural backgrounds, international students, and so on. Many higher education institutions have special admissions programs for prospective students who do not have basic entry requirements but show the potential of succeeding in a college environment.

Another major area of responsibility is the evaluation of admission and enrollment data to improve recruitment and admissions services. Directors conduct various forms of analyses, such as student needs analyses, trend analyses, and satisfaction surveys. Based on the feedback, directors make adjustments where needed in staffing, customer services, or recruitment programs, as well as make recommendations to the administration for addressing market changes.

As leaders of admissions offices, directors are responsible for building a supportive and efficient team that provides quality services to students, parents, faculty, and others. Directors of Admissions supervise all activities performed by their professional and administrative support staff members. (Some part-time staff members are students.) Directors also provide ongoing training for staff to update or learn new skills, procedures, computer applications, and so on. In addition to performing job evaluations of staff members, directors make recommendations for staff promotions, demotions, or terminations to the administration.

In some institutions, Directors of Admissions are responsible for overseeing financial aid programs. They help students obtain scholarships, loans, fellowships, or other financial assistance for their school tuition and living expenses.

A Director of Admissions reports to the chief officer of enrollment management who may be a dean, vice president, or another executive-level administrator. Directors work 40 hours a week, sometimes working additional hours on evenings and weekends to complete their duties.

Salaries
Salaries for Directors of Admissions vary, depending on such factors as their experience, education, employer, and geographical location. According to the November 2004 *Occupational Employment Statistics* survey, by the U.S. Bureau of Labor Statistics (BLS), the estimated annual salary for most educational administrators—including the Director of Admissions—ranged between $38,910 and $128,180.

Employment Prospects
The BLS reports that opportunities for nonacademic administrators in higher education institutions should be favorable through 2012, partly due to the increase in student enrollments and the large number of administrators becoming eligible for retirement. Most openings for the Director of Admissions position become available as individuals retire, advance to higher positions, or transfer to other jobs.

Advancement Prospects
Directors of Admissions can become administrative deans, vice presidents, and college or university presidents. At the executive levels, advanced degrees are required. Directors also have the option to pursue careers in other areas of enrollment management services, as well as other administrative departments in higher education institutions.

Education and Training
Most employers require that applicants have a master's degree in student personnel, higher education administration, business administration, or another related field. Some employers prefer that directors have doctoral degrees. Employers sometimes choose candidates with bachelor's degrees if they have qualifying work experience.

Directors receive training on the job. Many pursue their own professional development through individual study, by enrolling in continuing education classes and professional seminars, and by participating in professional conferences.

Experience, Skills, and Personality Traits
Applicants generally need between five to eight years of work experience, with increasingly responsible supervisory and management experience in admissions or enrollment management. Having experience in higher education settings is preferable.

Directors of Admissions should have strong leadership, supervisory, and management skills along with superior communication, interpersonal, team-building, and conflict resolution skills. In addition, they need computer skills, including a knowledge of databases. Being independent, self-motivated, ethical, creative, dedicated, energetic, and organized are some personality traits that successful Directors of Admissions share.

Unions and Associations
Many Directors of Admissions are members of different professional associations to take advantage of education programs, networking opportunities, and other professional resources and services. Some societies that they join are the American Association of Collegiate Registrars and Admissions Officers, the Association of College Administration Professionals, and the American Association of University Administrators. See Appendix IV for contact information.

Tips for Entry
1. To find out if the field of enrollment management is right for you, obtain part-time work in the admissions office at the college that you attend.
2. Experts say that job seekers willing to relocate to another city or region may have better opportunities for securing a position.
3. You can learn about admissions offices at different colleges and universities on the Internet. To get a list of Web pages to read, enter the keyword *admissions office* in a search engine.

REGISTRAR

CAREER PROFILE

Duties: Administer student registration services; manage and maintain student academic records; oversee staff; perform other duties as required

Alternate Title(s): None

Salary Range: $47,000 to $83,000

Employment Prospects: Good

Advancement Prospects: Fair

Prerequisites:

Education or Training—Bachelor's or master's degree

Experience—Three to eight years of management and supervisory experience in the enrollment management field

Special Skills and Personality Traits—Leadership, administrative, management, computer, communication, interpersonal, and team-building skills; be analytical, organized, honest, reliable, and flexible

CAREER LADDER

```
┌──────────────────────────┐
│   Vice President of      │
│   Enrollment Management   │
└──────────────────────────┘

┌──────────────────────────┐
│        Registrar         │
└──────────────────────────┘

┌──────────────────────────┐
│    Assistant Registrar   │
└──────────────────────────┘
```

Position Description

Every higher education institution has a Registrar's Office that provides student enrollment services and maintains all records of admissions, registration, and student academic records. Overseeing the day-to-day administration of this office is the Registrar.

Registrars have several areas of responsibility that are generally the same regardless of the type of institution (two-year college, four-year college, or university) or whether an institution is public or private. One major responsibility is managing the student registration process for each school term—fall, spring, or summer. (Many campuses also have a short term between the fall and spring terms.) Under the Registrar's direction, staff members obtain proposed class offerings and schedules from each department on campus. The staff assigns classrooms and creates a master schedule; they then prepare a class schedule and distribute it to students near the end of the current term. The schedule announces the courses that each department plans to offer for the forthcoming term. Relevant information is given about each course, such as the name of the course, the number of units, the name of the instructor, if available, and the days and time a class would be held.

Most students preregister for classes, forwarding completed registration forms and their tuition fees to the Regis-

trar's Office. The office processes the forms and fees, then mails individual class schedules to students before the new term begins.

Another major responsibility is managing student records of current and former students. Most campuses now keep student records on computer databases which include information such as grades, attendance, transfer evaluations, admissions applications, enrollment records, and graduation certifications. The Registrar is responsible for the integrity and security of all student records for an institution.

Registrars are also responsible for directing the activities of the professional and support staff in their departments. (Staff may also include students who work part time.) Providing leadership, Registrars are expected to develop a strong collaborative team that offers superior service to students, faculty, administrators, and others. Registrars also provide in-service programs to help staff improve skills as well as learn new ones. In addition, they evaluate the job performance of their staff members, and make recommendations for staff promotions, demotions, or terminations to the administration.

Registrars work closely with faculty and administrators on their campuses. They communicate with appropriate personnel about changes in enrollment policies and procedures.

On occasion, Registrars are asked to compile statistical data that administrators would use for accreditation compliance requirements, institutional planning, annual reports, and so on. Registrars may also be asked to prepare data that might assist faculty in curriculum development.

Registrars perform many other duties, with the assistance of their staff. For example, Registrars:

- prepare and administer the budget for the Registrar's Office
- recruit and select new staff
- oversee the preparation of college catalogs
- respond to student requests for certification of academic status
- provide former students with transcripts and other student records
- provide faculty with class rosters
- process grades upon the completion of each term
- audit students' grades and credits to ensure that they have the requirements for graduation

Registrars work 40 hours a week, sometimes working evenings and weekends to complete their various tasks.

Salaries

Salaries for Registrars vary, depending on such factors as their experience, education, job duties, and employer. According to a 2004–05 salary survey by the College and University Professional Association for Human Resources, the median annual salary for Registrars ranged from $46,987 to $83,200.

Employment Prospects

The U.S. Bureau of Labor Statistics reports that opportunities for nonacademic administrators in higher education institutions should be favorable through 2012. This is partly due to the expected increase in student enrollments and the large number of administrators becoming eligible for retirement. Most openings for the Registrar position generally become available as individuals retire, advance to higher positions, or transfer to other jobs.

Advancement Prospects

Registrars can become administrative deans, vice presidents, and college (or university) presidents. For executive administrator positions, advanced degrees are required. Registrars also have the option to pursue careers in other areas of enrollment management services, as well as other administrative departments in higher education institutions.

Education and Training

Generally, candidates need either a bachelor's or master's degree in business administration, student personnel services, or a related field. Employers may consider candidates who have degrees in unrelated fields if they have qualifying work experience. Specialty colleges often give preference to qualified candidates who have degrees in their specialized fields. For example, a fine arts college might choose a qualified candidate who has a degree in one of the visual arts.

Experience, Skills, and Personality Traits

Depending on the size and type of college, candidates generally need three to eight years of management and supervisory experience in registration or student records functions, preferably in higher education environments. Employers look for candidates who have knowledge of academic regulations and issues in higher education, as well as technical experience with computerized registration systems.

To do their work effectively, Registrars must have strong leadership, administrative, and management skills along with computer, communication, interpersonal, and team-building skills. Successful Registrars share several personality traits, such as being analytical, organized, honest, reliable, and flexible.

Unions and Associations

Registrars join professional associations to take advantage of education programs, professional publications, networking opportunities, and other professional services and resources. They might join organizations that specifically service enrollment management officers, such as the American Association of Collegiate Registrars and Admissions Officers. They also join organizations that generally serve higher education administrators such as the Association of College Administration Professionals or the American Association of University Administrators. For contact information, see Appendix IV.

Tips for Entry

1. To find job listings for Registrars and other nonacademic job opportunities, check out professional journals, national newspapers, and major metropolitan newspapers. Also contact professional associations for higher education administrators.
2. As a college student, obtain a part-time or summer job in the Registrar's Office to gain experience.
3. You can learn about the Registrar's Office at different colleges and universities on the Internet. To get a list of Web pages to read, enter the keyword *registrar's office* in a search engine.

DIRECTOR OF STUDENT ACTIVITIES

CAREER PROFILE

Duties: Oversee the administration of student activity programs, the student union, and student organizations: perform duties as required

Alternate Title(s): Director of Student Life; Director of Campus Life; Assistant Dean/Director

Salary Range: $34,000 to $58,000

Employment Prospects: Good

Advancement Prospects: Fair

Prerequisites:

Education or Training—Master's degree

Experience—At least three years of managerial or supervisory experience in student affairs

Special Skills and Personality Traits—Report-writing, communication, decision-making, computer, leadership, management, interpersonal, and team-building skills; be tactful, organized, energetic, self-motivated, and creative

CAREER LADDER

```
┌─────────────────────────────────────┐
│          Dean of Students            │
└─────────────────────────────────────┘

┌─────────────────────────────────────┐
│   Director of Student Activities     │
└─────────────────────────────────────┘

┌─────────────────────────────────────┐
│ Assistant Director of Student Activities │
└─────────────────────────────────────┘
```

Position Description

Directors of Student Activities oversee the planning and organizing of a wide variety of educational, social, cultural, and recreational programs and activities that meet students' interests and needs. For example, activities may include concerts, movies, dances, career days, health fairs, intramural sports programs, student newspapers, and community service programs.

A program or activity may be sponsored by the student activities office, a student organization, or an academic department. Activities and programs are sometimes sponsored by campus organizations in collaboration with community organizations, local schools, or other outside groups. Directors ensure that all programs and activities are in compliance with the policies and regulations of their institutions.

Most programs and activities are held at an institution's student union. This is where students (as well as faculty and others) have access to food services, bookstores, recreational facilities, student organization offices, and so on. Staff members of the student activities office manage the student union, under the direction of the Director of Student Activities.

Supervising campus-sponsored student organizations is another responsibility of Directors of Student Activities.

These organizations include student government councils; honor societies; academic organizations; sororities and fraternities; musical groups, dance groups, and other performance organizations; political and issue-oriented groups; sports clubs; religious organizations; special interest organizations; and so on. Directors advise student organizations about their financial status, on planning activities, and on methods for improving their organizations. Directors also maintain contact with faculty advisers.

Directors of Student Activities are responsible for administering budgets for their offices. Each term, student activities offices receive funds raised by student activity fees which directors allocate accordingly to the student union, student organizations, student publications, cultural activities, intramural programs, and so forth. Furthermore, directors prepare budgets for their offices that they submit to executive-level administrators.

Another major responsibility is supervising the student activities office staff. The staff is made up of professionals and support workers. Some members are students who work part time. Directors are responsible for providing staff with job training and professional development programs. They also perform job evaluations and make recommendations for staff promotions, demotions, and terminations to the administration.

Directors of Student Activities have many other duties that include, but are not limited to:

- keeping a master schedule of events and activities
- assigning conference rooms and other space within the student union
- coordinating campus orientation programs for new students
- recruiting and selecting staff members
- producing and distributing information about upcoming programs and events
- assisting in development, or fund-raising activities, for community-based programs
- serving on campus councils and committees as representatives of the office of student activities
- representing the college at professional conferences related to student services or student affairs

The Director of Student Activities reports to the dean of students or other senior-level administrator. Directors often work more than 40 hours a week. They typically work many evenings and weekends to attend meetings, participate in professional conferences, supervise student activities, appear at student functions, and so on.

Salaries
Salaries for Directors of Student Activities vary, depending on such factors as their experience, education, job duties, and employer. According to a 2004–05 salary survey by the College and University Professional Association for Human Resources, the median annual salary for Directors of Student Activities ranged from $34,000 to $57,789.

Employment Prospects
The U.S. Bureau of Labor Statistics reports that opportunities for nonacademic administrators in higher education institutions should be favorable through 2012, partly due to the expected increase in student enrollments and the large number of administrators becoming eligible for retirement. Most openings for the Director of Student Activities position generally become available as individuals advance to higher positions, transfer to other jobs, or retire.

Advancement Prospects
Directors of Student Affairs can become deans of students, vice presidents of student affairs, and college or university presidents. Master's or doctoral degrees are usually required for executive-level positions.

Education and Training
In general, applicants should have a master's degree, preferably in student personnel, counseling, or related field. Candidates with a doctoral degree in college student personnel, higher education administration, or related fields are preferred by many employers.

Many directors pursue professional development through individualized study, by enrolling in continuing education courses and professional workshops, and by participating in professional conferences.

Experience, Skills, and Personality Traits
Employers generally require a minimum of three years of professional experience with student activities. They look for candidates who have experience with budget and human resource management. Candidates also demonstrate a knowledge and sensitivity to issues and behaviors that shape and affect students' college experience.

Directors of Student Activities need strong report-writing, communication, decision-making, and computer skills, along with leadership, management, interpersonal, and team-building skills. Being tactful, organized, energetic, self-motivated, and creative are some personality traits that successful Directors of Student Activities share.

Unions and Associations
Directors of Student Activities join professional associations to take advantage of other networking opportunities and professional resources and services. Some organizations that they might join are the College and University Professional Association for Human Resources, the ACPA: College Student Educators International, the National Association of Student Personnel Administrators, the Association of College Administration Professionals, and the American Association of University Administrators. See Appendix IV for contact information for these organizations.

Tips for Entry
1. As a college student, find out if the field of student affairs might interest you. Volunteer or obtain part-time jobs in the student affairs office.
2. Some employers allow candidates to substitute a combination of education and experience for the work experience requirement.
3. Use the Internet to learn more about student affairs in higher education. You might start by visiting Student Affairs.com at http://www.studentaffairs.com. To find other Web sites, enter one of these keywords in a search engine: *student affairs* or *office of student activities*.

ATHLETIC DIRECTOR

CAREER PROFILE

Duties: Plan and direct intercollegiate athletic programs; supervise coaches; perform duties as required

Alternate Title(s): Athletic Administrator

Salary Range: $53,000 to $141,000 or more

Employment Prospects: Fair

Advancement Prospects: Fair

Prerequisites:

Education or Training—Master's degree

Experience—Supervisory and management experience in college athletic departments; coaching experience preferred

Special Skills and Personality Traits—Leadership, supervisory, communication, interpersonal, team-building, report-writing, financial management, computer fund-raising, and community relations skills; be fair, honest, open-minded, optimistic, even-tempered, dedicated

CAREER LADDER

```
Administrative Dean or Vice President
```

```
Athletic Director
```

```
Assistant Athletic Director
```

Position Description

Athletic Directors at colleges and universities are in charge of all intercollegiate sports, such as football, basketball, baseball, softball, soccer, golf, fencing, tennis, gymnastics, swimming, rowing, and track and field. Some athletic departments have two directors—one for women's sports, and the other for men's sports. On some campuses, the women's athletic administrator is a senior executive under the Athletic Director.

Athletic Directors are responsible for planning, administering, and evaluating all intercollegiate athletic programs. Working with the coaching staff, directors develop objectives and strategic plans to meet the goals (such as gender equity) of their departments. They also make sure that the athletic departments are compatible with the missions, policies, and regulations of their institutions. In addition, directors ensure that all athletic programs comply with the regulations and standards of the athletic conferences in which their institutions are members.

Athletic Directors are also responsible for overseeing the activities of the coaching staffs of the different sports. Additionally, they supervise administrative staffs that may include assistant athletic directors, support workers, busi-

ness managers, publicists, and others. On a regular basis, Athletic Directors conduct performance reviews of the different personnel. They also make recommendations for promotions, demotions, or terminations of coaching and administrative staff to the administration.

In addition, Athletic Directors are business managers. Their duties include, but are not limited to:

- managing and preparing budgets
- coordinating student athlete recruiting plans
- recruiting and selecting coaching and other athletic department staff
- overseeing development, or fund-raising, plans to raise resources for the various athletic programs
- scheduling games, meets, and other sports events
- overseeing ticket sales for athletic events
- supervising public relations
- supervising the maintenance of gymnasiums, playing fields, swimming pools, and other facilities

As representatives of their institutions, Athletic Directors participate in meetings held by intercollegiate conferences and professional organizations. They also actively participate in community activities and projects, serving on committees, boards, and task forces.

Some Athletic Directors are responsible for planning and administering intramural sports programs. (In an intramural program, students on campus form coeducational or single-sex teams, such as in volleyball, and play against each other.) Some Athletic Directors assume teaching responsibilities, teaching one or more classes in physical education, health education, teacher education, or other departments.

Athletic Directors report to an executive administrator, such as the vice president for student affairs or the president.

Athletic Directors often put in more than 40 hours a week to complete their various tasks. They spend many evenings and weekends attending meetings, participating in professional conferences, meeting with boosters and donors, appearing at school and community functions, and completing various tasks.

Salaries
Salaries for Athletic Directors vary, depending on such factors as their experience, education, employer, and size of athletic program. According to a 2004–05 salary survey by the College and University Professional Association for Human Resources, the median annual salary for Athletic Directors ranged from $52,511 to $141,400 per year.

Employment Prospects
Athletic Directors are hired by public and private institutions. They work for two-year colleges, four-year colleges, and universities. Most opportunities, become available as administrators retire, resign, or transfer to other institutions.

Advancement Prospects
Athletic Directors can become administrative deans, vice presidents, and college or university presidents. Becoming an executive administrator requires an advanced degree. Many Athletic Directors realize advancement through salary increases, with professional recognition, and by obtaining positions in institutions of their choice.

Athletic Directors can also pursue other career paths, such as becoming coaches and administrators in professional sports organizations.

Education and Training
Depending on the institution, Athletic Directors must have a minimum of either a bachelor's or master's degree, preferably in athletic administration or a related field. Most four-year colleges and universities prefer that candidates have an advanced degree.

Directors generally receive on-the-job training. Many pursue professional development through individualized study, with continuing education courses and professional workshops; and by participating in professional conferences.

Experience, Skills, and Personality Traits
In general, Athletic Directors have previous management and supervisory experience in positions of increasing responsibility. They have demonstrated success in handling gender equity, financial management, and other matters related to running a successful athletic department. Many employers prefer that prospective Athletic Directors have coaching or athletic administrative experience at the intercollegiate conference level in which their institutions participate.

Because they work with students, coaches, administrators, boosters, and others, Athletic Directors need superior leadership, supervisory, communication, interpersonal, and team-building skills. They also need strong report-writing, financial management, computer, fund-raising, and community relations skills to perform their jobs effectively. Successful Athletic Directors share several personality traits, such as being fair, honest, open-minded, optimistic, even-tempered, and dedicated.

Unions and Associations
Athletic Directors join professional associations to take advantage of networking opportunities and other professional services and resources. Many are members of the National Association of Collegiate Directors of Athletics and the National Association of Collegiate Women Athletic Administrators. Many directors also belong to associations that serve specific sports. In addition, some are members of societies, such as the Association of College Administration Professionals, that serve higher education administrators. See Appendix IV for contact information for the above organizations.

Tips for Entry
1. Obtain practical experience in the different areas of running a college athletic department, such as coaching, fund-raising, public relations, and facilities management.
2. Network with colleagues to learn about job openings.
3. Talk with colleagues who are familiar with the athletic departments in which you are interested. Learn about people, issues, politics, and other matters within the department.
4. To learn more about intercollegiate athletics on the Internet, visit the National Collegiate Athletic Association Web site at http://www.ncaa.org.

DIRECTOR OF PUBLIC SAFETY

CAREER PROFILE

Duties: Oversee law enforcement and administrative operations; provide direction and guidance to police and civilian staff; perform duties as required

Alternate Title(s): Director of Campus Security, Director of Campus Safety, Chief of Police

Salary Range: $40,000 to $87,000

Employment Prospects: Good

Advancement Prospects: Fair

Prerequisites:

    Education or Training—A college degree

    Experience—Law enforcement or security background, preferably in campus settings; supervisory and management experience

    Special Skills and Personality Traits—Leadership, communication, interpersonal, team-building, report-writing, computer, supervisory, and program management skills; be honest, dedicated, organized, personable, innovative, and flexible

    Special Requirements—Police officer certification may be required

CAREER LADDER

```
┌─────────────────────────────────────────┐
│        Director of Public Safety         │
│  (for larger public safety department)   │
└─────────────────────────────────────────┘

┌─────────────────────────────────────────┐
│        Director of Public Safety         │
└─────────────────────────────────────────┘

┌─────────────────────────────────────────┐
│    Assistant Director of Public Safety   │
└─────────────────────────────────────────┘
```

Position Description

The Director of Public Safety is in charge of the overall safety and security of the campus environment for all students, faculty, administrators, employees, and visitors. He or she is responsible for coordinating all campus safety and security programs and activities.

Public safety departments differ from campus to campus. Some departments are composed solely of security officers. They enforce the campus rules and regulations. Any individuals suspected of criminal or illegal activities can be questioned and held by security officers until local law enforcement officers arrive on the scene.

Other departments are composed of police officers who enforce local and state laws in addition to institutional rules and regulations. Campus police officers have the authority to arrest people suspected of criminal or illegal activities. They also can conduct criminal investigations for prosecution. Some public safety departments have both law enforcement and security forces. A Director of Public Safety who oversees law enforcement officers is also known as the chief of (campus) police.

Most campus public safety departments provide the following protective services:

- patrol units (vehicle, foot, bicycle, and other types)
- security services for campus facilities (such as art museums and science laboratories), construction projects, special campus events, and visiting dignitaries
- security technology systems, such as burglar alarm systems and access card systems
- crime prevention programs and services such as a campus escort service, a bicycle registration program, and a rape prevention program
- traffic and parking enforcement
- emergency services during medical emergencies, fires, floods, civil disturbances, and other crises
- safety and environmental health inspections of campus facilities and grounds

Directors of Public Safety oversee all field operations. They may supervise armed or unarmed officers. (On many campuses, the security staff includes students who work part time.) Directors also supervise unit supervisors, dispatch staff, and support staff. As part of their duties, directors provide staff members with in-service training.

They perform many administrative duties, which vary with the different directors. One general task that most directors do is the management and preparation of department budgets. Another general duty is overseeing the record keeping of criminal and security incident statistics. As mandated by law, Directors of Public Safety prepare annual crime reports for their campuses.

Their responsibilities also include maintaining a working relationship with local, state, and federal law enforcement agencies. In addition, Directors of Public Safety represent their institutions at meetings with community organizations, law enforcement agencies, and other groups.

The Director of Public Safety reports to the dean of students or other executive-level administrator.

Directors of Public Safety are on call 24 hours a day.

Salaries

Salaries for Directors of Public Safety vary, depending on such factors as their experience, education, employer, and geographical location. Generally, directors in larger institutions earn higher salaries. According to a 2004–05 salary survey by the College and University Professional Association for Human Resources, the median annual salary for campus security directors ranged from $40,111 to $87,048 per year.

Employment Prospects

Directors of campus public safety or security are employed by two-year colleges as well as four-year colleges and universities. Most opportunities become available as directors retire, resign, or transfer to other campuses.

Advancement Prospects

Directors of Public Safety realize advancement through pay increases, professional recognition, and transfers to other institutions.

Other careers that they might pursue include becoming private campus security consultants. They might also become professors in criminal justice, police science, or another related field.

Education and Training

Most employers require an associate's or bachelor's degree along with qualifying work experience. Some employers prefer that candidates have a master's degree. Degrees may be in any field, although most employers prefer a degree in criminal justice, police science, industrial security, business management, public management, or a related field.

Directors of campus police forces are usually required to have completed police academy training.

New directors usually receive on-the-job training during their first few months in employment. Directors typically participate in professional training workshops and continuing education classes to learn new skills and knowledge.

Special Requirements

Directors in charge of campus enforcement officers must be certified as police officers or be certifiable within a certain time period after their appointments. For campus security programs, directors may be required to obtain professional certification as a Certified Protection Professional (CPP).

Experience, Skills, and Personality Traits

In general, candidates must have several years of experience in law enforcement, industrial security, the military, or a combination in such fields. Their work history should also show progressively responsible managerial or supervisory experience.

Directors of Public Safety must have strong leadership, communication, interpersonal, and team-building skills to establish effective relationships with their staff as well as students, faculty, administrators, and others. In addition, directors need report-writing and computer skills along with supervisory and program management skills. Successful directors share several personality traits, such as being honest, dedicated, organized, personable, innovative, and flexible.

Unions and Associations

Many Directors of Public Safety belong to professional associations to take advantage of networking opportunities and other professional services and resources. Some national groups that directors may join are the International Association of Campus Law Enforcement Administrators, International Association of Chiefs of Police, and ASIS International. They may also join societies for higher education administrators, such as the Association of College Administration Professionals. See Appendix IV for contact information for the above organizations.

Tips for Entry

1. As a college student, gain work experience by obtaining part-time work as a campus security officer.
2. Early in your career as a police officer, seek a mentor. Choose an administrator whom you respect and trust, and from whom you would like to learn.
3. You can learn more about campus security on the Internet. You might start by visiting the International Association of Campus Law Enforcement Administrators Web site at http:///www.iaclea.org.

DEAN OF STUDENTS

CAREER PROFILE

Duties: Oversee the administration of all student services; provide leadership and supervision to program directors and their staffs; recommend student personnel policies; perform other duties as required

Alternate Title(s): None

Salary Range: $39,000 to $128,000

Employment Prospects: Fair

Advancement Prospects: Fair

Prerequisites:

Education or Training—Master's or doctoral degree

Experience—Extensive administrative, management, and supervisory experience in student affairs programs

Special Skills and Personality Traits—Leadership, management, supervisory, computer, communication, mediation, interpersonal, and team-building skills; be energetic, creative, innovative, self-motivated, organized

CAREER LADDER

```
┌─────────────────────────────────────┐
│   Vice President of Student Affairs  │
└─────────────────────────────────────┘

┌─────────────────────────────────────┐
│          Dean of Students            │
└─────────────────────────────────────┘

┌─────────────────────────────────────┐
│  Assistant Dean of Students or       │
│  Program Director (such as           │
│  Director of Student Affairs)        │
└─────────────────────────────────────┘
```

Position Description

Every higher education institution has an administrative department that is responsible for the well-being of the student body and for providing a supportive learning environment. On most campuses, this department is called the *Office of Dean of Students*. As administrator of this office, the Dean of Students oversees different student services that assist students with handling campus life so that they can successfully complete their academic and personal goals. The types of student services vary from campus to campus. They include (but are not limited to):

- enrollment services—recruitment, admissions, enrollment, registration, and student records
- financial aid services
- "new student" orientation programs
- housing services
- academic and personal support services—such as academic counseling, personal counseling, career service programs, and study skills programs
- student health services
- student judicial affairs
- student activities, which includes the development of social, cultural, educational, and recreational programs and activities; supervision of student organizations, sororities, and fraternities; and direction of the student union
- intercollegiate sports programs for both men and women
- public safety department

The various student services are run by different directors who are under the leadership and direction of the Dean of Students. The Dean of Students meets with directors on a regular basis to stay up-to-date with what is happening with the different operations. The Dean of Students also advises and assists directors on numerous policy, administrative, and program matters such as student personnel policies, fiscal management, human resources management, and program development.

Deans of Students are responsible for the quality of student services. Thus, they conduct reviews of the various student services and individual programs on a regular basis to ensure they are providing satisfactory services to students, faculty, and others. Deans also make sure that the services and programs are in compliance with the missions, policies, and regulations of their institutions, as well as with any local, state, and federal laws. Deans also do a continuing assessment of each service and program to evaluate whether the need for and cost of a service or program is justified.

Other general responsibilities of Deans of Students include: administering and preparing budgets for the overall operation of student services; directing the activities of the professional and support staff within the Office of Dean of Students; and assisting in the recruitment and selection of student service directors and the office administrative staff.

As representative of student service operations, Deans of Students serve on various administrative committees and councils on campus. They recommend and assist in the development of effective student personnel policies for their campuses. On occasion, Deans of Students speak to community organizations on behalf of their institutions regarding student programs and activities. They may also represent their institutions at meetings and conferences with educational agencies and professional associations.

Deans work more than 40 hours a week. They work many evenings and weekends to attend meetings, appear at student activities and functions, participate in professional conferences, complete reports, and so on.

Salaries

Salaries for Dean of Students vary, depending on such factors as experience, education, employer, and geographical location. According to the November 2004 *Occupational Employment Statistics* survey by the U.S. Bureau of Labor Statistics, the estimated annual salary for most educational administrators in higher education ranged between $38,910 and $128,180.

Employment Prospects

Deans of Students are employed by two-year colleges, four-year colleges, and universities. Most opportunities, however, become available as administrators advance to other positions, transfer to other institutions, retire, or resign.

Advancement Prospects

Deans of Students can advance to such policy-making positions as vice presidents of student affairs, which generally require doctoral degrees. They can also become, if desired, presidents of higher education institutions. Many Deans of Students realize advancement through pay increases, with professional recognition, and by transferring to other institutions.

Education and Training

Employers generally require that Deans of Students have at least a master's degree in college student personnel, higher education administration, or related field. Many employers, however, prefer candidates with doctoral degrees.

Many Deans of Students pursue professional development through individual study, enrollment in continuing education classes and professional workshops, and participation in professional conferences.

Experience, Skills, and Personality Traits

Deans of Students have extensive administrative, management, and supervisory experience. Generally, employers look for candidates who have held positions with increasing levels of responsibility in student affairs. The qualifying number of years (about six to 10 years) varies with the different institutions.

To perform their work effectively, Deans of Students must have excellent skills in leadership, management, and supervision. They should also have good computer skills, as well as communication, mediation, interpersonal, and team-building skills. Being energetic, creative, innovative, self-motivated, and organized are some personality traits that successful Deans of Students share.

Unions and Associations

Deans of Students join professional associations to take advantage of services such as training programs, networking opportunities, professional resources, and job listings. Some of the organizations that they might join are:

- ACPA: College Student Educators International
- National Association of Student Personnel Administrators
- College and University Professional Association for Human Resources
- National Association for Women in Education
- Association of College Administration Professionals

For contact information, see Appendix IV.

Tips for Entry

1. Talk with current and former Deans of Students and find out what different career paths they traveled to arrive at the Dean of Students position.
2. Job descriptions for the Dean of Students positions differ from one campus to the next. Be sure to get a job description from the human resources department for the position for which you wish to apply.
3. On the Internet, you can visit Web pages of college and university Dean of Students offices. To get a list of Web pages to read, enter the keyword *Dean of Students office* in a search engine.

DIRECTOR OF DEVELOPMENT

CAREER PROFILE

Duties: Develop and implement fund-raising programs and activities; manage day-to-day operations; perform duties as required

Alternate Title(s): Director of Annual Giving, or other title that reflects a fund-raising program

Salary Range: $30,000 to $140,000

Employment Prospects: Good

Advancement Prospects: Fair

Prerequisites:

Education or Training—Bachelor's or master's degree

Experience—Three to five years of experience in increasingly responsible positions, preferably in higher education settings

Special Skills and Personality Traits—Organization, management, team-building, computer, grant-writing, interpersonal, communication, and social skills; be honest, caring, enthusiastic, persistent, loyal, flexible, creative

CAREER LADDER

```
┌─────────────────────────────────────┐
│  Vice President of Development or     │
│  Vice President of Advancement        │
└─────────────────────────────────────┘

┌─────────────────────────────────────┐
│     Director of Development           │
└─────────────────────────────────────┘

┌─────────────────────────────────────┐
│        Assistant Director             │
└─────────────────────────────────────┘
```

Position Description

The Director of Development oversees fund-raising programs that are used to seek donations and endowments from alumni, parents, businesses, foundations, and other sources. The money helps pay for general operations, construction projects, athletic programs, student services, and other needs that a college or university may have.

Many academic institutions have more than one Director of Development to create and implement strategic fund-raising plans. Some fund-raising officers are in charge of all fund-raising programs and activities for individual colleges (such as the college of engineering) or major student services (such as library services). Other officers are in charge of different fund-raising programs, such as:

- annual giving programs for soliciting yearly gift donations
- corporate and foundation relations programs for seeking major grants from corporations and foundations
- major and planned gifts programs for pursuing large cash gifts, real estate, securities, and property, which may be given all at once or distributed in increments over several years or upon the death of the donors

- capital campaigns for raising a specific dollar amount over a certain period of time

The different Directors of Development perform general duties that are the same regardless of their roles. They evaluate the potential amount of money that can be raised with a fund-raising activity. They identify potential donors, as well as meet with donors in either a business or social setting.

In addition, Directors of Development coordinate and direct all marketing and public relations activities for their fund-raising programs or activities. For example, they might develop seminars and information packets for potential donors, or produce newsletters to keep donors up-to-date with campus activities. Directors of Development are also responsible for managing the day-to-day activities of the development offices. They develop, implement, and evaluate administrative operating plans. They administer and prepare program budgets. In addition, they represent their institutions at community meetings and professional conferences.

Another major responsibility is overseeing the office personnel, which includes professional and support staff, as well as volunteers. Directors provide leadership and supervision as they direct the activities of their staff members. They also plan and conduct in-service training for staff members and volunteers. In addition, directors assist in the recruitment and selection of their staffs. They also recruit on an ongoing basis for volunteer leaders, especially before major fund-raising campaigns.

Directors of Development report to an executive administrator (such as the vice president of institutional advancement). They typically work more than 40 hours a week. They often work evenings and weekends, meeting with donors, attending fund-raising events, conducting training workshops, or completing other tasks.

Salaries

Salaries for Directors of Development vary, depending on such factors as their experience, education, job duties, and employer. According to the Career Prospects in Virginia Web site (http://www.ccps.virginia.edu/career_prospects), development professionals with a few years of experience can earn between $30,000 and $50,000 while senior development executives can earn between $75,000 to $140,000.

Employment Prospects

In addition to being employed by colleges and universities, Directors of Development are employed by hospitals, schools, churches, and nonprofit organizations.

Openings generally become available when directors advance to higher positions, transfer to other jobs, or retire. Employers may create additional positions, if funding is available.

Advancement Prospects

With advanced education and experience, Directors of Development can become executive vice presidents of development in higher education institutions. Many Directors of Development realize advancement through pay increases, professional recognition, and transfers to other institutions.

Directors of Development can also continue their careers in other settings, such as schools, hospitals, museums, and nonprofit organizations.

Education and Training

Depending on the institution, applicants must have either a bachelor's or a master's degree, in any field. Employers may waive the education requirement if a candidate has excellent qualifying experience.

Many Directors of Development pursue professional development through individual study, enrollment in continuing education classes and professional workshops, and participation in professional conferences.

Experience, Skills, and Personality Traits

Applicants generally need between three to five years of fund-raising experience in positions of increasing responsibility.

To handle their work effectively Directors of Development need strong organization, management, and team-building skills. They also need good computer and grant-writing skills. In addition, they should have outstanding interpersonal, communication, and social skills as they must be able to build positive relationships with alumni, donors, faculty, administrators, and others. Some personality traits that successful Directors of Development share are: being honest, caring, enthusiastic, persistent, loyal, flexible, and creative.

Unions and Associations

Many Directors of Development join professional associations to take advantage of networking opportunities, education programs, and other professional resources and services. They join societies, such as the Association of Fundraising Professionals, that serve development officers, as well as organizations that serve higher education administrators, such as the Association of College Administration Professionals. See Appendix IV for contact information for these organizations.

Tips for Entry

1. To gain experience, participate in fund-raising activities for your school or for nonprofit organizations in your community.
2. As a college student, volunteer or obtain part-time work in your college development department.
3. To enhance your employability, obtain professional certification, such as the Certified Fund Raising Executive (CFRE) granted by the Association of Fundraising Professionals.
4. Learn more about the fund-raising field on the Internet. You might start by visiting these Web sites: Council for Advancement and Support of Education, http://www.case.org, and Association of Fundraising Professionals, http://www.afpnet.org.

ACADEMIC DEAN

CAREER PROFILE

Duties: Provide academic and administrative leadership to an academic division or college in a higher education institution; oversee daily operations and personnel; perform duties as required

Alternate Title(s): A title that reflects the school or college being administered, such as Dean of College of Liberal Arts or Dean, College of Architecture

Salary Range: $39,000 to $128,000

Employment Prospects: Fair

Advancement Prospects: Fair

Prerequisites:

Education or Training—Doctoral degree

Experience—Be a full professor; have administrative experience as a department chair or higher

Special Skills and Personality Traits—Leadership, administrative, management, fund-raising, communication, interpersonal, and computer skills; be organized, analytical, honest, fair, innovative, energetic, and flexible

CAREER LADDER

```
┌─────────────────────────────┐
│   Provost or Vice President of │
│      Academic Affairs          │
└─────────────────────────────┘

┌─────────────────────────────┐
│      Dean (Academic)          │
└─────────────────────────────┘

┌─────────────────────────────┐
│ Department Chair or Assistant Dean │
└─────────────────────────────┘
```

Position Description

Academic Deans provide leadership and supervision to academic units, which are composed of departments and schools. In community colleges, the academic units are called *divisions*. In four-year colleges and universities, the academic units are called *colleges*. For example, a university might be comprised of four colleges, the college of letters and science, college of education and human service, college of nursing, and college of business administration. An Academic Dean is usually known by the name of the college that he or she leads—such as *Dean of College of Education and Human Service.*

The responsibilities and duties of deans vary from one institution to the next. In general, deans are responsible for overseeing all personnel, programs, and services related to their academic units. They direct and coordinate activities of department chairs in matters such as curriculum and personnel. Deans review the different academic programs within their units. On occasion, they recommend additional courses to be taught in a department.

Academic Deans also perform evaluations of faculty members, assessing their performances and achievements.

Deans make recommendations to the administration about faculty appointments, promotions, tenure, and sabbatical leaves. Furthermore, deans are responsible for providing professional development for the faculty.

Deans also lead and encourage fund-raising efforts for their academic units. For example, they inspire (and assist) faculty members to write proposals for research grants. Deans also participate in fund-raising activities, which may include meeting with prospective donors in business or social settings.

Academic Deans perform various administrative duties that include (but are not limited to):

- supervising support staff in their office
- managing and developing annual budgets
- coordinating the scheduling of courses
- administering collective bargaining agreements
- recruiting and selecting faculty members and administrative staff
- coordinating student recruitment activities
- enforcing institutional policies and regulations

Additionally, Academic Deans serve on various faculty, student, and administrative committees. Most Academic Deans are part of a provost's council that develops and recommends academic polices for the institution. Furthermore, as representatives of their institutions, deans participate in meetings with community organizations, educational agencies, and professional associations.

Academic Deans generally work long days. They attend frequent meetings and social engagements connected to their academic units and institutions in the evenings and on weekends.

Salaries
Salaries for Academic Deans vary, depending on such factors as their experience, education, employer, and geographical location. According to the November 2004 *Occupational Employment Statistics* survey by the U.S. Bureau of Labor Statistics, the estimated annual salary for most educational administrators in higher education ranged between $38,910 and $128,180.

Employment Prospects
Most opportunities, become available as administrators retire, resign or advance to other positions. Competition is keen.

Advancement Prospects
Academic Deans are part of a traditional career ladder, in which deans can advance to assistant provost, provost, and president. Many deans realize advancement through increases in salary and with professional recognition. Some deans choose to return to teaching and researching after serving one or more terms in this position.

Other career options for deans include becoming consultants, administrators, and professionals with government agencies, private industry, professional associations, and nonprofit institutions.

Education and Training
Academic Deans usually have doctoral degrees in their disciplines. For example, the dean who oversees his or her university's college of business administration might have a doctoral degree in economics.

Deans typically learn their duties and tasks on the job. Many deans participate in professional development workshops and classes.

Experience, Skills, and Personality Traits
Candidates must hold the academic rank of full professor and have academic tenure, or have the appropriate academic credentials to be granted tenure. Academic credentials include classroom teaching experience, recognized scholarly and professional accomplishments, along with successful administrative experience. Furthermore, candidates should have considerable administrative experience at the level of department chair or higher. Employers typically prefer candidates with a successful record of working with a diversified population, encouraging faculty development and scholarship, and performing successful fundraising.

To do their work effectively, Academic Deans must have strong leadership, administrative, management, and fundraising skills along with communication, and interpersonal skills. In addition, they should have computer skills. Successful Academic Deans share several personality traits, such as being organized, analytical, honest, fair, innovative, energetic, and flexible. They are committed to providing the best academic opportunities for all students.

Unions and Associations
Academic Deans join professional associations to take advantage of professional services such as education programs, professional publications, and networking opportunities. Some organizations that deans belong to are:

- American Association of University Administrators
- Association of College Administration Professionals
- National Association for Women in Education
- American Conference of Academic Deans
- National Association of Scholars

For contact information, see Appendix IV.

Tips for Entry
1. As you begin your teaching career in higher education, volunteer to serve on administrative committees in your department, academic unit, and institution.
2. Use your network to help you learn about job opportunities, as well as about key people, issues, the political climate, and other information regarding an institution where you may be interested in applying for a position.
3. Learn more about the Academic Dean profession on the Internet. You might start by visiting the American Conference of Academic Deans Web site at http://www.acad-edu.org. To find other relevant Web sites, enter the keyword *academic dean* in a search engine.

PROVOST

CAREER PROFILE

Duties: Provide overall academic leadership for an institution; administer all academic programs; perform duties as required

Alternate Title(s): Executive Vice President and Provost

Salary Range: $94,000 to $199,000

Employment Prospects: Fair

Advancement Prospects: Fair

Prerequisites:

Education or Training—A doctoral degree

Experience—Extensive instructional and administrative experience; be a full professor

Special Skills and Personality Traits—Leadership, administrative, supervisory, communication, interpersonal, team-building, and computer skills; be honest, fair, innovative, energetic, patient, flexible, decisive, organized

CAREER LADDER

```
┌─────────────────────────────┐
│         President           │
└─────────────────────────────┘

┌─────────────────────────────┐
│          Provost            │
└─────────────────────────────┘

┌─────────────────────────────┐
│  Dean, Assistant Provost, or│
│ Vice President of Academic  │
│           Affairs           │
└─────────────────────────────┘
```

Position Description

Provosts are the chief academic officers at two-year colleges, four-year colleges, and universities. Their role is to manage the overall academic programs and to advise presidents on academic matters. Provosts also assist presidents in making both academic and administrative policies, which are based on the missions and goals established by the governing board of trustees. When presidents must be absent from their duties, Provosts usually serve as acting chief executive officers.

Provosts are responsible for the overall design and implementation of curriculum and academic standards for the various programs that are offered at their institutions. Depending on their missions, institutions may offer various academic degree, professional certificate, continuing education, vocational, nondegree, and other types of programs.

Provosts are also responsible for building and supporting positive environments that encourage superior teaching and scholarship. They are generally expected to raise and expand their institutions' academic standing statewide, regionally, nationally, and internationally. Thus, they continually look for ways to improve existing academic programs and to introduce new academic offerings that would benefit the student body. Many Provosts also develop educational partnerships with local educational institutions, community organizations, businesses, and industries. For example, a community college Provost and local school superintendents might develop a program that allows qualifying high school seniors to enroll in one or more courses at the community college for their elective classes.

Another major responsibility is providing support and guidance to academic deans. Provosts coordinate and direct the activities of the various academic deans. They also advise deans about instructional programs, academic policies, and administrative matters such as personnel and fiscal management. In addition, Provosts provide academic leadership and advocacy to the faculty.

Provosts are responsible for the day-to-day administration of the academic operations at their institutions. This includes all academic units (departments, divisions, schools, and colleges), libraries, museums, and other cultural and educational units. Their administrative duties include, but are not limited to:

- overseeing central administration planning and fiscal management
- developing annual academic budgets
- directing the process of faculty appointments, evaluation, and professional development

- ensuring that academic programs are in compliance with institutional policies and regulations, as well as with any government laws and guidelines
- serving as liaison officers with accreditation agencies which evaluate academic programs
- performing fund-raising duties

In some institutions, Provosts are in charge of overseeing the administration of student support and student affairs services. This includes enrollment services, student organizations, health services, instructional resources, and other services.

Provosts also maintain positive relationships with the local communities. Provosts network with community leaders, business leaders, social service agencies, community groups, and so on. In addition, they participate in community events, as well as serve on boards, task forces, and committees of local agencies and organizations.

Provosts put in long hours in order to fulfill their duties and responsibilities. They often spend evenings and weekends attending meetings, participating in conferences, meeting with donors, making presentations at conferences, and appearing at social or political functions.

Salaries

Salaries for Provosts vary, depending on such factors as their experience, size and type of institution, and geographical location. According to a 2004–05 salary survey by the College and University Professional Association for Human Resources, the median annual salary for chief academic officers ranged from $93,725 to $199,000.

Provosts usually receive additional compensation in the form of moving allowances, expense accounts, payment for professional dues, and other benefits.

Employment Prospects

Most job opportunities become available when Provosts retire, resign, or transfer to other institutions. Those willing to relocate to another city or region may have better chances of obtaining positions.

Advancement Prospects

Provosts can become presidents of single institutions or college systems. Those who have chosen the Provost position as their highest career goal realize advancement through pay increases, with professional recognition, and by transfers to other institutions with more complex responsibilities and challenges.

Provosts can pursue other career paths such as becoming consultants and chief executive officers with government agencies, private industry, educational organizations, and professional associations.

Education and Training

Most higher education institutions require that Provosts hold doctoral degrees.

Provosts generally pursue professional development through individual study, enrollment in continuing education classes and professional workshops, and participation in professional conferences.

Experience, Skills, and Personality Traits

Employers choose candidates who have a distinguished record of teaching, research, and scholarship as well as senior-level administrative experience. Candidates at the four-year college and university level should be full professors or have the qualifications to be appointed as such.

To perform their work well, Provosts must have outstanding leadership, administrative, and supervisory skills. They should also have superior communication, interpersonal, and team-building skills. In addition, they should be proficient with computers. Being honest, fair, innovative, energetic, patient, flexible, decisive, and organized are some of the personality traits that successful Provosts share.

Unions and Associations

Many Provosts belong to professional associations to take advantage of professional services and resources such as education programs and networking opportunities. Some organizations that they might join are the American Association of University Administrators, the Association of College Administration Professionals, the American Conference of Academic Deans, and the National Association for Women in Education. For contact information, see Appendix IV.

Tips for Entry

1. Read biographies about different Provosts, as well as network with current and past Provosts. Learn what different career paths they traveled to reach the position of Provost.
2. Check professional associations for job listings. Many of them post vacancy announcements on their Web sites.
3. You can learn about different Provost offices on the Internet. To find relevant Web pages, enter the keywords *provost office* or *office of the provost* in a search engine.

PRESIDENT

CAREER PROFILE

Duties: Provide educational leadership; oversee all academic, administrative, and other operations; perform duties as required

Alternate Title(s): Chief Executive Officer (CEO), Chancellor

Salary Range: $130,000 to $272,000

Employment Prospects: Fair

Advancement Prospects: Fair

Prerequisites:

Education or Training—Doctoral degree

Experience—Extensive administrative experiences in progressively responsible executive-level positions

Special Skills and Personality Traits—Administrative, leadership, team-building, communication, interpersonal, and social skills; be dedicated, honest, ethical, analytical, approachable, flexible, creative, and resourceful

CAREER LADDER

```
┌─────────────────────────────────┐
│    Chancellor, college system    │
└─────────────────────────────────┘

┌─────────────────────────────────┐
│            President             │
└─────────────────────────────────┘

┌─────────────────────────────────┐
│             Provost              │
└─────────────────────────────────┘
```

Position Description

The chief executive officer of a higher education institution is its President, who is strongly committed to providing and promoting academic excellence. He or she is given the authority to develop and implement policies and programs that would best fulfill the missions and goals established by the governing board of trustees.

Presidents are responsible for the overall operations of two-year colleges, four-year colleges and universities. They oversee several areas of operations that include (but are not limited to):

- academic programs (all degree and nondegree programs)
- student services—such as admissions, housing services, student health services, and extracurricular programs
- administrative services—such as human resources, financial services, legal relations, and information systems
- external affairs—such as development (or fund-raising), alumni relations, and community relations

Presidents have many different responsibilities that vary from one institution to the next. The priority of responsibilities also varies, depending on the needs of their campuses.

One general responsibility of all Presidents is developing plans to meet the needs of their institutions. This includes long-range and short-term plans for instruction, student enrollment, human resources, new facilities, and so on. They also ensure that all programs and services are in compliance with institutional policies and standards, governmental laws and regulations, and requirements of accreditation agencies.

Another general responsibility is overseeing the development and management of institutional budgets, which typically involve millions of dollars. The budgets cover salaries, operation costs, academic programs, student services, athletic programs, and so forth. In addition, Presidents are responsible for broadening their institution's financial base. This includes overseeing development, or fund-raising, activities such as capital campaigns, annual fund-raising drives, major gifts from prospective donors, and grants from corporations and philanthropic foundations.

Their job also involves promoting positive community relations. Presidents network with community leaders, business leaders, social service agencies, community groups, and others. They participate on boards, task forces, and committees for community organizations, educational agencies, and professional associations. In addition, they represent their institutions at educational conferences, professional meetings, community events, and other functions.

Executive-level administrators—provosts, vice presidents, deans, program directors, and specialists—assist Presidents with their various responsibilities. Some administrators make up a President's executive council to advise the President as well as offer policy and program recommendations. Presidents also have their own professional and support staffs.

In private colleges and universities, most Presidents report directly to boards of trustees (or boards of directors), while in public institutions, Presidents report to chancellors and/or boards of trustees.

Presidents work very long hours each day. They often work evenings and weekends completing their various tasks, participating in meetings, attending conferences, meeting with donors, and appearing at community functions.

Salaries

Salaries for Presidents vary, depending on such factors as their experience, size and type of institution, and geographical location. According to a 2004–05 salary survey by the College and University Professional Association for Human Resources, the median salary for chief executive officers of college systems ranged from $130,000 to $270,000, and for Presidents of single institutions, from $135,375 to $272,251.

Presidents also receive additional compensation in other forms, such as expense accounts and a housing allowance.

Employment Prospects

Most job opportunities become available when Presidents retire, resign, or transfer to other institutions. Those willing to relocate to other cities and regions may have better chances of obtaining positions.

Advancement Prospects

Presidents can become chancellors who administer college systems. Most Presidents realize advancement through pay increases, with professional recognition, and by transfers to other institutions with more complex responsibilities and challenges.

Other career paths available for Presidents include becoming consultants and chief executive officers with government agencies, educational organizations, professional associations, and private industry.

Education and Training

Employers generally prefer to hire applicants who possess a doctorate. If they have qualifying experience, applicants with a master's degree may qualify for positions in two-year colleges.

Many Presidents pursue professional development through individual study, enrollment in continuing education classes and professional workshops, and with participation in professional conferences.

Experience, Skills, and Personality Traits

Employers seek applicants who have a work history of extensive administrative, management, and academic experiences, as well as proven educational leadership and working relationships with boards of trustees.

To do their work effectively, Presidents must have superior administrative leadership skills. Team-building, communication, interpersonal, and social skills are also important as they must be able to relate well with boards, staff, administrators, faculty, students, alumni, local communities, educational agencies, and other constituents. Being dedicated, honest, ethical, analytical, approachable, flexible, creative, and resourceful are some personality traits that successful college and university Presidents share.

Unions and Associations

Presidents join various professional associations to take advantage of professional services and resources such as networking opportunities and education programs. Some national societies that they might join are the American Association of University Administrators, the Association of College Administration Professionals, and the National Association of Scholars. For contact information, see Appendix IV.

Tips for Entry

1. Learn what career paths various Presidents have traveled to reach their positions. You might read biographies about college and university Presidents, as well as network with current and past Presidents.
2. Presidents have risen through the academic ranks as well as within the ranks of nonacademic administrators.
3. You can learn more about college and university Presidents and their offices on the Internet. To get a list of relevant Web sites to read, enter either of these keywords in a search engine: *college president* or *university president*.

EDUCATIONAL ASSISTANTS

CHILD CARE AIDE

CAREER PROFILE

Duties: Assist in the care, supervision, and education of infants, toddlers, and preschoolers; perform duties required

Alternate Title(s): Child Care Worker, Teaching Assistant, Nursery School Aide

Salary Range: $12,000 to $30,000

Employment Prospects: Excellent

Advancement Prospects: Good

Prerequisites:

Education or Training—High school diploma; classroom or on-the-job training

Experience—Some child care experience is preferred

Special Skills and Personality Traits—Reading, writing, math, communication, interpersonal teamwork, and self-management skills; be mature, patient, open-minded, enthusiastic, and energetic

Special Requirements—Childhood Development Associate certificate preferred

CAREER LADDER

```
┌─────────────────────────────────┐
│     Early Childhood Teacher      │
└─────────────────────────────────┘

┌─────────────────────────────────┐
│         Child Care Aide          │
└─────────────────────────────────┘

┌─────────────────────────────────┐
│            Trainee               │
└─────────────────────────────────┘
```

Position Description

Child Care Aides assist in the care and education of infants, toddlers, and preschoolers in child care facilities. Today, more and more parents must leave their babies and preschool children with child care providers so that they may go to work or school. The child care providers not only are entrusted with caring and protecting children but also with developing and stimulating their social, mental, emotional, and physical growth. Many of these providers are child care centers run by individuals, franchises, churches, community agencies, and public schools. Some child care centers are run on-site by companies and government agencies for their employees, clients, or customers. Child care centers may have programs for infants, toddlers, and preschoolers as well as after-school child care programs for children up to 12 years old.

Under the supervision of child care teachers, Child Care Aides perform a variety of tasks. With infants, Child Care Aides feed them, change their diapers, bathe them, and dress them. Showing them love and warmth, Child Care Aides hold the babies regularly through the day. They play with the babies, sing songs, and talk to them to encourage laughter and smiles, as well as to help in their development and growth.

With toddlers and preschoolers, Child Care Aides participate in their games and activities. They read books to the children; listen to their imaginary stories; teach them songs; show them how to draw shapes; play make-believe games with them; play catch and other outside games with them; and help them learn to count and say their ABCs. Furthermore, Child Care Aides help to build children's self-confidence and encourage them to discover, explore, create, and use their imagination.

Child Care Aides are also responsible for supervising children outdoors to make sure that they are playing safely and behaving appropriately. Under teachers' directions, aides help children learn good habits and social skills—for example, washing hands, waiting their turn, getting along with others, and saying "please" and "thank-you."

In addition, Child Care Aides help prepare and serve snacks and meals to children. They help keep classrooms neat and tidy. They may wash dishes, wash toys, change bed or crib sheets, or clean bathrooms.

Child Care Aides are constantly on the move—standing, bending, walking, stooping, and lifting—throughout the day. Each day is different from the other, yet Child Care

Aides are ready to face any and all joyous, tearful, or chaotic situations.

Child Care Aides work full time or part time. Some work early morning and late evening hours to accommodate the work schedules of the child care center's clients.

Salaries
Salaries for Child Care Aides vary, depending on such factors as their experience, education, employer, and geographical location. The U.S. Bureau of Labor Statistics (BLS) reports in its November 2004 *Occupational Employment Statistics* (OES) survey that the estimated annual salary for most child care workers ranged between $12,330 and $26,100 and for most teacher assistants, between $13,150 and $29,850. The estimated annual mean wage for teacher assistants in child day care services was $17,790.

Employment Prospects
According to the BLS's November 2004 OES survey, about 532,400 child care workers were employed in the United States.

Job are readily available for qualified Child Care Aides due to the high turnover rate. The BLS predicts that employment of child care workers should increase by 10 to 20 percent through 2012. In addition, opportunities become available as employees transfer to other occupations or leave the workforce for various reasons.

Advancement Prospects
For many individuals, becoming a Child Care Aide is the first stepping-stone to a career in early childhood care and education. With continuing education and experience, Child Care Aides can become preschool, kindergarten, or elementary school teachers, as well as early childhood program administrators. Another career option for Child Care Aides is to own child care businesses.

Education and Training
Child Care Aides need a high school or general equivalency diploma. Many employers require that they also complete a minimum of early childhood education (ECE) units, which cover topics in child growth and development.

Generally, Child Care Aides receive on-the-job training.

Special Requirements
Most employers prefer that Child Care Aides have a Child Development Associate (CDA) certificate, a nationally recognized professional credential for either a center-based, family child care, or home visitor setting. The CDA is a vol-

untary certification, which may be obtained through training programs sponsored by colleges, professional associations, or community agencies.

Many Child Care Aides obtain certification in first aid and cardiopulmonary resuscitation (CPR) skills.

Experience, Skills, and Personality Traits
No previous work experience is necessary; but applicants should have some experience taking care of infants, toddlers, and preschool children.

Child Care Aides must have adequate reading, writing, and math skills. Having strong communication, interpersonal, and teamwork skills is also essential. In addition, they need excellent self-management skills, such as the ability to follow instructions, get to work on time, and handle stressful situations. Being mature, patient, open-minded, enthusiastic, and energetic are some personality traits that successful aides share.

Unions and Associations
Local, state, and national early childhood organizations, such as the National Association for the Education of Young Children, provide many professional services and resources for Child Care Aides. These include networking opportunities, training workshops, education programs, career counseling, and job listings. See Appendix IV for contact information for the above organization.

Tips for Entry
1. As a student, you can find out if early childhood education is the field for you by volunteering at a nearby child care center or preschool. Call or visit the program and ask to speak to the director.
2. Talk with friends and relatives who have preschool children in early childhood programs. They may be able to tell you of job openings or persons to contact.
3. Some states, in collaboration with the U.S. Department of Labor, offer an apprenticeship program for child care workers. Contact your state employment office to find out if a program is available in your area.
4. In most states, the minimum age for being a Child Care Aide is 18 years old. If you're younger than 18, the requirement may be waived if you have a high school diploma or are enrolled in an occupational training program.
5. You can learn more about early childhood education on the Internet. To find pertinent Web sites, enter either of these keywords in a search engine: *early childhood education* or *early childhood career.*

TEACHER AIDE (K–12)

CAREER PROFILE

Duties: Provide teachers with instructional and clerical support; perform duties as required

Alternate Title(s): Paraeducator, Instructional Assistant, Teacher Assistant, Paraprofessional, Bilingual Assistant, Special Education Paraeducator

Salary Range: $13,000 to $30,000

Employment Prospects: Excellent

Advancement Prospects: Poor prospects without additional education

Prerequisites:

Education or Training—A high school or general equivalency diploma; on-the-job training

Experience—One or more years of working with children

Special Skills and Personality Traits—Communication, reading, writing, math, teamwork, interpersonal, and self-management skills; be patient, fair, flexible, creative, and trustworthy

Special Requirements—Some states or schools require a license, certification, or permit

CAREER LADDER

```
+---------------------+
|      Teacher        |
+---------------------+

+---------------------+
|    Teacher Aide     |
+---------------------+

+---------------------+
|      Trainee        |
+---------------------+
```

Position Description

Teacher Aides work in public and private schools, providing teachers with much needed instructional and clerical support. Responsibilities and tasks for Teacher Aides vary and differ from school to school, and also vary among Teacher Aides within a school. Some Teacher Aides work extensively with students with limited English proficiency while others work exclusively with special education students (children with disabilities). Other Teacher Aides perform only noninstructional tasks such as supervising children during recess.

In general, instructional Teacher Aides assist teachers with classroom instruction under the teachers' supervision and direction. Teacher Aides might assist teachers with class demonstrations, such as science experiments, or operate audiovisual equipment, such as film projectors and cassette players, for teachers. Teacher Aides might circulate around the classroom to check students' work to make sure they understand the day's lesson and to help students when needed. For limited-English-proficient students, bilingual Teacher Aides may explain or clarify instructions and lessons in students' native languages.

Teachers sometimes have their aides tutor students individually or in small groups by reviewing past lessons or providing extra practice for math, reading, or other skills. Teacher Aides may also be directed to coordinate discussion groups with the task of encouraging all students to participate. In addition, Teacher Aides help monitor student behavior as well as maintain class order and discipline. Teacher Aides give teachers feedback on students with whom they have worked, either orally or in notes.

Many Teacher Aides help teachers with lesson preparations. For example, teachers might have aides type activity sheets, photocopy student records, or collate tests. Teacher Aides may be asked to obtain textbooks, audiovisual equipment, and other materials from the appropriate school offices. Many teachers also ask their assistants to help create and put up classroom decorations, bulletin boards, and learning centers.

Many Teacher Aides are responsible for maintaining student files and performing other clerical duties. For example, many take care of daily attendance tasks, such as taking roll, collecting absence and tardy notes, and recording attendance.

They also collect permission slips for student activities (such as field trips), as well as collect fees for lunch programs and other school programs and activities. Many Teacher Aides score tests, assignments, and homework in accordance with the teachers' answer keys. Some Teacher Aides record assignment grades and test scores in the teacher's grade book or computer files. Some Teacher Aides are also responsible for keeping inventory of classroom supplies and informing teachers when new supplies are needed.

Teacher Aides perform many other duties as requested, such as: supervising students during recesses and lunch breaks, performing housekeeping tasks to maintain a safe and clean classroom, arranging field trips, and contacting parents about participating in class activities.

Teacher Aides work part time or full time during the school year. Most Teacher Aides work between three and eight hours each school day.

Salaries

Salaries for Teacher Aides vary, depending on such factors as their experience, education, employer, and geographical location. According to the November 2004 *Occupational Employment Statistics* (OES) survey, by the U.S. Bureau of Labor Statistics (BLS), the estimated annual salary for most teacher assistants ranged between $13,150 and $29,850. The estimated annual mean wage for those working in elementary and secondary schools was $20,710.

Employment Prospects

In addition to public and private elementary, middle, and high schools, Teacher Aides are employed by preschools, child care facilities, and community colleges. The BLS reports in its November 2004 OES survey that an estimated 997,460 teacher assistants worked in elementary and secondary schools.

The BLS expects employment for this occupation to increase by 21 to 35 percent through 2012. In addition to new positions, Teacher Aides are needed to replace those who retire, transfer to other occupations, or return to school to become teachers. Opportunities typically are better in areas that are experiencing rapid expansion of population and school enrollments. However, the number of jobs available in a school is tied to its particular needs as well as the limitations of its budget.

Teacher Aides are especially in demand to help special education students as well as students with limited English proficiency. Public schools may need additional Teacher Aides to help students prepare for standardized testing that is required by the federal No Child Left Behind (NCLB) Act.

Advancement Prospects

Opportunities for Teacher Aides are generally limited to pay raises and receiving more complex responsibilities. For many educators, the Teacher Aide position had been the first stepping-stone in their careers.

During teacher shortages, many schools encourage Teacher Aides to pursue their bachelor's degrees and teaching credentials. Many public schools offer tuition reimbursement plans and other incentives in return for a teaching commitment for a certain length of time.

Education and Training

Educational requirements vary from school to school. Minimally, applicants must possess a high school or general equivalency diploma. An increasing number of employers prefer applicants who have completed one or more years of college.

To work in public schools that receive Title I funds from the federal government, applicants must fulfill one of the following requirements:

- complete two years of college
- possess at least an associate degree
- pass a formal local or state assessment

Teacher Aides typically learn their duties on the job. More schools are providing Teacher Aides with preservice training in addition to their on-the-job training. Some schools provide Teacher Aides with in-service training throughout the school year to enhance and improve their skills.

Special Requirements

State licensure or certification for Teacher Aides in public schools vary from state to state. For example, as of January 2005, Teacher Aides in Texas and New York were required to possess state certification, while in Kansas only special education Teacher Aides were required to obtain licensure. For specific information for the state where you wish to work, contact the state board of education. See Appendix III for a list of state boards.

Private schools may have their own licensure or certification for Teacher Aides.

Experience, Skills, and Personality Traits

Many employers require applicants to have one or more years of experience working with children. In addition, they should have knowledge of the subject matter in which they would be helping students, be familiar with how schools are organized and run, as well as have an understanding of teaching methods and materials. In addition, they have—or show they are able to learn—various skills, such as simple recordkeeping, operating audiovisual equipment, and using office equipment.

Teacher Aides must have adequate communication, reading, writing, and math skills, as well as teamwork and interpersonal skills. They should also have good self-management skills—getting to work on time, taking initiative, understanding and following directions, and so on. For those working with bilingual or ESL students, Teacher Aides must be proficient in a second language such as Spanish, Russian, Vietnamese, or Korean. (Most schools require that bilingual aides pass an oral and written language competency test.)

Some personality traits that successful Teacher Aides share include being patient, fair, flexible, creative, and trustworthy. Additionally, they are able to motivate and inspire children to learn.

Unions and Associations

Many Teacher Aides in public schools belong to a union, such as the American Federation of Teachers, which negotiates wages and working conditions with school administrations.

Teacher Aides are eligible to join local, state, and national educator associations in the areas of their interests, such as the Council for Exceptional Children, the National Association for the Education of Young Children, or the National Association for Bilingual Education. These organizations provide professional services and resources such as education programs, networking opportunities, and job listings.

See Appendix IV for contact information for the above organizations.

Tips for Entry

1. You can start obtaining work experience while in the middle grades and high school. For example, you might volunteer as a student aide, tutor, or peer counselor with the lower grades. Or, you might volunteer or work part time for a library, recreational center, Sunday school, scout troop, or other youth group.

2. Enhance your employability by completing an associate's degree program that prepares you to become a Teacher Aide.

3. Contact public and private schools directly to learn about job openings and requirements.

4. Learn how to use computers as more and more teachers are incorporating computers with their instruction.

5. You can learn more about education on the Internet. One place to start is at *Education World,* an on-line resource for educators. Its URL is http://www.education-world.com. To learn more about specific educational areas, such as special education, bilingual education, or early childhood education, use those terms as keywords in a search engine.

CAREER GUIDANCE TECHNICIAN

CAREER PROFILE

Duties: Collect, organize, and distribute resources about careers and education; help students, teachers, counselors, and other school staff use the available resources; provide clerical support; perform duties as required

Alternate Title(s): Career Guidance Specialist

Salary Range: $15,000 to $36,000

Employment Prospects: Poor

Advancement Prospects: Poor, without further education

Prerequisites:

Education or Training—A high school or general equivalency diploma

Experience—Two years of office clerk experience, or equivalent education and experience

Special Skills and Personality Traits—Reading, research, problem-solving, communication, listening, interpersonal, and teamwork skills; be enthusiastic, patient, tactful, courteous, flexible, organized, resourceful

CAREER LADDER

> **Lead Career Guidance Technician**

> **Career Guidance Technician**

> **Trainee**

Position Description

Many public and private middle-level schools and high schools have career centers where students can learn about possible options for themselves after high school graduation. These centers are usually part of school counseling departments and are run by Career Guidance Technicians under the direction of the school counselors.

Career centers provide a variety of resources for students, teachers, and other school staff that may include:

- encyclopedias, dictionaries, handbooks, books, videos, and other reference materials about occupations, careers, labor market information, and job search skills
- catalogs, directories, pamphlets, brochures, and applications for two-year colleges, four-year colleges, universities, technical schools, and vocational programs
- announcements, flyers, brochures, and pamphlets about scholarships, financial aid, college admission tests, apprenticeships, and military information
- computer programs on careers and colleges
- access to relevant Web sites on the Internet

Career Guidance Technicians are responsible for displaying information (catalogs, brochures) about scholarships, schools, tests, etc. as they are received in the mail. Technicians also make sure resources are current and remove old items. Many technicians contact schools, test services, community organizations, employment centers, and other sources to request current information. In addition, many technicians browse through catalogs and advertisements and suggest to counselors any books, software, and other materials that may be useful to the career center.

Most Career Guidance Technicians are responsible for training students, school staff, and others on using the career center. They may give tours of the center. They may also teach individuals how to run the different computer programs and how to access the Internet to obtain career information.

Career Guidance Technicians also help students with specific questions about occupations, colleges, vocational schools, and so on. They might suggest to students which resources (books, computer programs, Internet, and so on) to research; they might help students with the research; they might do the research themselves.

Career Guidance Technicians are responsible for providing clerical support to the career center. They answer phones—taking messages, routing calls, and responding to informational requests about services and programs—as well as receive and route mail. They type and proofread letters, memos, reports, and related materials; they may also compose routine correspondence. Some Career Guidance Technicians also maintain student files.

Career Guidance Technicians' other duties may include scheduling appointments for students, counselors, and outside visitors and making arrangements for guest speakers and field trips. Career Guidance Technicians also keep inventory of all items in the career center, and make sure all equipment is maintained and in working order. In addition, they keep the center clean, neat, and tidy.

Career Guidance Technicians work part time or full time, during the school year.

Salaries

Salaries for Career Guidance Technicians vary, depending on such factors as their experience, education, job duties, and geographical location. According to the November 2004 *Occupational Employment Statistics* survey, by the U.S. Bureau of Labor Statistics, the estimated annual salary for most general office clerks—which includes Career Guidance Technicians—ranged between $14,560 and $36,260. The estimated annual mean wage for those working in elementary and secondary schools was $24,940.

Employment Prospects

Career Guidance Technicians are employed by private and public schools, colleges, and universities.

Opportunities generally become available as Career Guidance Technicians transfer to other occupations, retire, or leave the workforce for other reasons. More and more schools are creating career centers to meet the growing interest for helping middle school, junior high, and high school students evaluate career goals. However, the creation of new positions depends on the availability of funding.

Advancement Prospects

Most Career Guidance Technicians realize advancement by receiving pay increases and higher-level responsibilities, such as supervisory duties. Experienced Career Guidance Technicians can obtain positions in community college, college, university, or private career guidance centers, where salaries are higher and responsibilities more complex. Another career option is to pursue further education and obtain a master's degree in counseling and become voca-

tional or school counselors in schools, colleges, and private practice.

Education and Training

Applicants need at least a high school or general equivalency diploma. Most employers prefer applicants with an associate's degree or some college training. Career Guidance Technicians receive on-the-job training.

Experience, Skills, and Personality Traits

Many employers require that applicants have two years of office work experience or equivalent education and experience. They should also have a general understanding of how a career center works.

To complete their duties effectively, Career Guidance Technicians must have competent reading and research skills, as well as adequate problem-solving, communication, listening, interpersonal, and teamwork skills.

Successful Career Guidance Technicians share several personality traits such as being enthusiastic, patient, tactful, courteous, flexible, organized, and resourceful.

Unions and Associations

Many Career Guidance Technicians in public schools belong to a union, such as the American Federation of Teachers, which negotiates wages and working conditions with school administrations. In addition, Career Guidance Technicians might join local, state, and national organizations, such as the National Career Development Association. By joining professional association, they can take advantage of education programs, networking opportunities, and other professional resources and services.

See Appendix IV for contact information for the above organizations.

Tips for Entry

1. In middle school or high school, visit your career center or one at a local community college. Talk with the Career Guidance Technician and learn more about his or her job. If possible, volunteer to work in the career center to obtain hands-on experience.
2. Contact schools directly to learn about job openings and requirements.
3. On the Internet, you can learn more about career guidance. To find relevant Web sites, use either of these keywords in a search engine: *career guidance* or *career guidance center.*

INSTRUCTIONAL ASSISTANT (COMMUNITY COLLEGE)

CAREER PROFILE

Duties: Provide faculty members with instructional and nonteaching support; tutor individuals and small groups; perform duties as required

Alternate Title(s): Instructional Aide, Lab Assistant, Educational Assistant

Salary Range: $13,000 to $30,000

Employment Prospects: Fair

Advancement Prospects: Poor

Prerequisites:

Education or Training—An associate's or bachelor's degree in an appropriate discipline

Experience—One to two years of relevant work experience; one year of prior teaching or tutoring experience with adult students

Special Skills and Personality Traits—Leadership, communication, interpersonal, customer service, organizational, teamwork, computer, and self-management skills; be patient, dependable, courteous, friendly, energetic, adaptable, creative, and self-motivated

CAREER LADDER

Lead Instructional Assistant

Instructional Assistant

Instructional Assistant (entry-level)

Position Description

Instructional Assistants who work in public and private community colleges are responsible for providing tutorial services to students. They might work with students who need remedial, reinforcement, or enrichment assistance in learning concepts and skills.

Community colleges are two-year academic institutions that serve the educational needs of the local communities as well as provide training for the local professions, businesses, industries, and government agencies. In some locations, these colleges are known as junior colleges or technical colleges. Community colleges offer academic programs that lead to associate's degrees as well as prepare students to transfer to four-year colleges and universities. These colleges also have established vocational and technical programs in such areas as aviation, dental hygiene, police science, registered nursing, culinary arts, and automotive services. In addition, they offer a variety of adult education programs that fulfill the various needs of students who wish to obtain their high school or general equivalency diploma, improve their English-language skills, or learn a subject or skill for recreational purposes.

Depending on their expertise and interests, Instructional Assistants may be assigned to work in an academic, vocational, or adult education department. They provide instructional support to one or more faculty members. Instructional Assistants perform their job in classroom and office settings. Many of them are assigned to work in learning centers, which are also known as tutoring centers or learning labs. Some learning centers are centered on an academic or vocational discipline, such as science or the culinary arts, while other centers are general learning resource centers that offer testing services, learning resources, and other services. In general learning centers, Instructional Assistants may also help students develop or improve their study skills, library skills, or computer skills.

Instructional Assistants work with students individually as well as in small groups. Under the technical direction of faculty, Instructional Assistants help students with classroom assignments. They answer questions, clarify instructions, provide explanations of concepts and modeling of skills, and review students' work. To help reinforce students' understanding of concepts and skills, Instructional Assistants may provide additional exercises or activities.

Instructional Assistants are expected to develop and maintain cooperative relationships with students under their tutelage. At the community college level, they work with a diverse group of students, who range in age from teenagers to the elderly and come from different socioeconomic, ethnic, and cultural backgrounds. In addition, students vary in skill level as well as in their learning aptitudes and styles. As professionals, Instructional Assistants adapt their teaching styles to meet the unique needs and differences of their students.

Instructional Assistants monitor the progress of the students assigned to them, and provide their instructors with regular updates. They also inform the instructors of any particular needs or problems that their students may have. These assistants may provide such information in person, by e-mail, by telephone, or in written reports.

Many instructors have Instructional Assistants help them with such administrative tasks as recording student attendance, correcting tests, preparing student grades, contacting absent students, scheduling student appointments, and maintaining student records. In addition, Instructional Assistants may support faculty by helping them with the planning and preparation of student instructional materials, study aids, and bulletin board displays. On occasion, many Instructional Assistants are requested to assist with classroom supervision. For example, Instructional Assistants may monitor students during examinations, conduct laboratory sessions, or substitute for an instructor who must be suddenly absent.

Instructional Assistants are assigned to perform a variety of nonteaching duties as well. Examples of such duties include:

- maintaining classroom and/or laboratory facilities and equipment
- maintaining a supply of classroom materials, reference materials, and other supplies
- training students and faculty in the use of classroom and laboratory equipment, machinery, and materials
- responding to questions relating to general information about classes, the department, or the institution
- participating in staff meetings
- helping in the recruitment, selection, training, and supervision of student assistants
- preparing routine correspondence and reports
- keeping accurate and up-to-date records, files, and databases
- photocopying and collating student materials

Instructional Assistants are expected to keep up with new knowledge and technology within their discipline as well as stay up-to-date with successful instructional techniques and skills for teaching adult learners.

Instructional Assistants are classified staff employees at community colleges. They may be contracted to work for eight to 12 months. They work varied hours, depending on the needs of students and faculty. Some assistants work afternoon and evening hours.

Salaries

Salaries for Instructional Assistants vary, depending on such factors as their experience, education, employer, and geographical location. According to the U.S. Bureau of Labor Statistics, in its November 2004 *Occupational Employment Statistics* survey, the estimated annual salary for most teacher assistants, in general, ranged between $13,150 and $29,850. The estimated mean annual salary for those working in junior colleges was $24,710.

Employment Prospects

According to the American Association of Community Colleges, there are about 1,100 community colleges in the United States. Many of these institutions hire Instructional Assistants to support faculty in their academic, vocational, and adult education programs. Opportunities generally become available as individuals transfer to other occupations, advance to higher positions, or leave the workforce. New positions are occasionally created to fill student needs, as long as funding is available.

Advancement Prospects

As Instructional Assistants gain experience, they may advance to positions in which they hold higher-level responsibilities and earn greater pay. Lead and supervisor opportunities are available, but limited.

Many Instructional Assistants use their experience as a stepping-stone to other educational careers, by becoming teachers, administrators, instructional designers, technology specialists, and so on.

Education and Training

Many employers prefer to hire applicants who possess either an associate's or bachelor's degree in an appropriate discipline. Some employers are willing to hire applicants with a high school diploma if they have qualifying work experience and abilities as well as knowledge about the subject matter in which they would be tutoring.

New employees receive on-the-job training.

Experience, Skills, and Personality Traits

Applicants should be knowledgeable about the subject matter in which they would be assisting. Employers generally require a minimum of one to two years of work experience in a relevant setting; for example, applicants for a position in a science lab may have prior experience working in a chemistry laboratory. In addition, applicants should have at least one year of work experience teaching, tutoring, or aiding in the instruction of adult students. Having teaching experience in the subject area in which an individual will work is highly desirable.

Because they work with students from diverse academic, socioeconomic, cultural, and ethnic backgrounds, Instructional Assistants need effective leadership, communication, interpersonal, and customer service skills. Strong organizational, teamwork, and computer skills are also important for Instructional Assistants. Furthermore, they must have excellent self-management skills, including the ability to work independently, understand and follow instructions, prioritize multiple tasks, and meet deadlines.

Some personality traits that successful Instructional Assistants share include being patient, dependable, courteous, friendly, energetic, adaptable, creative, and self-motivated.

Unions and Associations

Many Instructional Assistants belong to an employee union that represents them in contract negotiations with their employers. The union seeks to get the best contract terms in regards to pay, benefits, and working conditions. It also handles any grievances that officers may have against their employers.

Tips for Entry

1. Gain experience by volunteering or obtaining a job as a tutor or teacher aide, especially in a community-based setting such as a community center, youth agency, church group, or senior citizen center.

2. Enroll in courses or workshops that provide instruction on theory and techniques of teaching adults.

3. Check the deadline for submission of applications. Some schools require that applications actually be in the personnel office by the deadline.

4. You can learn more about teaching adults on the Internet. To find relevant Web sites, enter either of these keywords into a search engine: *teaching adults* or *adult learners.*

RESEARCH TECHNICIAN

CAREER PROFILE

Duties: Provide research and laboratory support to university faculty; conduct experiments and tests; perform duties as required

Alternate Title(s): Research Associate, Research Analyst, Research Specialist, Laboratory Technician; Chemical Technician, or other title that reflects a particular occupation

Salary Range: $20,000 to $69,000

Employment Prospects: Fair

Advancement Prospects: Fair

Prerequisites:

Education or Training—A bachelor's degree, usually required

Experience—One or more years of work experience required

Special Skills and Personality Traits—Writing, computer, communication, interpersonal, teamwork, organizational, problem-solving, and self-management skills; be cooperative, detail-oriented, focused, flexible, persistent, self-motivated, and creative

CAREER LADDER

```
┌─────────────────────────────┐
│    Research Specialist       │
└─────────────────────────────┘

┌─────────────────────────────┐
│    Research Technician       │
└─────────────────────────────┘

┌─────────────────────────────┐
│         Trainee              │
└─────────────────────────────┘
```

Position Description

Many Research Technicians are employed in public and private research universities where they provide professors with essential research and laboratory support on their various research projects. These professional technicians work on research that may lead to scientific and technological discoveries and inventions that benefit society in medicine, health, education, biotechnology, agriculture, energy, the environment, telecommunications, space exploration, and other areas. Like the professors for whom they work, Research Technicians specialize in different scientific and engineering disciplines, such as chemistry, biology, agricultural science, geography, or mechanical engineering.

Research Technicians conduct experiments and tests under the supervision of principal investigators, who are the faculty members responsible for the overall management of the research projects. Technicians may be involved with basic or applied research. Principal investigators who perform basic research seek to gain further knowledge and understanding about a particular subject. For example, microbiology professors might conduct research to understand how a particular microorganism works. Those who are conducting applied research focus on using basic research to develop products and processes for practical uses. For example, applied researchers might work on the development of pest-resistant crops, food processing techniques, or drugs to cure cancer.

Research Technicians may be assigned to work with one or several professors. Their job may also require them to work on one or more research projects. Depending on their projects, Research Technicians may handle plants and animals.

Research Technicians perform a variety of duties every day. Many tasks are specific to their specialty and work setting. Other tasks are similar in type, regardless of the field. Under the direction of the principal investigators, technicians might be assigned any of the following duties:

• obtain and compile data, which may involve gathering specimens and performing library searches for relevant information

- review research literature, such as scientific journals, abstracts, and manuals
- prepare data (or specimens) for experiments and tests
- set up, operate, and adjust laboratory instruments
- monitor tests or experiments
- monitor product quality to ensure compliance to standards and specifications
- verify information and check calculations
- analyze and interpret data on tests or experiments
- maintain accurate, detailed records of work activities
- prepare technical summaries and reports
- provide oral progress reports at meetings
- clean and maintain the laboratory as well as the lab equipment and instruments
- maintain an adequate inventory of laboratory supplies

As technicians gain experience, they are usually given the autonomy to correct technical problems and recommend resolutions to principal investigators. They are also assigned more complex duties, such as designing and manufacturing tools for experiments or assisting with the preparation of research plans and major reports. Some senior technicians are involved in the training and supervision of lower-level technicians, clerical assistants, and student research workers.

Research Technicians work in offices and laboratories. Some technicians, such as those working on agricultural and marine research, perform many of their duties outdoors. Occasionally, some technicians travel to remote locations to gather data or perform experiments.

Technicians may be exposed to dust, fumes, toxic chemicals, radiation, infectious agents, extreme temperatures, and other hazards. To prevent risks of contamination or injury, they wear protective clothing and follow strict safety procedures.

Research Technicians work part time or full time. Some technicians work irregular hours or are assigned to shifts to monitor experiments. They may work evenings, nights, or weekends.

Salaries

Salaries vary for Research Technicians, depending on such factors as their education as well as the amount of funding available for a research project. Compensation may be provided from grant funds, departmental operating budgets, or a combination of these sources.

The U.S. Bureau of Labor Statistics reported, in its November 2004 *Occupational Employment Statistics* survey, the following estimated annual salary ranges for most workers in these general occupations:

- agricultural technicians, $19,890 to $48,410
- biological technicians, $22,730 to $54,400
- chemical technicians, $23,870 to $57,910
- mathematical technicians, $26,630 to $68,910
- social science research assistants, $20,060 to $52,630

Employment Prospects

In the United States, many Research Technicians are employed by public and private research universities. According to the Association of American Universities, as of 2002, U.S. research universities performed 54 percent of the country's basic research and contributed to 13 percent of the total research and development conducted in the United States.

Positions usually become available when individuals transfer to other occupations or when new research projects are starting. Most Research Technicians are hired for the length of a research project, which may be funded for one or several years. They may be offered further employment on other projects if funding is available.

Research Technicians can also find employment with government agencies and research laboratories, nonprofit organizations, private firms (such as drug companies and chemical manufacturers), and research and testing services. Opportunities are particularly favorable in the chemical, pharmaceutical, and biotechnology industries.

Advancement Prospects

Advancement opportunities for Research Technicians in academic settings are limited to supervisory positions.

Some Research Technicians return to school to pursue higher degrees to obtain higher-level jobs with private companies or government agencies. Individuals who earn a doctoral degree may pursue careers as professors or research scientists, which involve leading their own research projects.

Education and Training

The minimum requirement for many Research Technician positions is a bachelor's degree in an appropriate discipline. A master's degree may be preferred for some positions. Some employers will hire applicants with an associate's degree in applied science or technology if they have qualifying work experience.

Experience, Skills, and Personality Traits

For entry-level positions, applicants should have at least one year of work experience in technical research, which may have been gained as an intern, student research assistant, lab technician, or other position. Applicants should also be knowledgeable about the subject matter as well as about the research methods and procedures with which they would be working.

Research Technicians need strong writing, computer, and communication skills for their work. Their work also requires that they have effective interpersonal and teamwork skills, as they must be able to work well with professors and others. In addition to excellent organizational and problem-solving skills, Research Technicians must possess adequate self-management skills, including the ability to work independently, understand and follow complex instructions, meet deadlines, and prioritize multiple tasks. Being cooperative, detail-oriented, focused, flexible, persistent, self-motivated, and creative are some personality traits that successful Research Technicians share.

Unions and Associations

Some Research Technicians are members of a union that represents them in contract negotiations with their employers. The union seeks to get the best contract terms in regards to pay, benefits, and working conditions. It also handles any grievances that technicians may have against their employers.

Research Technicians are eligible to join professional associations that serve their particular disciplines. For example, chemical technicians may join the American Chemical Society, while biological technicians may join such organizations as the American Institute of Biological Sciences or the American Society of Microbiology.

See Appendix IV for contact information for the above organizations.

Tips for Entry

1. As an undergraduate student, obtain as much research experience as you can through internships or summer employment.
2. Some employers may require that interested parties apply online through their Web site.
3. Many employers reject applicants because they have incomplete applications. Hence, go over your application. Make sure you have answered all the questions completely, provided accurate information, and have attached any requested documents.
4. Use the Internet to prepare yourself for a job interview. You can learn more about a school, academic department, professor, and research subject. Enter a name or topic into a search engine to obtain a list of relevant Web sites to visit.

SCHOOL CLASSIFIED STAFF

SCHOOL BUS DRIVER

CAREER PROFILE

Duties: Safely transport children to and from school and their homes; perform bus inspections; enforce school regulations; perform other duties as required

Alternate Title(s): None

Salary Range: $13,000 to $35,000

Employment Prospects: Good

Advancement Prospects: Poor

Prerequisites:

Education or Training—High school or general equivalency diploma

Experience—Six months or more of driving experience

Special Skills and Personality Traits—Leadership, communication, interpersonal, and self-management skills; be independent, flexible, calm, patient, tolerant, pleasant, courteous, and stable

Special Requirements—Commercial driver's license (CDL) with a passenger or school bus endorsement; school bus driver certification; first aid and CPR certificates

CAREER LADDER

```
┌─────────────────────────────┐
│   Lead School Bus Driver    │
└─────────────────────────────┘

┌─────────────────────────────┐
│     School Bus Driver       │
└─────────────────────────────┘

┌─────────────────────────────┐
│          Trainee            │
└─────────────────────────────┘
```

Position Description

Every school day in the United States, School Bus Drivers transport millions of students in school buses to public and private schools (preschools to high schools), as well as bring them back home. They also transport students, teachers, and chaperones to and from field trips, games, and other school events.

School Bus Drivers' primary responsibility is the safety of all children and adults riding on their buses. They have been trained to drive in any kind of traffic, observing all traffic laws, as well as to operate the school buses in a safe and efficient manner in sun, fog, wind, rain, snow, or any other weather condition. They are also trained to handle emergency evacuations and provide first aid treatment in emergency situations.

These classified staff members are also responsible for enforcing school rules and policies. Following standard procedures, they maintain discipline and control student behavior as they see fit. For example, they may assign students who are causing trouble to certain seats or refer misbehaving students to school administrators.

Most School Bus Drivers are assigned two or more routes, or runs, to complete in the morning and afternoon.

The drivers follow a time schedule for each route, which is usually about one hour long. Some School Bus Drivers are assigned to transport special education students—children with disabilities. They drive specially-designed school buses that have seat belts or other passive restraint systems, and which have the ability to accommodate wheelchairs.

School Bus Drivers follow standard procedures for transporting, loading, and unloading passengers. They pick up and drop off students at designated bus stops and passenger loading zones. When necessary, the drivers escort students safely across the street.

On preschool and kindergarten routes, School Bus Drivers make sure that parents, or other designated persons, are at the stops to pick up their children. If no one is at the stop or home to pick up a child, the School Bus Driver notifies the bus dispatcher or school office. The School Bus Driver may try to deliver the child again after completing his or her route, or bring the child back to the school office to be picked up by the parents.

In addition, School Bus Drivers are responsible for the safe operating condition of their buses. They perform inspections before beginning their first route, as well as after each run. For example, they make sure their buses have gasoline, oil, and fluids; the tires are full of air and the windshields are clean; and the lights, horns, fuses, engine, doors, emergency equipment are in working order. If anything needs maintenance or repair, the drivers get it fixed immediately.

School Bus Drivers sweep out the interiors of the buses, if necessary. In addition, they check for belongings that children may have left behind, and bring them to the school office. Some School Bus Drivers are also responsible for washing their buses on a regular basis.

As part of their job, they complete a daily record of their hours, bus mileage, number of runs, number of students per busload, and so on. School Bus Drivers are also responsible for keeping driving licenses and professional certifications up-to-date. In most schools, drivers participate in routine emergency exit drills for school bus riders.

School Bus Drivers work full time or part time. Most begin their workdays at 6:00 A.M. Many full-time employees have other duties in addition to driving a bus; for example, some train new School Bus Drivers while others work on the maintenance crew. Some School Bus Drivers hold down other part-time positions, such as playground supervisors, food service workers, and custodians.

Salaries

Salaries for School Bus Drivers vary, depending on such factors as their experience, employer, and geographical location. The U.S. Bureau of Labor Statistics (BLS) reports in its November 2004 *Occupational Employment Statistics* (OES) survey that the estimated annual salary for most School Bus Drivers ranged between $13,110 and $35,150.

Employment Prospects

School Bus Drivers work for public and private schools, as well as for school transportation contractors. According to the BLS's November 2004 OES survey, about 475,700 School Bus Drivers were employed in the United States.

Job opportunities for School Bus Drivers are good because of the high turnover rate. Positions are particularly favorable for part-time positions and in fast-growing suburban areas. The BLS expects employment for bus drivers to increase by 10 to 20 percent through 2012.

Advancement Prospects

School Bus Drivers can become dispatchers and trainers as well as advance to lead and supervisor positions. Those interested in administrative roles can work their way up to branch, district, and regional managers with school transportation contractors, or to transportation directors in public school districts. Another career option is to apply for positions with public or private bus transit systems.

Education and Training

School Bus Drivers need at least a high school or general equivalency diploma. In most states, they must complete a preservice school bus safety and training program that includes classroom training and behind-the-wheel training. Many drivers are also required to complete in-service training each year.

Special Requirements

School Bus Drivers must hold a commercial driver's license (CDL) with a passenger or school bus endorsement. In most states, School Bus Drivers need a school bus driver certification, which is granted upon completion of a preservice training program. Furthermore, School Bus Drivers must have valid first aid and cardiopulmonary resuscitation (CPR) certificates.

Experience, Skills, and Personality Traits

In general, School Bus Drivers should have six months or more driving experience. They must also be able to pass a background check and a drug screening.

To complete their daily duties effectively, School Bus Drivers need adequate leadership skills, communication skills, interpersonal skills, and self-management skills—they should be able to follow instructions, work under stressful conditions, and so on. Successful School Bus Drivers share several personality traits such as being independent, flexible, calm, patient, tolerant, pleasant, courteous, and stable.

Unions and Associations

Many School Bus Drivers in public schools join a union, such as the American Federation of Teachers, which negotiates wages and working conditions with school administrations. School Bus Drivers are also eligible to join the National Association for Pupil Transportation which provides opportunities for networking, training programs, and other professional services.

See Appendix IV for contact information for the above organizations.

Tips for Entry

1. During School Bus Driver shortages, many employers provide free training for CDL exams. Some employers offer incentives such as sign-up bonuses and part-time positions in other areas to encourage qualified individuals to apply.
2. Contact the employers for whom you would like to work to learn about job vacancies, job requirements, and application processes.
3. On the Internet, you can learn more about School Bus Drivers and school bus safety. To start, use the keyword *school bus* in any search engine to find relevant Web sites.

SCHOOL SECRETARY (MAIN OFFICE)

CAREER PROFILE

Duties: Provide clerical and administrative support to school administrators; perform duties as required

Alternate Title(s): Administrative Assistant

Salary Range: $17,000 to $54,000

Employment Prospects: Fair

Advancement Prospects: Fair

Prerequisites:

Education or Training—High school diploma; business training preferred; some college or other postsecondary training may be required

Experience—Clerical or secretarial experience, preferably in school settings

Special Skills and Personality Traits—Reading, writing, math, computer, telephone, interpersonal, communication, public relations, organizational, critical-thinking, decision-making, and self-management skills; be pleasant, cooperative, detail-oriented, dependable, honest, composed, adaptable, open-minded, and self-motivated

CAREER LADDER

```
┌─────────────────────────────────┐
│   Administrative Assistant or   │
│      Executive Secretary        │
└─────────────────────────────────┘

┌─────────────────────────────────┐
│        School Secretary         │
└─────────────────────────────────┘

┌─────────────────────────────────┐
│  School Secretary (entry-level) │
└─────────────────────────────────┘
```

Position Description

School Secretaries have been described as being the glue that holds a school together. Their job is to help school administrators oversee the day-to-day operations of individual schools as well as whole school districts. Most School Secretaries perform as administrative aides to principals, superintendents, or other administrators. Some work exclusively for one administrator, while others provide clerical and administrative services for several administrators.

Much of a School Secretary's job is done in a busy office. Most School Secretaries work in the school main office. They perform a wide array of duties every day, and each day is different from the next. Along with performing clerical functions, they handle a wide range of administrative details that often involve conducting research to resolve problems as well as making decisions on their own. Some of their many clerical and administrative duties include:

• composing, typing, and distributing correspondence, memorandums, reports, school bulletins, meeting minutes, press releases, and other materials

• preparing statistical and confidential reports about students and school personnel

• organizing and maintaining paper or electronic filing and record-keeping systems for students' records, class lists, attendance reports, employee time records, and inventory records

• processing student enrollments, transfers, and withdrawals

• compiling and processing student grades, attendance records, and other required forms or reports for district offices and governmental agencies

• arranging for substitute teachers

• managing daily schedules for administrators

• maintaining a schedule of school activities and events

• scheduling and preparing agendas for committee, school board, faculty, and other meetings

• preparing payrolls

• processing and distributing mail, faxes, and e-mail to administrators, faculty, and staff

• answering phones and making sure messages are given to the appropriate personnel

- duplicating and assembling reports, forms, test materials, schedules, and other materials for meetings, school activities, and other purposes
- ordering and distributing school supplies to teachers, administrators, and staff
- training and supervising office staff

In some schools, School Secretaries are responsible for monitoring daily attendance. They also check in students who are late to school as well as check out students who must leave early. Other tasks include verifying any unexcused absences and printing and distributing the daily attendance report to teachers.

Many School Secretaries help administrators maintain school financial accounts for various school activities, such as lunch programs, school clubs, school dances, and athletic events. Their tasks may include balancing budgets, collecting money from students, teachers, and parents, preparing funds for banking, issuing checks, and recording financial transactions.

Their job also involves daily contact with the general public. School Secretaries screen telephone calls as well as school visitors, such as parents, the media, and vendors. They determine the nature of each visitor's business and direct the visitor to the appropriate personnel or location. Many School Secretaries often play a public relations role for their school. They answer requests from the public, the media, and others for general information about school practices, policies, and activities. They may provide the information in person, in writing, by telephone, or by e-mail.

School Secretaries are in contact with students throughout the day. Like other classified staff members, School Secretaries are expected to be a positive role model to students. Many of them, in fact, take time out of their schedule to talk with students who are having problems or who just come by to visit. At most schools, School Secretaries supervise students who are waiting in the main office to see a school administrator or the school nurse, or to be picked up by a parent or other family member. These secretaries may also oversee students who are being disciplined through office detention.

School Secretaries interact with parents and guardians on a regular basis. The School Secretary is often the staff member contacted by parents to ask school-related questions. When students have become ill or have gotten in trouble, it is usually the School Secretary's job to call the parents or guardians and inform them about their children's situations and arrange for them to pick up their children or to meet with school administrators or teachers. School Secretaries may also be asked by teachers to contact parents and schedule them to assist in the classroom, on field trips, or other school activities.

Many School Secretaries find themselves handling any number of unexpected situations every day. For example,

School Secretaries have unplugged toilets, driven sick children home, monitored classrooms for teachers who must handle emergencies, and dealt with law enforcement officers. In addition, School Secretaries must occasionally deal with children, parents, and other adults who are expressing strong emotions, such as being sad, upset, frustrated, angry, or hostile.

School Secretaries work 40 hours a week, but put in additional hours when required.

Salaries

Annual earnings for School Secretaries vary, depending on such factors as their education, experience, job duties, employer, and geographical location. Executive secretaries and administrative assistants usually earn the highest salaries in schools. According to the November 2004 *Occupational Employment Statistics* (OES) survey, by the U.S. Bureau of Labor Statistics (BLS), the estimated annual salary for most secretaries, in general, ranged from $16,810 to $40,730. The estimated annual mean wage for School Secretaries was $27,670. The estimated annual salary for most executive secretaries and administrative assistants ranged from $24,030 to $54,110.

Employment Prospects

The BLS reported in its November 2004 OES survey that about 221,440 secretaries were employed in elementary and secondary schools in the United States. Opportunities generally become available when individuals retire, advance to higher positions, or transfer to other occupations.

Many schools also employ secretaries for positions in their academic departments (such as an English department), counseling offices, or other departments. In addition, secretaries are employed in school district offices.

Advancement Prospects

As School Secretaries gain additional training and experience, they may earn higher wages as well as be assigned to more complex responsibilities. Secretaries may seek promotions to become administrative assistants or executive secretaries to the top educational administrators within the school or school district.

Education and Training

Minimally, School Secretaries must possess a high school or general equivalency diploma. Many employers prefer to hire applicants who have completed some postsecondary training in a vocational school, college, or other institution.

New employees usually learn on the job. Many School Secretaries enroll in workshops, classes, and seminars to update their skills and expertise throughout their careers.

Experience, Skills, and Personality Traits

Applicants generally need several years of clerical and administrative experience. Having two or more years of experience in school settings is preferred.

School Secretaries need effective reading, writing, math, computer, and telephone skills to perform their various duties well. They also need excellent interpersonal, communication, and public relations skills, as they must be able to maintain positive relationships with administrators, staff, students, parents, and the general public. Having strong organizational, critical-thinking, and decision-making skills is important as well. In addition, School Secretaries need strong self-management skills, which include the ability to work independently, handle stressful situations, organize and prioritize multiple tasks, follow instructions, and meet deadlines.

Some personality traits that successful School Secretaries have in common are being pleasant, cooperative, detail-oriented, dependable, honest, composed, adaptable, open-minded, and self-motivated.

Unions and Associations

School Secretaries are usually members of a union such as the National Education Association or the Service Employees International Union that represents them in contract negotiations with their employers.

School Secretaries may join professional associations to take advantage of networking opportunities, professional certification, education programs, and other professional services and resources. For example, these school employees might join the National Association of Educational Office Professionals or professional societies that serve the interests of secretaries in general such as the International Association of Administrative Professionals.

See Appendix IV for contact information for the above organizations.

Tips for Entry

1. If you are a high school student, you may be able to gain practical experience by becoming an office aide. Contact your work experience counselor.
2. Talk with different school secretaries to learn more about their job. Also ask them to recommend courses you might take to prepare yourself for a career. If you can, sit in a school office for a day to help you determine if it is the right work setting for you.
3. Some schools maintain a pool of clerical and secretarial support for temporary positions.
4. Use the Internet to learn more about schools where you would like to work. You may sometimes find job listings at a Web site. To find the Web site for a school, enter its name into a search engine.

SCHOOL SECURITY PROFESSIONAL

CAREER PROFILE

Duties: Provide security services on a school campus; perform patrol duties; perform duties as required

Alternate Title(s): School Resource Officer, School Police Officer, School Security Officer, Campus Monitor, or other title that reflects a specific occupation

Salary Range: $13,000 to $69,000

Employment Prospects: Good

Advancement Prospects: Good

Prerequisites:

Education or Training—Law enforcement or security training required

Experience—Two or more years of law enforcement or security work experience usually required; prior work experience with children preferred

Special Skills and Personality Traits—Leadership, teamwork, communication, interpersonal, conflict resolution, and self-management skills; be fair, calm, friendly, tactful, honest, trustworthy, observant, patient

Special Requirements—Police officer certification for law enforcement positions; driver's license; firearms certification may be required

CAREER LADDER

Lead, Senior, or Supervisory Officer

Journey Officer

Trainee or Recruit

Position Description

Many public and private schools employ School Security Professionals to prevent crime and violence on their campuses. They work in elementary, middle-level, and high schools, and may be law enforcement officers, security officers, or paraeducators. Their job is to assist with the supervision of students before, during, and after school, and to protect the safety and welfare of students, teachers, staff, visitors, and school property. When necessary, they intervene or investigate reports of various types of school and student-related incidents, including student mischief, bullying, loitering, arguments, fights, unsafe play, substance abuse, weapons possession, violence, and crime.

In general, School Security Professionals are assigned to patrol specific areas of a school campus that may include common areas, hallways, bathrooms, parking lots, and the campus perimeter. They are responsible for enforcing school policies and rules. Those who are law enforcement officers also ensure that appropriate laws and regulations are observed on school campuses.

They perform their duties on foot, by bicycle, or in a vehicle throughout the school day. They stop students who are out of class to check their authorized hallway passes. They also make sure that visitors are permitted to be on campus. Additionally, these professionals watch for nonstudents loitering on campus or cruising in vehicles around or near the school, and keep an eye out for safety hazards, vandalism, illegally parked vehicles, use of illegal substances (drugs, alcohol, cigarettes), and inappropriate activity.

In some schools, School Security Professionals are assigned to screen students and visitors prior to entering school buildings or before attending athletic events or other school functions. They use standard screening procedures as well as electronic and imaging technologies to look for firearms, knives, explosives, and other weapons.

School Security Professionals are specifically trained to work with children and teenagers, and are expected to be a positive role model to students. They maintain high visibility on campus and become familiar with the students, while gaining their trust as adult figures to whom students can come for help.

Every school and school district has its own unique security program that employs one or more of the following types of School Security Professionals.

- school police officers: Some public school districts maintain their own police departments, which are separate from any local police agencies. School police officers, like all other police, have full police authorities, such as enforcing criminal and traffic laws and regulations, making arrests, and investigating criminal activity. Their main priority is to respond to incidents that occur within their school district. School Police may provide classroom presentations and advise students and parents on law enforcement matters.
- school resource officers (SROs): These are commissioned officers who are part of a local law enforcement agency, such as a police department or sheriff's office. In addition to performing patrol and investigative duties, SROs are responsible for developing and implementing educational programs on campus that address crime prevention, substance abuse, gangs, and other issues. They also act as a resource to students, teachers, administrators, parents, and the community in regards to law enforcement and community problems.
- school security officers: These non-police-officers are employed by a school or school district, and are sometimes known by such other job titles as school safety officer, security aide, or campus supervisor. In some schools, security officers have completed the necessary training that grants them limited powers to arrest individuals suspected of committing a crime.
- campus monitors: These personnel are usually categorized as paraeducators. They are assigned to oversee students on playgrounds, in cafeterias and other lunch areas, and in bus lines. In elementary schools, they may be known as playground supervisors, lunchroom monitors, and bus monitors.

Security officers and campus monitors are authorized to give students warnings about their behavior, as well as refer students to appropriate school personnel for counseling and discipline. Depending on the situation, these School Security Professionals may intervene alone or assist other school personnel. Many of them have the authority to contact law enforcement personnel for immediate assistance in very critical situations.

School Security Professionals normally report to a school principal, an assistant principal, or other school administrator. They may be assigned to one or more schools.

Depending on a school's policy, School Security Professionals wear a uniform or dress in civilian clothing. In some schools, law enforcement officers or security officers carry firearms on campus.

School Security Professionals work full time or part time. In addition to school hours, many of them work several hours at night or on weekends during school events such as athletic games, dances, and concerts. On forces that provide 24-hour security services, school police or security officers may be assigned to shifts that include working nights and weekends.

Salaries

Salaries for School Security Professionals vary, depending on such factors as their occupation, rank, experience, employer, and geographical location. Law enforcement officers typically earn higher wages than security officers. The U.S. Bureau of Labor Statistics reports, in its November 2004 *Occupational Employment Statistics* survey, the following estimated annual salary ranges for most professionals working in these occupations:

- security guards: $14,360 to $34,080
- police and sheriff's patrol officers: $27,210 to $69,310
- teacher assistants (which includes campus monitors) $13,150 to $29,850

Employment Prospects

School resource officers are employees of police or sheriff's departments, while school police officers, security officers, and campus monitors are school employees. Some security officers are part of private security firms that provide security services on a contractual basis to schools.

Since the 1990s, there has been a growing concern by parents, teachers, administrators, and the general public about violence and crime in the schools, which has led to an increase in the employment of School Security Professionals. However, the ability to create new or additional positions depends on the availability of funding. Most opportunities become available as staff members transfer to other occupations, advance to higher positions, or leave the workforce due to retirement or for other reasons. When schools are facing budget constraints, school security services may be reduced or cut.

Advancement Prospects

School Security Professionals can develop a satisfying and diverse law enforcement or security career, according to their interests and ambitions. Some of them use their experience as a stepping-stone for a career with other law enforcement agencies. Advancement opportunities for security officers are limited to those found with lead and supervisor positions. Law enforcement officers can rise through the ranks of their agency; for example, a police officer can seek promotions to become a detective, sergeant, lieutenant, and so on, up to police chief. Experienced School Security Professionals may seek positions as school security directors or become school security consultants.

Education and Training

Minimally, applicants must possess a high school or general equivalency diploma. Some employers prefer to hire applicants who have completed some college work. Applicants for law enforcement positions may be required to possess an associate's or bachelor's degree in law enforcement, criminal justice, or another related field.

Law enforcement officers must have successfully completed training at a law enforcement academy agency. Some employers require security officers to receive several weeks of training at a police academy. All School Security Professionals participate in regular training programs on issues pertaining to school security, juvenile law, child abuse, child psychology, youth gangs, drug abuse, parent relations, stress management, and other topics.

Special Requirements

Applicants for law enforcement positions must possess the peace officer standard and training (POST) certificate, which is earned upon completion of basic training at a police academy.

Applicants for positions as security officers or campus monitors are usually required to possess a valid driver's license along with current first aid and cardiopulmonary resuscitation (CPR) certification. For armed security positions, candidates must qualify for firearms certification.

Experience, Skills, and Personality Traits

Requirements vary for the different school security positions. In general, law enforcement and security officer applicants should have at least two years of experience working in their field. Some employers require three or more years of work experience. Employers usually prefer that applicants have prior work experience with children and teenagers as well as be knowledgeable about student behavior and nonphysical disciplinary practices for maintaining student discipline and order.

School Security Professionals need excellent leadership, teamwork, communication, interpersonal, and conflict resolution skills to perform their job effectively. They also need strong self-management skills, which include the ability to work independently, make mature decisions, handle stressful situations, and prioritize and organize tasks. Being fair, calm, friendly, tactful, honest, trustworthy, observant, and patient are some personality traits that successful School Security Professionals share.

Unions and Associations

School Security Professionals may join various professional associations to take advantage of networking opportunities, education programs, and other professional resources and services. Two national societies that specifically serve School Security Professionals are the National Association of School Resource Officers and the National Association of School Safety and Law Enforcement Officers.

Many individuals also join professional associations that serve their particular occupation. Police officers might belong to such associations as the American Federation of Police and Concerned Citizens, the Fraternal Order of Police, or the International Association of Women Police. Security officers might belong to such groups as the International Foundation for Protective Officers or the National Police or Security Officers Association of America. Additionally, many School Security Professionals are eligible to join a union, such as the National Education Association or the Service Employees International Union, that serves school classified personnel.

See Appendix IV for contact information for the above organizations.

Tips for Entry

1. To become a law enforcement officer, you must be a U.S. citizen. You must also meet a minimum age requirement, which varies with every employer. Additionally, you must be in good physical condition as well as be of high moral character.

2. Contact schools directly to learn about job vacancies and application processes for school security, school police, or campus monitor positions.

3. You can learn more about school security and safety on the Internet. You might start by visiting these Web sites: National Association of School Resource Officers, http://www.nasro.org; National School Safety and Security Services, http://www.schoolsecurity.org; and Center for the Prevention of School Violence (North Carolina Department of Juvenile Justice and Delinquency Prevention), http://www.ncdjjdp.org/cpsv/cpsv.htm.

CAFETERIA MANAGER

CAREER PROFILE

Duties: Oversee the daily operations of a school's food service program; supervise and train staff; set up and enforce safe and sanitary standards; perform other duties as required

Alternate Title(s): Food Service Manager, School Nutrition Manager, Cafeteria Director

Salary Range: $17,000 to $42,000

Employment Prospects: Fair

Advancement Prospects: Fair

Prerequisites:

Education or Training—High school or general equivalency diploma

Experience—Three years of work experience; supervisory experience preferred

Special Skills and Personality Traits—Leadership, program management, interpersonal, teamwork, math, communication and report-writing skills; be independent, self-disciplined, organized, fair, flexible, and hardworking

CAREER LADDER

```
┌─────────────────────────────┐
│    Food Service Director     │
└─────────────────────────────┘

┌─────────────────────────────┐
│     Cafeteria Manager        │
└─────────────────────────────┘

┌─────────────────────────────┐
│  Lead Food Service Worker or │
│      Assistant Manager       │
└─────────────────────────────┘
```

Position Description

School cafeterias are run by Cafeteria Managers who oversee—as well as assist—their staff in food preparation, serving meals, storing food and supplies, and keeping the equipment and facilities safe and clean. Depending on the size of their school, Cafeteria Managers may supervise a staff as few as two or as many as 15 or more. They make sure that their staff follows standard procedures for safety and quality control at all times.

Cafeteria Managers complete many different duties each day, including:

- estimating the amount of foods to be prepared
- making sure that equipment and supplies needed for the day are available
- supervising the preparation, cooking, and serving of foods
- assigning tasks to different staff members
- completing required paperwork for nutritional and fiscal accountability

Cafeteria Managers also maintain inventories of foodstuff and supplies; estimate the quantities of food and supplies to be ordered; order food and supplies; receive deliveries; and evaluate the quality of fresh foods, baked goods, and other foodstuff. In addition, they arrange for equipment maintenance and repairs, as well as for outside maintenance services, such as waste removal and pest control. Furthermore, Cafeteria Managers make sure that their food service programs are in compliance with federal, state, and local laws, regulations, and health codes.

Their responsibilities include staff training and development along with providing daily guidance to their staff. In addition, they plan work schedules, complete time sheets, and perform staff evaluations. As leaders, Cafeteria Managers try to create a relaxed environment so that their staff can work together efficiently.

Many Cafeteria Managers help in the planning of school menus, which are the responsibility of nutrition specialists, food service directors, or registered dietitians. Nutritional analyses are performed on each dish and food to make sure that menus are well-balanced and follow dietary guidelines established by the U.S. Department of Agriculture. Additionally, menus are developed to offer several selections, including vegetarian, low fat, and ethnic—such as Italian, Chinese, or Mexican—dishes. In some schools, Cafeteria Managers encourage students to participate in the development of the school menus.

In many schools, Cafeteria Managers run food service programs that participate in the federal government's school meals programs which provide low-cost or free meals to children who meet eligibility guidelines. Cafeteria Managers are responsible for keeping accurate records of the meals sold in order to receive reimbursements for each meal they serve that meets federal guidelines. They may also be responsible for reviewing and approving family applications for free meals.

Cafeteria Managers may be under the supervision of their school principal or an administrator, such as a food service director, who manages several school cafeterias. Most Cafeteria Managers work full time during the school year.

Salaries

Salaries for Cafeteria Managers vary, depending on such factors as their experience, education, job duties, employer, and geographical location. According to the November 2004 *Occupational Employment Statistics* (OES) survey, by the U.S. Bureau of Labor Statistics (BLS), the estimated annual salary for most first-line supervisors or managers of food service workers ranged between $16,590 and $41,910. The estimated annual mean wage for managers in elementary and secondary schools was $26,080.

Employment Prospects

Cafeteria Managers are employed by public and private schools. The BLS reports in its November 2004 OES survey that about 41,110 first-line supervisors were employed in elementary and secondary schools.

Most opportunities become available as Cafeteria Managers retire, advance to higher positions, or transfer to other occupations.

Advancement Prospects

Many school Cafeteria Managers achieve advancement by receiving higher salaries and obtaining positions with increasingly complex responsibilities. With additional education and experience, Cafeteria Managers can advance to higher positions—field managers, nutrition specialists, and food service directors. Another option is to pursue careers in other food service settings.

Education and Training

Cafeteria Managers must have at least a high school or general equivalency diploma. Many Cafeteria Managers have an associate's degree in food service management or have completed college training in food management, dietetics, and supervision.

Most schools require Cafeteria Managers to complete annual in-service training or other training provided by professional organizations.

Experience, Skills, and Personality Traits

Most employers require that Cafeteria Managers have at least three years of previous experience preparing and serving food in large quantities, preferably in an institutional setting. Many employers also prefer that entry-level managers have previous supervisory experience or training in methods and techniques used in supervision.

Along with leadership and program management skills, Cafeteria Managers need interpersonal and teamwork skills in order to work with people of various personality types. In addition, they need strong math, communication, and report-writing skills.

Being independent, self-disciplined, organized, fair, flexible, and hardworking are some personality traits that successful Cafeteria Managers share. Furthermore, they are committed to contributing to children's academic success by providing them with healthy and tasty meals.

Unions and Associations

Many Cafeteria Managers join the School Nutrition Association, a national organization, along with other local and state food service association. These professional associations provide education programs, job listings, net-working opportunities, and other professional services and resources.

Many Cafeteria Managers in public schools are eligible to join a union, such as the National Education Association, the American Federation of Teachers, or the Service Employees International Union.

See Appendix IV for contact information for the above organizations.

Tips for Entry

1. Contact schools and school districts directly to learn about job vacancies and requirements.
2. Learn how to use a computer, because many school cafeterias now use computers for meal planning, gathering statistics, completing paperwork, and so on.
3. You can learn more about school nutrition programs on the Internet. To find pertinent Web sites, use either of these keywords in a search engine: *school nutrition program* or *child nutrition*.

SCHOOL CUSTODIAN

CAREER PROFILE

Duties: Provide janitorial services; perform daily and weekly routine cleaning and maintenance duties; perform other duties as required

Alternate Title(s): Janitor

Salary Range: $13,000 to $32,000

Employment Prospects: Good

Advancement Prospects: Fair

Prerequisites:

Education or Training—High school diploma

Experience—Prior janitorial work experience preferred

Special Skills and Personality Traits—Communication, interpersonal, teamwork, reading, writing, math, problem-solving, critical-thinking, and self-management skills; be friendly, pleasant, patient, flexible, cooperative, reliable, and organized

CAREER LADDER

```
┌─────────────────────────────────────┐
│   Crew Leader or Head Custodian      │
└─────────────────────────────────────┘

┌─────────────────────────────────────┐
│              Custodian               │
└─────────────────────────────────────┘

┌─────────────────────────────────────┐
│        Custodian (entry-level)       │
└─────────────────────────────────────┘
```

Position Description

School Custodians provide a valuable service to public and private schools. They are responsible for maintaining a safe and healthy learning environment for students and teachers by keeping school buildings and facilities clean and orderly.

School Custodians perform routine daily and weekly cleaning duties, which are usually done after school hours. They service classrooms, offices, hallways, bathrooms, locker rooms, gyms, auditoriums, teacher's lounges, and other facilities. Their housekeeping tasks involve sweeping, vacuuming, mopping, and scrubbing floors; sanitizing restrooms, cafeterias, kitchens, and other food areas; cleaning walls, doors, chalkboards, windows, and mirrors; emptying pencil sharpeners and wastebaskets; disinfecting drinking fountains; refilling soap dispensers and replacing light bulbs; dusting furniture, equipment, and machines; and so on. They also perform routine maintenance duties, such as making minor repairs to plumbing or electrical systems. They report any major maintenance needs or equipment malfunctions to their supervisors.

During school breaks, School Custodians do a more thorough and extensive cleaning of school facilities. For example, during the summer break, they may be scheduled to strip, seal, and wax floors, shampoo carpets, paint walls, and disinfect lockers.

Most, if not all, schools employ one or more School Custodians who work during school hours. These School Custodians do spot cleaning as it is needed throughout the day. Many School Custodians are responsible for regulating the heat, ventilation, and air conditioning systems to ensure that classrooms and other facilities receive uniform temperatures as well as healthful indoor air quality and ventilation. In some schools, School Custodians use a computer to control these systems.

School Custodians also respond to emergencies during school hours, such as broken windows, clogged toilets, and spills of toxic materials. In addition, School Custodians may provide personal services to administrators, teachers, staff, and students. For example, a School Custodian might assist an administrator with finding lost keys, change a flat tire for a staff member, or help a student get his car out of the mud.

Many School Custodians assist in providing school security. Due to the nature of their work, they are able to keep an eye open for such problems as vandalism, safety hazards, student misbehavior, or unauthorized school visitors, and make reports to the appropriate school administrators. School Custodians may be called upon to help in disruptive or violent situations on campus until the proper authorities arrive on the scene. Like all classified staff, School Custodians are expected to be positive role models for students.

School Custodians are assigned numerous other tasks; for example, they might:

- mow lawns
- exterminate pests, such as insects and rats
- clear snow or debris from sidewalks
- open and lock up buildings
- perform routine maintenance on vacuums, buffers, and other custodial equipment and tools
- maintain storage areas for custodial supplies, tools, and equipment
- set up rooms for special events
- move furniture or equipment for student activities
- deliver or pick up items off campus for administrators or faculty
- provide escort service for students, parents, faculty, staff, and visitors when necessary

Head custodians oversee the custodial staff. They are in charge of scheduling, assigning, and supervising the activities of the staff. They are also responsible for performing inspections, maintaining the inventory of supplies, screening and hiring new employees, training employees, and preparing various reports. Some head Custodians continue doing janitorial duties.

School Custodians are continuously performing physical work. Most of their work is done indoors. Their various tasks may involve bending, stretching, stooping, kneeling, crouching, and crawling. They occasionally push, pull, carry, and lift objects and materials weighing up to 40 to 50 pounds or more. Their work exposes them to dust, fumes, toxic chemicals, machinery noises and vibrations, as well as other hazards. To prevent risks of contamination or injury, they wear protective clothing and follow strict safety procedures.

School Custodians may work alone or in teams, and they may be assigned to maintain more than one school. On a large custodial staff, members are divided into crews and supervised by lead custodians. The crew leaders report to the head custodian, who is usually under the direction of a school principal or other administrator.

School Custodians work part time or full time. They may be hired as temporary or permanent employees. Some positions are year-round, while other positions are for nine or 10 months. School Custodians may be assigned to day or night shifts.

Salaries

Salaries for School Custodians vary, depending on such factors as their experience, employer, and geographical location. According to the November 2004 *Occupational Employment Statistics* survey, by the U.S. Bureau of Labor Statistics (BLS), the estimated annual salary for most janitors, in general, ranged between $13,140 and $31,930. The estimated annual mean wage for School Custodians was $24,340.

Employment Prospects

According to the BLS's November 2004 OES survey, an estimated 353,310 janitors were employed by elementary and secondary schools.

Job opportunities for School Custodians typically become available when individuals retire or transfer to other occupations. School administrators occasionally hire additional custodial staff to meet demands if funding is available. Some schools have a difficult time filling and retaining custodial staff due to the nature of the low pay of this job.

The BLS reports that the job growth, in general, for building maintenance workers should increase by 10 to 20 percent through 2012. Opportunities for custodians are available with various types of employers, such as colleges and universities, hospitals, restaurants, shopping centers, apartment complexes, office buildings, factories, and government agencies. Custodians can also find employment with firms that offer building maintenance services on a contractual basis.

Advancement Prospects

With experience and training, School Custodians can advance to lead and supervisory positions. Advancement opportunities are typically more available in larger schools or school districts. Individuals with entrepreneurial ambitions may establish their own cleaning business.

Some School Custodians return to school to gain the appropriate training and credentials to serve in other educational roles, by becoming teacher's aides, teachers, administrators, informational technology specialists, and so on.

Education and Training

Applicants are usually required to possess a high school or general equivalency diploma.

New employees generally receive on-the-job training, while working under the supervision of experienced custodians. Custodians also receive training when they are assigned to work with new job procedures, new chemicals, and new equipment, or to learn about various health and safety issues such as ergonomics, asbestos handling, and building security.

Experience, Skills, and Personality Traits

Many employers prefer to hire applicants with previous custodial work experience, especially in school settings. In general, applicants should be knowledgeable about operating machinery, equipment, tools, and cleaning materials that are used in custodial work. They should also be able to perform minor repair work.

To perform their job well, School Custodians must have adequate reading, writing, and math skills. They also need strong problem-solving, critical-thinking, communication, interpersonal, and teamwork skills. Additionally, they should have excellent self-management skills, such as the ability to follow and understand instructions, prioritize multiple tasks, meet deadlines, handle stressful situations, and work independently. Being friendly, pleasant, patient, flexible, cooperative, reliable, and organized are some personality traits that successful School Custodians have in common.

Unions and Associations

Most School Custodians belong to a union, such as the National Education Association or American Federation of Teachers, that represents school classified staff. A union represents its membership in contractual negotiations for better pay, benefits, and working conditions. (See Appendix IV for contact information for the above organizations.)

Tips for Entry

1. Appearance counts. Dress neatly and appropriately when you go to apply for jobs as well as for job interviews.
2. Apply directly to schools where you would like to work.
3. Some schools take applications for substitute custodians. They hire these individuals on a temporary basis when employees must be absent for several days or weeks.
4. Many schools require applicants to pass a physical exam, TB test, and fingerprint clearance.
5. Use the Internet to learn more about schools where you would like to work. To find a particular school, enter its name in a search engine.

CLASSIFIED STAFF IN HIGHER EDUCATION

ADMINISTRATIVE SUPPORT PROFESSIONAL

CAREER PROFILE

Duties: Provide clerical, secretarial, and/or administrative support; perform duties as required

Alternate Title(s): Administrative Support Assistant, Program Assistant; a title that reflects an occupation such as Office Assistant or Administrative Secretary

Salary Range: $16,000 to $69,000

Employment Prospects: Good

Advancement Prospects: Good

Prerequisites:

Education or Training—High school diploma; business or secretarial training may be required

Experience—Varies with the different occupations

Special Skills and Personality Traits—Writing, math, telephone, computer, teamwork, interpersonal, communication, customer service, organizational, problem-solving, and self-management skills; be enthusiastic, diplomatic, discreet, reliable, flexible, detail-oriented, self-motivated

CAREER LADDER

```
┌─────────────────────────────────────┐
│     Administrative Assistant         │
└─────────────────────────────────────┘

┌─────────────────────────────────────┐
│            Secretary                 │
└─────────────────────────────────────┘

┌─────────────────────────────────────┐
│  Receptionist, Office Clerk, or      │
│        Information Clerk             │
└─────────────────────────────────────┘

┌─────────────────────────────────────┐
│   Clerical Trainee or Assistant      │
└─────────────────────────────────────┘
```

Position Description

Administrative Support Professionals in colleges and universities provide essential office and administrative support to faculty, administrators, professionals, specialists, technicians, and others. These classified employees work in academic departments, administrative departments, business offices, student services, and research centers and laboratories. In medical research universities, Administrative Support Professionals also work in the various hospital departments and physician offices.

Administrative Support Professionals perform a wide range of clerical, secretarial, and administrative duties every day to ensure that all campus operations, academic programs, and research projects run efficiently and effectively. The following are some of the more common Administrative Support Professionals found in academic institutions.

Data input operators enter information from source documents, such as student applications or medical records, into computer database. They are responsible for verifying that entered data is accurate and complete. They also update data by changing or adding new information to files.

Receptionists are usually the first employees that visitors meet in a work unit. They are responsible for greeting and screening visitors, and directing them to the appropriate staff member upon determining their business needs. Receptionists also answer telephones for their work unit, and take messages or direct calls to the proper parties. Many are also assigned to process and distribute incoming mail as well as perform other general office duties.

General office clerks, or office assistants, work under the supervision of senior office assistants or office managers. They are assigned routine clerical tasks such as answering telephones, sorting and distributing mail, running errands, making photocopies, compiling reports, filing documents, taking inventory of supplies, processing requisitions and forms, typing letters and reports, and entering information into databases.

Junior office clerks follow detailed work instructions, and their work is checked for accuracy and completeness. As clerks gain experience and training, they advance to more responsible and complex duties. For example, senior office clerks might assist with designing brochures and other materials, scheduling meetings for faculty or administrators, ordering supplies, researching information for reports, composing standard correspondence, and supervising student workers.

Record clerks are responsible for processing, maintaining, and updating records that hold essential information about individuals. For example, record clerks in the registrar's office take care of student records, which contain registration data, transcripts, and other information about students.

Accounting clerks assist with keeping track of financial records for a work unit. Following established procedures, they perform routine accounting and bookkeeping duties, such as maintaining records, posting transactions to accounts, reconciling bank statements, preparing invoices, and compiling routine numerical data for reports. They are also responsible for verifying amounts and other data for accuracy and making the necessary corrections.

Secretaries perform a wide variety of clerical and secretarial duties in a work unit. They provide direct support to one or more faculty members or administrators, or to their whole unit's staff. In addition to routine general office tasks, secretaries are responsible for handling a wide range of administrative details that often involve conducting research and making decisions to resolve problems. Some of their higher-level tasks include preparing correspondence from dictation or notes, preparing reports, organizing paper and electronic filing and record-keeping systems, making travel arrangements, scheduling meetings, recording minutes at meetings, keeping track of financial accounts, handling and processing administrative forms, and maintaining the inventory of office supplies. Some secretaries supervise and direct the work of subordinate Administrative Support Professionals.

Executive secretaries and *administrative assistants* provide support to the top managers and executive officers of academic institutions, such as program directors, administrative deans, academic deans, provosts, or presidents. They perform advanced secretarial and administrative work that involves interpreting policies, guidelines, and practices, taking initiative, and using independent judgment.

Examples of their duties include coordinating personnel matters and business affairs, keeping track of budgets, maintaining an administrator's calendar, preparing meeting agendas and minutes, managing the distribution of internal communications to and from administrators, composing correspondence, directing the preparation of reports and other materials, researching information, and calculating statistics for reports. Some administrative assistants are also assigned the responsibility to serve as the communication link to faculty, staff, students, alumni, organizations, and the general public.

Some secretaries and administrative assistants work in legal, medical, or scientific offices on college campuses. These Administrative Support Professionals are trained in the use of terminology, documents, procedures, and systems that are particular to those specialized areas.

Office supervisors, or office managers, are responsible for overseeing all the office operations of their work units, which are generally large centralized offices. They are responsible for the direction and supervision of office staff. Some of their major duties include planning and scheduling the work of their staff, monitoring the quality of the work performed by their staff, developing and revising job procedures, preparing budget recommendations, coordinating complex projects, evaluating job performances, and making decisions or offering recommendations to hire, promote, or terminate office employees.

Depending on their work unit, Administrative Support Professionals may interact with students, faculty, administrators, staff, alumni, visitors, and the general public. Those working in medical centers may be in regular contact with patients.

All Administrative Support Professionals operate a variety of general office equipment, including telephone systems, fax machines, photocopiers, scanners, calculators, printers, and typewriters. Most of them also use a computer to perform many of their tasks, and work with word processing, spreadsheet, desktop publishing, business, and other software.

Administrative Support Professionals work full time or part time. They may be required to work additional hours to meet project deadlines.

Salaries

Salaries for Administrative Support Professionals in academic institutions vary, depending on their position, education, experience, employer, and geographical location. Secretaries, administrative assistants, and office supervisors typically earn higher salaries, while data input operators, receptionists, and junior office clerks earn lower salaries. According to the November 2004 *Occupational Employment Statistics* survey by the U.S. Bureau of Labor Statistics, the estimated annual salary for most office and administrative support occupations ranged from $15,520 to $42,560. The estimated annual salary for most administrative assistants and executive secretaries ranged from $24,030 to $54,110, and for office supervisors, from $25,550 to $69,000.

Employment Prospects

In general, most opportunities in colleges and universities become available as Administrative Support Professionals advance to higher positions, retire, or transfer to other jobs. On occasion, additional positions are created in an institution to meet staffing needs, if funding is available.

Advancement Prospects

Administrative Support Professionals can advance in any number of ways, depending on their interests and ambitions. With experience and additional training, Administrative Support Professionals can advance through the ranks as receptionists and junior clerks to become senior office clerks, office specialists, or secretaries, and then continue to advance to become office managers and executive assistants. Experienced professionals may seek positions as business operations managers and directors.

Many Administrative Support Professionals have continued their education and obtained bachelor's and advanced degrees to pursue careers as administrators, educators, professionals, scientists, technicians, and so forth.

Education and Training

Educational requirements vary for the different positions as well as with different employers. For many positions, a high school or general equivalency diploma is the minimum requirement as long as the applicant fulfills the experience requirement. Some employers prefer to hire applicants who have completed some business or secretarial training at a postsecondary institute. An associate's or bachelor's degree may be required for higher-level administrative support positions.

Experience, Skills, and Personality Traits

Requirements vary for the different occupations. For example, applicants for entry-level office assistant positions may need six months to one or more years of clerical experience. Employers usually allow a combination of education and experience to substitute for either the education or experience requirement. Having previous experience working in an academic setting is desirable.

Regardless of their position, Administrative Support Professionals need to possess adequate writing, math, telephone, and computer skills. They also need excellent teamwork, interpersonal, communication, and customer service skills, as they must be able to work well with coworkers, faculty, administrators, students, the general public, and others. In addition, they must have strong organizational, problem-solving, and self-management skills.

Successful Administrative Support Professionals have several personality traits in common, such as being enthusiastic, diplomatic, discreet, reliable, flexible, detail-oriented, and self-motivated.

Unions and Associations

Administrative Support Professionals may join professional associations to take advantage of networking opportunities, professional certification, education programs, and other professional services and resources. For example, they might join the National Association of Educational Office Professionals, the International Association of Administrative Professionals, or the National Association of Executive Secretaries and Administrative Assistants. Many Administrative Support Professionals are members of a union, such as the National Education Association, that represents them in contract negotiations with their employers. For contact information for the above organizations, see Appendix IV.

Tips for Entry

1. In high school, you can begin gaining valuable experience by working as an office aide in your school's main office or another school department.
2. Job titles vary, so read job vacancy announcements carefully to find out if you meet the requirements as well as possess the appropriate skills and knowledge for a position.
3. Many academic institutions maintain a list of eligible administrative support personnel. As temporary vacancies become available, job candidates are culled from the list.
4. If you are an employee of your state, you may be able to transfer to vacant positions for which you qualify at state-operated colleges and universities.
5. Most colleges and universities maintain a Web site on which they post information about job vacancies, selection processes, and employee benefits. To find a particular Web site, enter the name of the institution in a search engine.

SECURITY SERVICES PROFESSIONAL

CAREER PROFILE

Duties: Maintain peace and order on a college or university campus; enforce governmental laws and regulations as well as institutional policies and rules; perform patrol duties; perform other duties as required

Alternate Title(s): A title that reflects an occupation, such as Public Safety Officer or Security Officer

Salary Range: $14,000 to $69,000

Employment Prospects: Good

Advancement Prospects: Good

Prerequisites:

Education or Training—High school diploma; police academy training for police officers

Experience—Previous law enforcement or security experience in an educational setting preferred

Special Skills and Personality Traits—Leadership, decision-making, writing, communication, interpersonal, teamwork, and self-management skills; be calm, composed, friendly, cooperative, tactful, honest, ethical, organized

Special Requirements—Police officer certification for police officers; firearms certification may be required for security officers; driver's license

CAREER LADDER

```
┌─────────────────────────────────────┐
│ Lead, Senior, or Supervisory Officer │
└─────────────────────────────────────┘

┌─────────────────────────────────────┐
│           Journey Officer            │
└─────────────────────────────────────┘

┌─────────────────────────────────────┐
│          Trainee or Recruit          │
└─────────────────────────────────────┘
```

Position Description

Most, if not all, colleges and universities have a security services department to ensure the safety and protection of all life and property on campus. Every department has its own unique staffing of Security Services Professionals. A department may consist of only police officers or security officers, or have both a police and a security force. The name of the department typically reflects its composition. For example, a campus security department is usually composed of security officers, whereas a campus police department that utilizes both police and security officers is sometimes called a public safety department.

Security Services Professionals, whether they are police officers or security officers, are responsible for carrying out patrol duties. They are assigned areas, or beats, on campus to patrol, which they complete on foot, on bicycles, or in marked vehicles. Along with maintaining a visible presence on campus, the officers check buildings, grounds, and facilities for criminal and suspicious activity as well as for violations of laws, regulations, policies, and rules. They also watch for fire and safety hazards and make reports to the proper authorities or campus personnel.

The various professionals have distinct enforcement responsibilities. Security officers are responsible for enforcing only institutional policies and rules, while police officers have the additional responsibility to ensure that federal, state, and local laws and regulations are being followed. In some cities, the jurisdiction of campus police officers includes areas surrounding their campuses.

Campus police officers have the power to discharge general police duties, such as deterring and preventing unlawful behavior, issuing citations, serving warrants, apprehending offenders, making arrests, preserving crime scenes, investigating crimes, conducting surveillance, and testifying in court. Campus security officers generally do not have any police powers, but they may stop and question individuals who are acting suspiciously. These officers may detain individuals whom they believe may be committing or have committed a crime until police officers have arrived on the scene. Police officers and security officers may be required to carry firearms on their job, depending on the institution's policy.

Security Services Professionals are expected to interact with students, faculty, and staff in a respectful and professional way. As part of their duty, they respond to a wide range of requests for service from students, faculty, and others on campus. The requests may be about criminal or noncriminal matters. For example, an officer might check out a report of vandalism in the student union, a complaint of loud music in a dormitory, or a call for emergency medical assistance in a classroom. Furthermore, on most campuses, Security Services Professionals provide escort service for anyone who does not wish to walk alone on campus during certain hours, particularly after dark.

Security Services Professionals complete other tasks that vary depending on their occupation and level of responsibility. For example, they might:

- perform traffic duty, which includes enforcing traffic laws and regulations, directing traffic, issuing traffic citations, and investigating traffic accidents
- provide security at games, dances, graduations, and other campus events
- screen visitors for firearms and other contraband
- coordinate medical emergency situations
- make presentations to students, faculty, and staff on such topics as alcohol abuse, drugs, crime prevention, sexual assault, and traffic safety
- assist other law enforcement agencies with their cases

Both police and security officers are responsible for preparing accurate and detailed reports of their activities, including daily logs, incident reports, and investigative reports. They also maintain records and files about incidents, criminal records, lost and found items, and so on.

Security Services Professionals typically wear uniforms. On campuses that employ both law enforcement and security officers, the officers wear different-colored uniforms to differentiate them.

Police and security officers operate various types of equipment, such as two-way radios, emergency medical equipment, riot control equipment, and standard office machines. Their job requires them to sit, stand, walk, run, and climb for long periods of time. When necessary, they lift, carry, or drag heavy objects or people. On occasion they must handle people who are angry, hostile, upset, or disturbed.

Security Services Professionals in higher education work a 40-hour week schedule. Many are assigned to rotating shifts, which may include working nights, weekends, and holidays. They sometimes work overtime to deal with emergencies and other unexpected situations.

Salaries

Earnings for police officers and security officers vary, depending on such factors as their rank, experience, education, employer, and geographical location. According to the November 2004 *Occupational Employment Statistics* survey by the U.S. Bureau of Labor Statistics, the estimated annual salary for most police patrol officers ranged between $27,210 and $69,310, and for most security guards, between $14,360 and $34,080.

Employment Prospects

In general, openings become available as officers retire, advance to higher positions, or transfer to other jobs. Typically, larger campuses employ a greater number of Security Services Professionals than smaller campuses. The ability of a department to create additional positions or to maintain current staffing levels is dependent on funding availability.

Advancement Prospects

Higher education security and law enforcement officers can develop a satisfying and diverse career, according to their interests and ambitions. Law enforcement officers can rise through the ranks as detectives, sergeants, lieutenants, to police chief. Some officers use their campus police experience as a stepping-stone for a career with other law enforcement agencies at the local, state, or federal level.

Advancement opportunities for security officers are limited to those found with lead and supervisor positions. Some officers obtain training to become law enforcement officers. Other security officers stay in the field and eventually become high-level security managers and consultants.

Education and Training

Minimally, applicants for law enforcement or security positions must possess a high school diploma or general equivalency diploma. Some employers prefer to hire applicants who have completed some college work.

Police recruits receive several weeks of training at a police academy, where they study such topics as criminal procedure law, the role of campus law enforcement, crisis intervention, and multicultural diversity. If their position requires them to be armed, recruits then complete training on the use of firearms.

Security officer trainees also go through specialized training that includes such areas as crime prevention, first aid, defensive tactics, traffic control, and evidence gathering.

Special Requirements

Applicants for law enforcement positions must possess the POST (peace officer standard and training) certificate, which is earned upon completion of basic training at a police academy. Those applying for armed security positions must qualify for firearms certification. Candidates for either a police or security officer position are usually required to possess a valid driver's license.

Experience, Skills, and Personality Traits

Many employers prefer to hire applicants with previous law enforcement or security experience. Having experience in a higher education setting is desirable. Many employers allow candidates to substitute a college degree in law enforcement, criminal justice, or another related field for one or more years of experience. Some employers may hire individuals without work experience if they have recently completed or are about to complete training at a police academy.

To perform their duties effectively, campus Security Services Professionals need strong leadership, decision-making, writing, communication, interpersonal, and teamwork skills. They must also have excellent self-management skills, such as the ability to work independently, follow and understand instructions, handle stressful situations, and prioritize and organize tasks. Being calm, composed, friendly, cooperative, tactful, honest, ethical, and organized are some personality traits that successful professionals share.

Unions and Associations

Many Security Services Professionals are members of a union that represents them in contract negotiations with their employers. In addition, many belong to professional associations to take advantage of networking opportunities and other professional resources and services. For example, the International Association of Campus Law Enforcement Administrators specifically serves the interests of campus law enforcement staff members.

Police officers may also join general law enforcement societies such as the Fraternal Order of Police, the International Association of Women Police, or the American Federation of Police and Concerned Citizens. Security officers are eligible to join such groups as the International Foundation for Protection Officers or the National Police and Security Officers Association of America. For contact information for these organizations, see Appendix IV.

Tips for Entry

1. If you are a college student, you might join the campus student security patrol to determine if this is the right field for you.
2. To become a law enforcement officer, you must be a U.S. citizen. You must also meet a minimum age requirement, which varies with every employer. Additionally, you must be in good physical condition as well as be of high moral character.
3. Some campuses maintain a pool of qualified candidates whom they contact for temporary positions.
4. For information about job vacancies and application procedures, contact the human resources department at institutions where you would like to work.
5. Many higher education security, police, and public safety departments have Web sites, which often include job recruitment information. To find the Web site for the organization that interests you, enter its name in a search engine.

COOK

CAREER PROFILE

Duties: Follow standard recipes to prepare and cook a variety of foods and dishes; clean and maintain utensils, equipment, and work areas; perform other duties as required

Alternate Title(s): Chef; a title that reflects a specific job such as Grill Cook or Pastry Chef

Salary Range: $12,000 to $56,000

Employment Prospects: Good

Advancement Prospects: Good

Prerequisites:

Education or Training—High school diploma; cooking apprenticeship or formal training

Experience—One or more years of work experience for entry-level positions

Special Skills and Personality Traits—Leadership, teamwork, time-management, organizational, communication, interpersonal, customer service, reading, writing, math, computer, and self-management skills; be courteous, respectful, flexible, efficient, inspirational, creative

CAREER LADDER

```
┌─────────────────────────────────┐
│   Line Cook or Chef Specialist   │
└─────────────────────────────────┘

┌─────────────────────────────────┐
│            Prep Cook             │
└─────────────────────────────────┘

┌─────────────────────────────────┐
│    Apprentice or Assistant Cook  │
└─────────────────────────────────┘
```

Position Description

Cooks in colleges and universities are responsible for preparing thousands of tasty, appealing, and nutritious meals every day for students, faculty, employees, and visitors. They prepare a wide variety of foods and dishes, including soups, stews, casseroles, roasts, fried foods, pizzas, ethnic dishes, vegetarian dishes, sandwiches, salads, breads, pastries, and cookies, among others.

The number and types of food service operations that are available in academic institutions vary from campus to campus. Cooks work in kitchens of student cafeterias, dormitory dining halls, faculty dining rooms, restaurants, delis, coffee houses, snack bars, catering services, and other food service operations. The Cooks at each establishment deal with different amounts of food production. For example, cafeteria cooks prepare large quantities of menu items, which are limited in number and vary each day, while restaurant cooks prepare items on the menu as they are ordered by customers.

Regardless of the operations in which they work, Cooks perform similar routines. They read food orders to determine which foods or dishes to make. Following standard recipes, they gather, measure, and mix ingredients, then use the proper technique (such as roasting, grilling, sautéing, or baking) to cook the ingredients. Cooks are expected to prepare meals quickly so that they are served to customers in a timely manner. It is also the cooks' job to ensure the quality of the foods and their preparation, as well as to make sure that foods and dishes are presented in an appetizing and healthful manner.

Cooks also clean and inspect cooking utensils, equipment, and work areas to maintain the highest levels of food safety, sanitation, and cleanliness. Many of them assist in training and supervising food preparation workers and lower-level Cooks in the preparation, cooking, and handling of food. They may also be involved in testing new recipes.

The job titles *cook* and *chef* are used interchangeably, but "chef" usually refers to experienced Cooks. Some people think of chefs as having higher-level culinary skills than Cooks, and that they perform managerial duties.

In many food service operations, several Cooks and chefs work together in the kitchens, each performing specific tasks according to their skill levels and specialties. Apprentice or assistant cooks help Cooks by performing basic tasks, such as weighing ingredients, peeling vegetables, cutting meat, cleaning work areas, and storing supplies. Prep cooks are responsible for assembling, decorating, and garnishing prepared foods. They may also be responsible for the production of cold foods, such as sandwiches and salads.

Line cooks and specialist chefs are responsible for preparing certain foods on the menu, and usually hold a job title that reflects the cooking technique or food in which they specialize. For example, grill cooks are responsible for grilling meats and vegetables, fry cooks handle deep-fried items, and pastry chefs specialize in desserts, pastries, and baked goods. Line cooks may supervise and instruct lower-level cooks and food preparation workers as well as assist in planning menus.

Head cooks and executive chefs are in charge of the kitchens. They provide direction and supervision to all the kitchen staff. They handle such tasks as keeping track of food costs, maintaining inventory of supplies, and ordering food, ingredients, supplies, and equipment. They also help food services managers to plan meals and develop new recipes.

Cooks are on their feet for most of their work day. They stand, walk, stoop, and bend for long periods of time. Their job often requires them to push, pull, and lift objects weighing up to 50 pounds or more. They work near hot stoves, ovens, steam cookers, and toasters all day, as well as handle knives, food choppers, blenders, grinders, and other kitchen equipment, Hence, Cooks follow safety measures and procedures to prevent burns, cuts, and other injuries.

Cooks work part time or full time. Their schedules may include working early mornings, evenings, weekends, and holidays. Some of them work a rotating schedule and are assigned to different shifts and days off.

Salaries

Salaries for Cooks in academic institutions vary, depending on such factors as their experience, education, employer, and geographical location. The U.S. Bureau of Labor Statistics (BLS) reported in its November 2004 *Occupational Employment Statistics* survey that the annual salary for most institutional cooks ranged from $12,270 to $29,050, and for chefs and head cooks, from $18,090 to $56,060.

Employment Prospects

Cooks in food service operations at colleges and universities may be employed by the institutions or by companies such as Aramark that provide food services on a contractual basis. In addition to higher education institutions, Cooks can find employment with food service operations in schools, hospitals, department stores, large companies, correctional facilities, country clubs, hotels, resorts, casinos, and other institutions. Cooks can also seek positions in restaurants, private residences, and catering services.

The BLS reports that the overall employment for Cooks, chefs, and food preparation workers should increase by 10 to 20 percent through 2012 in the United States. However, job growth among institutional and cafeteria cooks is expected to show little or no growth. Most opportunities in colleges and universities will become available as Cooks retire, advance to higher positions, or transfer to other jobs. Keep in mind that when academic institutions face tight budgets, fewer workers are usually hired and current staff may be laid off.

Advancement Prospects

As Cooks gain higher-level skills and experience, they advance through the ranks as assistant cooks, line cooks, specialist chefs, head cooks, and executive chefs. Those interested in administrative and management responsibilities may seek opportunities as food service managers. To advance to chief cook and food service management positions, a Cook may be required to obtain additional training from an accredited culinary school or other institution.

Cooks with entrepreneurial interests may start their own restaurants or catering services. Another career option may be for Cooks to become instructors in culinary schools or culinary vocational programs in high schools or community colleges.

Education and Training

Minimally, applicants need a high school or general equivalency diploma. For higher-level cooking positions, employers may prefer to hire candidates who have an associate's or bachelor's degree in the culinary or hospitality fields or who have completed a training program from a professional culinary institute.

Many Cooks begin their careers as apprentices or interns, and learn cooking skills under experienced Cooks and chefs. Some Cooks start their careers by enrolling in a formal culinary training program through a high school, community college, professional culinary institute, or independent cooking school. Most training programs include an apprenticeship, internship, or field practicum in which students can have experience working in real-life situations.

Most food service operations in higher education institutions provide their Cooks with regular in-service training. Some employers send selected Cooks to training programs sponsored by professional culinary institutes and professional associations.

Experience, Skills, and Personality Traits

For entry-level positions, applicants usually need one or more years of work experience as a food preparation worker or short-order cook. They should be knowledgeable about sanitation and safety measures in the kitchen and with food handling as well as the basic procedures and equipment used to prepare, cook, and present large quantities of food.

To perform their job well, Cooks must have strong leadership, teamwork, time management, and organizational skills. They also need strong communication, interpersonal, and customer service skills, as they constantly deal with people of different backgrounds. Having reading, writing, math, and computer skills is also essential. In addition, Cooks need adequate self-management skills, including the ability to work independently, handle stressful situations, meet deadlines, prioritize multiple tasks, and understand and follow instructions. Successful Cooks have several personality traits in common, such as being courteous, respectful, flexible, efficient, inspirational, and creative.

Unions and Associations

Cooks in academic institutions may be members of a union that represents them in contract negotiations for better pay, benefits, and working conditions. Many Cooks join professional societies to take advantage of networking opportunities, job listings, training programs, and other professional services and resources. The American Culinary Federation is one association that is available at the national level. See Appendix IV for contact information.

Tips for Entry

1. As a high school student, gain experience in the food industry through entry-level jobs such as a food preparation worker, fast-food cook, or waiter.
2. Enhance your employability and advancement prospects by obtaining professional certification, from recognized organizations such as the American Culinary Federation.
3. Do your research before applying for a job or going to a job interview. For example, you might visit the food service operation where you would like to work to get an idea of the meals it serves.
4. Some institutions accept applications for entry-level food service workers on a continuous basis.
5. Use the Internet to learn more about food service operations on college and university campuses. You might start by visiting these Web sites: National Association of College and University Food Services, http://www.nacufs.org, and American Culinary Federation, http://www.acfchefs.org.

BUILDING TRADES WORKER

CAREER PROFILE

Duties: Perform a specialty trade; install, maintain, and repair buildings and infrastructure

Alternate Title(s): Electrician, Painter, or other title that reflects a specific occupation

Salary Range: $18,000 to $70,000

Employment Prospects: Good

Advancement Prospects: Fair

Prerequisites:

Education or Training—Informal on-the-job training or formal apprenticeship program

Experience—One or more years of journey-level work experience

Special Skills and Personality Traits—Teamwork, interpersonal, communication, math, writing, reading, computer, self-management skills; be flexible, self-motivated, creative, dependable, cooperative, persistent, alert, assertive

Special Requirements—Professional licensure or certification may be required

CAREER LADDER

```
┌─────────────────────────────┐
│  Crew Leader or Supervisor   │
└─────────────────────────────┘

┌─────────────────────────────┐
│    Journey Trades Worker     │
└─────────────────────────────┘

┌─────────────────────────────┐
│ Apprentice or Helper Trades Worker │
└─────────────────────────────┘
```

Position Description

Colleges and universities employ Building Trades Workers to provide maintenance and repair of campus buildings as well as mechanical, electrical, and utility systems, security systems, roof drainage systems, windows, painted surfaces, and built-in furniture. These skilled specialists contribute to keeping academic institutions healthy, safe, comfortable, and attractive places for students, faculty, employees, and visitors to learn, work, live, and play.

Building Trades Workers perform routine maintenance, following daily, weekly, monthly, and annual schedules. They also complete service jobs in support of such campus activities as athletic games, public events, conferences, and commencement exercises. In addition, they work on renovations and respond to emergencies as they occur.

The type and number of Building Trades Workers vary from one academic institution to the next. The following are some of the different craftspeople who are employed as classified staff at many colleges and universities.

Electricians install, maintain, modify, and repair all types of electrical systems and equipment on campus. For example, they might troubleshoot electrical malfunctions, plan the layout of new electrical installations, rewire a building's electrical system, install low-voltage wiring for security systems, and test electrical equipment for safety,

Heating, ventilation, and air conditioning (HVAC) mechanics perform the maintenance, service, and repair of heating and cooling systems and equipment on campus. They make sure all systems are working efficiently and maintain a comfortable indoor level of coolness and heat. HVAC mechanics may be responsible for refrigeration systems and equipment as well.

Plumbers install, alter, maintain, and repair water lines, sewers, water heaters, toilet fixtures, laboratory equipment, drinking fountains, and other types of plumbing fixtures and appliances in campus buildings and structures.

Locksmiths install, adjust, change, maintain, and repair locks, locking systems, and security devices for buildings, offices, rooms, furniture, safes, and vehicles. They also cut and issue keys. Some locksmiths work with computerized access control systems and are responsible for programming, troubleshooting, and repairing these systems.

Carpenters perform a variety of skilled carpentry work that may include installing, building, repairing, and maintaining internal and external structures, such as doors, window frames, walls, floors, and fences. They also build, install, and repair shelves, cabinets, furniture, and partitions, as well as build scaffolds and forms or molds for the construction of structures.

Glaziers are responsible for selecting, cutting, installing, and replacing all types of glass for windows, skylights, display cases, building fronts, walls, tabletops, and so on. Their work orders may involve replacing broken glass, installing new mirrors in bathrooms, and installing specially treated glass for improving security, appearance, or energy management.

Roofers maintain and repair the roofs of campus buildings and other structures. They may also waterproof, dampproof, or soundproof structures.

Painters are responsible for the application of paint, varnish, stain, and other finishes to exterior and interior surfaces, including walls, doors, trims, hallways, stairwells, and furnishings. They may also provide general maintenance on street painting, campus crosswalks, and parking lots.

Masons do masonry work to maintain, alter, repair, and renovate campus buildings, grounds, and equipment. Their work ranges from laying bricks, tiles, cinder blocks, or stone, to applying plaster or stucco, to finishing surfaces of poured concrete. For example, their work projects may involve plastering interior walls, building concrete retaining walls, installing tiled shower stalls, laying stone pathways, repairing brick structures, or finishing concrete floors.

In addition to performing duties required of their specialty, Building Trades Workers complete general tasks that are common to all tradespeople. They follow work orders, which include instructions, specifications, drawings, and blueprints. They provide estimates for cost, time, and materials for work projects, and may advise in the selection and storage of building materials. They also troubleshoot problems and recommend solutions when they are unable to complete the repairs. When needed, they consult with other trades workers.

All Building Trades Workers are responsible for inspecting completed work, and making sure it is compliant with requirements and specifications as well as with applicable building and safety codes and regulations. In addition, they are responsible for cleaning, maintaining, and servicing their tools, equipment, and work areas. Furthermore, they perform administrative tasks such as preparing standard reports and maintaining records and logs. They may also supervise and train apprentices and helpers.

All Building Trades Workers are constantly standing, walking, bending, stooping, twisting, climbing, kneeling, and reaching. They occasionally push, pull, lift, and carry objects weighing up to 50 pounds or more. Their work exposes them to various hazards, such as dust, fumes, toxic chemicals, and machinery noises and vibrations. To prevent risks of contamination or injury, they wear protective clothing and follow strict safety procedures.

Building Trades Workers may work alone or in teams. On a large staff, members are divided into crews and supervised by lead craftspersons. The crew leaders report to supervisors, who are usually under the direction of the physical plant (or facilities management and services) director.

Skilled Trades Workers in higher institutions generally work 40 hours a week, but put in additional hours when required. Some positions require working shifts, which includes working nights, weekends, and holidays.

Salaries

Salaries for Building Trades Workers in higher education vary, depending on their occupation, experience, employer, geographical location, and other factors. The U.S. Bureau of Labor Statistics (BLS) reported in its November 2004 *Occupational Employment Statistics* survey that the estimated annual salary for most of the these occupations, in general, ranged as follows:

- carpenter, $21,810 to $59,980
- electrician, $25,730 to $70,200
- glazier, $20,560 to $60,490
- heating, air conditioning, and refrigeration mechanic, $22,830 to $56,460
- locksmith, $18,120 to $49,590
- mason (brick or block), $24,270 to $64,040
- mason (cement), $19,920 to $53,780
- mason (stucco and plasterers), $20,600 to $55,710
- mason (stone), $20,750 to $58,330
- painter, $19,840 to $52,870
- plumber, $24,260 to $70,310
- roofer, $19,480 to $53,700

Employment Prospects

Most opportunities in colleges and universities become available as Building Trades Workers retire, advance to higher positions, or transfer to other jobs. Employers may create additional jobs if funding is available. According to the BLS, employment for installation, maintenance, and repair occupations in the educational services industry is expected to grow by about 17 percent through 2012.

Opportunities in general for Building Trades Workers is expected to be favorable through 2012 because a large number of craftspeople are becoming eligible for retirement. In addition, fewer young people are training to be skilled trades workers.

Advancement Prospects

In academic institutions, Building Trades Workers advance through the ranks as crew leaders and supervisors, building trades managers, and physical plant department directors. Many craftspersons realize advancement by earning higher wages or through job satisfaction and professional recognition.

Education and Training

Minimally, applicants must possess a high school or general equivalency diploma. For some positions, employers may require that applicants have completed two years of college or technical training.

Building Trades Workers generally receive training through informal on-the-job training or formal apprenticeship programs. In apprenticeship programs, apprentices are employed full time as they learn on the job under journey or master trades workers. They also complete a minimum number of hours each year in classroom instruction, studying such subjects as mathematics and blueprint reading. For most skilled trades, apprenticeship programs are three to five years in length. Apprentices in programs registered with the U.S. Department of Labor are certified as journey level trades workers upon successful completion of their apprenticeships.

Apprenticeship programs may be sponsored by local unions or companies, or as a joint venture between a union and a company.

Special Requirements

Plumbers and electricians may be required to possess professional licensure.

Many employers prefer to hire applicants who hold a valid state driver's license or who are willing to obtain one within a certain time period.

Experience, Skills, and Personality Traits

Employers typically hire applicants who are journey Building Trades Workers with a few years of work experience related to the position for which they are applying. They are expected to be knowledgeable about the applicable safety codes and regulations pertaining to their line of work, such as plumbing or masonry.

Because they need to work well with coworkers, supervisors, and other people, Building Trades Workers need excellent teamwork, interpersonal, and communication skills. Having basic math, writing, reading, and computer skills is also important. In addition, these professionals must have strong self-management skills, such as the ability to work independently, follow and understand instructions, meet deadlines, handle stressful situations, and prioritize multiple tasks. Being flexible, self-motivated, creative, dependable, cooperative, persistent, alert, and assertive are some personality traits that successful Building Trades Workers share.

Unions and Associations

Building Trades Workers in higher education typically belong to a union that represents them in contract negotiations for better wages, employee benefits, and working conditions. The union also handles any grievances that trades workers may have about their employers.

Tips for Entry

1. To learn about apprenticeship programs in your area, talk with a school counselor or a job counselor at your state employment office. You may also be able to obtain information from a local union.
2. Working in temporary positions for academic institutions is one way for supervisors and managers to get to know you. You also gain valuable work experience which you can put on your résumé.
3. Develop a network of people—such as former coworkers and bosses, job counselors, friends, and hiring hall staff—whom you can contact about job openings.
4. Many college and university building trades departments have Web sites. To obtain a list of sites, enter one of these keywords in a search engine: *university building trades department* or *college building trades department*.

GROUNDSKEEPER

CAREER PROFILE

Duties: Perform routine gardening and grounds maintenance duties as required; may perform specialized function, such as pest control; perform other duties as required

Alternate Title(s): Grounds Maintenance Worker; a title that reflects a specialized function, such as Gardener or Irrigation Specialist

Salary Range: $15,000 to $33,000

Employment Prospects: Good

Advancement Prospects: Fair

Prerequisites:

Education or Training—High school diploma

Experience—No prior work experience needed for entry-level positions but experience usually preferred

Special Skills and Personality Traits—Reading, writing, math, self-management, and teamwork skills; be self-motivated, dependable, resourceful, cooperative

Special Requirements—Driver's license or pesticide applicator's permit may be required

CAREER LADDER

Specialist or Lead Groundskeeper

Groundskeeper (journey-level)

Groundskeeper Trainee

Position Description

Groundskeepers in colleges and universities are responsible for keeping campuses safe, clean, and attractive. These classified personnel may care for and maintain hundreds of landscaped acres throughout their campuses, as well as all athletic fields, recreational areas, woodland areas, arboretums, and gardens that belong to their institutions. They also maintain parking lots, roads, sidewalks, and pathways on campus. In addition, they prepare campuses for graduations and other special events.

Groundskeepers work in crews and are assigned to maintain a specific area of a campus. They perform daily, weekly, monthly, and seasonal routines, under the direction of crew leaders and the managers of the grounds maintenance departments. Their job assignments may involve the care and maintenance of turf (or lawns), trees, ornamental shrubs, plants, and flower beds. Some of their tasks may include mowing and edging lawns or fields; planting, fertilizing, cultivating, and watering lawns and a wide variety of plants, shrubs, trees, and flowers; trimming and pruning

trees and plants; removing weeds and brush; raking leaves; mulching; applying pesticides and herbicides; and installing irrigation and sprinkler systems.

Groundskeepers are also responsible for the upkeep of the grounds in their assigned areas. They may perform such tasks as removing plant debris from roofs, sewers, streets, and sidewalks; picking up and removing trash and litter from lawns, building entrances, parking lots, and roads; transporting litter, debris, and trash to the incinerator or dump; cleaning spills or stains in parking lots; filling potholes in streets; and cleaning street gutters and drains. In addition, they may be involved in repairing road signs, sidewalks, parking lots, fences, planters, benches, fountains, and so on. During winter, some Groundskeepers remove ice and snow from walkways, parking lots, and building entrances.

Another essential duty for Groundskeepers is equipment maintenance. They maintain a variety of mechanical and power tools and equipment, such as shovels, rakes, clippers, trimmers, saws, lawnmowers, and snowblowers, which they use to perform their various tasks. Some grounds staff are also responsible for maintaining trucks, small riding mowers, tractors, and other vehicles that they use for their work.

Grounds maintenance trainees perform basic ground work duties under the immediate supervision of experienced Groundskeepers. As they receive more training and gain experience, they are assigned to perform more complex tasks. Some senior Groundskeepers specialize in performing specific functions, such as pest control, irrigation, tree trimming, pruning, turf management, or horticultural work. Specialists usually hold a title, such as irrigation specialist, gardener, or pruner, that reflects their specialty.

Supervisory groundskeepers are responsible for the overall daily administration of the grounds maintenance at their campus. Some of their duties include inspecting grounds for future landscaping needs, preparing cost estimates for proposed projects, setting job priorities, planning work schedules, providing staff training and supervision, performing job evaluations, and reviewing work for quality and compliance with departmental procedures, institutional policies, and governmental regulations.

Groundskeepers mostly work outdoors in all types of weather, including rain, snow, and high temperature. Their work is physically demanding, which often requires long periods of walking, standing, bending, stooping, kneeling, crouching, crawling, and reaching. They also push, pull, and lift objects weighing up to 50 pounds or more. Some tasks require workers to handle toxic chemicals, such as fertilizers and pesticides. To ensure their safety, they wear protective clothing and follow standard procedures for handling dangerous chemicals.

Groundskeepers may be part-time or full-time classified staff employees. Some are hired for seasonal employment.

Salaries

Salaries for Groundskeepers in higher education vary, depending on such factors as their experience, education, employer, and geographical location. According to the November 2004 *Occupational Employment Statistics* survey, by the U.S. Bureau of Labor Statistics (BLS), the estimated annual salary for most groundskeeping workers ranged between $14,710 and $33,230.

Employment Prospects

The grounds maintenance department in colleges and universities is usually part of the physical plant division. Instead of employing in-house staff, some higher education institutions outsource their grounds maintenance services.

In addition to academic institutions, Groundskeepers are employed by schools, corporations, shopping malls, parks, apartment complexes, private home owners, and other organizations. Opportunities in general are favorable for Groundskeepers, as turnover is high because of low wages and the hard physical labor involved in this line of work. According to the BLS, employment for grounds maintenance workers is expected to increase by 21 to 35 percent through 2012.

Opportunities in colleges and universities usually become available as Groundskeepers retire, advance to higher positions, or transfer to other occupations. The ability of an institution to hire new or additional Groundskeepers as well as maintain the current level of its grounds maintenance staff is dependent on the availability of funds.

Advancement Prospects

Groundskeepers may be promoted to crew leader and supervisor positions. To advance to grounds manager positions, Groundskeepers usually need education beyond high school as well as extensive experience. With additional training and experience, Groundskeepers can become irrigation specialists, pest control specialists, gardeners, and tree trimmers.

Groundskeepers with entrepreneurial ambitions may start their own businesses, and offer lawn care and gardening services.

Education and Training

Minimally, applicants must possess a high school or general equivalency diploma. Some employers will hire applicants without such a diploma if they have qualifying work experience.

New employees usually receive on-the-job training from experienced Groundskeepers. Workers continually receive formal instruction or hands-on training to learn new job assignments.

Special Requirements

Applicants may be required to possess a valid driver's license. They may also need to possess the proper certification if their duties include the application of pesticides.

Experience, Skills, and Personality Traits

Entry-level positions may require little or no work experience; however, applicants should be able to identify plants and trees, have a basic knowledge of horticultural and goundskeeping practices, and be skilled in the use of common tools and equipment.

Groundskeepers need adequate reading, writing, and math skills. They must also have effective self-management skills, such as being able to work independently, prioritize multiple tasks, follow and understand instructions, and meet deadlines. In addition, they should have strong teamwork skills. Being self-motivated, dependable, resourceful, and cooperative are some personality traits that successful Groundskeepers share.

Unions and Associations

Groundskeepers in academic settings usually belong to a union that represents them in contract negotiations for better pay, benefits, and working conditions. A union also handles any grievances that its members may have against their employers.

Supervisory and administrative grounds staff are eligible to join the Professional Grounds Management Society to take advantage of networking opportunities and other professional resources and services. For contact information, see Appendix IV.

Tips for Entry

1. Learn as much as you can about horticulture and gardening. For example, you might grow a garden, read horticulture books, visit arboretums, enroll in gardening classes, or obtain a job at a nursery or with a grounds maintenance business.

2. Many colleges and universities hire Groundskeepers on a temporary basis throughout the year.

3. To enhance your employability and advancement prospects, obtain professional certification from such professional associations as the Professional Grounds Management Society.

4. Use the Internet to learn more about grounds maintenance in academic institutions. To get a list of relevant Web sites, enter either of these keywords in a search engine: *university grounds maintenance department* or *college grounds maintenance department.*

SCHOOL SPECIALISTS IN STUDENT SERVICES AND SPECIAL EDUCATION–RELATED SERVICES

SCHOOL NURSE

CAREER PROFILE

Duties: Provide first aid treatment; monitor students' health; provide health assessments and evaluations; provide health education and health counseling; perform other duties as required

Alternate Title(s): None

Salary Range: $28,000 to $49,000

Employment Prospects: Good

Advancement Prospects: Fair

Prerequisites:

Education or Training—Bachelor's degree; for school licensure, completion of an accredited school nurse program

Experience—One year of work experience as a registered nurse

Special Skills and Personality Traits—Communication, interpersonal, teamwork, problem-solving, organizational, and record-keeping skills; be calm, patient, sympathetic, caring, trustworthy, and respectful

Special Requirements—Registered nurse license; school nurse certification

CAREER LADDER

```
┌─────────────────────────────┐
│     Lead School Nurse       │
└─────────────────────────────┘

┌─────────────────────────────┐
│       School Nurse          │
└─────────────────────────────┘

┌─────────────────────────────┐
│         Student             │
└─────────────────────────────┘
```

Position Description

School Nurses contribute to a successful learning environment in public and private schools by promoting and providing quality health care to students. Based on school campuses, these registered nurses are especially trained to address the physical, mental, emotional, and social health of children and teenagers. Some School Nurses work in early childhood programs where they provide services to infants, toddlers, and pre-schoolers.

School Nurses coordinate various health services and health education programs on campuses throughout the school year. One area of responsibility is providing first aid treatment to students when they become ill or injured. Many School Nurses are also responsible for administering prescribed medications to students during the school day.

Another area of responsibility is monitoring students' health and maintaining their health records. School Nurses make sure that all students have received necessary immunizations, and notify parents to have their children get essential shots. Each year, School Nurses conduct or arrange for vision, hearing, scoliosis, growth, and other mandated screenings. When needed, School Nurses provide parents with referrals to medical doctors, opthalmologists, and other health care professionals.

If School Nurses suspect that students have disabilities that may be causing learning problems, they can refer students to a school assessment team. The team determines if students have any disabilities that may qualify them for the school's special education program.

In many schools, School Nurses may be part of a student assessment team to provide student health assessments and evaluations. School Nurses may also participate in developing Individualized Education Programs (IEPs) for special education students. An IEP outlines the goals and objectives for instruction and related services that School Nurses or other school specialists might provide.

Most School Nurses provide health education services to students, parents, and school staff. They are resource persons for teachers in health instruction. They may plan and conduct in-service training for teachers and other school staff. Some School Nurses are responsible for planning and teaching health classes to students. Many School Nurses also participate in developing health curriculum for their schools or districts. In addition, many School Nurses help school administrators develop procedures for school safety, accident prevention, and other health policies. For example, School Nurses may help plan in the control and prevention of colds, flu, and other communicable diseases.

Many School Nurses provide health counseling to students, individually or in small groups. They cover issues such as mental health problems, substance abuse, eating disorders, and pregnancy so that students can make responsible decisions about their health and lifestyles.

School Nurses perform various other duties. For example, they may assist in the investigation of cases of suspected child abuse and neglect.

School Nurses may be assigned to one or more schools. They may be full-time or part-time employees. Most School Nurses are contracted to work nine or 10 months. Many of them obtain summer jobs (such as nursing positions at summer camps) to supplement their income.

Salaries

Salaries for School Nurses vary, depending on such factors as their experience, education, employer, and geographical location. School Nurses typically earn lower wages than nurses working in hospitals and other settings. The Nurses for a Healthier Tomorrow, a coalition of nursing organizations, reports that most School Nurses earn between $28,000 and $49,000 per year.

Employment Prospects

School Nurses work for public and private schools, from preschools to high schools. Opportunities generally become available as individuals retire or transfer to other occupations. Most positions become available as School Nurses retire, resign, or advance to other positions. With the increasing number of students with special needs, the demand for School Nurses should be steady. However, the creation of new opportunities depends on the availability of school funding.

Advancement Prospects

Promotions within the school settings are limited to few supervisory and administrative positions; and those are mostly found in large schools and school districts. With additional education and licensure, School Nurses can become school nurse practitioners, which leads to higher pay and complex responsibilities.

Another career option is to work in other settings—hospitals, rehabilitation facilities, nursing homes, and so on. School nurses can also pursue other nursing specialties, such as clinical nurse specialists, certified nurse-midwives, or nurse practitioners. Still other options include becoming community college instructors or university professors.

Education and Training

School Nurses must have graduated from an accredited nursing program in which they earned a diploma, associate's degree, or bachelor's degree in nursing, depending on their state's requirement for registered nurses. In most states, a bachelor's degree is needed to obtain school nurse licensure.

To obtain school nurse licensure, registered nurses must complete an accredited school nurse program, which includes course work in education, health education, prevention of illness, health promotion, and health maintenance. In addition, students complete a supervised field practicum in one or more school settings.

Special Requirements

Most employers require that School Nurses be state licensed registered nurses. In addition, many states require that School Nurses in public schools and some private schools be licensed by the state board of education. Requirements for registered nurse and School Nurses licensure vary from state to state. For specific information, contact the nursing and education licensing boards for the state in which you wish to work.

Experience, Skills, and Personality Traits

Many schools require at least one year of work experience as a registered nurse, preferably in a school or other public health setting. Also, many schools prefer hiring School Nurses with some teaching experience.

To complete their many duties, School Nurses need effective communication, interpersonal, teamwork, problem-solving, organizational, and record-keeping skills.

Successful School Nurses share many personality traits, such as being calm, patient, sympathetic, caring, trustworthy, and respectful. They also genuinely enjoy being around schoolchildren and care for their well-being.

Unions and Associations

School Nurses might join the National Association of School Nurses, the American Nurses Association, or the American School Health Association in addition to other health care provider organizations. These professional associations provide School Nurses with services such as networking opportunities, information resources, education programs, and job listings. School Nurses in public schools may be represented by a union such as the National Education Association, which represents its members in contract negotiations for better pay, employee benefits, and working conditions.

For contact information for the above organizations, see Appendix IV.

Tips for Entry

1. In high school, you can begin preparing for a nursing career by taking classes in science, biology, chemistry, mathematics, psychology, and English.
2. Get experience working with children in health care settings. For example, you might volunteer at a hospital or health clinic.
3. As a nursing student, gain practical experience working in pediatrics as well as in community or public health settings.
4. To learn more about the School Nurse profession on the Internet, visit the National Association of School Nurses Web site at http://www.nasn.org.

EDUCATIONAL DIAGNOSTICIAN

CAREER PROFILE

Duties: Provide student assessments; help develop education plans for individual students; provide consultation services to parents and school staff; perform other duties as required

Alternate Title(s): Learning Disabilities Teacher-Consultant

Salary Range: $27,000 to $73,000

Employment Prospects: Good

Advancement Prospects: Fair

Prerequisites:

Education or Training—Master's degree; completion of an approved certification program

Experience—Three years as a classroom teacher

Special Skills and Personality Traits—Leadership, teamwork, interpersonal, and communication skills; be careful, logical, thorough, and sympathetic

Special Requirements—Teaching credential with an Educational Diagnostician (or Learning Disabilities Teacher-Consultant) endorsement

CAREER LADDER

```
┌─────────────────────────────────────┐
│     Student Services Coordinator     │
└─────────────────────────────────────┘

┌─────────────────────────────────────┐
│      Educational Diagnostician       │
└─────────────────────────────────────┘

┌─────────────────────────────────────┐
│               Teacher                │
└─────────────────────────────────────┘
```

Position Description

Educational Diagnosticians are specialists who determine if students' academic failures are due to learning problems, and if the basis of their learning problems is a learning disorder, or disability. A learning disability is caused by a condition, such as dyslexia, brain dysfunction, brain injury, or developmental aphasia, which affects the way the brain is able to process information. Thus a student with a learning disability would have trouble performing one or more of these skills: listening, speaking, reading, writing, spelling, or math. Learning disabled students may also have problems with paying attention, coordination, and self-control.

The job duties of Educational Diagnosticians vary from school to school; but, in general, their primary function is to perform student assessments as part of teams, which may be composed of teachers, administrators, school psychologists, school social workers, school nurses, and other school specialists. Different assessment teams determine whether students are eligible for special education, bilingual education, or other programs that may help students succeed academically in school. Team members work together to obtain an in-depth assessment of students referred by teachers, parents, administrators, or other school specialists. Each team member performs a student assessment according to his or her expertise.

When performing student assessments, Educational Diagnosticians administer several standardized tests to determine students' achievement levels in reading, writing, and math, as well as general information in science, social studies, and other subjects. They assess students' cognitive and sensory abilities in areas such as reasoning, comprehension, visual processing, and short-term memory. Upon completion of their assessments, Educational Diagnosticians write reports of their findings with recommendations to help the students succeed in school.

Many student assessments are performed for placement in special education programs. When a student is placed in a special education program, then the assessment team develops an Individualized Education Program (IEP) for the student. In general, the IEP describes the annual goals and learning objectives for the student, the types and amounts of special education instruction and related services (such as occupational therapy) that are needed, and the evaluation procedures for measuring the student's progress.

Educational Diagnosticians also provide consultation services to parents, teachers, and other school staff. For example, they might help individual teachers modify teaching methods and techniques for more effective instruction. Or, Educational Diagnosticians might help instructional supervisors develop in-service workshops that cover topics such as dyslexia, teaching strategies, and current laws such as the Individuals with Disabilities Act (IDEA).

As part of their job. Educational Diagnosticians write required correspondence, reports, and proposals. They also complete forms and other paperwork in compliance with federal and state laws as well as local education agency policies and procedures. In addition, they keep up with current legislation and research on testing methods, learning disabilities, and other topics and issues relevant to their field through individual study or continuing education.

Educational Diagnosticians may be assigned to one or more schools in a school system. They work 40 hours a week, and on occasion may work longer to attend meetings, complete paperwork, confer with parents, and so on.

Salaries

Salaries for Educational Diagnosticians vary, depending on such factors as their experience, education, job duties, employer, and geographical location. Most of them earn a salary based on their school's teacher or counselor pay schedule. According to the November 2004 *Occupational Employment Statistics* survey, by the U.S. Bureau of Labor Statistics, the estimated annual salary for most school counselors ranged between $26,610 and $72,970.

Employment Prospects

In addition to public and private schools. Educational Diagnosticians are employed by hospitals, corporate settings, private practices, and state and federal agencies.

The National Clearinghouse for Professions in Special Education reports that the job outlook for Educational Diagnosticians in schools looks favorable. Most positions become available as Educational Diagnosticians retire, resign, or advance to other positions. Because of the growing number of students who demonstrate learning problems, Educational Diagnosticians are continually needed to perform assessments and re-evaluations. Some experts report a shortage of this occupation in some states. However, the creation of new positions in schools is dependent on available funding.

Advancement Prospects

For many Educational Diagnosticians, advancement is realized by earning higher wages and receiving higher-level responsibilities such as supervisory or administrative tasks.

With advanced training and licensure. Educational Diagnosticians can become principals and school district administrators. Other career options include becoming professors, researchers, and consultants.

Education and Training

Most schools require that Educational Diagnosticians have a master's degree in education. To be licensed, Educational Diagnosticians must complete an accredited certification program, which includes a supervised internship and courses such as educational assessment, psychology of learning, and teaching strategies in special education.

Special Requirements

In public schools, Educational Diagnosticians must hold a valid teaching license, as well as hold an Educational Diagnostician, or learning disabilities teacher-consultant, endorsement. For specific information, contact the board of education for the state in which you wish to teach. See Appendix III for a list of state boards.

Experience, Skills, and Personality Traits

Most schools require that Educational Diagnosticians have three or more years of classroom teaching experience. To complete their various duties, Educational Diagnosticians need strong leadership, teamwork, interpersonal, and communication skills. Successful Educational Diagnosticians share several personality traits such as being careful, logical, thorough, and sympathetic.

Unions and Associations

The Council for Educational Diagnostic Service and the Learning Disabilities Association of America are two national associations that Educational Diagnosticians might join. These organizations offer the opportunity to network with colleagues, as well as to obtain services such as professional resources and education programs. For contact information for the above groups, see Appendix IV.

Tips for Entry

1. Talk with Educational Diagnosticians to learn more about their jobs.
2. As graduate students, attend professional conferences for Educational Diagnosticians to network with professionals in the field. Some of your contacts may be able to help you find a position when you begin your job search.
3. You can learn more about learning disabilities on the Internet. You might start by visiting the Learning Disabilities Association of America Web site http://www.ldanatl.org.

SCHOOL PSYCHOLOGIST

CAREER PROFILE

Duties: Provide psycho-educational assessments, counseling, crisis intervention, and consultation services; perform other duties as required

Alternate Title(s): None

Salary Range: $33,000 to $97,000

Employment Prospects: Good

Advancement Prospects: Fair

Prerequisites:

Education or Training—Master's, education specialist's, or doctoral degree; for school licensure, completion of an accredited credential program

Experience—Internship for one school year

Special Skills and Personality Traits—Interpersonal, teamwork, leadership, social, communication, organizational, time-management, and report-writing skills; be tactful, flexible, dependable, patient, and compassionate

Special Requirements—School Psychologist credential; may need state occupational license

CAREER LADDER

```
┌─────────────────────────────┐
│  Lead School Psychologist   │
└─────────────────────────────┘

┌─────────────────────────────┐
│    School Psychologist      │
└─────────────────────────────┘

┌─────────────────────────────┐
│           Intern            │
└─────────────────────────────┘
```

Position Description

School Psychologists are specialists in education as well as in child psychology and development. While working in school settings, they collaborate with parents, teachers, and other school staff to help preschoolers, children, and teenagers succeed academically, socially, and emotionally.

These school specialists may provide consultation, evaluation, intervention, prevention, and research and planning services to schools. Their responsibilities vary, according to the needs of the schools for which they work.

The primary responsibility for most School Psychologists is performing student assessments. For example, they may evaluate a student to determine his or her social and emotional development, mental health status, ability to learn, or eligibility for special services.

When performing assessments, School Psychologists use a combination of methods that include observing students in classrooms and playgrounds and reviewing students' school records. They also interview students and their parents and teachers, as well as have them complete questionnaires. In addition, School Psychologists administer a battery of tests to assess different areas such as intelligence, academic achievement, motor functioning, visual-motor perception, sensory impairments, emotional functioning, and personal adjustment.

In most schools, School Psychologists are part of assessment teams with teachers, administrators, and other specialists, such as social workers, speech-language pathologists, and school nurses. Each team member performs an assessment on a referred student according to his or her expertise. With the completed assessments, the team develops an intervention plan that may include placement of a student in a bilingual education, special education, or another program.

When students are placed in special education programs, School Psychologists—along with parents, teachers, and other school specialists who will be providing related services—develop Individualized Education Programs (IEPs) that outline the goals and learning objectives for the students. The IEPs also describe what related services, such as counseling, are to be provided.

Another area of responsibility for many School Psychologists is providing direct services to students and their families. They might provide individual or group counseling to students to help them with personal, social, or emotional problems. They might do interventions with students and their families to help solve conflicts that are related to learning and personal adjustment. School Psychologists also provide crisis intervention for all students and school staff after critical events, such as the sudden death of a student or in the aftermath of an act of violence in the school or community.

School Psychologists also provide consultation services to parents, teachers, and other school staff. For example, School Psychologists might work with parents to develop a behavior management plan for their children, or they might advise classroom teachers on strategies for motivating students in their classes. In addition, many School Psychologists develop and conduct workshops for teachers and parents. They cover such topics as child development, learning disabilities, substance abuse, self-esteem, and preventing crises.

Some School Psychologists are responsible for helping administrators develop school programs that provide students with a safer and better learning environment. The specialists may perform such tasks as evaluating academic programs, researching effective behavior management strategies, and identifying community services. Many School Psychologists also work with the school and community to design programs that help students who are at risk of failing in school.

As part of their job, School Psychologists write required correspondence, reports, and proposals. They also fill out forms and other paperwork in compliance with federal and state laws as well as local education agency policies and procedures. In addition, through independent reading, continuing education, and professional networking, they keep up with current issues, changes in state and federal laws, and developments in areas such as intervention strategies and working with parents.

School Psychologists may be assigned to work in one or more schools. They are employed part time or full time and often create their own work schedule. Usually, School Psychologists work more than a 40-hour week to complete paperwork, meet with parents, attend meetings, do research, and so on.

Salaries

Salaries for School Psychologists vary, depending on such factors as their experience, education, employer, and geographical location. Those with doctoral degrees typically earn higher wages. According to the U.S. Bureau of Labor Statistics (BLS), in its November 2004 *Occupational Employment Statistics* survey, the estimated annual salary for most School Psychologists ranged between $33,380 and $96,720.

Employment Prospects

Besides public and private schools, School Psychologists are employed by health centers, hospitals, clinics, private practices, community agencies, and universities.

The BLS reports that employment for School Psychologists is expected to increase by 21 to 35 percent through 2012. According to the National Association of School Psychologists, the job market is promising throughout the country due to the large number of School Psychologists becoming eligible for retirement within the next few years.

Advancement Prospects

Advancement opportunities are limited to few supervisory and administrative positions with student services or special education services. For many School Psychologists, advancement is realized by earning higher wages or taking on greater responsibilities.

An alternative career option for School Psychologists is to work in different settings, such as residential treatment facilities or community mental health centers. Some other options are: to work for private practices, start their own practices, or become researchers or university professors. To work independently in private practice, hospitals, and clinics, School Psychologists must possess a doctorate.

Education and Training

In addition to earning a master's degree in school psychology or a related field, future School Psychologists must complete a two- or three-year program that leads to an advanced graduate certificate, education specialist's degree, or doctoral degree. Their post master's degree program must include a field practicum. To obtain school licensure in some states, a one-year internship must be completed.

Special Requirements

In public schools, School Psychologists must hold a School Psychologist credential. To work in private schools, School Psychologists may need to be licensed from the state board of psychology. For more information about requirements, contact the education and psychology licensing boards for the state in which you wish to work. See Appendix III for a list of state boards of education.

Some states accept the professional credential of Nationally Certified School Psychologist (NCSP) granted by the National Association of School Psychologists as an alternative route to certification as a School Psychologist in public schools.

Experience, Skills, and Personality Traits

Entry-level applicants typically have gained practical experience through internships or a field practicum, which was part of their educational program.

Because they must work well with students, parents, school staff, and others, School Psychologists need strong interpersonal, teamwork skills, leadership, social, and communication skills. They also need organizational, time-management, and report-writing skills to complete their various duties. Some personality traits that successful School Psychologists share are being flexible, tactful, dependable, patient, and compassionate.

Unions and Associations

In addition to state and local professional organizations, School Psychologists might join the National Association of School Psychologists and the American Psychological Association. These associations provide a variety of services, such as networking opportunities, professional resources, continuing education programs, and job listings. (For contact information, see Appendix IV.)

Tips for Entry

1. Get experience working with children with disabilities. For example, you might volunteer in special education classrooms and with groups such as the Special Olympics.

2. Before committing yourself to a graduate or doctorate program in school psychology, be sure you know what the field is about. Talk with School Psychologists to learn what their workday is like, what challenges they face, and so on.

3. Some states will grant emergency or provisional licenses to individuals who have not completed their school psychology program, if they have been offered positions at schools that cannot find qualified, credentialed School Psychologists.

4. Learn more about school psychology on the Internet. You might start by visiting these Web sites: National Association of School Psychologists, http://www.nasponline.org, and School Psychology Resources Online, http://www.schoolpsychology.net.

SCHOOL SOCIAL WORKER

CAREER PROFILE

Duties: Provide counseling, referrals, and other social work services to students and their families; provide student assessments; perform other duties as required

Alternate Title(s): None

Salary Range: $23,000 to $58,000

Employment Prospects: Good

Advancement Prospects: Limited

Prerequisites:

Education or Training—Bachelor's or master's degree; for school licensure, completion of an accredited credential program

Experience—Previous social work experience with children, adolescents, and their families

Special Skills and Personality Traits—Communication, listening, interpersonal, teamwork, organizational, and report-writing skills; be independent, responsible, committed, sympathetic, sensitive, objective, respectful

Special Requirements—School Social Worker certification; may need a state license or be state certified or registered

CAREER LADDER

```
┌─────────────────────────────────┐
│   Lead School Social Worker      │
└─────────────────────────────────┘

┌─────────────────────────────────┐
│     School Social Worker         │
└─────────────────────────────────┘

┌─────────────────────────────────┐
│ Graduate Student or Social Worker│
└─────────────────────────────────┘
```

Position Description

School Social Workers are another type of school specialist who work in public and private school settings to help students who are at risk of failing. They work with students who have learning, emotional, behavioral, or health problems. The students may be preschoolers (including infants and toddlers), children, or teenagers.

Typically, School Social Workers act as school liaisons between schools and families. They contact parents to discuss students' problems and to get their support for students' needs. School Social Workers may identify community resources that can help students and their families with their problems, providing referrals as well.

School Social Workers generally manage a caseload that may include both general education students and special education students. Each case begins with an assessment to determine a student's needs and what resources would best meet those needs. Through individual or small group work, these social workers help students deal with homelessness,

child abuse, neglect, family conflicts, pregnancy, substance abuse, and other issues.

Most School Social Workers are part of assessment teams that determine if students are eligible for special education programs or other programs. Social Workers are responsible for providing social history assessments that cover areas such as students' family life, school history, and emotional behavior.

School Social Workers perform other duties, which vary from school to school. They might:

- assist in developing Individualized Education Programs (IEPs) for special education students
- plan and facilitate in-service workshops for teachers, covering topics such as violence prevention, parenting issues, and compulsory attendance
- help develop school programs such as peer counseling
- provide consultations with individual teachers
- give classroom presentations on topics such as substance abuse

- monitor student attendance records
- network with social agencies, employment offices, health care providers, community agencies, and so on

Furthermore, School Social Workers help all students and staff during critical times, such as after an act of violence, natural disaster, or other crisis in the school or community.

In addition, School Social Workers are responsible for completing various reports, forms, and other paperwork in compliance with state and government laws and local education agencies' policies and procedures. Through independent study, continuing education, and professional networking, they stay current with school issues, changes in legislation, and new research in their field.

School Social Workers may be assigned to one or more schools. Some School Social Workers work exclusively with special education students. Most School Social Workers work beyond their 40-hour week to meet with parents, attend meetings, handle emergencies, and complete various tasks.

Salaries
Salaries for School Social Workers vary, depending on such factors as their education, experience, employer, and geographical location. According to the U.S. Bureau of Labor Statistics, in its November 2004 *Occupational Employment Statistics* survey, the estimated annual salary for most social workers, in general, ranged between $23,470 and $58,410.

Employment Prospects
School Social Workers are mostly employed by local education agencies, including local school districts, regional school agencies, and special education agencies.

Opportunities vary nationwide. In general, the field of school social work is growing steadily, partly due to the increasing enrollment in special education programs. However, the ability to create new positions or hire replacements in a school district is dependent on the availability of funding.

Advancement Prospects
For many School Social Workers, advancement is realized by earning higher wages and receiving higher-level responsibilities such as supervisory or administrative tasks. In some states, School Social Workers can become school administrators with advanced education and licensure.

School Social Workers might choose to work in other settings, such as health care, family services, or corrections. Some other career paths they might pursue are becoming university professors or researchers, or going into private practice.

Education and Training
Educational requirements vary from state to state. Most states require School Social Workers to have a master's degree in social work (MSW) earned from a graduate program accredited by a nationally recognized agency such as the Council of Social Work Education. MSW graduates are trained to perform assessments and case management; individual, family, and group counseling; and supervisory and administrative duties. In some states, School Social Workers must complete an accredited education program that leads to school licensure.

Special Requirements
Some states require School Social Workers to be licensed, certified, or registered with the state social work licensing board. Other states require social work certification from the state board of education. Many states require both a state license and school social work certification. Contact the social work and teacher licensing boards for the state in which you wish to practice for information. See Appendix III for a list of state teacher licensing boards.

Experience, Skills, and Personality Traits
Typically, employers choose candidates who have previous social work experience providing services to children, adolescents, and their families. Many schools hire MSW graduates who completed their field placement in school, child welfare, or similar settings.

Because they must work well with students, parents, school staff, and others, School Social Workers need excellent communication, listening, interpersonal, and teamwork skills. They also need strong organizational and report-writing skills in order to complete their various duties.

Successful School Social Workers have several personality traits in common, such as being independent, responsible, committed, sympathetic, sensitive, and objective.

Unions and Associations
Most School Social Workers join professional associations to take advantage of professional resources and services such as education programs, networking opportunities, and job listings. Two national groups that many join are the School Social Work Association of America and the National Association of Social Workers. For contact information, see Appendix IV.

Tips for Entry
1. Gain experience working with children and adolescents in school, community, or other settings.
2. To enhance your employability, you may want to obtain the Certified School Social Work Specialist credential granted by the National Association of Social Workers. To learn more, visit NASW at its Web site at http://www.naswdc.org.
3. Learn more about social work and school social work on the Internet. You might start by using these keywords in a search engine to find relevant Web sites: *social work* or *school social work*.

SPEECH-LANGUAGE PATHOLOGIST

CAREER PROFILE

Duties: Provide assessments and treatments for speech and language disorders; perform other duties as required

Alternate Title(s): None

Salary Range: $36,000 to $84,000

Employment Prospects: Good

Advancement Prospects: Fair

Prerequisites:

Education or Training—Master's degree; for school licensure, completion of an accredited certification program

Experience—Clinical field placement

Special Skills and Personality Traits—Interpersonal, teamwork, communication, report-writing, organizational, and management skills; be warm, patient, tolerant, persistent, resourceful, and creative

Special Requirements—A state license or other requirement; school credential; Certificate of Clinical Competence in Speech-Language Pathology (CCC-SLP) certification

CAREER LADDER

```
┌─────────────────────────────────────┐
│  Lead Speech-Language Pathologist    │
└─────────────────────────────────────┘

┌─────────────────────────────────────┐
│    Speech-Language Pathologist       │
└─────────────────────────────────────┘

┌─────────────────────────────────────┐
│         Graduate Student             │
└─────────────────────────────────────┘
```

Position Description

Speech-Language Pathologists are employed by many public and private schools to help students who are at risk of failing because of speech and language disorders. For example, students may be unable to speak clearly, may have stuttering or other speech problems, may have trouble understanding and producing language, or may have an attention, memory, or other cognitive communication disorder. Students' speech and language problems may be congenital, developmental, or acquired, and may have resulted from a cleft palate, stroke, brain injury, cerebral palsy, voice pathology, emotional problems, or mental retardation.

These school specialists are assigned to work with preschoolers, elementary-age children, or teenagers. They are responsible for diagnosing students for speech and language disorders, and for providing intervention when needed. They develop treatment plans that fit each student's particular needs.

They work with students individually or in small groups, one or more times a week. Speech-Language Pathologists also work with teachers to develop teaching strategies that may help students improve their communication development and participation in class. Additionally they collaborate with students' families to provide treatment plans, as well as give them progress reports. They also provide families with counseling related to speech and language issues. When needed, they may refer students and families with other complicated issues to other professionals, such as the school social worker or school psychologist.

Another major responsibility for Speech-Language Pathologists is conducting thorough and balanced assessments. Usually, they are part of assessment teams, which vary and differ from school to school. Some teams provide assessments to develop intervention strategies for teachers to address the learning needs and interests of students. Other teams do evaluations to determine if students have disabilities that qualify them for special education programs or other programs. Some teams develop Individualized Education Programs (IEPs) for special education students.

Speech-Language Pathologists use a variety of tools when doing an assessment. That includes reviewing pertinent school records, collecting and reviewing samples of students' work, observing students, and sometimes interviewing students. Speech-Language Pathologists may have parents and teachers complete checklists, surveys, and questionnaires about the students along with interviewing the teachers and parents.

Speech-Language Pathologists also administer standardized tests to measure skills such as language comprehension; following directions; use of syntax, semantics, and morphology; and auditory processing of language. In addition, they diagnose functions such as articulation, fluency, and swallowing.

Speech-Language Pathologists perform various other duties as required. For example, they might conduct in-service workshops and provide consultation services to school staff; or they might be assigned the case manager for individual IEPs, which involves such tasks as scheduling and coordinating assessments, monitoring progress of each IEP, and completing documentation.

Speech-Language Pathologists must complete a lot of paperwork in compliance with federal and state laws as well as local education agency policies and procedures. For example, they prepare assessment reports, IEPs, lesson plans, treatment notes, and progress reports, and fill out various forms. Speech-Language Pathologists also are responsible for keeping up with current legislation and developments in their field.

Speech-Language Pathologists may be employed part time or full time by schools. Some are in private practices and work for schools on a contractual basis.

Salaries

Salaries for Speech-Language Pathologists vary, depending on such factors as their education, experience, employer, and geographical location. The U.S. Bureau of Labor Statistics (BLS) reports in its November 2004 *Occupational Employment Statistics* (OES) survey that the estimated annual salary for most Speech-Language Pathologists ranged between $35,820 and $84,310. The estimated annual mean salary was $51,920 for those who worked in elementary and secondary schools.

Employment Prospects

Besides schools, Speech-Language Pathologists work for hospitals, home care health agencies, adult day care centers, rehabilitation centers, health care facilities, industry, research laboratories, and private practices.

An estimated 49,250 Speech-Language Pathologists were employed in elementary and secondary schools, according to the BLS's November 2004 OES survey. The BLS also reports that employment for this occupation is expected to increase by 21 to 35 percent through 2012. Opportunities should be favorable in school settings. This is partly due to the growing number of special education students who need related services, which must be provided to all eligible schoolchildren between the ages of three and 21.

Advancement Prospects

Advancement opportunities in schools are limited to lead and supervisor positions. With additional education and credentials, Speech-Language Pathologists can become school administrators.

Another career option is to work in other settings, such as hospitals and rehabilitation centers. Some other career paths include becoming university professors, academic researchers, or laboratory researchers.

Education and Training

Speech-Language Pathologists need at least a master's degree in speech-language pathology to obtain both a state license and the Certificate of Clinical Competence in Speech-Language Pathologic (CCC-SLP) certification, which is granted by the American Speech-Language-Hearing Association. In many states, Speech-Language Pathologists must complete an approved teacher education program leading up to school licensure. The program generally includes a supervised field practicum and course work in areas such as education, psychology, and classroom instruction and management.

Special Requirements

In most states, Speech-Language Pathologists must either register with the state or hold a state license. Many states also require school-based Speech-Language Pathologists to hold a pupil services or clinical rehabilitative services credential. Some states require them to hold a teaching license as well. Speech-Language Pathologists may also be required to possess the CCC-SLP certification. To learn about requirements for the state in which you wish to practice, contact the state's education and speech-language pathologist licensing boards. See Appendix III for a list of state education boards.

Experience, Skills, and Personality Traits

Entry-level Speech-Language Pathologists must have completed clinical field placement in school settings. In some states, they must also have previous teaching experience.

Some skills that Speech-Language Pathologists need for their work are interpersonal, teamwork, communication, report-writing, organizational, and management skills.

Successful Speech-Language Pathologists share several personality traits, such as being warm, patient, tolerant, persistent, creative, and resourceful. In addition, they enjoy working with children.

Union and Associations

The American Speech-Language-Hearing Association and the Council for Exceptional Children are two national professional associations that Speech-Language Pathologists might join. These organizations provide services such as professional resources, continuing education programs, and networking opportunities. See Appendix IV for contact information.

Tips for Entry

1. In high school, you can begin preparing for a career in speech-language pathology by taking science, English, and speech classes.
2. To obtain licensure, individuals must also pass a national examination on speech-language pathology.
3. When you begin your job search, network with colleagues, professors, alumni, friends, and others who may know about job openings.
4. You can learn more about speech-language pathology on the Internet. To start, use the keyword *speech-language pathology* in any search engine to find relevant Web sites.

SCHOOL OCCUPATIONAL THERAPIST

CAREER PROFILE

Duties: Provide student assessments, intervention, and treatment plans; perform other duties as required

Alternate Title(s): None

Salary Range: $38,000 to $83,000

Employment Prospects: Good

Advancement Prospects: Fair

Prerequisites:

Education or Training—Bachelor's or master's degree in occupational therapy

Experience—Clinical internship in school settings

Special Skills and Personality Traits—Interpersonal, teamwork, problem-solving, communication, organizational, and management skills; be patient, respectful, tactful, creative, and energetic

Special Requirements—State license; school credential and professional certification

CAREER LADDER

```
┌─────────────────────────────────────────┐
│   Lead School Occupational Therapist     │
└─────────────────────────────────────────┘

┌─────────────────────────────────────────┐
│      School Occupational Therapist       │
└─────────────────────────────────────────┘

┌─────────────────────────────────────────┐
│                 Intern                   │
└─────────────────────────────────────────┘
```

Position Description

School Occupational Therapists are specialists who help students at risk of failing because they have insufficient motor and self-help skills to function in the school environment. For example, students may have difficulty processing sensory information or may need assistance to move about. It is the job of these school-based occupational therapists to analyze and adapt daily activities in the school setting so that students can develop needed skills to succeed academically, socially, and personally.

School Occupational Therapists are assigned a caseload of students who may range in age from infants to young adults. Some specialists work exclusively with students in special education programs. (Those working with infants and toddlers may conduct their activities in private homes or child care settings.) They are responsible for screening and evaluating skills that can affect school performance. They also identify students' weak and strong areas, as well as develop intervention plans and monitor students' progress.

These specialists work with students individually or in small groups. They create purposeful and age-appropriate activities that help students develop and practice the skills they lack or in which they are limited—such as motor, visual perception, handwriting skills, organizational, con-

centration, problem-solving, and daily living skills. The therapy is incorporated into daily lessons as well as play activities. Students may do paper-and-pencil exercises and physical exercises, as well as use computers.

School Occupational Therapists also help students by rearranging their work spaces or modifying their environment in the classroom in other ways. In addition, they provide students with adaptive equipment, such as special seats, splints, and wheelchairs, and instruct them and their teachers and parents on their use.

As part of their duties, School Occupational Therapists communicate with parents. They inform parents of their children's progress. They also suggest activities that parents can do with their children at home to develop and improve their skills.

School Occupational Therapists also provide consultation services to teachers and other school staff. For example, they might suggest strategies for teachers to use with students who have short attention spans. Or, they might help school administrators make schools more accessible to children in wheelchairs and walkers.

School Occupational Therapists usually are part of student assessment teams that may be composed of general education teachers, special education teachers, parents, school psychologists, school nurses, and other school specialists. Some teams use student assessments to develop intervention strategies for general education teachers. Other teams do evaluations to determine if students have disabilities that qualify them for special education programs. Some teams develop Individualized Education Programs (IEPs) for special education students. The IEPs outline the goals and objectives for instruction and related services, such as those offered by the Occupational Therapist.

Their job requires completing assessment reports, IEPs, treatment notes, progress reports, forms, and other paperwork in compliance with federal and state laws as well as local education agency policies and procedures. School Occupational Therapists also are responsible for keeping up with current legislation and developments in their field.

School Occupational Therapists may be assigned to work at one or more schools. They may be part-time or full-time employees. Some School Occupational Therapists work for private practices and so provide their services on a contractual basis.

Salaries

Salaries for School Occupational Therapists vary, depending on such factors as their experience, education, employer, and geographical location. The U.S. Bureau of Labor Statistics (BLS) reports, in its November 2004 *Occupational Employment Statistics* survey, that the estimated annual salary for most occupational therapists ranged between $38,130 and $83,150. The estimated annual mean wage for professionals working in elementary and secondary schools was $51,410.

Employment Prospects

Besides private and public schools, School Occupational Therapists work in child care centers, community agencies, and private practices. Opportunities for School Occupational Therapists are favorable because of the demand for services in growing special education programs. The BLS reports that employment for occupational therapists, in general, should increase by 21 to 35 percent through 2012.

Advancement Prospects

Promotions in schools are limited to lead and supervisory positions. With continuing education and additional licensure, School Occupational Therapists can become school administrators such as special education directors. They can also become university professors and researchers, or start their own private practice.

Education and Training

School Occupational Therapists need either a bachelor's or master's degree in occupational therapy. Occupational ther-

apy majors study subjects such as anatomy, kinesiology, neurology, psychology, and occupational therapy theory and techniques. They also complete clinical internships.

In many states, School Occupational Therapists must complete an approved teacher education program leading up to school licensure, which includes a supervised field practicum.

Special Requirements

School Occupational Therapists must hold a state license for occupational therapists. To work in public schools, they must also be licensed by the state board of education. In addition, schools may require these specialists to hold the Occupational Therapist Registered (OTR) certification, granted by the National Board for Certification in Occupational Therapy, Inc.

For specific information about licensing and certification, contact the occupational therapy and education licensing agencies for the state where you wish to practice. See Appendix III for a list of state boards of education.

Experience, Skills, and Personality Traits

Entry-level applicants must have completed a clinical internship, preferably in a school setting.

To perform their work effectively, School Occupational Therapists need strong interpersonal, teamwork, problem-solving, communication, organizational, and management skills. Being patient, respectful, tactful, creative, and energetic are a few of the personality traits that successful School Occupational Therapists share.

Unions and Associations

Occupational Therapists might join the American Occupational Therapy Association and the Council for Exceptional Children as well as local and state professional associations. These groups provide opportunities for networking with colleagues and taking advantage of continuing education programs and other professional services. See Appendix IV for contact information for the above groups.

Tips for Entry

1. You can prepare for a career in occupational therapy while in high school by taking these courses: biology, chemistry, physics, health, art, and social studies.
2. Talk with School Occupational Therapists to learn more about their profession. Call local school district offices to find out how to contact professionals in your area.
3. Learn more about occupational therapy on the Internet. You might start by visiting the American Occupational Therapy Association Web site at http://www.aota.org.

ART THERAPIST

CAREER PROFILE

Duties: Use the combination of art and therapy to provide intervention and treatment plans; provide student assessments; perform other duties as requested

Alternate Title(s): None

Salary Range: $25,000 to $60,000

Employment Prospects: Fair

Advancement Prospects: Fair

Prerequisites:

    Education or Training—Master's degree in art therapy, art, or related field

    Experience—Internship in school settings or other settings with children

    Special Skills and Personality Traits—Interpersonal, teamwork, organizational, communication, and report-writing skills; be calm, patient, attentive, trustworthy, and compassionate

    Special Requirements—A state art therapist or counseling license; school credential in some states; Registered Art Therapist (ATR) or Registered Art Therapist, Board Certified (ATR-BC) certification

CAREER LADDER

```
┌─────────────────────────────────┐
│     Owner of private practice    │
└─────────────────────────────────┘

┌─────────────────────────────────┐
│         Art Therapist            │
└─────────────────────────────────┘

┌─────────────────────────────────┐
│        Graduate Student          │
└─────────────────────────────────┘
```

Position Description

Art Therapists are specialists who work in school settings. They help children—preschoolers to high schoolers—whose behavioral problems, emotional problems, or developmental disabilities are interfering with their ability to learn successfully. As mental health professionals, Art Therapists incorporate art and its creative process with traditional therapy.

Art has proven to be a useful tool in the assessment of children's mental health as well as in intervention. Many children often are unable or unwilling to express themselves verbally. Art, as a form of communication, may be one way that children can express their thoughts and emotions. Through their artwork and the artistic process, children may be able to express feelings that are too difficult to talk about while gaining insight into what may be troubling them.

Art Therapists work with individual students or with small groups of students. They give crayons, paints, chalk, clay, and other art materials to students, and encourage the students to express themselves in any art form. They might direct students in the type of project to do or have them decide on their own. Therapists also nurture students' creativity, letting them discover positive self-expression through personal artwork. In so doing, the students' confidence and self-esteem increase.

When an artwork (drawing, painting, sculpture, collage, etc.) is completed, the Art Therapist studies the piece and determines what symbolic images or themes may be present. Depression, aggression, fear, frustration, or other emotions, for example, may be expressed through color, form, and other art elements. The Art Therapist discusses the artwork with the child.

Art Therapists also use the art process to help children develop, improve, and maintain abstract thinking skills, social skills, communication skills, and coping skills along with discovering personal feelings and self-awareness.

Many Art Therapists work exclusively with special education students. Their duties may include being part of assessment teams that determine if students are eligible for special education programs. Art Therapists may also help in developing Individualized Education Programs (IEPs) for special education students with whom they will work. The IEPs outline the goals and learning objectives for instruction as well as for treatment plans by art therapists and other specialists.

Many Art Therapists provide consultation services to parents, teachers, and other school staff. Some may plan and conduct in-service workshops for teachers and administrators.

As part of their job, Art Therapists complete reports and fill out forms and other paperwork in compliance with federal and state laws as well as local education agency policies and procedures. They also provide oral or written progress reports for parents. In addition, Art Therapists make sure they have a sufficient supply of art media and materials for sessions and maintain safe and usable art tools and equipment.

Art Therapists are employed part time or full time by schools. Some Art Therapists have private practices and provide services on a contractual basis. In addition, many Art Therapists continue with their careers as artists.

Salaries

Salaries for Art Therapists vary, depending on such factors as their experience, job duties, employer, and geographical location. The American Art Therapy Association reports that the median annual income for Art Therapists ranges between $28,000 and $38,000. Entry-level salaries generally start at about $25,000 per year, while top salaries for salaried administrators range between $40,000 and $60,000.

Employment Prospects

Besides schools, Art Therapists work in residential facilities, adult day care centers, hospitals, mental health facilities, rehabilitation centers, and correctional institutions. Some Art Therapists have their own private practices.

Art therapy is a small, but growing field. Schools are reporting increased use of Art Therapists as part of the related services that schools offer with special education programs.

Advancement Prospects

Art Therapists who work for schools have few opportunities to advance to supervisory and administrative positions. Promotions, however, may mean leaving clinical practice. Those with advanced degrees have the option to teach and do research at the college and university level. With state licensure, Art Therapists can go into private practice.

Education and Training

Art Therapists must have a master's degree in art therapy, in art with an emphasis in art therapy, or in a related field with at least 21 semester units in art therapy. Most art therapy graduate programs are two years long and include course work in art therapy, psychology, and studio art, as well as a supervised field practicum.

Special Requirements

To work in public schools, Art Therapists may be required to possess a school specialist credential. To find out what may be required for the state where you wish to practice, contact the state education board. See Appendix III for a list of state boards.

Most Art Therapists obtain professional certification through the Art Therapy Credentials Board, Inc. The Registered Art Therapist (ATR) and Registered Art Therapist, Board Certified (ATR-BC) credentials are recognized standards for the profession. To qualify for the ATR credential, individuals must complete 1,000 hours of postgraduate paid experience under the supervision of an ATR.

Experience, Skills, and Personality Traits

Entry-level Art Therapists in school must have completed an internship, preferably in a school setting or other settings that involved working with children.

Art Therapists need interpersonal, teamwork, organizational, communication, and report-writing skills to complete the many different tasks they must perform. Successful Art Therapists share several personality traits such as being calm, patient, attentive, trustworthy, and compassionate.

Unions and Associations

Art Therapists might join the American Art Therapy Association or the National Coalition of Creative Arts Therapies Associations. Both organizations provide professional services such as education programs, professional resources, and opportunities for networking with colleagues. For contact information, see Appendix IV.

Tips for Entry

1. Get experience working in a special education program, hospital, rehabilitation center, or other setting to find out if art therapy is the right field for you.
2. Use the Internet as a tool when you do a job search. For example, you might create your own home page to post your resume.
3. Develop a network of professional contacts whom you can call, write, or e-mail about job openings.
4. Use the Internet to learn more about art therapy. You might start by visiting the American Art Therapy Association Web site at http://www.arttherapy.org.

COUNSELORS

SCHOOL COUNSELOR

CAREER PROFILE

Duties: Provide academic, vocational, and personal counseling services to students; provide consultation and case management services; perform other duties as required

Alternate Title(s): Guidance Counselor; a title, such as Elementary School Counselor or High School Counselor, that reflects a school level

Salary Range: $27,000 to $73,000

Employment Prospects: Good

Advancement Prospects: Fair

Prerequisites:

Education or Training—Bachelor's or master's degree; for licensed School Counselors, completion of an educational administration program

Experience—One to five years of classroom teaching experience

Special Skills and Personality Traits—Organizational, time-management, writing, communication, interpersonal, teamwork, conflict resolution, and computer skills; caring, gentle, firm, nonjudgmental, tolerant, patient, and flexible

Special Requirements—School counseling credential

CAREER LADDER

```
┌─────────────────────────────┐
│   Senior School Counselor   │
└─────────────────────────────┘

┌─────────────────────────────┐
│      School Counselor       │
└─────────────────────────────┘

┌─────────────────────────────┐
│      Classroom Teacher      │
└─────────────────────────────┘
```

Position Description

School Counselors are responsible for addressing the educational, vocational, social, and personal needs of schoolchildren. These professional counselors work with teachers, administrators, and families to help students succeed in school. They may be assigned to work with elementary, middle, junior high, or high school students.

Because students' development and interests differ with age, School Counselors at the different school levels focus on different needs. Elementary and middle school counselors do more individual and small group counseling around personal and social matters. They also do large group guidance activities in the classrooms, covering topics such as life skills, coping skills, and career exploration.

High School Counselors mostly address academic and vocational needs. In particular, they help high school students explore vocational and career options. For example, they might advise students about different types of colleges, technical schools, and apprenticeships; arrange for job shadowing or college tours; or assist with admissions applications and financial aid forms. High school counselors also help students develop job search skills such as resume writing and interviewing techniques.

Another major responsibility of School Counselors is to provide consultation services to teachers, administrators, school psychologists, school social workers, and other school staff. They conduct consultations with families, community agencies, social service agencies, and others. In addition, School Counselors provide in-service training to teachers and administrators on child development issues, behavioral management techniques, and other topics.

Case management is another area of responsibility for most School Counselors. This includes coordinating meetings between parents, teachers, and other school personnel regarding individual children. It also involves helping families obtain services for their children through referrals to social service agencies, community agencies, health care professionals, and other agencies.

Counselors perform many other duties that may include:

- providing special services, such as alcohol and drug prevention programs or peer mediation programs
- providing crisis counseling to students and school staff when critical events occur
- developing a network of therapists, health care professionals, social service agencies, and others to refer students and their families
- performing student assessments as part of pupil services or special services teams
- coordinating and administering standard tests
- operating career guidance centers
- following up on students with attendance problems
- registering and scheduling new students
- participating in school meetings and on school committees
- sponsoring extracurricular activities

Most School Counselors have a 10-month school schedule, usually from September to June. They frequently work long days to complete their many tasks.

Salaries

Salaries for School Counselors vary, depending on such factors as their education, experience, employer, and geographical location. The U.S. Bureau of Labor Statistics (BLS) reports in its November 2004 *Occupational Employment Statistics* (OES) survey that the estimated annual salary for most School Counselors ranged between $26,610 and $72,970. The estimated annual mean wage was $52,590.

Employment Prospects

School Counselors are employed in both public and private school systems. According to the BLS's November 2004 OES survey, about 119,700 counselors were employed in elementary and secondary schools throughout the United States. It reports that employment for School Counselors should increase by 10 to 20 percent through 2012. In addition to job growth, opportunities will become available as counselors retire, advance to higher positions, or transfer to other jobs. However, the ability for employers to hire new or additional School Counselors depends on the availability of funds.

Advancement Prospects

School Counselors can advance to supervisory and management positions as instructional supervisors in counseling, directors of guidance and counseling, and directors of pupil services.

With additional education and licensure, they can become school psychologists, school social workers, or school administrators. Other options include specializing in other counseling fields such as rehabilitation counseling, career counseling, and marriage and family therapy.

Education and Training

Most employers prefer to hire applicants who possess a master's degree in counseling, educational psychology, or another related field.

Licensed School Counselors must have completed an approved school guidance and counseling program which leads to licensure in the state where they practice. The program includes course work in developmental guidance and counseling, child psychology, individual and group counseling techniques, and pupil appraisal and evaluation techniques. It also includes a supervised field practicum in school settings.

Special Requirements

In public schools, School Counselors must hold a valid school counselor credential. Some states require that public School Counselors also hold a teaching credential. For specific information, contact the state board of education in the state where you wish to work. See Appendix III for a list of state boards.

Many private schools require state licensure or professional certification from school accreditation organizations, professional associations, or other recognized organizations.

Experience, Skills, and Personality Traits

Generally, schools require that School Counselors have one to five years of classroom teaching experience. Employers may accept previous school counseling experience or supervised school counseling internship as a substitution for some or all of the teaching requirement.

To perform their jobs effectively, School Counselors need adequate organizational, time-management, and writing skills. They also need strong communication, interpersonal, teamwork, and conflict resolution skills to work well with students, teachers, administrators, parents, and others. In addition, School Counselors should have sufficient computer skills, including knowledge of computer databases and the Internet. Successful School Counselors share several personality traits, such as being caring, gentle, firm, nonjudgmental, tolerant, patient, and flexible.

Unions and Associations

School Counselors join professional associations to take advantage of services such as professional resources, continuing education programs, and networking opportunities. At the national level, they might join the American School Counselor Association and the American Counseling Association.

Many School Counselors also join educator organizations that serve their particular interests, such as the Council for Exceptional Children, the National Association for the Education of Young Children, or the National Middle School Association.

School Counselors in public schools are eligible to join their school's teacher union, such as the American Federation of Teachers or the National Education Association.

For contact information for the above organizations, see Appendix IV.

Tips for Entry

1. You can gain valuable experience by participating in peer counseling programs sponsored by your school, community center, church, youth agency, or other community organization.
2. Join professional associations, and network with members to learn about current or upcoming job vacancies. Many organizations have student memberships.
3. Before you apply for a position, do your homework about a school and the community it serves. For example, learn what types of problems and issues that the school is handling.
4. Use the Internet to earn more about the school counseling field. To get a list of relevant Web sites, enter either of these keywords in a search engine: *school counselors* or *school counseling.*

CAREER COUNSELOR
(COLLEGE OR UNIVERSITY)

CAREER PROFILE

Duties: Provide career counseling and job search coaching; perform other duties as required

Alternate Title(s): Career Adviser, Career Development Counselor

Salary Range: $27,000 to $73,000

Employment Prospects: Fair

Advancement Prospects: Fair

Prerequisites:

Education or Training—Master's degree

Experience—Prior experience in career counseling and career programs; experience working in college settings

Special Skills and Personality Traits—Organizational, project management, writing, communication, presentation, interpersonal, teamwork, customer service, and computer skills; be patient, objective, friendly, tactful, sincere, trustworthy, flexible, and creative

CAREER LADDER

```
┌─────────────────────────────┐
│   Senior Career Counselor    │
└─────────────────────────────┘

┌─────────────────────────────┐
│      Career Counselor        │
└─────────────────────────────┘

┌─────────────────────────────┐
│           Intern             │
└─────────────────────────────┘
```

Position Description

Career Counselors in colleges and universities are responsible for providing career services to students and alumni. These professional counselors work in career centers, which house a variety of career and job resources.

Career Counselors are involved in different areas of work. One major area is providing career counseling services to clients. They hold individual sessions as well as conduct workshops and seminars to discuss various career development issues. In addition, Career Counselors help clients develop a career plan to meet their career objectives.

Career Counselors assist many clients who are unsure of what career choices to make. They interview clients and administer self-assessment tools to determine their interests, aptitudes, talents, and skills. The counselors evaluate the information and scores and discuss the results with their clients; they also offer clients suggestions of possible career choices.

Career Counselors also provide clients with information about occupations, careers, job markets, job trends, employers, graduate programs, and financial aid. In addition, they show individuals how to use the resources that are available in the career centers so that they can research on their own about careers, jobs, and employers.

Developing job search plans for full-time employment is another area in which Career Counselors provide assistance. They might advise students on how to focus their job search in order to reach employers for whom they wish to work. They might review students' resumes and make suggestions for improvements. They might conduct mock job interviews to help students prepare and practice for their real-life interviews. Career Counselors can also help individuals evaluate actual job offers.

Another aspect of the college or university Career Counselor's job is to help with the development and implementation of programs and services for their career centers. For example, many four-year colleges and universities offer internship and cooperative education programs that provide students with the opportunity to gain work experience in their chosen fields. These counselors also plan and coordinate campus-wide events such as job recruitment fairs and career information days. This usually involves working with other staff members, faculty, other campus organizations, and employers.

Career Counselors perform various other duties that vary from one counselor to the next. For example, they may be involved in creating instructional aids for their center, developing job opportunities for students, or maintaining their center's career resources. All counselors are responsible for staying current with the latest career counseling and labor market trends.

In many college and university career centers, Career Counselors are assigned to provide services to certain majors or to certain schools and colleges (such as a school of business or college of architecture). In small colleges, one full-time Career Counselor may be responsible for providing all services offered by the career centers.

Career Counselors in higher education work full time or part time. Some counselors work early evening hours to accommodate clients who work or attend classes during the day.

Salaries

Salaries for Career Counselors in higher education institutions vary, depending on such factors as their education, experience, employer, and geographical location. According to the November 2004 *Occupational Employment Statistics* survey by the U.S. Bureau of Labor Statistics, the estimated annual salary for most educational and vocational counselors ranged between $26,610 and $72,970.

Employment Prospects

Career Counselors work for public and private two-year colleges, four-year colleges, and universities. Most job opportunities become available as counselors retire, resign, or advance to other positions.

Opportunities vary from institution to institution. Generally, an increase in student enrollment often goes hand in hand with the addition of full-time and part-time counseling positions. However, the creation of new positions is dependent on available funding.

Advancement Prospects

Career Counselors can advance to supervisory and administrative positions within career centers. With advanced degrees and extensive experience, they can pursue positions such as directors of student affairs, deans of students, vice presidents of student affairs, and college or university presidents.

They can also follow other paths such as becoming college professors, consultants, or private career counselors.

Education and Training

Most employers prefer that Career Counselors have a master's degree in counseling, higher education, student affairs, or a related field. Some employers accept candidates with bachelor's degrees if they are currently enrolled in an appropriate master's program.

Experience, Skills, and Personality Traits

Applicants should have previous experience in career development counseling, preferably in college settings.

To perform their work effectively, Career Counselors must have strong organizational, project management, writing, communication, and presentation skills. They also need strong interpersonal, teamwork, and customer service skills. In addition, they should have adequate computer skills including the ability to utilize databases and the Internet.

Successful Career Counselors share several personality traits such as being patient, objective, friendly, tactful, sincere, trustworthy, flexible, and creative.

Unions and Associations

Many Career Counselors belong to professional associations to take advantage of networking opportunities and other professional resources and services. At the national level, they might join the American Counseling Association and the National Career Development Association. For contact information, see Appendix IV.

Tips for Entry

1. In college, volunteer or work in your career center or with a student affairs program to gain experience working in college settings.
2. Contact the career center or personnel department of each institution where you would like to work. Find out if positions are currently available or will be in the near future. Also find out to whom you can submit a resume or application.
3. Many Career Counselors obtain professional certification to enhance their employability. For certification information, visit the National Board for Certified Counselors, Inc., and Affiliates Web site at http://www. nbcc.org.
4. Use the Internet to learn more about career centers in higher education institutions. To find a particular Web site, enter the institution's name plus the keyword *career center* or *career services* in a search engine. Example: *San Jose State University Career Center.*

EMPLOYMENT COUNSELOR

CAREER PROFILE

Duties: Provide career development and employment counseling; perform other duties as required

Alternate Title(s): Job Counselor, Employment Specialist

Salary Range: $27,000 to $73,000

Employment Prospects: Fair

Advancement Prospects: Fair

Prerequisites:

Education or Training—Master's or bachelor's degree

Experience—Vocational counseling or related experience

Special Skills and Personality Traits—Organizational, time-management, writing, communication, interpersonal, teamwork, customer service, and computer skills; be patient, objective, friendly, tactful, sincere, trustworthy, flexible, and creative

CAREER LADDER

```
┌─────────────────────────────────┐
│  Senior Employment Counselor    │
└─────────────────────────────────┘

┌─────────────────────────────────┐
│     Employment Counselor        │
└─────────────────────────────────┘

┌─────────────────────────────────┐
│           Trainee               │
└─────────────────────────────────┘
```

Position Description

Employment Counselors help individuals identify and pursue their career goals, as well as find jobs that match their goals. In public job service offices, community agencies, private practices, and other settings, Employment Counselors work with people of all ages, backgrounds, and circumstances. For example, clients may be high school dropouts with no job skills, recent college graduates, wives who are reentering the workforce, retirees looking for part-time work, parolees, laid-off workers wishing to learn new job skills, recent immigrants, or full-time workers wanting to change careers.

As trained professionals, Employment Counselors establish a trusting and open relationship with each of their clients. Through individual and group counseling sessions, Employment Counselors support, encourage, and motivate their clients to achieve their career and job goals.

Because they handle many different clients at the same time who may require different services, Employment Counselors' jobs involve case management. For example, Employment Counselors in public employment services may manage a caseload of 200 or more clients. The counselors coordinate services with appropriate representatives of social service agencies, health centers, community agencies, and other organizations to help their clients achieve their goals.

In initial meetings with clients, Employment Counselors determine their eligibility for services and what types of services they would need. They recognize any special needs that clients may have, such as physical or mental disabilities, limited English proficiency, or health problems. These counselors provide clients with educational, occupational, and labor market information to help them decide on their immediate job and career goals.

With clients who are unsure of their career or job goals, Employment Counselors may have them take several standard tests and inventories to identify their interests, skills, aptitudes, and needs. Counselors interpret the tests and explain the results to the clients. Together, Employment Counselors and clients develop a realistic job and career plan for the clients. This includes obtaining any education, training, and services (such as rehabilitative, psychological, or social services) that would help them attain their goals.

As part of their services, Employment Counselors provide clients with suitable job referrals. They review job orders at their agencies for job vacancies that match their clients' interests and experiences. They give their clients information about particular jobs—name of employer, address, and phone number—so that they can contact the employers about the openings.

These counselors perform various other duties that vary from one counselor to the next. For example, Employment Counselors may be involved in developing job opportunities, performing outreach activities about their agency, or conducting in-service workshops for staff members.

Employment Counselors are also responsible for keeping up with current regulations and laws that affect employment and training, job service, and employee rights. In addition, they keep up with current information about occupations, labor markets, and job trends. Furthermore, they are responsible for developing a network of public agencies, community agencies, institutions, business organizations, and other groups for client referrals.

Employment Counselors generally work 40 hours per week. They may work extra hours in the evenings and on weekends to attend meetings, conduct workshops, or perform other job tasks. Some counselors have evening and weekend counseling hours to accommodate clients who may work or attend school during the day.

Salaries

Salaries for Employment Counselors vary, depending on such factors as their education, experience, employer, and geographical location. According to the November 2004 *Occupational Employment Statistics* survey by the U.S. Bureau of Labor Statistics, the estimated annual salary for most vocational counselors ranged between $26,610 and $72,970.

Employment Prospects

Employment Counselors work for public job service offices, community agencies, military facilities, and private practices. Most job opportunities become available as Employment Counselors retire, resign, or advance to other positions.

Advancement Prospects

Advancement opportunities are limited to supervisory and administrative positions. Many counselors realize advancement through higher pay and more complex assignments.

Employment Counselors can also pursue other options such as becoming consultants, rehabilitation counselors, or teachers.

Education and Training

Depending on an employer's requirements, applicants need either a master's or bachelor's degree in counseling or a related field. Some employers accept candidates with bachelor's degrees in any field as long as they have completed appropriate counseling courses on human behavior and development, counseling strategies, ethical practice, and other core areas.

Experience, Skills, and Personality Traits

Employers generally require that Employment Counselors have previous vocational counseling or related experience with employment services. New counselors should be familiar with the principles and techniques of vocational guidance, as well as be able to interpret labor market information and laws and regulations regarding employment and training.

To perform their work effectively, Employment Counselors need adequate organizational, time-management, writing, and communication skills. They also need strong interpersonal and teamwork skills in order to establish and maintain positive working relationships with clients, coworkers, and others. Having good customer service skills and computer skills is also essential.

Successful Employment Counselors share personality traits such as being patient, objective, friendly, tactful, sincere, trustworthy, flexible, and creative.

Unions and Associations

Many Employment Counselors join professional associations to take advantage of networking opportunities and other professional resources and services. Two national societies that these professionals might join are the National Employment Counseling Association and the American Counseling Association. For contact information, see Appendix IV.

Tips for Entry

1. Obtain experience by volunteering or working in your school or college career center.
2. Successful job candidates must complete several steps in a selection process, which may include a job application, job interview, written test, medical examination, and background investigation.
3. To enhance your employability, you might obtain professional certification granted by the National Board for Certified Counselors, Inc., and Affiliates. For information, visit its Web site at http://www.nbcc.org.
4. Use the Internet to learn more about employment counseling. To get a list of relevant Web sites, enter the keyword *employment counseling* in a search engine.

REHABILITATION COUNSELOR

Duties: Provide counseling services to individuals with disabilities; design, implement, and coordinate rehabilitation treatment plans; perform other duties as required

Alternate Title(s): Vocational Rehabilitation Counselor

Salary Range: $19,000 to $48,000

Employment Prospects: Excellent

Advancement Prospects: Good

Prerequisites:

Education or Training—A master's degree in rehabilitation counseling

Experience—Previous experience working with individuals with disabilities

Special Skills and Personality Traits—Management, organizational, writing, communication, interviewing, interpersonal, and teamwork skills; be sincere, patient, trustworthy, creative, flexible, and energetic

Special Requirements—State licensure, certification, or registration may be required; professional certification from CRCC may be needed

```
┌─────────────────────────────────┐
│   Lead Rehabilitation Counselor  │
└─────────────────────────────────┘

┌─────────────────────────────────┐
│     Rehabilitation Counselor     │
└─────────────────────────────────┘

┌─────────────────────────────────┐
│              Intern              │
└─────────────────────────────────┘
```

Position Description

Rehabilitation Counselors work with clients who have physical, mental, emotional, cognitive, or developmental disabilities. Their job is to use the counseling process to help clients achieve their goals to lead productive and independent lives. These counselors work with different age groups, ranging from preschoolers to the elderly. Their clients may have been born with disabilities or became disabled as a result of illness, disease, injury, or stress.

Rehabilitation Counselors are responsible for designing rehabilitation treatment plans that allow their clients to take control of their lives. A treatment plan generally includes a variety of services, such as vocational training, job placement, personal counseling, medical care, and independent living services, that will help a client achieve specific personal, career, and independent living objectives. The plan also identifies any environmental modifications and assistive devices (such as wheelchairs) that a client may need to work independently at his or her job, school, or home.

To create the most effective rehabilitation treatment plans for their clients, Rehabilitation Counselors conduct thorough appraisals of their clients' abilities, interests, goals, and so on. They also interview their clients' friends, families, teachers, and others, as well as review their clients' school and medical records. In addition, the counselors consult physicians, social workers, occupational therapists, mental health counselors, and other professionals who may help them develop realistic plans that address emotional, interpersonal, and other issues related to their clients' disabilities.

Rehabilitation Counselors are also responsible for implementing and coordinating their clients' treatment plans. They identify the appropriate health, vocational, social, and other services that can meet their clients' needs, and refer their clients to these programs and professionals. Some counselors are involved in job placement for their clients as well. Additionally, Rehabilitation Counselors follow up on their clients' progress with their treatment plan. Furthermore, Rehabilitation Counselors provide their clients with vocational and other counseling services.

Rehabilitation Counselors perform other duties that may include:

- developing job opportunities in the community for their clients
- providing counseling to nondisabled clients served by their agencies
- supervising rehabilitation counselor aides and other support staff
- writing correspondence and reports
- completing required paperwork
- participating in community functions and events to promote their agencies and the services that are available to the community
- keeping up with current trends in their field as well as with their own professional development

Rehabilitation Counselors usually work 40 hours per week. Some counselors meet with clients during the evening or on the weekend to accommodate their clients' schedules. Their job involves some local travel, for such purposes as to talk with families, to observe their clients at their workplace, and to participate in training workshops.

Salaries

Salaries for Rehabilitation Counselors vary, depending on such factors as their experience, employer, and geographical location. According to the November 2004 *Occupational Employment Statistics* (OES) survey, by the U.S. Bureau of Labor Statistics (BLS), the estimated annual salary for most Rehabilitation Counselors ranged between $18,610 and $48,290.

Employment Prospects

Some employers of Rehabilitation Counselors include state rehabilitation agencies, community rehabilitation programs, educational institutions, independent living centers, drug and alcohol rehabilitation programs, correctional facilities, residential care facilities, and worker's compensation insurance companies. The BLS reported in its November 2004 OES survey that about 116,560 Rehabilitation Counselors were employed in the United States.

The BLS predicts that this occupation should be one of the fastest-growing occupations in the United States through 2012. The increasing demand for Rehabilitation Counselors is partly due to legislation requiring equal employment rights for people with disabilities, as well as to advances in medical technology that have been able to save many lives. In addition to job growth, replacements will be needed as Rehabilitation Counselors retire, advance to higher positions, or leave the field.

Advancement Prospects

Depending on their interests and ambitions, Rehabilitation Counselors may become specialists with specific disability groups (such as the learning disabled or visually impaired) or in an area of service delivery (such as case management, vocational assessment, or career development). They may also advance to supervisory and administrative positions within their organizations. Other career options include going into private practice, conducting research, or teaching. A doctorate is usually required to teach in four-year colleges and universities.

Education and Training

Most employers require applicants to possess a master's degree in rehabilitation counseling, counseling and guidance, counseling psychology, or another related field. Some employers accept candidates with a bachelor's degree in rehabilitation services, or another appropriate field if they have qualifying work experience. If hired, they are usually expected to obtain their master's degree within a specific time frame.

The master's program in rehabilitation counseling is generally 18 to 24 months long, which includes a supervised clinical practicum.

Special Requirements

Rehabilitation Counselors may be required to be licensed, certified, or registered as professional counselors in the state where they work. For specific information, contact the state board that grants licenses to professional licensed counselors in the state where you wish to practice.

Many employers require that Rehabilitation Counselors possess the Certified Rehabilitation Counselor designation, granted by the Commission on Rehabilitation Counselor Certification (CRCC). This is a voluntary professional certification. For more information visit the CRCC Web site at http://www.crccertification.com.

Experience, Skills, and Personality Traits

Employers typically require that applicants have previous experience working with persons with disabilities. Entry-level applicants may have gained work experience through internships, volunteer work, or paid work experience.

To perform their job effectively, Rehabilitation Counselors need strong management, organizational, writing, communication, and interviewing skills. They also need excellent interpersonal and teamwork skills in order to maintain positive working relationships with clients, coworkers, and others. Being sincere, patient, trustworthy, creative, flexible, and energetic are some personality traits that successful Rehabilitation Counselors share.

Unions and Associations

Many Rehabilitation Counselors join professional associations to take advantage of education programs, networking opportunities, and other professional services and resources. The National Rehabilitation Counseling Association, the American Rehabilitation Counseling Association, and the International Association of Rehabilitation Professionals are some societies that serve the interests of Rehabilitation Counselors. For contact information, see Appendix IV.

Rehabilitation Counselors who work for government agencies may be eligible to join a union that negotiates contracts with their employers.

Tips for Entry

1. Many employers keep applications of qualified applicants on file for several months. Thus, make a point of calling regularly about the status of your application.
2. Take advantage of job listings that are available through professional associations, college career centers, and state employment agencies.
3. Contact your local or state vocational rehabilitation office about job openings.
4. Use the Internet to learn more about rehabilitation counseling. You might start by visiting these Web sites: National Rehabilitation Counseling Association, http://nrca-net.org, and RehabJobs.com, http://www.rehabjobs.com. Also visit the Rehabilitation Services Administration (RSA), a federal agency within the U.S. Department of Education. First go to http://www.ed.gov. Click on the link *Offices,* next click on the link for *Office of Special Education and Rehabilitative Services,* then the link for *RSA.*

CURRICULUM AND INSTRUCTIONAL DEVELOPERS

CURRICULUM SPECIALIST

CAREER PROFILE

Duties: Develop curriculum frameworks for a subject area such as language arts, science, music, or physical education; be a resource to teachers and administrators regarding curriculum and instruction for subject area; perform other duties as required

Alternate Titles(s): Curriculum Supervisor, Curriculum Coordinator

Salary Range: $28,000 to $83,000

Employment Prospects: Good

Advancement Prospects: Fair

Prerequisites:

Education or Training—Master's degree

Experience—Classroom teaching experience

Special Skills and Personality Traits—Writing, analytical, organizational, management, leadership, communication, interpersonal, and team-building skills; be confident, dedicated, creative, energetic, and enthusiastic

Special Requirements—School administrator credential with a curriculum specialist endorsement

CAREER LADDER

```
┌─────────────────────────────────────┐
│       Curriculum Coordinator         │
│          (district-level)            │
└─────────────────────────────────────┘

┌─────────────────────────────────────┐
│        Curriculum Specialist         │
└─────────────────────────────────────┘

┌─────────────────────────────────────┐
│  Department Head or Classroom Teacher │
└─────────────────────────────────────┘
```

Position Description

In public schools, Curriculum Specialists are district-level administrators who develop curriculum standards for all the subjects that are taught in their schools. Teachers use these standards as guidelines for creating units of study and daily lesson plans for their classes.

Curriculum Specialists are assigned to subject areas—such as mathematics, social studies, foreign language, art, technology, or language arts—in which they had taught as classroom teachers. They are responsible for developing curriculum standards for each subject taught in their subject area. These specialists describe the concepts and skills that students should learn in a subject throughout the school year as well as from one grade level to the next. They also define the student learning objectives that should be accomplished in a subject.

Curriculum Specialists base district standards on curriculum frameworks established by state and federal educational agencies. Specialists are continually modifying district curriculum standards because of changes in educational programs and priorities.

Curriculum Specialists also serve as resources to teachers and administrators. They are available to assist on curriculum and instruction questions related to their subject areas. For example, a Social Studies Curriculum Specialist in a K–8 school system helps teachers from kindergarten through eighth grade who teach social studies classes.

Curriculum Specialists perform many other duties, such as:

- training teachers in the newest teaching methods
- evaluating teachers in their subject area
- evaluating new textbooks, supplementary materials, and other instructional materials
- administering budget for assigned subject areas
- processing orders for instructional supplies, equipment, and textbooks
- coordinating with community organizations and agencies about specific activities related to a subject area (such as essay contests, science fairs, and field trips)
- planning special school-wide events such as math contests, knowledge bowls, art contests, and band performances

Furthermore, Curriculum Specialists are responsible for staying current with developments in the content of their particular subject areas as well as with curriculum and instruction trends.

Curriculum Specialists work 40 hours a week on a 12-month schedule. Most Curriculum Specialists travel from school to school. In some school districts, Curriculum Specialists are assigned to cover all subject areas at one school.

Salaries

Salaries for Curriculum Specialists vary, depending on such factors as their experience, employer, and geographical location. The U.S. Bureau of Labor Statistics (BLS) reported in its November 2004 *Occupational Employment Statistics* survey that the estimated annual salary for most instructional coordinators, which includes Curriculum Specialists, ranged between $27,830 and $82,690.

Employment Prospects

According to the BLS, employment for instructional coordinators is expected to increase by 21 to 35 percent through 2012. The need for qualified Curriculum Specialists partly stems from the continuing emphasis to improve the quality of education along with developing curricula that meet governmental standards. In addition to job growth, openings will become available as Curriculum Specialists retire, advance to higher positions, or transfer to other jobs. However, the ability for schools to hire new or additional staff depends on the availability of funding.

Advancement Prospects

Curriculum Specialists can advance to higher administrative positions such as district-level curriculum coordinators, directors of curriculum and instruction, assistant superintendents, and superintendents. Another career option is to become school principals or assistant principals.

Curriculum Supervisors can also follow other career paths such as becoming instructional technologists, software developers, textbook editors, or textbook authors. Another option is to become curriculum developers for publishers, software companies, businesses, corporations, or state or federal education agencies.

Education and Training

Most employers prefer to hire applicants who possess a master's degree or higher in education.

To obtain their state licensure, Curriculum Specialists must complete an approved education program that includes courses in curriculum and instruction, human resource development, instructional technology, and other areas. In addition, they must participate in a supervised practicum.

Special Requirements

In public schools, Curriculum Specialists hold a school administrator credential with a curriculum specialist endorsement. For specific information, contact the state board of education in the state where you wish to work. See Appendix IV for a list of boards.

Experience, Skills, and Personality Traits

Curriculum Specialists generally are selected from the ranks of classroom teachers who have taught several years. In addition, they are experts in the curriculum and instruction of their subject areas.

Curriculum Specialists need superior writing, analytical, organizational, management, and leadership skills to do their work effectively. Additionally, they need excellent communication, interpersonal, and team-building skills.

Successful Curriculum Specialists share several personality traits such as being confident, dedicated, creative, energetic, and enthusiastic.

Unions and Associations

Curriculum Specialists join different professional associations to take advantage of networking opportunities and other professional services and resources. Many join organizations that serve their particular subject area, such as the International Reading Association, the National Council for the Social Studies, the Council for Exceptional Children, or MENC: The National Association for Music Education.

Curriculum Specialists are also eligible to join school administrator societies such as: Association for Supervision and Curriculum Development, American Association of School Administrators, National Association of Elementary School Principals, and National Association of Secondary School Principals.

For contact information for the above organizations, see Appendix IV.

Tips for Entry

1. As teachers, participate on curriculum committees.
2. Having strong instructional technology skills may enhance your chances of employment.
3. You can read about different state and local curriculum frameworks on the Internet. To find a list of relevant Web sites, enter the keyword *curriculum framework* in a search engine.

TEXTBOOK EDITOR

CAREER PROFILE

Duties: Manage textbook projects; edit manuscripts; perform other duties as required

Alternate Title(s): Development Editor; Acquisition Editor; a title (such as ESL Editor, Elementary Math Editor, or College Social Science Editor) that reflects a subject area

Salary Range: $26,000 to $82,000

Employment Prospects: Fair

Advancement Prospects: Good

Prerequisites:

Education or Training—Bachelor's degree

Experience—Publishing experience is desirable; teaching experience in subject matter usually preferred

Special Skills and Personality Traits—Writing, analytical, problem-solving, communication, interpersonal, teamwork, organizational, and project management skills; be tactful, friendly, enthusiastic, energetic, self-motivated, and creative

CAREER LADDER

```
┌─────────────────────────┐
│      Senior Editor      │
└─────────────────────────┘

┌─────────────────────────┐
│     Textbook Editor     │
└─────────────────────────┘

┌─────────────────────────┐
│     Assistant Editor    │
└─────────────────────────┘
```

Position Description

In educational publishing houses, Textbook Editors are responsible for the development of textbooks and supplementary materials (such as workbooks, tests, software, and maps). Editors who create materials for K–12 students work for school publishers, whereas those working on materials for university and college students are employed by higher education publishers.

Textbook Editors, specialize in subject areas, such as elementary language arts, secondary mathematics, college biology, special education, and adult ESL (English as a second language). Most editors manage one or more editorial projects at a time, with each project usually at a different point in its development. A project may be one proposed textbook title or a series of several proposed titles. Ideas for textbooks are proposed by Textbook Editors, marketing staff, vice presidents, or other staff within a publishing house. Textbook Editors also acquire book proposals from authors who submit original ideas that fit publishers' needs.

For each project, editors determine the goals, objectives, and contents for textbooks and ancillary materials, such as teacher's guides, student workbooks, and teacher resource books. Textbook Editors also find and assign authors to write all or parts of manuscripts. They provide authors with working guidelines from which to develop manuscripts. Textbook Editors keep in constant communication with authors to track their progress and to ensure that they are able to make writing deadlines.

Manuscripts usually go through draft and revision stages. Textbook Editors review manuscript drafts carefully, providing authors with detailed comments and suggestions for necessary revisions. If needed, Textbook Editors send manuscript drafts to subject experts to review content for accuracy.

When authors have finished writing manuscripts, Textbook Editors then edit manuscripts for content as well as for adherence to the publisher's own styles, formats, and standards. When needed, a Textbook Editor rewrites parts or all of a manuscript. Edited manuscripts are released to production departments where manuscripts are physically prepared for printing. (During the production stage, the book design, page design and layout, illustrations, and other physical features of textbooks are created.) Textbook Editors usually review manuscripts again, but in the form of galley and page proofs which show how actual book pages will look. Textbook Editors make sure that manuscript copy has been transferred completely and accurately. They also edit text further on pages where the text runs too long. Textbook Editors may also send proofs to authors to review to make corrections and comments.

Textbook Editors are assigned other responsibilities that differ from one editor to the next. For example, an editor might be responsible for conducting photo research, supervising freelance editors, giving presentations at educator conferences, or writing promotional copy for new books.

Textbook Editors have a 40-hour schedule, but often work longer hours to meet deadlines.

Salaries

Salaries for Textbook Editors vary, depending on such factors as their education, experience, employer, and geographical location. According to the November 2004 *Occupational Employment Statistics* survey by the U.S. Bureau of Labor Statistics, the estimated annual salary for most editors, in general, ranged between $26,490 and $82,070.

Employment Prospects

Opportunities are available for staff and freelance positions, however the competition is strong. Most staff openings for Textbook Editors become available as editors retire, advance to higher positions, or transfer to other jobs. As their companies grow, employers create additional positions as long as funds are available.

Advancement Prospects

Textbook Editors can advance to supervisory and administrative positions as senior editors, managing editors, executive editors, editorial directors, and up to executive-level positions as vice presidents and publishers. Many editors pursue advancement by accepting jobs at different publishing houses. Some editors choose to become freelance editors or to start their own businesses offering editorial development services to publishers.

Education and Training

Employers generally require that Textbook Editors have a bachelor's degree, preferably in the field in which they would be working. For example, an editor who edits college math textbooks has a bachelor's degree in mathematics.

Publishers may waive the requirement if candidates have qualifying work experience.

Experience, Skills, and Personality Traits

Applicants need one or more years of teaching experience, preferably in the subject areas for which they are applying. Alternatively, they should be knowledgeable with the subject matter as well as familiar with the pedagogy, curriculum, and instruction for a subject area. In addition, candidates should have publishing experience.

Textbook Editors need excellent writing, analytical, and problem-solving skills to do their work effectively. Strong communication, interpersonal, and teamwork skills are needed as they must work well with authors, editors, production staff, and others. In addition, Textbook Editors should have strong organizational and project management skills. Being tactful, friendly, enthusiastic, energetic, self-motivated, and creative are some personality traits that successful Textbook Editors share.

Unions and Associations

Many Textbook Editors belong to professional associations to take advantage of networking opportunities, education programs, and other professional resources and services. They may join societies such as the Association of Educational Publishers that serve their general editorial interests. They may also join associations for their particular subject area, such as TESOL, Inc., National Council of Teachers of English, American Chemical Society, or American Association of Adult and Continuing Education. For contact information, see Appendix IV.

Tips for Entry

1. In high school, gain valuable experience by working on your school paper, yearbook, or other publication.
2. As a teacher, you can gain publishing experience by doing freelance or consulting work for educational publishers. Many companies hire teachers for writing assignments or for reviewing manuscripts.
3. Find out who the editorial directors are at the publishing houses where you would like to work. Then send each one a query letter about job openings, along with your resume. Follow up with a call a few days later.
4. Use the Internet to learn about various educational publishers. To find relevant Web sites, enter the keyword *educational publisher* in a search engine.

INSTRUCTIONAL DESIGNER

CAREER PROFILE

Duties: Develop and design technology-based instructional materials; manage instructional projects; perform other duties as required

Alternate Title(s): Courseware Developer, Distance Education Specialist

Salary Range: $28,000 to $83,000

Employment Prospects: Good

Advancement Prospects: Fair

Prerequisites:

Education or Training—Bachelor's or master's degree

Experience—Prior experience in the design and delivery of distance education in appropriate work settings; teaching experience preferred

Special Skills and Personality Traits—Analytical, writing, organizational, project management, communication, interpersonal, and teamwork skills; be patient, tolerant, tactful, flexible, self-motivated, energetic, enthusiastic, and creative

CAREER LADDER

```
┌─────────────────────────────────────┐
│    Senior Instructional Designer     │
└─────────────────────────────────────┘

┌─────────────────────────────────────┐
│       Instructional Designer         │
└─────────────────────────────────────┘

┌─────────────────────────────────────┐
│               Intern                 │
└─────────────────────────────────────┘
```

Position Description

Instructional Designers provide the basic framework for the development and design of training videotapes, satellite television courses, on-line courses, and other instructional materials. Many Instructional Designers are part of training departments of businesses, corporations, government agencies, and other organizations where they help in the creation of instructional materials (and sometimes curriculum) for technical training programs. Many Instructional Designers work in higher educational institutions where they help faculty with creating technology resources (such as web pages) for their courses as well as assist in the design and development of on-line courses. Some Instructional Designers work in educational publishing companies and software companies, providing instructional expertise for the development of software and courseware projects.

Most Instructional Designers work as part of a team of experts, each responsible for different aspects of the project. Other team members would include editorial, graphic design, and technical personnel. The team also includes one or more subject matter experts who are responsible for providing the content matter. When the content is highly technical, subject matter experts provide instructional objectives and other instructional guidance. For example, if an art professor asks an Instructional Designer to design an on-line course on 16th-century Italian art, the professor would provide him or her with content materials, learning objectives, lesson activities, and other information.

When developing materials, Instructional Designers look at instruction from the perspective of the learners in order to meet their specific needs. A project usually begins with a needs assessment to determine the direction and design of the project. Instructional Designers identify important information, such as the target audience, the settings in which the proposed material would be used, the educational goals and objectives, the appropriate instructional strategies to use, and the most effective media and formats for presenting instruction.

Instructional Designers also work on the creation of instructional projects. They might write or edit text, develop layouts, make videotapes, write programming codes, and so on. Instructional Designers often have the responsibility of managing projects through completion. This includes creating deadline schedules, answering questions from outsiders about the project, and tracking the project's progress. Furthermore, it involves testing the instruction with sample learners to evaluate whether it has met learning objectives. The material is revised and retested until the evaluation is satisfactory.

Instructional Designers' responsibilities vary according to their expertise. Beginning developers generally work on parts of a project under the direction of senior Instructional Designers. As they become more experienced, they are given the responsibility of developing entire courses and becoming team project leaders. Senior Instructional Designers have higher-level responsibilities that include supervising team project leaders, managing projects, and directing needs assessments.

Instructional Designers are also responsible for keeping up with new technologies as well as with their professional development. They read books, magazines, and journals about technology as well as about education. They join professional associations, participate in professional conferences, and network with colleagues. In addition, they enroll in training workshops and continuing education courses.

They work 40 hours a week and often work evenings and weekends to meet deadlines.

Salaries

Salaries for Instructional Designers vary, depending on such factors as their education, experience, employer, and geographical location. According to the November 2004 *Occupational Employment Statistics* survey by the U.S. Bureau of Labor Statistics, the estimated annual salary for most instructional coordinators, which include Instructional Designers, ranged between $27,830 and $82,690.

Employment Prospects

Instructional Designers work for colleges and universities, educational publishers, businesses, corporations, government, the military, nonprofit organizations, and various other types of organizations and agencies. Many Instructional Designers work for courseware development businesses that provide contractual services to different organizations. Some Instructional Designers are self-employed.

Opportunities generally become available as individuals advance to higher positions, transfer to other jobs, or retire. Employers create additional positions as demands for instructional design services increase, as long as funding is available.

Advancement Prospects

Instructional Designers can advance to become lead developers, project managers or other administrative positions. They can also become self-employed, as well as start their own companies.

Education and Training

The education requirement varies from one employer to the next. In general, the minimum requirement for Instructional Designers is a bachelor's degree in instructional technology, instructional design, educational media, or other related field. More and more employers, however, are requiring or preferring candidates with master's degrees.

Experience, Skills, and Personality Traits

Requirements vary among the different types of employers. In general, employers look for candidates who have prior experience in their particular work settings. They also prefer candidates who have teaching experience and are knowledgeable about educational multimedia design principles. Furthermore, candidates have a working knowledge of appropriate technology such as HTML programming, authoring software, and Web-based instructional systems.

To perform their work effectively, Instructional Designers need superior analytical, writing, organizational, and project management skills. In addition, they need excellent communication, interpersonal, and teamwork skills as they must work well with faculty, project team members, and others on a daily basis.

Successful Instructional Designers share several personality traits such as being patient, tolerant, tactful, flexible, self-motivated, energetic, enthusiastic, and creative.

Unions and Associations

Many Instructional Designers belong to professional associations to take advantage of networking opportunities, certification programs, and other professional resources and services. Some national societies include International Society for Performance Improvement, American Society for Training and Development, Association for the Advancement of Computing in Education, and Association for Educational Communications and Technology. For contact information, see Appendix IV.

Tips for Entry

1. In middle school or high school, you can start gaining teaching experience by volunteering or getting a part-time job as a tutor, coach, teacher aide, summer camp counselor, or Sunday school teacher.
2. Ask professors and college career counselors for help in obtaining appropriate internships.
3. Keep up with advances in technology and update your skills as needed.
4. Use the Internet to learn more about the instructional design field. To get a list of relevant Web sites, enter the keywords *instructional designers* or *instructional design* in a search engine.

EDUCATIONAL SOFTWARE DEVELOPER

CAREER PROFILE

Duties: Design educational software; manage projects; perform others duties as required

Alternate Title(s): Courseware Developer, Software Engineer

Salary Range: $47,000 to $115,000

Employment Prospects: Good

Advancement Prospects: Fair

Prerequisites:

Education or Training—Bachelor's degree

Experience—One or more years of experience with specific programming languages; a background in education

Special Skills and Personality Traits—Organizational, management, interpersonal, teamwork, self-management skills; be patient, tolerant, flexible, self-motivated, confident, energetic, and enthusiastic

CAREER LADDER

```
┌─────────────────────────────────┐
│   Senior Software Developer      │
└─────────────────────────────────┘

┌─────────────────────────────────┐
│  Educational Software Developer  │
└─────────────────────────────────┘

┌─────────────────────────────────┐
│            Intern                │
└─────────────────────────────────┘
```

Position Description

Educational Software Developers are responsible for the creation of software that helps students learn concepts and skills of mathematics, English, history, astronomy, and other subjects. These professionals may be involved in developing software for any age or grade level, from preschoolers to university students. They are usually employed by book publishers or software companies. They may be staff members or independent contractors.

Educational Software Developers generally are responsible for managing a project from start to finish. They take an idea for a software program—such as teaching simple fractions by showing equal segments of pizza pies—and begin to define the product from the eyes of the learners. These developers ask questions, such as: What type of students would be using the software? What concepts and skills should the students be learning? What are the learning objectives that should be achieved with the software? What types of activities and exercises can be used to motivate students, and to keep their interest throughout the whole program?

Most educational software today is multimedia, meaning that a combination of text, sounds, animation, graphic arts, and video is used. Educational software also allows for users to interact with the content. Thus developers determine how the software should look, how the user should move around in the program, and what type of interactions the user should be doing. Software developers may also research the marketability of the proposed product as well as the competition it would be facing.

Once the parameters of the product are defined, the development of the product begins. In staff positions, most Educational Software Developers are part of teams, in which each team member (such as a graphic artist, software engineer, writer, instructional designer, or video artist) brings his or her own expertise to the project.

Software developers are sometimes designated the project managers. They are responsible for tasks such as creating deadline schedules, preparing budgets, and keeping track of the project's progress. They also coordinate testing sessions with sample users to evaluate the products, reviewing and retesting them until evaluations are satisfactory.

Educational Software Developers also contribute to the creative development of projects. Depending on their interests and skills, they might write text, design exercises and tests, write programming codes, create graphics, and so on. On simple projects, software developers who have the expertise might create the products all by themselves.

Educational Software Developers typically work long hours to meet deadlines.

Salaries

Salaries for Educational Software Developers vary, depending on such factors as their experience, responsibilities, employer, and geographical location. According to the November 2004 *Occupational Employment Statistics* survey by the U.S. Bureau of Labor Statistics (BLS), the estimated annual salary for most computer applications software engineers, a category that includes software developers, ranged between $47,340 and $114,690.

Employment Prospects

The BLS projects that the software publishing industry will be the fastest growing industry in the United States through 2012. The agency also describes the market for educational software as expected to show robust growth within this time period.

Most openings for Educational Software Developers will become available as employees retire, advance to higher positions, or transfer to other jobs. Employers will create additional positions as their companies grow and expand, as long as funds are available.

Advancement Prospects

Educational Software Developers can advance to become lead developers, project managers, or other administrative positions. Another option is to pursue careers in the other areas of educational software development, such as programming, graphic arts, or curriculum development. They can also become self-employed educational software developers or consultants, as well as start their own software companies.

With their skills and experience, Educational Software Developers can become developers of games and other types of software.

Education and Training

Most employers require that Educational Software Developers have a bachelor's degree, preferably in computer science. However, employers usually waive the education requirement if candidates have qualifying experience.

Educational Software Developers are expected to keep up with their skills and professional development. They may do so through self-study, continuing education courses, networking with colleagues, and participating in professional conventions.

Experience, Skills, and Personality Traits

In general, educational software companies require that candidates have one or more years experience with specific programming languages. Candidates should also have a background in education, or at the minimum a basic understanding of educational theory for the target audiences of the software they would be developing.

To do their work effectively, Educational Software Developers need adequate organizational, management, interpersonal, and teamwork skills. They also should have superior self-management skills—the ability to meet deadlines, manage several duties at the same time, take the initiative to seek new work and update skills, and work well under pressure.

Successful Educational Software Developers share several personality traits, such as being patient, tolerant, flexible, self-motivated, confident, energetic, and enthusiastic.

Unions and Associations

Many Educational Software Developers belong to professional associations that allow them to take advantage of training programs, networking opportunities, and other professional resources and services. Some general computing associations that they might join are the Association for Computing Machinery and Computer Society, a division of the Institute of Electrical and Electronics Engineers.

Many self-employed developers and business owners belong to the Educational Software Cooperative. Educational Software Developers who sell their own software might join the Association of Shareware Professionals.

For contact information for the above organizations, see Appendix IV.

Tips for Entry

1. To gain experience, obtain internships with educational software companies or educational publishers that develop software.
2. Take courses in education. Also, volunteer or get a job as a tutor, teacher aide, recreation leader or similar position to get teaching experience.
3. You can learn more about various educational software companies on the Internet. To find pertinent Web sites, enter either of these keywords in a search engine: *educational software* or *educational software company*.

EDUCATIONAL AND INSTRUCTIONAL TECHNOLOGY SPECIALISTS

INSTRUCTIONAL TECHNOLOGY SPECIALIST (K–12 SCHOOLS)

CAREER PROFILE

Duties: Provide technology training and support to teachers; manage computer lab; perform other duties as required

Alternate Title(s): Educational Technologist, Technology Teacher

Salary Range: $33,000 to $57,000

Employment Prospects: Fair

Advancement Prospects: Fair

Prerequisites:

Education or Training—Master's degree

Experience—Classroom teaching experience integrating technology with curriculum and instruction

Special Skills and Personality Traits—Organizational, management, problem-solving, communication, interpersonal, and leadership skills; be patient, courteous, flexible, adaptable, creative, and positive

Special Requirements—A teaching credential may be required

CAREER LADDER

```
┌─────────────────────────────────────┐
│        Technology Director           │
└─────────────────────────────────────┘


┌─────────────────────────────────────┐
│ Instructional Technology Specialist  │
└─────────────────────────────────────┘


┌─────────────────────────────────────┐
│         Classroom Teacher            │
└─────────────────────────────────────┘
```

Position Description

Instructional Technology Specialists are responsible for the coordination of technology training in public and private elementary, middle-level, and high schools. They are experts in integrating technology into curriculum. Their job is to provide training and support to teachers on how to use computers, software, the Internet, and other technology as tools to enhance their lessons and instruction.

Instructional Technology Specialists work with teachers and administrators to evaluate the technology training needs of teachers, and then plan training sessions and workshops accordingly.

These specialists also provide consultation services to teachers in designing effective technology strategies for their instruction. For example, a specialist and a fifth grade teacher might brain-storm ways that students can use a digital camera for classroom assignments. Technology specialists often collaborate with teachers on preparing lesson plans, showing how teachers can integrate various technologies to teach, reinforce, and enrich their lessons. Some-

times, Instructional Technology Specialists coteach classes in order to model the use of technology for the teachers.

In many schools, Instructional Technology Specialists manage the computer labs. This includes overseeing the use of the Internet by teachers, students, and other staff members. Specialists also make sure all hardware, networks, providers, and so on are running correctly, and that they are maintained and repaired as needed. They also set up equipment and install software, as well as troubleshoot hardware, software, or network problems. Additionally, they organize, store, and maintain an inventory of hardware, software, manuals, computer supplies, and other materials. Instructional Technology Specialists may also supervise and train student aides.

Many Instructional Technology Specialists are responsible for providing technical support to teachers and administrators as the need arises. Some schools have computer specialists who provide technical support so that Instructional Technology Specialists may focus on curriculum and instruction.

Some Instructional Technology Specialists are also part-time computer teachers at their schools. They are responsible for teaching one or more technology classes in a grading period. Some computer teachers/Instructional Technology Specialists collaborate with other teachers to develop technology projects that combine both subject area and computer lab curriculum.

All Instructional Technology Specialists perform many administrative tasks. For example, they submit requisitions for hardware, software, and other products; complete required reports and paperwork; and assist in the preparation of grant proposals. Other duties vary from one school to the next. For example, they might design school Web sites, oversee technology needs for administrative networks, or assist in the planning of school-wide technology plans. These specialists are also responsible for staying current with new instructional technologies, as well as keeping up their professional development.

Instructional Technology Specialists may hold full-time or part-time positions. Some Instructional Technology Specialists are assigned to two or more schools.

Salaries

Salaries for Instructional Technology Specialists vary, depending on such factors as their education, experience, employer, and geographical location. Specific salary information for this occupation is unavailable, but many schools base the wages of technology specialists on their teacher salary schedule. According to the 2003–04 salary survey by the American Federation of Teachers, the average annual salary for teachers in public school ranged from $33,236 to $56,516.

Employment Prospects

The instructional technology field is relatively new, but continues to expand as more schools build and develop their technology resources. Most opportunities become available as Instructional Technology Specialists advance to higher positions, transfer to other jobs, or retire. Schools may create additional positions to meet growing demands, as long as funding is available.

Advancement Prospects

Instructional Technology Specialists can advance through the ranks as instructional technology coordinators, technology directors, chief information officers, and assistant superintendents for technology. Advanced degrees and school administrator licensure may be required for executive-level positions.

Other career options are to obtain Instructional Technology Specialist positions in other settings, such colleges, universities, business, industry, government, or health institutions.

Education and Training

Most employers require or prefer that Instructional Technology Specialists have a master's degree in instructional technology or a related field with acceptable course work in instructional technology.

Special Requirements

Instructional Technology Specialists are generally required to hold valid teaching credentials. For specific information, contact the state board of education for the state in which you wish to teach. See Appendix III for a list of boards.

Experience, Skills, and Personality Traits

Most employers require that applicants have previous classroom teaching experience that includes the integration of technology into their lesson plans and teaching.

To perform their jobs effectively, Instructional Technology Specialists need strong organizational, management, problem-solving, communication, interpersonal, and leadership skills. Successful Instructional Technology Specialists have several personality traits in common, such as being patient, courteous, flexible, adaptable, creative, and positive.

Unions and Associations

Instructional Technology Specialists may join professional associations to take advantage of networking opportunities, and other professional resources and services. Some national societies are International Society for Technology in Education, International Technology Education Association, Association for Educational Communications and Technology, and Association for the Advancement of Computing in Education. See Appendix IV for contact information.

Tips for Entry

1. Get experience working in school computer labs. While in high school, you might become a student aide. While in college, you might become a volunteer, intern, or paid assistant.
2. As a teacher, keep a portfolio of lesson plans, class projects, videotapes, and other items that show how you have used technology in the classroom. You can then show your portfolio to prospective employers when you are ready to apply for Instructional Technology Specialist positions.
3. Use the Internet to learn more about the field of instructional technology. To get a list of relevant Web sites, enter the keyword *instructional technology* in a search engine.

SPECIAL EDUCATION TECHNOLOGY SPECIALIST

CAREER PROFILE

Duties: Provide assistive technology services to special education students; perform other duties as required

Alternate Title(s): Assistive Technology Specialist

Salary Range: $33,000 to $57,000

Employment Prospects: Fair

Advancement Prospects: Fair

Prerequisites:

Education or Training—Bachelor's or master's degree

Experience—Previous experience working with disabled children in school or other settings

Special Skills and Personality Traits—Organizational, management, problem-solving, observation, communication, interpersonal, and computer skills; be analytical, patient, self-motivated, resourceful, patient, and creative

Special Requirements—A teaching credential may be required

CAREER LADDER

```
┌─────────────────────────────────────────┐
│  Lead Assistive Technology Specialist or │
│         Program Coordinator              │
└─────────────────────────────────────────┘

┌─────────────────────────────────────────┐
│     Assistive Technology Specialist      │
└─────────────────────────────────────────┘

┌─────────────────────────────────────────┐
│                Trainee                   │
└─────────────────────────────────────────┘
```

Position Description

Special Education Technology Specialists provide assistive technology services in public and private schools. These professionals seek ways to use technology to help students with learning, emotional, or physical disabilities succeed in school.

Assistive technology is defined as any item, device, or equipment that helps special education students function independently in the school environment. For example, students with a speech impairment may be accommodated with an electronic device so that they can communicate with their teacher and classmates.

Technology specialists are usually part of student assessment teams that are composed of general education teachers, special education teachers, parents, school psychologists, and other school specialists. The teams develop Individualized Education Programs (IEPs) that outline the goals and objectives for instruction and related services such as those offered by Special Education Technology Specialists.

As members of student assessment teams, Special Education Technology Specialists provide expertise in assessing and evaluating whether students with disabilities need assistive technology. They observe students in classrooms as well as interview their teachers to learn about the daily activities and tasks that students do. Specialists may also administer tests to assist them with their assessments.

When it is determined that special education students require assistive technology, technology specialists consider possible accommodations that range from no-technology solutions to high-technology solutions. A no-technology solution may be a referral to services such as occupational therapy, or it may be a modification of a student's environment or the way a student performs his or her tasks. For example, a learning disabled student's work area is rearranged so that he or she can better focus on his or her lessons. Low-technology solutions include the use of items such as adapted spoon handles, pencil grips, special-lined paper, or Velcro fasteners. Medium-technology solutions include the use of equipment such as wheelchairs, while high-technology solutions include the use of computers, talking calculators, and other electronic technology.

Technology specialists are responsible for ordering assistive devices as well as installing them or providing for their installation. They also train students (and their teachers and families) how to use their assistive devices properly.

Accurate record keeping is an important part of Special Education Technology Specialists' work. They maintain daily records of their staff meetings, in-service sessions, and training sessions with students, teachers, and parents. They also keep statistics on the number of students that are referred to them, as well as maintain an inventory of assistive devices on hand. In addition, they complete paperwork in compliance with federal and state laws as well as with local education agency policies and procedures.

Special Education Technology Specialists may be assigned to work at one or more schools. They may be part-time or full-time employees.

Salaries

Salaries for special education technologists vary, depending on such factors as their education, experience, employer, and geographical location. Salary information for this occupation is unavailable. Some schools base the wages of their technology specialists on their teacher salary schedule. According to the 2003–04 salary survey by the American Federation of Teachers, the average annual salary for teachers in public school ranged from $33,236 to $56,516.

Employment Prospects

Special Education Technology Specialists are employed by private and public schools. Some work for consulting services or are self-employed consultants.

Although this is a relatively new occupation, opportunities should continually grow due to the steady increase in students who require special education services. Keep in mind that the ability for a school to hire new or additional Special Education Technology Specialists is dependent on the availability of funds.

Advancement Prospects

Promotions are limited to lead and supervisory positions. With additional education and licensure, technology specialists can become special education directors and other school administrators.

Another option is to work in other settings such as hospitals, developmental centers, and vocational rehabilitation agencies. Technology specialists can also pursue careers as university professors, researchers, or private consultants.

Education and Training

Education requirements vary from one employer to the next. In general, Special Education Technology Specialists possess either a bachelor's or master's degree in such disciplines as special education, vocational counseling, or adaptive physical education.

Special Requirements

Some states may require that Special Education Technology Specialists hold valid teaching credentials. For specific information, contact the state board of education for the state in which you wish to work. See Appendix III for a list of boards.

Experience, Skills, and Personality Traits

Employers typically look for candidates who have previous experience working with special education children in schools or other settings. Specialists with backgrounds in special education as teachers, school occupational therapists, school speech language pathologists, or other related professions have the best chances of being hired.

To do their work effectively, Special Education Technology Specialists need excellent organizational, management, problem-solving, observation, communication, and interpersonal skills. In addition, they need strong computer skills. Successful Special Education Technology Specialists share several personality traits such as being analytical, patient, self-motivated, resourceful, patient, and creative. They are dedicated to helping children with disabilities become confident users of technology so that they can succeed in school and other endeavors.

Unions and Associations

Special Education Technology Specialists may join professional associations to take advantage of networking opportunities, education programs, and other professional resources and services. Some national societies include Alliance for Technology Access, Technology and Media Division (part of the Council for Exceptional Children), and Rehabilitation Engineering and Assistive Technology of North America. For contact information, see Appendix IV.

Tips for Entry

1. Get experience working with children who have disabilities.
2. Take courses in special education technology if they are offered at your school.
3. To enhance their employability, many technologists obtain voluntary certification from the Rehabilitation Engineering and Assistive Technology Society of North America. For information visit its Web site at http://www.resna.org.
4. You can learn more about assistive technology on the Internet. To get a list of relevant Web sites, enter the keyword *assistive technology* in a search engine.

INSTRUCTIONAL TECHNOLOGY COORDINATOR (SCHOOL-WIDE LEVEL)

CAREER PROFILE

Duties: Oversee the school-wide instructional technology plan; perform other duties as required

Alternate Title(s): None

Salary Range: $28,000 to $83,000

Employment Prospects: Good

Advancement Prospects: Fair

Prerequisites:

Education or Training—Bachelor's or master's degree

Experience—Knowledgeable of educational technology; have supervisory and management experience; having teaching experience is preferred

Special Skills and Personality Traits—Organizational, supervisory, management, writing, leadership, communication, interpersonal, and presentation skills; be patient, positive, enthusiastic, self-motivated, energetic, flexible, and creative

Special Requirements—A teaching or school administrator credential may be required

CAREER LADDER

```
┌─────────────────────────────────────┐
│        Director of Technology         │
└─────────────────────────────────────┘

┌─────────────────────────────────────┐
│  Instructional Technology Coordinator │
│         (school-wide level)           │
└─────────────────────────────────────┘

┌─────────────────────────────────────┐
│  Instructional Technology Coordinator │
│          (building level)             │
└─────────────────────────────────────┘
```

Position Description

Instructional Technology Coordinators are educational managers based in the central or district office of public and private school systems. They are responsible for overseeing their school system's plan for integrating technology—computers, software, the Internet, and so on—into the curriculum. They may report to a director of technology, assistant superintendent, or other higher-level administrator.

Instructional Technology Coordinators work with principals, teachers, curriculum specialists, school-level technology managers, and others to develop and implement goals and strategies to use technology effectively at the different grade levels as well as in special education, bilingual, and other education programs. As the educational technology leaders, coordinators continually evaluate the effectiveness of technology plans and make recommendations for improvements and modifications to superintendents or school boards.

Instructional Technology Coordinators perform a wide range of duties that vary from one coordinator to the next. For example, they:

- manage instructional technology budgets
- conduct assessments of new technology needs in schools
- plan in-service technology workshops for teachers, administrators, and others
- provide consultations on technology-related issues and problems to teachers, administrators, school boards, and others
- disseminate technology information to teachers and administrators that may be useful for instruction
- assist in the development and implementation of plans for the acquisition and maintenance of school-wide technology infrastructure
- maintain an inventory of computer software and hardware
- coordinate purchase requisitions for equipment and supplies
- seek grant sources in both the public and private sectors
- prepare grant proposals
- develop and maintain community relations through presentations to parent and civic groups
- prepare administrative reports and paperwork

- keep up to date with new developments in educational and instructional technologies
- participate in conferences and meetings sponsored by educational agencies and professional associations

Technology Coordinators typically work more than 40 hours a week, often working evening and weekend hours to meet all the demands of their jobs.

Salaries

Salaries for Instructional Technology Coordinators vary, depending on such factors as their education, experience, employer, and geographical location. Specific salary information for this occupation is unavailable. In general, most instructional coordinators earned an estimated annual salary that ranged between $27,830 and $82,690, according to the November 2004 *Occupational Employment Statistics* by the U.S. Bureau of Labor Statistics.

Employment Prospects

Most opportunities become available as Instructional Technology Coordinators retire, resign, or transfer to other schools. As more schools integrate technology into their systems, the demand for experienced educational technology managers should grow as well.

Advancement Prospects

With advanced degrees and appropriate licensure, Instructional Technology Coordinators can advance to the positions of technology directors, chief information officers, and assistant superintendents of technology. Many Instructional Technology Coordinators realize advancement by way of receiving higher salaries, gaining professional recognition, and becoming educational technology managers in larger school systems.

Education and Training

Employers require either a bachelor's or master's degree. The degree may be in any discipline as long as candidates have qualifying work experience. Many employers prefer that applicants have master's or higher degrees in educational technology.

Special Requirements

Public school districts may require Instructional Technology Coordinators to hold a valid teaching or school administra-tor credential. For specific licensure requirements, contact the central office for the school district where you would like to work.

Experience, Skills, and Personality Traits

Employers look for candidates who have an overall knowledge of educational technology, and whose work history shows increasingly responsible supervisory and management experience. Many employers prefer that candidates have teaching experience.

To perform their work effectively, Instructional Technology Coordinators need excellent organizational, supervisory, management, and writing skills. They also need effective leadership, communication, interpersonal, and presentation skills, as they must work well with teachers, students, administrators, staff, and others. Successful coordinators share several personality traits, such as being patient, positive, enthusiastic, self-motivated, energetic, flexible, and creative.

Unions and Associations

Many Instructional Technology Coordinators belong to various professional associations to take advantage of education programs, networking opportunities, and other professional resources and services. Some national societies include: Association for Educational Communications and Technology, Association for the Advancement of Computing in Education, International Society for Technology in Education, and American Association of School Administrators. For contact information, see Appendix IV.

Tips for Entry

1. Keep up with new developments in educational and instructional technology.
2. Join professional organizations to take advantage of their services. Many organizations have student memberships. Attend conferences and network with professionals.
3. Learn about everything in technology that you can, including programming, networks, software, wiring, computer troubleshooting, basic repairs, and so on.
4. Learn more about educational technology on the Internet. You might start by visiting these Web sites: the Snorkel, http://www.thesnorkel.org, and Instructional Technology Education Association, http://www.iteaconnect.org.

INSTRUCTIONAL TECHNOLOGY SPECIALIST (HIGHER EDUCATION)

CAREER PROFILE

Duties: Provide technology support to faculty; assist in the development and design of technology based instructional materials; perform other duties as required

Alternate Title(s): Courseware Designer, Instructional Technologist, Academic Technology Specialist, Instructional Designer

Salary Range: $28,000 to $83,000

Employment Prospects: Good

Advancement Prospects: Fair

Prerequisites:

　Education or Training—Bachelor's or master's degree

　Experience—One or more years of work experience in instructional technology in academic settings; teaching experience is preferred

　Special Skills and Personality Traits—Communication, interpersonal, customer service, organizational, management, teamwork, writing, and presentation skills; be patient, tactful, energetic, enthusiastic, creative, flexible

CAREER LADDER

```
┌─────────────────────────────────────┐
│  Department Coordinator or Director  │
└─────────────────────────────────────┘

┌─────────────────────────────────────┐
│  Instructional Technology Specialist │
└─────────────────────────────────────┘

┌─────────────────────────────────────┐
│              Intern                  │
└─────────────────────────────────────┘
```

Position Description

Instructional Technology Specialists in higher education institutions are responsible for providing technology support to professors, teaching assistants, librarians, and other faculty who wish to use technology to enhance their instruction. For example, an English professor might have a web site for his or her courses, while a history instructor might have his or her students use the Internet to complete assignments. On many campuses, Instructional Technology Specialists are available to provide faculty—professors, instructors, lecturers, teaching assistants, and other academic professionals—with the necessary technology support.

These specialists are usually based in information technology services centers on academic campuses. Most specialists are assigned to work with faculty from the various academic departments on campus. Some are assigned to work with faculty in specific departments (such as history) or individual schools (such as liberal arts).

Instructional Technology Specialists generally work in a consultant role, providing assistance to individual faculty members with their teaching projects. Upon assessing the faculty member's interests and project needs, the specialists advise on appropriate hardware, software, and peripherals (such as scanners and digital cameras) to use for completing teaching projects. They also help faculty develop and design computer-assisted instruction and presentations, which may include the use of interactive web-based applications.

Instructional Technology Specialists are also available to brainstorm about technology solutions to instructional problems. For example, a specialist and architecture lecturer might consider the use of electronic mail or video conferencing to improve communication with the lecturer's students. Furthermore, faculty members may request Instructional Technology Specialists to coteach a class session (in the computer lab or regular classroom) to instruct students on how to use the Internet, software databases, or other technology to perform specific tasks for student assignments.

Instructional Technology Specialists perform various duties, such as:

- assisting with the development and design of new services and procedures for their centers
- supervising interns
- developing and conducting training workshops and individual training sessions for faculty
- reviewing and evaluating articles and other information about new software and hardware
- maintaining equipment in their centers

Instructional Technology Specialists work 40 hours a week, but sometimes work additional hours to complete projects.

Salaries

Salaries for Instructional Technology Specialists vary, depending on such factors as their education, experience, and employer. Specific salary information for this occupation is unavailable. A general idea of their earnings may be gained by looking at the wages of instructional coordinators, a similar occupation. According to the November 2004 *Occupational Employment Statistics* survey by the U.S. Bureau of Labor Statistics, the estimated annual salary for most instructional coordinators ranged between $27,830 and $82,690.

Employment Prospects

Instructional Technology Specialists work for public and private two-year colleges, four-year colleges, and universities. This position is relatively new in academic settings. Until the 1990s, Instructional Technology Specialists were mostly employed in business and industry.

The demand for qualified Instructional Technology Specialists in academic settings is high throughout the United States. Many campuses find it difficult to recruit and retain specialists because of the growing demand for this profession in business and industry, where the salary rate is much higher.

Advancement Prospects

Advancement opportunities are limited to coordinator or director positions. With advanced degrees, Instructional Technology Specialists can pursue faculty and higher-level administrative positions on campus.

Education and Training

Instructional Technology Specialists have either bachelor's or master's degrees in instructional technology, educational media, or another related field. Most employers prefer candidates with master's or higher degrees. Many employers accept candidates who have degrees in unrelated fields as long as they have qualifying work experience.

Experience, Skills, and Personality Traits

In general, candidates need one or more years of experience in instructional technology in academic settings. Many employers require or prefer that candidates have some teaching experience.

Instructional Technology Specialists need excellent communication, interpersonal, and customer service skills to work well with faculty, staff, and others. They also need strong organizational, management, teamwork, writing, and presentation skills. Successful Instructional Technology Specialists share several personality traits such as being patient, tactful, energetic, enthusiastic, creative, and flexible.

Unions and Associations

Instructional Technology Specialists may join professional associations to take advantage of networking opportunities and other professional services and resources. Some national societies are Association for Educational Communications and Technology, American Society for Training and Development, Association for the Advancement of Computing in Education, and International Society for Performance Improvement. For contact information for these societies, see Appendix IV.

Tips for Entry

1. As a college student, obtain a part-time job in the instructional technology center.
2. Get as much teaching experience as possible so you have an understanding of what faculty want to accomplish with their instruction.
3. Contact professional associations for job listings. Many of them post job announcements on their Web sites.
4. The *Chronicle of Higher Education* is a valuable source for job listings. You can access its online version at http://chronicle.com/jobs.
5. Use the Internet to learn more about instructional technology in higher education. For a list of Web sites of different instructional technology centers, enter the keyword *instructional technology center* in a search engine.

LANGUAGE TECHNOLOGY SPECIALIST (HIGHER EDUCATION)

CAREER PROFILE

Duties: Provide technology support to foreign language faculty; conduct training workshops; perform other duties as required

Alternate Title(s): Language Technology Consultant, Modern Languages Instructional Technology Specialist, Language Lab Director (or Lab Coordinator)

Salary Range: $28,000 to $83,000

Employment Prospects: Fair

Advancement Prospects: Poor

Prerequisites:

Education or Training—Bachelor's degree or higher

Experience—Previous work experience in higher education language labs; one or more years of teaching a foreign language; instructional technology experience

Special Skills and Personality Traits—Proficient in a foreign language; communication, interpersonal, teamwork, leadership, organizational, and writing skills; be analytical, energetic, creative, patient, and respectful

CAREER LADDER

```
┌─────────────────────────────────┐
│     Language Lab Director        │
└─────────────────────────────────┘

┌─────────────────────────────────┐
│  Language Technology Specialist  │
└─────────────────────────────────┘

┌─────────────────────────────────┐
│   Language Lab Staff Member      │
└─────────────────────────────────┘
```

Position Description

In higher education institutions, Language Technology Specialists provide support to faculty in foreign language departments who seek ways to use technology to enhance their instruction. For example, a Spanish language professor might have students communicate with native speakers in Spanish-speaking countries through the Internet.

Language Technology Specialists are experts in instructional technology, and are knowledgeable of second-language acquisition principles, methods, and techniques. (Many specialists are proficient in one or more foreign languages.) Usually based in language lab centers, these specialists provide several roles.

One role is that of instructional technology consultant. Upon request, Language Technology Specialists meet with individual faculty members and assess their needs for appropriate academic technologies, such as using specific instructional software in the classroom or developing web sites for their courses. Specialists also assist faculty with developing and designing computer-based and multimedia instructional materials. In addition, they help faculty identify appropriate technical resources (such as hardware, digital cameras, and application software) for their teaching projects. Furthermore, Language Technology Specialists provide faculty members with general information on trends and innovations in instructional technology as it relates to language instruction.

Being trainers is another role that Language Technology Specialists perform. They plan and conduct individual training sessions and group training workshops on various topics that meet the needs of the faculty. For example, specialists might hold individual sessions on using a type of instructional software; conduct small workshops about using new computer operating systems in the language lab; or provide longer workshops about such topics as the integration of multimedia technology with instruction.

Many Language Technology Specialists also provide technical support in language labs. They assist with the installation and maintenance of software, operating systems, and microcomputer workstations; provide technical assistance to support staff, faculty, and students; and perform technical troubleshooting.

Some Language Technology Specialists are foreign language department faculty members, and thus responsible for teaching one or more classes per semester. Other specialists hold the position of language lab director (or coordinator), and are responsible for administering the daily operations of the lab. Their administrative duties include developing and evaluating policies and procedures for the daily use of the language lab. They also select, train, and supervise student assistants. Additionally, they maintain an inventory of equipment, software, supplies, and other materials; repair and service equipment; maintain accurate records of student attendance; and prepare required reports and paperwork.

Language Technology Specialists typically work 40 hours a week. Some positions are based on one-year or longer contracts, which are usually renewable.

Salaries

Salaries for Language Technology Specialists vary, depending on such factors as their education, experience, responsibilities, and employer. Specific salary information for this occupation is unavailable. A general idea of their earnings may be gained by looking at the wages of instructional coordinators, a similar occupation. According to the November 2004 *Occupational Employment Statistics* survey by the U.S. Bureau of Labor Statistics, the estimated annual salary for most instructional coordinators ranged between $27,830 and $82,690.

Employment Prospects

Language Technology Specialists work for foreign language institutes, two-year colleges, four-year colleges, and universities. Although this is a relatively new profession, opportunities should grow in the coming years as more higher education institutions convert from analog language labs to computer-assisted language learning centers, and as more faculty choose to integrate technology into their instruction.

Advancement Prospects

Promotions are limited to language lab coordinator and director positions. Finding work in these administrative positions may require transferring to other institutions.

With doctoral degrees, Language Technology Specialists can become professors in foreign language, instructional technology, or other disciplines in which they are interested.

Education and Training

The education requirement varies from one employer to the next. Most employers prefer that Language Technology Specialists have advanced degrees in a foreign language, educational technology, or a related field. Many employers accept candidates with bachelor's degrees if they have qualifying work experience.

Experience, Skills, and Personality Traits

Language Technology Specialists generally have previous work experience in higher education foreign language labs, and have one or more years of experience teaching a foreign language. In addition, they have experience in integrating instructional technologies into the foreign language curriculum. Many specialists are proficient in a foreign language that is taught at their institutions.

Having excellent communication, interpersonal, teamwork, and leadership skills is essential to Language Technology Specialists as they must be able to work well with staff, faculty, and students. They also have strong organizational and writing skills.

Successful Language Technology Specialists share several personality traits such as being analytical, energetic, creative, patient, and respectful.

Unions and Associations

Many Language Technology Specialists belong to professional associations to take advantage of education programs, professional publications, networking opportunities and so on. Some national societies include:

- International Association for Language Learning Technology
- Computer Assisted Language Instruction Consortium (CALICO)
- Computer-Assisted Language Learning Interest Section, a special interest group of TESOL, Inc.

For contact information for these organizations, see Appendix IV.

Tips for Entry

1. Become proficient in a second language.
2. Gain experience working as a part-time lab assistant in language labs while you are in college.
3. Contact foreign language departments or foreign language labs directly to learn about job openings.
4. Many foreign language labs have Web sites on the Internet. To get a list of relevant sites to read, enter any of these keywords in a search engine: *college language lab, university language lab,* or *foreign language lab.*

LIBRARIANS

PUBLIC LIBRARIAN

CAREER PROFILE

Duties: Help patrons access and use library resources; develop and maintain library collections; oversee library programs; perform other duties as required

Alternate Title(s): A title that reflects an area of specialty, such as Reference Librarian, Technical Service Librarian, Children's Librarian, or Special Collections Librarian

Salary Range: $30,000 to $71,000

Employment Prospects: Good

Advancement Prospects: Good

Prerequisites:

Education or Training—Master's degree in library science

Experience—Work experience in public library settings preferred

Special Skills and Personality Traits—Writing, communication, self-management; interpersonal, public service, teamwork, computer, and online skills; be courteous, friendly, enthusiastic, energetic, organized, resourceful, patient, and tolerant

Special Requirements—State or local Public Librarian certification may be required; a driver's license may be required

CAREER LADDER

```
┌─────────────────────────────────────────┐
│  Senior Librarian or Library Director     │
└─────────────────────────────────────────┘

┌─────────────────────────────────────────┐
│              Librarian                    │
└─────────────────────────────────────────┘

┌─────────────────────────────────────────┐
│     Intern or Assistant Librarian         │
└─────────────────────────────────────────┘
```

Position Description

Most communities in the United States have a public library that offers patrons free access to library collections of books, magazines, newspapers, videos, recordings, computer databases, and other print and nonprint materials. Public Librarians manage all library collections and ensure that they are readily available to library patrons.

Public Librarians perform various duties that are generally divided into public, technical, or administrative services. In the area of public services, one of their duties is to provide reference services to library patrons. Being familiar with a wide variety of scholarly and public information sources, librarians can direct patrons to print and nonprint resources that may have the information that patrons want. Public Librarians also provide search services that range from looking up a fact in an encyclopedia to an in-depth search of Internet resources. Public Librarians might assist patrons in person, over the telephone, by fax, or by E-mail.

Public Librarians also teach patrons how to use the library facilities. They give tours, describing the various collections that are available. They explain how to look up book titles, subjects, and authors in the library catalog, which most libraries now have on computer systems. Public Librarians also demonstrate how to use microfilm and microfiche machines as well as how to access CD-ROM and on-line databases and the Internet.

Many Public Librarians plan and coordinate programs and special events to promote reading and the use of library resources. These might include such programs as children's reading programs, author readings, adult literacy reading programs, video or film programs, reading groups, and workshops on using the Internet. Many Public Librarians solicit the help and input of parents, teachers, community organizations, and the general public to develop programs that meet the needs of children, teenagers, and adults in their communities.

Public Librarians assist patrons directly in many other ways, such as recommending books to read, checking out and checking in books, and borrowing books from other libraries for patrons through an interlibrary loan system.

In the area of technical services, Public Librarians maintain adequate and up-to-date library collections that support the needs of their patrons. Their duties include:

- analyzing library collections and recommending materials that should be discarded as well as new materials that should be acquired
- reading book reviews, software reviews, publishers' catalogs, and other sources to learn about new materials to add to collections
- purchasing print and nonprint materials for library collections
- classifying and cataloging materials so that they can be easily found by patrons
- compiling lists of the different print and nonprint materials in the library

Public Librarians are also responsible for performing a variety of administrative services. They develop, implement, and evaluate information systems. They negotiate contracts with various vendors for materials, equipment, and services. They select, train, and supervise library assistants, library clerks, and other support staff. Many librarians train and supervise volunteers. Public Librarians also prepare budgets, financial reports, and other reports that library directors or library boards may request. Additionally, librarians maintain accurate records of circulation, materials, and personnel. Many librarians have fund-raising duties that include writing grant proposals, soliciting gifts from donors, and participating in fund-raising activities.

In small libraries, Public Librarians usually handle all aspects of library work. In large library systems, many librarians specialize in the different public, technical, or administrative services. Public Librarians may also specialize in overseeing particular collections such as children's services, audiovisual collections, government documents collections, special collections, or bookmobile services.

Public libraries may be part of city or county government services. A large library system is typically composed of a main library and library branches in different city neighborhoods or different cities within a county. Public Librarians may be assigned to work at more than one branch.

Public Librarians work full time or part time. Their work schedules may include evening and weekend hours.

Salaries

Salaries for Public Librarians vary, depending on such factors as their experience, responsibilities, employer, and geo-

graphical location. According to the November 2004 *Occupational Employment Statistics* survey by the U.S. Bureau of Labor Statistics (BLS), the estimated annual salary for most librarians ranged between $29,890 and $71,270.

Employment Prospects

The BLS reports that employment for librarians is expected to increase by 10 to 20 percent through 2012. In addition to job growth, openings will become available as librarians retire, advance to higher positions, or transfer to other jobs. Some experts in the field expect a shortage of qualified librarians in the coming years due to the large number of librarians who are becoming eligible for retirement and the fewer number of students that are entering librarian programs. Bear in mind that the ability for a library to hire new or additional staff, as well as to keep current levels of staffing, is dependent on the availability of funds.

Advancement Prospects

Public Librarians can pursue supervisory and administrative positions all the way up to the top position of public library director. Public Librarians can also follow other librarian career paths by becoming academic librarians, research librarians, law librarians, or specialist librarians. Public Librarians can pursue other related careers such as systems analyst, database specialist, web developer, network administrator, information broker, archivist, museum curator, or research analyst careers.

Education and Training

Most employers require or prefer that Public Librarians have a master's degree in library science from a library school accredited by the American Library Association (ALA). Some employers hire Public Librarians with bachelor's or associate's degrees as long as they have qualifying work experience and have completed required courses in librarianship. They may also be required to complete a master's degree in library science within a certain time period.

Special Requirements

In some states, Public Librarians are required to hold state or local certification. The requirements for certification vary with the different states. For specific information, contact the state board or commission that oversees public libraries in the state where you wish to work.

Depending on their responsibilities, Public Librarians may be required to hold valid driver's licenses.

Experience, Skills, and Personality Traits

Employers hire candidates for entry-level positions who demonstrate a knowledge of professional library principles, methods, and techniques that include print and electronic resources. Having work experience in public library settings is generally preferred.

To do their work effectively, Public Librarians need strong writing, communication, and self-management skills (such as the ability to manage multiple tasks, set priorities, plan and organize work, and meet deadlines). They also need excellent interpersonal, public service, and teamwork skills for their job. Furthermore, they need excellent computer skills along with effective online skills for searching CD-ROM and Internet databases. Being courteous, friendly, enthusiastic, energetic, organized, resourceful, patient, and tolerant are some personality traits that Public Librarians share.

Unions and Associations

Most Public Librarians join professional associations to take advantage of professional resources, continuing education programs, job listings, networking opportunities and so on. Some national societies are American Library Association, Public Library Association, and American Society for Information Science and Technology. For contact information, see Appendix IV.

Tips for Entry

1. Volunteer or obtain library assistant jobs in public libraries to gain work experience.
2. Many colleges and universities offer graduate library science programs but not all are accredited by the ALA. Keep in mind that more and more employers prefer candidates who have graduated from ALA-approved library schools. For more information, visit the ALA Web site at http://www.ala.org.
3. Many public library systems need on-call librarians to substitute for staff members who must be absent. Contact public library personnel departments for information and job applications.
4. The selection process for Public Librarians may take several weeks to establish eligibility. You must be able to pass all steps of the selection process that includes an application, oral interview, examination, and background investigation.
5. Use the Internet to explore the array of services that various public libraries provide throughout the United States. To get a list of relevant Web sites, enter the keyword *public library* in a search engine.

CHILDREN'S LIBRARIAN

CAREER PROFILE

Duties: Help patrons access and use library resources; develop and maintain library collections; oversee children's programs; perform other duties as required

Alternate Title(s): Children Services Librarian

Salary Range: $30,00 to $71,000

Employment Prospects: Good

Advancement Prospects: Good

Prerequisites:

Education or Training—Master's degree in library science

Experience—Professional librarian with experience working with child patrons

Special Skills and Personality Traits—Interpersonal, communication, public service, writing, organizational, management, teamwork, computer, and online skills; be courteous, patient, creative, enthusiastic, friendly, energetic, and dependable

Special Requirements—State or local Public Librarian certification may be required

CAREER LADDER

```
┌─────────────────────────────────────┐
│  Senior Librarian or Library Director │
└─────────────────────────────────────┘

┌─────────────────────────────────────┐
│         Children's Librarian          │
└─────────────────────────────────────┘

┌─────────────────────────────────────┐
│     Graduate Student or Librarian     │
└─────────────────────────────────────┘
```

Position Description

Children's Librarians specialize in managing the library collections in the children's department of public libraries. The children's collection includes both print and nonprint materials such as books, magazines, recordings, videos, and CD-ROM databases. Some children's collections also include toys and games. Many Children's Librarians also maintain lists of appropriate Web sites on the Internet of topics that might interest child patrons.

Children's Librarians have many responsibilities, which include providing children's reference services to library patrons. They assist children and other patrons with their research needs, using resources in both the children's and adult sections. They direct patrons to possible sources in books, magazines, microfilm, microfiche, computer databases, and the Internet. These librarians also provide search services for their patrons, using both print and electronic resources. In addition, they teach children and other patrons how to use the library resources. For example, a Children's Librarian might show a patron how

to use the children's catalog on the library's computer system.

Children's Librarians are also responsible for developing quality collections that meet the developmental, cultural, recreational, and educational needs of the children in their communities. In many libraries, the collection includes materials in different foreign languages. Many Children's Librarians confer with local teachers so that they can select materials that would support class assignments and projects. Furthermore, Children's Librarians regularly evaluate the children's collections to make sure that materials are up-to-date and useful.

Another responsibility of Children's Librarians is planning and coordinating programs that develop children's enjoyment of reading as well as promote the use of library resources. For example, public libraries might offer storytelling programs, puppet shows, author readings, film programs, and arts and crafts programs.

Many Children's Librarians work closely with parents, teachers, social agencies, and other community organizations to develop programs that serve the educational, health, and other needs of children and their families. Thus, many public libraries also offer homework tutoring programs, family literacy programs, and children's workshops on topics such as first aid and safety.

Children's Librarians perform various other duties that vary from one librarian to the next. For example, they may be involved with developing budgets, improving work procedures, writing grant proposals, or supervising support staff and volunteers. They also keep up with current trends in children's literature and developments in the field of librarianship.

In some public libraries, Children's Librarians are responsible for the youth services department, which provides resources that meet the specific needs of teenagers. Some Children's Librarians provide support for adult reference services, filling in for reference librarians when needed.

Children's Librarians work full time or part time. They have flexible work schedules that may include evening and weekend hours.

Salaries

Salaries for Children's Librarians vary, depending on their experience, employer, geographical location, and other factors. According to the November 2004 *Occupational Employment Statistics* survey by the U.S. Bureau of Labor Statistics (BLS), the estimated annual salary for most librarians ranged between $29,890 and $71,270.

Employment Prospects

The BLS reports that employment for librarians is expected to increase by 10 to 20 percent through 2012. Although the job growth is about average for this occupation, opportunities should be favorable because of the large number of librarians who are becoming eligible for retirement and the fewer number of students entering librarian programs. However, the ability for a library to hire new or additional staff, as well as to keep current levels of staffing, is dependent on the availability of funds.

Advancement Prospects

With experience and ambition, Children's Librarians can advance to supervisory and administrative positions as department managers, branch library managers, division heads, assistant library directors, and library directors. Advancement opportunities are usually better in large public library systems.

Children's Librarians can follow other librarian career paths by becoming specialists in technical services or cataloging. They can also become school library media specialists, academic librarians, research librarians, or specialist librarians. Additionally, they can pursue related careers by becoming systems analysts, web developers, curriculum developers, or children's book authors.

Education and Training

Most employers prefer to hire candidates who have a master's degree in library science from an institution accredited by the American Library Association.

Public libraries generally require that new employees complete orientation and training programs. Many public libraries provide ongoing in service training.

Special Requirements

Children's Librarians may be required to hold state or local certification for public librarians, depending on the state where they live. For specific information, contact the state board or commission that oversees public libraries in the state where you wish to work.

Experience, Skills, and Personality Traits

Employers typically look for professional librarians who have experience working with child patrons. They also demonstrate knowledge of children's literature and are familiar with the different children's services that are offered in public libraries.

In order to relate well with children, parents, library staff, and others, Children's Librarians need superior interpersonal, communication, and public service skills. They also need effective writing, organizational, management, and teamwork skills for their job. In addition, they must have excellent computer skills along with strong online skills for searching CD-ROM and Internet databases.

Successful Children's Librarians share personality traits such as being courteous, patient, creative, enthusiastic, friendly, energetic, and dependable.

Unions and Associations

Many Children's Librarians join professional associations to take advantage of networking opportunities and other professional resources and services. A national organization specifically for Children's Librarians is the Association for Library Services to Children, a division of the American Library Association. For contact information, see Appendix IV.

Tips for Entry

1. As a college student, obtain internships with children's departments in public libraries.
2. To learn about job vacancies, contact library science schools, professional associations, and state employment offices. Also contact the personnel office of the public libraries where you would like to work.
3. Enroll in classes about child development, teaching reading to children, and other such subjects to advance your professional growth.
4. Use the Internet to learn about different children's departments in public libraries. To get a list of Web sites to read, enter the keyword *children's library services* in a search engine.

LIBRARY MEDIA SPECIALIST

CAREER PROFILE

Duties: Manage the school library media center; help patrons access and use library resources; develop and maintain collections; perform other duties as required

Alternate Title(s): School Librarian

Salary Range: $30,000 to $71,000

Employment Prospects: Good

Advancement Prospects: Fair

Prerequisites:

Education or Training—Master's degree; completion of an accredited teacher education program

Experience—Classroom teaching experience

Special Skills and Personality Traits—Teaching, communication, interpersonal management, organizational, problem-solving, computer, and online skills; be caring, patient, curious, enthusiastic, flexible, creative, resourceful

Special Requirements—A library media specialist credential; a teaching credential may be required

CAREER LADDER

```
┌─────────────────────────────────────┐
│   Library Supervisor or Coordinator  │
│  (district- or central office–level) │
└─────────────────────────────────────┘

┌─────────────────────────────────────┐
│      Library Media Specialist        │
└─────────────────────────────────────┘

┌─────────────────────────────────────┐
│             Teacher                  │
└─────────────────────────────────────┘
```

Position Description

School librarians are usually known as Library Media Specialists. They are in charge of library media centers, which include book and other print collections as well as video, software, and other nonprint collections. These centers also have multimedia workstations for students to access the Internet and other electronic resources.

Library Media Specialists have many different responsibilities. One responsibility is providing reference services to students, such as helping them locate appropriate resources for assignments and research projects as well as for their personal pleasure. Specialists also teach students essential library skills such as searching for information in print and technology resources and evaluating the information they find. In addition, Library Media Specialists instruct students on how to properly use and care for computers, copiers, and other equipment in the library media centers.

Library Media Specialists also provide consulting services to teachers about how to use the various print and electronic resources in the library media centers. Many collaborate with teachers on lesson plans to reinforce and enhance class lessons with library materials. Specialists also provide in-service training to teachers, administrators, and other school staff.

Another major duty is developing and maintaining the library media center collections of print and nonprint materials. Library Media Specialists continually review collections and discard materials that are outdated or no longer have any useful value. They select and purchase new materials that support the school curriculum as well as the diverse backgrounds, learning styles, abilities, and interests of the students.

Also part of their job is making sure that center policies such as hours of operation, library rules, circulation procedures, and rules for Internet access are in place and are being followed by students, teachers, and others. Additionally, Library Media Specialists check out and check in books. Furthermore, they perform many administrative duties such as evaluating their centers' goals; overseeing budgets; writing reports and completing required paperwork; keeping inventory of hardware and other equipment; and maintaining accurate records on circulation, work schedules, and other matters. In addition, specialists train and supervise support staff, student aides, and volunteers.

Library Media Specialists work part time or full time. They typically have a 10-month work schedule, usually from September to June.

Salaries

Salaries for Library Media Specialists vary, depending on such factors as their education, experience, employer, and geographical location. According to the November 2004 *Occupational Employment Statistics* (OES) survey by the U.S. Bureau of Labor Statistics (BLS), the estimated annual salary for most librarians ranged between $29,890 and $71,270. The estimated annual mean wage for school librarians was $49,670.

Employment Prospects

The BLS reported in its November 2004 OES survey that about 62,590 librarians were employed in elementary and secondary schools. Most openings become available as Library Media Specialists retire, resign, or transfer to other jobs. Opportunities should be favorable for qualified librarians because a large number of librarians are becoming eligible for retirement within the coming years. However, the ability for schools to hire new or additional staff is dependent on the availability of funds.

Advancement Prospects

In library media centers with more than one staff member, Library Media Specialists can advance to supervisory and managerial positions. With additional licensure, specialists can become library supervisors or coordinators at the district (or central office) level. Those with higher administrative ambitions can pursue positions as principals, program directors, assistant superintendents, and school superintendents.

Library Media Specialists can pursue other librarian careers by becoming academic librarians, public librarians, research librarians, or special librarians.

Education and Training

Most employers prefer to hire applicants who possess a master's degree in library science from schools accredited by the American Library Association or the National Council for the Accreditation of Teacher Education.

Licensed Library Media Specialists must have completed an approved school library media program that leads to licensure in the state where they practice. The program also includes a supervised field practicum.

Special Requirements

In public schools, Library Media Specialists must hold a Library Media Specialist credential. They may also be required to hold a teaching credential. For specific information, contact the state board of education in the state where you wish to work. See Appendix III for a list of boards.

Many private schools require state licensure or professional certification from school accreditation organizations or other recognized organizations.

Experience, Skills, and Personality Traits

Most public schools require that Library Media Specialists have previous classroom teaching experience. The minimum number of years varies among different schools. Both public and private schools look for candidates who have traditional library skills as well as knowledge about technology to support curriculum and instruction programs.

To do their work effectively, Library Media Specialists need excellent teaching, communication, interpersonal, management, organizational, and problem-solving skills. They also need superior computer skills and effective online skills for searching CD-ROM and Internet databases.

Successful Library Media Specialists share several personality traits such as being caring, patient, curious, enthusiastic, flexible, creative, and resourceful.

Unions and Associations

Many Library Media Specialists join professional associations to take advantage of networking opportunities, education programs, and other professional resources and services. Some national societies include the American Association of School Librarians and the Association for Educational Communications and Technology. Public school librarians are eligible to join a teacher union, such as the American Federation of Teachers or the National Education Association. For contact information for these organizations, see Appendix IV.

Tips for Entry

1. To learn more about the profession, visit school library media centers at the different school levels. Talk with Library Media Specialists about their jobs. Also volunteer or intern at a school library media center during your undergraduate years in college.
2. Contact public and private schools where you would like to work. Be ready to complete job applications and to submit your resume.
3. Use the Internet to learn more about the Library Media Specialist profession. To get a list of relevant Web sites, enter the keyword *library media specialist* in a search engine.

ACADEMIC LIBRARIAN

CAREER PROFILE

Duties: Develop library collections; provide consultation services to faculty; teach students library research skills; perform public services, technical, and/or administrative duties

Alternate Title(s): A title that reflects a specialized area such as Public Services Librarian, Technical Services Librarian, Computer Services Librarian, or Special Collections Librarian

Salary Range: $30,000 to $71,000

Employment Prospects: Fair

Advancement Prospects: Good

Prerequisites:

Education or Training—Master's degree in library science

Experience—Previous work experience in an academic library setting; teaching experience preferred

Special Skills and Personality Traits—Analytical, writing, presentation, supervisory, teaching, organizational, communication, interpersonal, computer, and online skills; be courteous, energetic, organized, patient, flexible, and resourceful

CAREER LADDER

```
┌─────────────────────────────┐
│      Senior Librarian       │
└─────────────────────────────┘

┌─────────────────────────────┐
│     Academic Librarian      │
└─────────────────────────────┘

┌─────────────────────────────┐
│           Intern            │
└─────────────────────────────┘
```

Position Description

In large institutions, the academic library may be composed of a central library and branch libraries that are located throughout the campus. All academic libraries hold a vast number of diverse collections of print and nonprint materials that support the many different degree programs at their institutions. Most, if not all, academic libraries are part of integrated on-line library systems that allow access to library catalogs at other college and university libraries as well as other public and private library systems.

The responsibility of managing an academic library's various collections is shared by a staff of Academic Librarians. They work closely with faculty to develop collections that offer primary and secondary sources for research projects. Also in collaboration with the faculty, Academic Librarians develop educational programs that provide students with effective information literacy skills.

Like all professional librarians, Academic Librarians perform duties in three basic areas. One area is public services (or user services). Essentially, Academic Librarians provide reference services to students, faculty, and others, using the available print and electronic resources in their libraries. They also explain and demonstrate how to use the library resources and equipment. In addition, they teach students library research skills through seminars, workshops, and individual consultations.

Technical services is another area of responsibility that Academic Librarians have. Their duties include acquiring new library materials in all media formats (print, audio, video, software, and so on). They also classify and catalog materials so that patrons can easily find them, prepare new materials for distribution, and compile reading lists, among other tasks.

Academic Librarians are also responsible for administrative services. These duties include: coordinating library activities; supervising support staff; preparing budgets;

negotiating contracts for materials and equipment; administrating public relations activities and so forth.

Academic Librarians usually specialize in specific types of public, technical, or administrative services. For example:

* *Reference librarians* help students find appropriate print and electronic resources for their research projects.
* *Acquisition librarians* select and purchase print and nonprint materials for the libraries.
* *Technical services librarians* process new library materials, such as cataloging and classifying materials.
* *Computer services librarians* administer and maintain library's computer systems and other computer resources.
* *Special collections librarians* develop and promote use of their institutions' rare book and manuscript holdings.

In many higher education institutions, Academic Librarians' jobs are tenure-track positions. With tenure, Academic Librarians are assured of a job at an institution until they retire or resign.

Academic Librarians work part time or full time. Their work schedules may include evening and weekend hours.

Salaries

Salaries for Academic Librarians vary, depending on such factors as their education, experience, employer, and geographical location. The U.S. Bureau of Labor Statistics (BLS) reported in its November 2004 *Occupational Employment Statistics* (OES) survey that the estimated annual salary for most librarians ranged between $29,890 and $71,270. The estimated annual mean wage for librarians in colleges and universities was $51,550, and for those in junior colleges, $53,510.

Employment Prospects

According to the BLS's November 2004 OES survey, about 20,320 librarians were employed in colleges and universities and about 4,030 were employed in junior colleges. Employment for librarians, in general, is expected to increase by 10 to 20 percent through 2012. Openings will also become available to replace librarians who retire, advance to higher positions, or transfer to other jobs. However, the ability for employers to hire new or additional staff, as well as to keep current levels of staffing, is dependent on the availability of funds.

Advancement Prospects

Academic Librarians can advance to such supervisory and administrative positions as department heads and library directors. To obtain faculty or higher administrative positions (such as deans), a doctoral degree in library science is usually required.

Academic Librarians can follow other librarian career paths by becoming research librarians, law librarians, or specialist librarians (in private corporations). Academic Librarians can also pursue other related careers, such as archivist, research analyst, information broker, systems analyst, or network administrator careers.

Education and Training

Academic Librarians are required to have a master's degree in library science from a program accredited by the American Library Association.

Experience, Skills, and Personality Traits

In general, employers look for candidates who have previous experience in the academic library setting, and prefer those with some teaching experience. Candidates should have a strong background with electronic information and instructional technologies. Other requirements vary and depend on the type of position (such as special collections librarian) for which a candidate is applying.

Academic Librarians must have adequate analytical, writing, presentation, supervisory, teaching, and organizational skills. They also need good communication and interpersonal skills. In addition, they need excellent computer skills and online skills that include searching computer databases and the Internet. Successful Academic Librarians share various personality traits such as being courteous, energetic, organized, patient, flexible, and resourceful.

Unions and Associations

Many Academic Librarians belong to professional associations to take advantage of professional resources, continuing education programs, job listings, networking opportunities, and other services. Two national societies that many librarians join are the Association of College and Research Libraries and the American Society for Information Science and Technology. For contact information, see Appendix IV.

Tips for Entry

1. If you will be working part time while in college, try to obtain a job at your institution's library.
2. Attend professional conferences and network with your peers.
3. Many professional associations post job listings at their Web sites.
4. Use the Internet to learn more about academic libraries where you want to work. To find a particular Web site, enter the institution's name plus the keyword *library* in a search engine. Example: *Columbia University Library.*

LIBRARY TECHNICIAN

CAREER PROFILE

Duties: Assist librarians with providing user and technical services; perform other duties as required

Alternate Title(s): Library Technical Assistant, Library Assistant, Library Clerk

Salary Range: $15,000 to $41,000

Employment Prospects: Good

Advancement Prospects: Fair

Prerequisites:

Education or Training—High school diploma; some employers require an associate's or bachelor's degree

Experience—Prior general clerical or library experience usually required

Special Skills and Personality Traits—Computer, communication, interpersonal, customer service, teamwork, organizational, and self-management skills; be detail-oriented, accurate, calm, patient, flexible, friendly, tactful

CAREER LADDER

```
┌─────────────────────────────┐
│  Senior Library Technician  │
└─────────────────────────────┘

┌─────────────────────────────┐
│     Library Technician      │
└─────────────────────────────┘

┌─────────────────────────────┐
│        Library Aide         │
└─────────────────────────────┘
```

Position Description

Library Technicians assist librarians with running the day-to-day operations of libraries. These paraprofessionals work in school library media centers, academic (college or university) libraries, public libraries, and special libraries. (A special library focuses on the interests of the organization of which it is part, such as a corporation, law firm, government agency, hospital, museum, research institution, or professional association.)

Library Technicians perform a variety of tasks that are generally categorized as public (or user) services and technical services. Within the area of public services, Library Technicians help patrons locate library materials as well as show patrons how to use reference sources, indexes, and catalog systems. They also teach patrons how to use the library's computers, photocopiers, and audiovisual equipment.

In addition, Library Technicians provide patrons, the general public, and others with general information about library services, library policies, the location of departments, and so forth. They may respond to reference questions that require some research. Library Technicians refer difficult questions to appropriate staff members.

Library Technicians who staff the circulation desk perform such duties as checking books and other items in and out, processing overdue notices, collecting fees and fines from patrons, and issuing library cards.

Some Library Technicians in public libraries are responsible for operating bookmobiles. These are trucks stocked with book collections that some public libraries use to extend library services to remote areas or to schools, nursing homes, shopping centers, and other designated sites in the communities that the libraries serve. Some bookmobiles are also equipped with copiers and personal computers for their patrons' use. Library Technicians are responsible for maintaining the book collections, answering patrons' questions, checking out books, and so on. Some technicians are also responsible for driving and maintaining bookmobiles, and keeping track of their mileage.

In the area of technical services, Library Technicians help librarians acquire, prepare, and organize book collections, periodicals, tapes, and other materials. Their tasks may include sorting and shelving library materials, compiling special bibliographies and book lists, processing and preparing new library materials for circulation, and making minor repairs to damaged books.

In large libraries, technicians provide either public or technical services. Some further specialize by working in a particular department, such as the special collections, reference, acquisition, or cataloging department.

Many Library Technicians are responsible for administrative tasks that vary according to their experience and job level. For example, technicians may be assigned to maintain databases, compile library statistics, operate and maintain audiovisual equipment, supervise library aides and other support staff, and assist with the development of library procedures. Some Library Technicians assist with designing displays, bulletin boards, and posters to promote their library's services.

Most, if not all, Library Technicians are responsible for performing a variety of general office duties. They answer telephones, photocopy materials, sort and distribute mail, maintain office equipment, and monitor the inventory of office supplies.

Library Technicians work under the direction of librarians, but perform many of their duties independently. Many technicians have the authority to make autonomous decisions, such as when handling disruptive patrons or supervising volunteer library aides. Their job requires some physical activity. They carry and lift bcoks as well as stoop, bend, and reach for books. Their assignments may require them to sit at desks and work on computer terminals for hours, which may lead to such problems as eyestrain, back problems, and carpal tunnel syndrome. On occasion, technicians must deal with patrons who are upset, angry, distraught, or hostile.

Library Technicians may work part time or full time. Some technicians are hired on an on-call basis. School library technicians typically work regular school hours, whereas technicians in other settings may be assigned to work evenings and weekends.

Salaries
Salaries for Library Technicians vary, depending on such factors as their education, experience, job duties, employer, and geographical location. According to the November 2004 *Occupational Employment Statistics* survey, by the U.S. Bureau of Labor Statistics (BLS), the estimated annual salary for most library technicians ranged between $14,990 and $41,370.

Employment Prospects
The BLS predicts that employment of Library Technicians should increase by 10 to 20 percent through 2012. Because of the increasing use of computerized circulation and information systems, technicians are able to handle routine tasks that were once performed by librarians. This is expected to create a demand for more Library Technicians. In addition to job growth, opportunities will become available as technicians transfer to other occupations or leave the workforce for various reasons. However, a library's ability to hire new employees or maintain its current staff is dependent on its funding.

Opportunities are expected to be stronger in special libraries due to the growing number of people using them.

Advancement Prospects
With additional education and experience, Library Technicians can advance to supervisory and administrative positions. Promotion opportunities are generally more numerous in larger libraries. Some Library Technicians pursue a master's degree in library science to become librarians.

Many Library Technicians realize career advancement by earning higher wages, being assigned complex responsibilities, and enjoying professional recognition.

Education and Training
Minimally, applicants must have a high school or general equivalency diploma. Some employers prefer to hire applicants with at least an associate's degree or some college course work in library technology, while other employers require that applicants have a bachelor's degree. Technical libraries may require that applicants have training in appropriate fields.

New employees typically receive on-the-job training, in which they learn their duties and tasks from experienced technicians.

Experience, Skills, and Personality Traits
Depending on the setting, entry-level applicants may be required to have six months to three years of general clerical or library experience.

Library Technicians must have strong computer skills, including the ability to work with database software. They also need excellent communication, interpersonal, and customer service skills, as they must be able to work well with supervisors, coworkers, and patrons. Having teamwork, organizational, and self-management skills is also essential. Being detail-oriented, accurate, calm, patient, flexible, friendly, and tactful are some personality traits that successful Library Technicians share.

Unions and Associations
Many Library Technicians are members of professional associations to take advantage of networking opportunities, education programs, and other professional resources and services. Two national societies they might join are the Council on Library/Media Technicians and the American Library Association. For contact information, see Appendix IV.

Some Library Technicians belong to a union that represents them in contract negotiations with their employers.

Tips for Entry
1. As a high school student, gain experience by volunteering or getting a part-time job as a library aide in your school or public library.
2. Apply directly to the personnel departments of libraries where you would like to work.
3. Gain valuable training by enrolling in some or all courses of a library technology program at a community college.
4. Applicants for civil service jobs will need to pass civil service examinations for employment.
5. Learn more about Library Technicians on the Internet. You might start by visiting the Council on Library/Media Technicians Web site, http://colt.ucr.edu.

INDEPENDENT INSTRUCTORS

INDEPENDENT INSTRUCTOR

CAREER PROFILE

Duties: Prepare and provide instruction in a subject, craft, sport, or other area in which one is an expert; perform small business duties; perform other duties as required

Alternate Title(s): A title that reflects the subject being taught, such as Yoga Instructor, Guitar Teacher, or Flight Instructor

Salary Range: $17,000 to $62,000

Employment Prospects: Good

Advancement Prospects: Poor

Prerequisites:

Education or Training—Varies with each field

Experience—Extensive prior experience in the subject matter

Special Skills and Personality Traits—Leadership, communication, interpersonal, organizational, time-management, and small-business skills; be patient, calm, inspiring, flexible, creative, resourceful, self-disciplined

Special Requirements—Professional licensure or certification may be required; business licenses may be needed

CAREER LADDER

```
varies with each individual
```

```
Independent Instructor
```

```
Professional in one's field
```

Position Description

Independent Instructors are self-employed educators. They offer instruction for classes in nonacademic and nonvocational subjects in which students usually enroll for fun, self-enrichment, or professional development. Depending on their expertise and interests, these instructors teach topics and skills in a wide range of areas, such as music, art, crafts, cooking, dance, physical fitness, sports, flying, personal finance, self-improvement, CPR, business writing, or computing.

Independent Instructors generally offer instruction in two ways. They may give private lessons to individuals and small groups from their homes, offices, studios, or rental spaces. (Some instructors provide lessons in their students' homes.) They may teach classes, seminars, or workshops through educational programs sponsored by educational institutions, recreational centers, museums, community groups, professional associations, retail businesses, private companies, and other organizations. They work on a contractual basis and offer their courses to an organization for a specific time frame. For example, a scrapbooking instructor might teach a one-day workshop at a crafts store and a four-week course at a community college.

Independent Instructors are responsible for the development of each course they plan to offer. They define the objectives—what students will learn—and what type of assessment they will use to determine that students are meeting the objectives. They decide whether the course will be in the form of a class, seminar, or workshop, how many sessions will be needed, and the length of each session. In addition, they develop a course outline, which is the sequence of the concepts and skills to be covered at each meeting. Furthermore, instructors prepare lesson plans, which involves creating student materials as well as class exercises and enrichment activities that provide students with hands-on experience.

Instructors use teaching methods appropriate to the subject matter, such as lectures, demonstrations, modeling, group work, and individual instruction. They also adapt their teaching methods and materials to fit the varying abilities and interests of their students. Many instructors use computers and audiovisual equipment to augment their instruction.

Independents Instructors may be freelancers or business owners. The difference between the two is this: Business owners usually receive a wage or salary, while freelancers' income is based on their net profits from fees they receive from students or organizations. Freelancers' earnings come directly from the profits they makes after subtracting the cost of running a business.

As freelancers or business owners, Independent Instructors are responsible for running the various aspects of their businesses. If they offer private lessons, they develop policies on matters such as the maximum number of students they will teach, the criteria by which they will accept new students, lesson fees and forms of acceptable payment, and whether they will allow make-up lessons for absent students.

All Independent Instructors routinely attend to such financial tasks as planning a budget, keeping track of finances, collecting fees from students or organizations, and paying taxes and bills. Keeping required business licenses up to date, preparing correspondence and invoices, maintaining their office and equipment, and inventorying supplies are other essential tasks that they perform. If they hire teaching or office staff, the instructors are responsible for providing ongoing supervision and training.

Independent Instructors are also responsible for generating more business. For example, they might promote their business through a Web site, listings in telephone directories, or advertisements in local newspapers. They also continually query organizations where they might offer classes or workshops on a contractual basis. Some instructors join local business associations, community organizations, or professional associations to build a network of contacts and support.

Independent Instructors determine their own work schedules. Some instructors teach part time while they continue to work (full time or part time) at their regular occupations. Other teachers, such as sports instructors and music teachers, work part time so that they can practice for competitions or performances. Some instructors work as educational consultants, offering such services as developing educational or training programs and designing instructional materials.

Many Independent Instructors work more than 40 hours a week to complete their teaching and business tasks. Some instructors travel to other cities and states to conduct workshops, seminars, or classes.

Salaries

Earnings for Independent Instructors vary, depending on many factors. These may include the rates they charge for lessons, the demand for their type of instruction, their geographical location, their business costs, and their ambition to increase their business. Their annual earnings also vary from year to year, based on their net profit after subtracting total business costs from their gross earnings.

Formal salary surveys for Independent Instructors are unavailable. A general idea of what they make can be gained by looking at how much salaried self-enrichment instructors earn. According to the November 2004 *Occupational Employment Statistics* survey by the U.S. Bureau of Labor Statistics, the estimated annual salary for most self-enrichment instructors ranged between $16,890 and $62,100.

Employment Prospects

Contractual opportunities for Independent Instructors can be found with almost any organization or institution. The success of obtaining contractual opportunities as well as finding students for private lessons depends on instructors' ambitions and resourcefulness, the demand for the type of instruction they provide, and how much competition they have.

Advancement Prospects

Advancement opportunities are defined by an individual's interests and ambitions. Many Independent Instructors realize advancement by earning a higher income, having job satisfaction, and gaining professional recognition.

For some instructors, self-employment is part of their overall career development. They use it as a stepping-stone to pursue permanent, full-time teaching or education-related positions with schools, colleges, universities, or other organizations.

Education and Training

Independent Instructors typically possess the education and training required for their professions (such as musicians, pilots, and fitness trainers) or for the subjects they teach that are outside of their professional training. The amount and type of education and training varies with the different fields.

Depending on the subject matter, organizations may require Independent Instructors to minimally possess an associate's, bachelor's, or advanced degree. Some organizations allow instructors to substitute work experience for some or all of the educational requirement.

Special Requirements

Independent Instructors may be required to possess an occupational license, professional certification, or other type of certification to teach their particular subject matter. For example, flight instructors must hold the proper pilot, flight instructor, and medical certifications granted by the Federal Aviation Administration.

Business owners must obtain the necessary business licenses to operate in their state and community.

Experience, Skills, and Personality Traits

Independent Instructors typically have extensive experience with the subject matter in which they offer instruction.

Many of them have previous teaching experience that they may have gained as educators and trainers, as well as through direct supervision and training of employees.

Independent Instructors need excellent leadership, communication, and interpersonal skills to work well with students. Having strong organizational, time-management, and small-business skills is essential to succeed as freelancers and business owners. Being patient, calm, inspiring, flexible, creative, resourceful, and self-disciplined are some personality traits that successful Independent Instructors share.

Unions and Associations

Many instructors belong to professional associations that serve their particular fields to take advantage of networking opportunities, professional development, and other professional services and resources. For example, independent ski instructors might join the Professional Ski Instructors of America, whereas independent rescue instructors might belong to the International Rescue Instructors Association and independent pet dog trainers might be members of the National Association of Dog Obedience Instructors. For contact information for these organizations, see Appendix IV.

Tips for Entry

1. Gain teaching experience by volunteering to facilitate workshops or classes at senior centers, community centers, recreation centers, museums, or other organizations.
2. Contact continuing education programs in your area to learn about contractual teaching opportunities, requirements for instructors, and submitting course proposals.
3. Volunteer to give a workshop at a professional conference, community event, or other event to make yourself known with your targeted audience.
4. Be sure you understand the lifestyle and work that is involved in becoming self-employed. Read books about self-employment and talk with independent instructors or other self-employed professionals.
5. Use the Internet to learn more about starting a business. You might start by visiting the U.S. Small Business Administration Web site at http://www.sba.gov.

MUSIC TEACHER

CAREER PROFILE

Duties: Teach music lessons; develop curriculum and lesson plans; perform other duties as required

Alternate Title(s): Voice Teacher, Guitar Teacher, or other title that reflects the type of lessons being taught

Salary Range: $10 to $100 per hour

Employment Prospects: Good

Advancement Prospects: Poor

Prerequisites:

Education or Training—Extensive music training in the types of vocal and instrumental instruction being offered

Experience—Broad background in music with performance skills; teaching experience is helpful

Special Skills and Personality Traits—Communication, interpersonal, motivational, organizational, time-management, public relations, customer service, and small-business skills; be friendly, patient, calm, flexible, enthusiastic, trustworthy, creative, and resourceful

CAREER LADDER

```
┌────────────────────────────────────────┐
│        Owner of larger studio or        │
│   School Music Teacher or Professor     │
└────────────────────────────────────────┘

┌────────────────────────────────────────┐
│         Independent Music Teacher        │
└────────────────────────────────────────┘

┌────────────────────────────────────────┐
│              Music Teacher               │
└────────────────────────────────────────┘
```

Position Description

Independent Music Teachers operate their own studios, offering private music lessons to children and adults. They provide instruction for the various types of instruments—violin, bass, guitar, flute, clarinet, saxophone, trumpet, trombone, tuba, percussion, accordion, harp, organ, electronic keyboards, and so on. Some teachers offer vocal or singing instruction. In addition, many instructors specialize in teaching particular types of music such as jazz, classical, country, Afro-Cuban, or Latin. Some also offer instruction in music theory or music history.

Music Teachers provide individual and group lessons to beginning, intermediate, and advanced students. In group lessons, students are generally at the same skill level. Most teachers work out of their homes or in rented facilities. Some provide lessons in students' homes.

Independent teachers are responsible for developing their own curriculum—the skills that they teach, the order for teaching the skills, and the musical pieces that students practice. Teachers also create lesson plans and compile a repertoire of musical pieces which they assign to their students. Many instructors base their instruction on one or more method books, which consist of established, graded curriculum developed by recognized music educators. Some Music Teachers integrate technology, such as electronic keyboards and music instruction software, into their curriculum.

Students receive weekly lessons that are usually 30 to 60 minutes long. Within a lesson, Music Teachers review the previous week's lesson and teach a new lesson which builds on students' prior learning. They assign students new musical pieces that best match students' abilities, skill levels, and personal interests.

Music Teachers encourage their students to practice as much as possible during the week, and may help them establish a workable practice schedule. Many Music Teachers hold student recitals so that students can experience performing their music before the public. With intermediate and advanced students, Music Teachers might schedule performances for senior centers, child care centers, or other organizations.

Independent Music Teachers are responsible for running their own businesses. They establish studio policies such as the criteria by which they will accept new students, the maximum number of students they will teach, how students should pay for their lessons, and the number of weeks for a class term. These teachers also attend to various administrative tasks. For example, they schedule lessons, collect students' fees, do bookkeeping, pay bills, maintain student records, and clean studio space. In addition, independent teachers continually look for ways to bring in new students.

Making a steady income from private instruction is difficult, thus many independent teachers seek additional means of income. Some teachers offer music classes through continuing education programs, music stores, and other studios. Some work part time as Music Teachers in schools or colleges, while others hold jobs in customer service, clerical, sales, and other areas.

Independent teachers have flexible work schedules. They often hold lessons during evenings and on weekends to accommodate their students' schedules.

Salaries
Annual earnings for independent Music Teachers vary, depending on such factors as the rates they charge for lessons, the demand for their type of instruction, their geographical location, their business costs, and their ambition to increase their business. According to MENC: The National Association for Music Education, studio teachers generally earn between $10 and $100 per hour for music lessons.

Employment Prospects
Within any given community, opportunities for independent Music Teachers depend on the local demand for the types of music lessons that they offer, as well as the number of teachers within the area who provide similar music lessons. Private Music Teachers are usually in greater demand in rural areas, areas that are experiencing a rapid increase in population, and in communities that lack comprehensive music programs within their public schools.

Advancement Prospects
Advancement opportunities are defined by an individual's interests and ambitions. Many independent Music Teachers realize advancement through job satisfaction, professional recognition, and the growth of their music studios.

Those wishing more job and financial security can pursue music education careers in public or private schools, music schools, colleges, and universities. Depending on the institutional setting, they may need to obtain additional education and teaching credentials.

Education and Training
College degrees are not required to become an independent Music Teacher; however, many instructors have bachelor's or advanced degrees in music, education, or other related fields. Music Teachers without degrees should have an expansive knowledge of music. In addition they have extensive music training in the types of vocal and instrumental instruction they plan to offer.

Experience, Skills, and Personality Traits
Independent teachers should have a broad music background that includes several years of experience performing their instruments. Having teaching experience is helpful.

To work well with students, Music Teachers should have excellent communication, interpersonal, and motivational skills. As business owners, they should have adequate organizational, time-management, public relations, customer service, and small-business skills. Successful independent Music Teachers have several personality traits in common, such as being friendly, patient, calm, flexible, enthusiastic, trustworthy, creative, and resourceful.

Unions and Associations
Professional associations are available for the various types of Music Teachers, as well as societies that serve the interests of all music teachers. By joining professional organizations, independent teachers can take advantage of networking opportunities, education programs, and other professional resources and services.

The Music Teachers National Association and MENC: The National Association for Music Education are two national organizations that serve the general interests of music teachers. For contact information, see Appendix IV.

Tips for Entry
1. To enhance their credibility as a music educator, some instructors obtain professional certification from a recognized organization, such as the Music Teachers National Association.
2. Define your teaching philosophy: Why do you teach? What do you wish your students to achieve and learn? Your teaching philosophy not only guides you in developing your instructional style and curriculum, but also in preparing your business marketing plan.
3. The Internet has many resources available for independent Music Teachers. To get a list of relevant Web sites, enter any of these keywords in a search engine: *private music teacher, private music teaching,* or *private music instruction.*

DANCE TEACHER

CAREER PROFILE

Duties: Teach dance lessons; develop curriculum and lessons; perform other duties as required

Alternate Title(s): A title, such as Ballroom Dance Teacher, that reflects the form of dance being taught

Salary Range: $17,000 to $62,000

Employment Prospects: Good

Advancement Prospects: Poor

Prerequisites:

    Education or Training—Several years of dance training in chosen discipline; apprenticeship as a dance teacher

    Experience—Performance experience; teaching experience or equivalent training

    Special Skills and Personality Traits—Communication, interpersonal, motivational, customer service, organizational, management, and leadership skills; small-business and public relations skills (if studio owners); be friendly, positive, caring, enthusiastic, energetic, calm, patient, and creative

CAREER LADDER

```
┌─────────────────────────────────────┐
│         Dance Studio Owner           │
└─────────────────────────────────────┘


┌─────────────────────────────────────┐
│      Independent Dance Teacher       │
└─────────────────────────────────────┘


┌─────────────────────────────────────┐
│  Apprentice or Teaching Assistant    │
└─────────────────────────────────────┘
```

Position Description

Independent Dance Teachers offer dance lessons to students of all ages, from preschoolers to senior citizens. They may teach one or more forms of dance—ballet, tap dance, jazz dance, line dancing, ballroom dancing, social dancing, Hawaiian dance, country Scottish dancing, belly dancing, Latin dances, swing dance, square dancing, modern dance, folk dances, and so on. These independent instructors may have their own dance studios or work on a contractual basis at a dance school or at someone else's dance studio. Some independent teachers also offer dance classes through continuing education programs sponsored by community centers, colleges, or other organizations.

Instructors teach beginning, intermediate, and advanced students on a group basis. Upon request, Dance Teachers provide individual coaching to amateur and professional dancers, as well as offer private lessons to students of all abilities.

Dance Teachers are responsible for developing curriculum plans for their studios. If they work at other dance studios, they may assist with curriculum development. These instructors also teach classes according to the methods and philosophy of their employers. However, Dance Teachers each bring their own teaching styles to their lessons.

All Dance Teachers prepare for their classes, creating formal or informal lesson plans. They choose dances and music that match the ages, abilities, and interests of their students, and gather all necessary materials and equipment for their lessons. If musicians will be providing music for the lessons, then teachers must let the musicians know what songs to play, as well as provide them with music scores, if needed.

In general, lessons begin with warm-ups and a review of learned skills. Teachers then demonstrate new steps and movements, which are built upon their students' previous lessons. Dance Teachers observe students as they practice, giving them individual attention to help them execute new steps and movements correctly. Teachers also make sure that students are standing and moving properly so as to prevent injuries. Dance Teachers give students positive feedback throughout their lessons. Teachers also encourage students to practice their steps as often as they can throughout the week.

Studio owners are responsible for the success of their businesses. Whether they run their studios from their homes or rented facilities, they develop studio policies on matters such as tuition payments and make-up classes for absent students. They are also in charge of arranging class schedules, collecting fees, paying bills, keeping accurate records, cleaning and maintaining studio space. If they have additional teachers working for them, they provide them with ongoing supervision and training. Studio owners also continually look for ways to bring in new students.

Independent Dance Teachers have flexible hours, often teaching classes on evenings and weekends to accommodate the schedules of their students.

Salaries

Annual earnings for independent Dance Teachers vary, depending on such factors as the rates they charge for lessons, the demand for their type of instruction, their geographical location, their business costs, and their ambition to increase their business.

Formal salary information for independent Dance Teachers is unavailable. A general idea of what they may make can be gained by looking at how much salaried self-enrichment instructors earn. According to the November 2004 *Occupational Employment Statistics* survey by the U.S. Bureau of Labor Statistics, the estimated annual salary for most self-enrichment instructors ranged between $16,890 and $62,100.

Employment Prospects

In general, the competition for teaching positions in private dance studios is high. The opportunities are better for Dance Teachers who own studios. Their success as studio owners depends on factors such as the local demand for the types of dance lessons that they offer, the number of teachers within the area who provide similar dance lessons, and how well individual teachers run their businesses.

Advancement Prospects

Advancement opportunities are defined by an individual's interests and ambitions. Independent Dance Teachers generally realize advancement through job satisfaction, professional recognition, and the successful growth of their businesses. Those wanting more financial security may seek staff positions with dance schools. With additional education, they can pursue teaching careers at the school or college level. To teach in public schools may require obtaining teaching credentials.

Education and Training

College degrees are not required for becoming independent Dance Teachers; however, many do have bachelor's or advanced degrees in dance or related fields. In general, Dance Teachers have had several years of serious training in their discipline. In addition, most had served as apprentice teachers or obtained the appropriate training to teach their particular forms of dance.

Experience, Skills, and Personality Traits

Along with a solid foundation in the performance of their discipline, Dance Teachers have broad life experiences upon which to draw in order to reach the different abilities and personalities of their students. In addition, Dance Instructors have previous teaching experience or appropriate training in dance education.

To do their work effectively, Dance Teachers need excellent communication, interpersonal, motivational, customer service, organizational, management, and leadership skills. As studio owners, they should also have adequate small-business and public relations skills.

Successful Dance Teachers have several personality traits in common, such as being friendly, positive, caring, enthusiastic, energetic, calm, patient, and creative.

Unions and Associations

Professional associations are available for the various types of Dance Teachers. By joining professional organizations, independent teachers can take advantage of education programs, networking opportunities, and other professional resources and services. The Dance Educators of America, the National Dance Association, and the American Dance Guild are some national societies that serve the general interests of dance teachers. For contact information, see Appendix IV.

Tips for Entry

1. Contact Dance Teachers with whom you would like to train about an apprenticeship.
2. To gain teaching experience, volunteer to give dance lessons at a community center, church, youth group, or senior center.
3. Enroll in business courses to help you run a business effectively and successfully.
4. You can use the Internet to learn more about dance education. To get a list of relevant Web sites, enter any of these keywords in a search engine: *dance education, dance teacher,* or *dance studio.*

RIDING INSTRUCTOR

CAREER PROFILE

Duties: Teach riding and horsemanship lessons; develop curriculum and lesson plans; perform other duties as required

Alternate Title(s): None

Salary Range: $20 to $250+ per hour

Employment Prospects: Good

Advancement Prospects: Poor

Prerequisites:

Education or Training—Apprenticeship under experienced instructors

Experience—Competent rider; solid foundation in horsemanship and horse care

Special Skills and Personality Traits—Leadership, organizational, management, communication, interpersonal, and customer service skills; if owners—small-business and public relations skills; friendly, enthusiastic, flexible, patient, caring, energetic, and responsible

CAREER LADDER

```
┌─────────────────────────────────────┐
│  Riding School Manager or Owner      │
└─────────────────────────────────────┘

┌─────────────────────────────────────┐
│         Riding Instructor            │
└─────────────────────────────────────┘

┌─────────────────────────────────────┐
│        Apprentice or Intern          │
└─────────────────────────────────────┘
```

Position Description

Independent Riding Instructors offer private horse-back riding lessons to children, teenagers, and adults. They teach individuals how to ride their horses properly and safely, and how to give their horses the appropriate commands to go, stop, walk, change directions, trot, gallop, jump, and so forth. Riding Instructors teach lessons for one or more different types of riding activities—such as English-style or Western-style pleasure riding, trail riding, long distance riding, dressage, hunt seat riding, vaulting, and barrel racing. Some instructors also teach carriage driving.

Independent instructors may offer lessons at their own stables or through someone else's stables. Some instructors work on a contractual basis at riding schools, horse farms and stables, dude ranches, or other horse-related businesses. Some Riding Instructors consider teaching their primary focus, while others teach riding lessons as part of the overall horse training services that they provide customers. (Many Riding Instructors also continue to participate in horse shows and riding competitions.)

Riding Instructors develop a teaching philosophy upon which they build their curriculum and lessons as well as

their teaching methods and techniques. They teach lessons that are appropriate to the skill levels and abilities of their students. Beginning students, for example, learn basic horsemanship skills, such as correct riding posture; proper mounting and dismounting; and hand, leg, and voice commands. They also learn how to saddle their horses and prepare them for riding as well as to care for their horses and equipment afterward. Riding Instructors build up students' riding skills slowly and ensure that students learn proper and safe practices and use them as they develop their riding proficiency.

Many Riding Instructors perform other nonteaching duties. They may help with the feeding, grooming, exercising, and care of horses. They may also maintain stables and grounds, as well as assist with administrative tasks such as answering phones and keeping accurate records of their students' progress.

Independent instructors who own riding schools have the responsibility of operating their businesses. They develop school policies on matters such as student requirements, tuition payments, and make-up classes for absent students. They take charge of arranging schedules, collecting fees, paying bills and taxes, cleaning and maintaining stables and office space, and so on. They are also responsible for providing staff members with ongoing training and supervision. In addition, Riding Instructors continually look for ways to bring in new students.

Riding Instructors work flexible hours, often teaching classes on weekends to accommodate students' schedules.

Salaries

Annual earnings for independent Riding Instructors vary, depending on such factors as the rates they charge for lessons, the demand for their type of instruction, their geographical location, their business costs, and their ambition to increase their business. According to the Equine Science Department Web site at Southern Illinois University (http://www.siu.edu/departments/coagr/animal/esmain1.htm), in 2005, independent instructors generally earn $20 to $250 or more per hour for lessons.

Employment Prospects

Opportunities for independent Riding Instructors depend on various factors, such as the local demand for the types of riding lessons that they offer; the number of teachers within the area who provide similar lessons; and how well individual teachers run their businesses.

Advancement Prospects

Advancement opportunities are defined by an individual's interests and ambitions. Independent Riding Instructors generally realize advancement through job satisfaction, professional recognition, and the successful growth of their businesses. Those wanting more financial security may seek staff positions. Riding Instructors can also pursue other careers in the horse industry. For example, they may become horse trainers, farriers, or equine veterinarians.

Education and Training

There is no minimum educational requirement to become Riding Instructors, although they should have at least a high school diploma or general equivalency diploma. Riding Instructors typically complete internships or apprenticeships under experienced Riding Instructors.

Riding Instructors are responsible for their own professional growth through self-study and further training under master Riding Instructors. In addition, they participate in professional associations, attend professional conferences, and network with colleagues.

Experience, Skills, and Personality Traits

Riding Instructors are competent riders and have a solid foundation in horsemanship, including stable management, basic veterinary care, and an understanding of the psychology of the horse. Additionally, they are physically fit and have the stamina and endurance to perform their work.

To do their work well, Riding Instructors need leadership, organizational, management communication, interpersonal, and customer service skills. If they are business owners, they also need strong small-business and public relations skills.

Successful Riding Instructors share several personality traits such as being friendly, enthusiastic, flexible, patient, caring, energetic, and responsible. They love horses and enjoy teaching people how to ride and handle horses.

Unions and Associations

Professional associations are available for the various types of Riding Instructors. By joining professional organizations, independent instructors can take advantage of networking opportunities, certification programs, and other professional resources and services. The Certified Horsemanship Association, the American Riding Instructors Association, and the American Association of Riding Schools are some national societies that serve the general interests of Riding Instructors. For contact information, see Appendix IV.

Tips for Entry

1. Many 4-H organizations provide opportunities for young people to obtain academic and practical training in horsemanship, as well as experience in competition activities.
2. Contact local riding stables or horse farms directly about internship or apprenticeship positions.
3. To enhance your professional status, you might obtain instructor certification that is granted by a nationally recognized professional organization, such as the American Riding Instructors Association.
4. Use the Internet to learn more about Riding Instructors and the horse industry. To get a list of pertinent Web sites, enter any of these key words in a search engine: *riding instruction, riding instructor,* or *horse industry.*

FLIGHT INSTRUCTOR

CAREER PROFILE

Duties: Teach ground and flight lessons; develop curriculum and lesson plans; perform other duties as required

Alternate Title(s): Certified Flight Instructor, Authorized Flight Instructor

Salary Range: $25,000 to $50,000

Employment Prospects: Good

Advancement Prospects: Good

Prerequisites:

Education or Training—High school diploma

Experience—Experienced pilot

Special Skills and Personality Traits—Communication, interpersonal, motivational, leadership, public relations, small-business, organizational, and self-management skills; be patient, calm, flexible, responsible, creative, enthusiastic, energetic, and independent

Special Requirements—Hold appropriate FAA certification and ratings

CAREER LADDER

```
┌─────────────────────────────┐
│   Commercial Pilot or        │
│   Flight School Owner        │
└─────────────────────────────┘

┌─────────────────────────────┐
│   Flight Instructor          │
└─────────────────────────────┘

┌─────────────────────────────┐
│   Pilot                      │
└─────────────────────────────┘
```

Position Description

Independent Flight Instructors teach private flying lessons to people who want to become pilots. Normally working in small airports, they teach students how to fly single-engine planes, multiengine planes, helicopters, seaplanes, gliders, balloons, or airships. They provide both ground and flight instruction that students must complete to obtain pilot certificates, which are granted by the Federal Aviation Administration (FAA).

These certified instructors develop their own course outlines, while adhering to strict guidelines and requirements set by the FAA. They teach essential concepts and skills that individuals must know and master in order to become safe and competent pilots. In general, Flight Instructors cover subjects such as aerodynamics, aircraft construction, airport operations, navigation, weather, preflight preparation, cockpit management, safety, and federal aviation regulations. They teach students specific procedures and maneuvers such as preflight procedures, taxiing, takeoff, landing, turns, instrument maneuvers, navigating by landmarks, and postflight procedures. They create simulated emergency situations (such as becoming lost or going into a tailspin) so that students can recognize problems and know what emergency procedures to perform.

Like all teachers, Flight Instructors prepare lesson plans, instructional activities, and study materials. They provide instruction at a pace that fits the abilities and learning styles of their students, as well as use a variety of teaching methods to reinforce students' learning.

Flight Instructors sign off on the appropriate document for students to obtain their student pilot certificates when they are ready for solo flights. Flight Instructors monitor each student's progress and determine when a student is competent to pass the required test for the pilot certificate or rating that the student is seeking.

Furthermore, freelance Flight Instructors are responsible for running their own businesses. This includes collecting students' fees, keeping accurate records, doing bookkeeping, paying bills, and so on. They also continually look for ways to bring in new students.

Flight Instructors work long and irregular hours. They schedule lessons at times that are convenient for their students. They generally work more hours on weekends and during the summer months when the weather is clear and calm for flying.

Salaries

Annual earnings for independent Flight Instructors vary, depending on such factors as the rates they charge for lessons, the demand for their type of instruction, their geographical location, their business costs, and their ambition to increase their businesses. According to Aviation Career Guide.com (http://www.aviationcareerguide.com), in 2005, new flight instructors earn $12 to $20 per hour for flight lessons. Earnings for career Flight Instructors range between $25,000 and $50,000.

Employment Prospects

Within any community, opportunities for independent Flight Instructors depend on various factors, such as the local demand for the types of instruction they offer and the number of teachers in the area who offer similar lessons.

In general, opportunities are favorable for experienced instructors. Many instructors use their teaching time as a means to accumulate sufficient flight time and experience to qualify them for entry-level pilot positions with airlines, air charter services, corporate flight departments, and other employers.

Advancement Prospects

Advancement opportunities are defined by an individual's interests and ambitions. Independent instructors generally realize advancement through job satisfaction, professional recognition, and the successful growth of their businesses. Those wanting more financial security may seek staff positions with flight schools or fixed base operators. With additional education, Flight Instructors may teach in colleges and universities.

Flight Instructors can also pursue careers as pilots.

Education and Training

The minimum educational requirement for Flight Instructors is a high school diploma, but many Flight Instructors do have bachelor's or advanced degrees in various fields. (A college degree is generally required or preferred for commercial and airline pilot positions.)

To become a certified Flight Instructor, individuals must successfully complete a flight instructor training program. They study such topics as lesson planning, course development, and student evaluation.

Freelance instructors are responsible for their own professional development. They participate in professional associations, network with colleagues, enroll in training workshops, and read professional journals.

Special Requirements

Flight Instructors must hold the FAA flight instructor certificate and the appropriate flight instructor rating for each type of instruction that they offer. Additionally, they must possess an FAA medical certificate. To learn about FAA certification requirements, contact a local FAA office. You can also find information at the FAA Web site, http://www.faa.gov.

Experience, Skills, and Personality Traits

Flight Instructors are experienced pilots. They have the appropriate knowledge and skills proficiency in the flight ranking that they are teaching—such as recreational pilot, commercial pilot, multiple engine, or glider.

To work well with students, Flight Instructors need excellent communication, interpersonal, motivational, and leadership skills. To be successful freelancers, they need adequate small-business, public relations, organizational, and self-management skills—such as the ability to work well under pressure, make sound judgments, and follow directions.

Successful Certified Flight Instructors share several personality traits such as being patient, calm, flexible, responsible, creative, enthusiastic, and energetic.

Unions and Associations

Flight Instructors can join professional associations to take advantage of networking opportunities, education programs, job listings, and other professional resources and services. Two national societies that are available include the National Association of Flight Instructors and the Aircraft Owners and Pilots Association. For contact information, see Appendix IV.

Tips for Entry

1. You can start gaining experience working in the aviation field at an early age. Many airlines and fixed base operators hire young people for part-time and summer jobs.
2. The Internet offers many resources to learn about flight instruction. To find relevant Web sites, enter any of these keywords into a search engine: *flight instructor, flight instruction,* or *flying lessons.*

HEALTH EDUCATORS

HEALTH EDUCATOR

CAREER PROFILE

Duties: Develop, implement, and evaluate health education programs; provide instruction on health and health-related issues; coordinate community outreach activities; perform other duties as required

Alternate Title(s): Health Education Specialist; Prevention Educator; a title, such as Health Education Teacher or Substance Abuse Educator, that reflects a specific occupation

Salary Range: $24,000 to $69,000

Employment Prospects: Good

Advancement Prospects: Fair

Prerequisites:

Education or Training—Bachelor's or master's degree; for licensed school teachers, completion of an accredited teacher education program

Experience—Previous experience working with the target clientele in the appropriate settings

Special Skills and Personality Traits—Organizational, management, writing, computer, public speaking, interpersonal, teamwork, leadership, and communication skills; be caring, friendly, confident, tactful, respectful

Special Requirements—Teaching credential or other certification to teach in schools

CAREER LADDER

```
┌─────────────────────────────┐
│  Senior Health Educator or  │
│     Program Coordinator      │
└─────────────────────────────┘

┌─────────────────────────────┐
│       Health Educator        │
└─────────────────────────────┘

┌─────────────────────────────┐
│           Student            │
└─────────────────────────────┘
```

Position Description

Health Educators help people make informed decisions that affect their personal health as well as the health of their family and community. As advocates of health-related issues, Health Educators' goals are to promote healthy lifestyles and to prevent diseases, disabilities, and premature deaths. Through educational activities, Health Educators provide education on a wide range of health issues to people of different ages, backgrounds, and circumstances. They address topics such as nutrition, physical fitness, stress management, substance abuse, sexually transmitted diseases, prenatal care, preventative health, care, disease prevention, environmental health and patients' rights.

Health Educators work on health programs in a variety of settings. They work for government agencies (such as public health departments) and community organizations. Many work in health care settings such as hospitals and health centers. Some Health Educators are health education teachers and curriculum specialists in public and private schools. Others hold Health Educator positions in colleges and universities. Some Health Educators are employed by private companies.

Their tasks vary according to their positions, but some duties are the same regardless of their work setting. For instance, Health Educators:

- perform individual and/or community needs assessments
- develop and implement health education programs
- evaluate the effectiveness of health education programs
- provide instruction on health and health-related issues to their clientele through individual counseling, workshops, seminars, and classes
- serve as resources for individuals, employers, health care professionals, and others

- provide clients with referrals to medical professionals, health care organizations, community agencies, and other groups that may help individuals with their concerns
- coordinate community outreach activities to promote wellness, program services, or special program activities
- develop audio, visual, and print educational materials—such as brochures, pamphlets, and software
- write grant proposals for health education programs

Health Educators work part time or full time. At times they work evenings and weekends to complete paperwork, attend meetings, and give presentations.

Salaries

Salaries for Health Educators vary, depending on such factors as their education, experience, employer, and geographical location. According to the November 2004 *Occupational Employment Statistics* survey by the U.S. Bureau of Labor Statistics (BLS), the estimated annual salary for most Health Educators ranged between $23,740 and $68,830.

Employment Prospects

The BLS reports that employment of Health Educators is expected to increase by 21 to 35 percent through 2012. According to its November 2004 OES survey, about 46,300 Health Educators were employed in the United States. Opportunities will also become available as educators retire, advance to higher positions, or transfer to other jobs.

Advancement Prospects

Health Educators can advance to supervisory and administrative positions such as program coordinators and directors. With advanced degrees and extensive experience, ambitious Health Educators can pursue such positions as health department managers and directors.

Education and Training

The minimum requirement is a bachelor's degree in health education or another related field. Many employers require or prefer that Health Educators have master's degrees.

Health Educators who plan to obtain a teaching license must complete an accredited teacher education program that includes course work in pedagogy and instruction, as well as a supervised field practicum.

Special Requirements

Health Educators who plan to teach in public schools must hold teaching credentials. For specific information, contact the state board of education for the state where you wish to teach. See Appendix III for a list of boards.

Experience, Skills, and Personality Traits

For entry-level positions, employers generally look for candidates who have previous experience working with their target clientele—such as teenagers, the elderly, immigrants, or pregnant women. Employers also prefer that candidates have experience working in appropriate settings. Candidates' experience may have been in the form of paid employment, volunteer work, internship, or field practicum.

To do their work effectively, Health Educators need organizational, management, writing, computer, and public speaking skills. They also need interpersonal, teamwork, leadership, and communication skills in order to work well with the many different people they meet on the job. Being caring, friendly, confident, tactful, and respectful are some personality traits that successful Health Educators share.

Unions and Associations

Many Health Educators belong to professional associations to take advantage of networking opportunities and other professional resources and services. Some national societies that many educators join include American Association for Health Education, Society for Public Health Education, American Public Health Association, American College Health Association, and American School Health Association. For contact information, see Appendix IV.

Tips for Entry

1. You can obtain valuable work experience in college as a volunteer or employee for the health education services on your college campus. Many colleges, for example, have peer health educator programs.
2. Keep a portfolio of examples of your work from school projects and volunteer and paid experience. Also keep letters of recommendation from professors and employers in it. Bring your portfolio to your job interviews.
3. To enhance their employability, some Health Educators obtain the voluntary Certified Health Education Specialist (CHES) certification. For more information, visit the National Commission for Health Education Credentialing, Inc. Web site at http://www.nchec.org.
4. Use the Internet to learn more about Health Educators. To get a list of relevant Web sites, enter either of these keywords in a search engine: *health educator* or *health education*.

NUTRITIONIST

CAREER PROFILE

Duties: Develop, implement, and evaluate nutrition programs; provide information and advice about food and nutrition; perform other duties as required

Alternate Title(s): Nutritionist Specialist

Salary Range: $29,000 to $65,000

Employment Prospects: Good

Advancement Prospects: Fair

Prerequisites:

Education or Training—Bachelor's degree

Experience—Experience working with target clientele in appropriate work settings

Special Skills and Personality Traits—Organizational, management, writing, research, computer, interpersonal, counseling, and communication skills; small-business skills (if self-employed or a business owner); be friendly, tactful, trustworthy, tolerant, and caring

Special Requirements—Nutritionist license, certification, or registration may be required

CAREER LADDER

```
┌─────────────────────────────┐
│  Senior Nutritionist or     │
│  Program Coordinator        │
└─────────────────────────────┘

┌─────────────────────────────┐
│       Nutritionist          │
└─────────────────────────────┘

┌─────────────────────────────┐
│         Trainee             │
└─────────────────────────────┘
```

Position Description

Nutritionists are experts in the science of nutrition—the way humans, animals, and plants need and use food. Their job is to help people make wise choices about the food they eat.

Nutritionists work in a variety of settings. Some oversee the planning and preparation of healthy, balanced meals in hospitals, day care facilities, educational institutions, senior centers, and other institutions. Some are involved in nutrition education programs sponsored by public health departments, hospitals, and community agencies. Others work for food companies, providing analysis and testing of food products and recipes.

Some Nutritionists are self-employed nutrition counselors. They help individuals design food plans to lose or gain weight, deal with food allergies, or control diabetes, high blood pressure, or other health conditions.

Regardless of where they work, Nutritionists attend to many of the same duties.

• They perform needs assessments. For example, an independent Nutritionist performs a nutrition screening of his or her teenage client's diet to find out what nutrients the teenager may be lacking. Or, a Nutritionist in a public health agency surveys the elderly community to learn what nutrition programs they might need.
• They develop, implement, and evaluate nutrition programs for individuals or for groups. For example, one Nutritionist creates a food plan for a client with high blood pressure, while a Nutritionist in a school district plans weekly lunch menus.
• They provide information about food and nutrition to individuals, health professionals, organizations, companies, and communities. Nutritionists may act as resources, consultants, teachers, or trainers.
• They conduct outreach activities to promote nutrition and nutrition-related programs or events.
• They write about nutrition-related topics for newspapers, magazines, radio programs, and other media sources.
• They develop educational materials about nutrition—such as brochures, pamphlets, and software.

Additionally, their job includes preparing and maintaining accurate records. They write correspondence, prepare reports, and complete required paperwork. Many write grant proposals to fund nutrition education programs.

Nutritionists are also responsible for keeping up with current developments in their field as well as for nurturing their professional growth. They accomplish this by reading professional journals and books, enrolling in continuing education courses, participating in professional conferences, and networking with colleagues.

Depending on the nature of their job description, Nutritionists may work in offices as well as in kitchens. Their job may involve traveling to other locations.

Nutritionists work part time or full time. They sometimes work evenings and weekends to attend meetings, give presentations, facilitate workshops, and participate in conferences.

Salaries

Salaries for Nutritionists vary, depending on such factors as their education, experience, employer, and geographical location. According to the November 2004 *Occupational Employment Statistics* survey by the United States Bureau of Labor Statistics (BLS), the estimated annual salary for most Nutritionists ranged between $28,530 and $65,170.

Employment Prospects

The BLS reports that employment of Nutritionists should increase by 10 to 20 percent through 2012. Much of this will be due to the growing public interest in preventing disease through healthy eating habits. Opportunities will also become available as Nutritionists retire, advance to higher positions, or transfer to other jobs.

Advancement Prospects

Advancement opportunities are limited to supervisory and administrative positions. Advanced degrees are required for higher-level executive positions. The ultimate goal for some Nutritionists is to become self-employed consultants or business owners.

Education and Training

Nutritionists need at least a bachelor's degree in food and nutrition or other related field. Their studies include course work in foods, nutrition, chemistry, microbiology, physiology, statistics, and institutional food service management.

Nutritionists who are registered dietitians must have earned their degrees from accredited institutions approved by the American Dietetic Association.

Special Requirements

Many states require Nutritionists who provide nutritional counseling to be licensed, certified, or registered. Requirements vary with the different states. For more information, contact the state licensing board for Nutritionists and dietitians in the state where you wish to practice.

Experience, Skills, and Personality Traits

Employers generally hire entry-level Nutritionists who have previous experience working with the target clientele as well as in the employers' settings. Many employers prefer candidates who are registered dietitians.

To perform their work effectively, Nutritionists need organizational, management, writing, research, and computer skills. They also need interpersonal, counseling, and communication skills to maintain positive working relationships with clients, coworkers, and others. Self-employed Nutritionists should have adequate small-business skills. Being friendly, tactful, trustworthy, tolerant, and caring are a few personality traits that successful Nutritionists share.

Unions and Associations

Many Nutritionists belong to professional associations to take advantage of networking opportunities and other professional resources and services. Some organizations at the national level include American Dietetic Association, International and American Associations of Clinical Nutritionists, American Society for Nutrition, and American Public Health Association. For contact information, see Appendix IV.

Tips for Entry

1. Obtain work as a dietary aide or nutrition assistant in a hospital, health care facility, school, or other setting to learn if the nutrition field is right for you.
2. One valuable source for job announcements are professional associations. Many professional associations have job listings that they send by mail or e-mail to members, as well as job hotlines that are available to the general public. Some organizations also post job vacancies on their Web sites.
3. Use the Internet to learn more about the nutritionist profession. One place to start is a visit to the American Dietetic Association Web site at http://www.eatright.org.

CHILDBIRTH EDUCATOR

CAREER PROFILE

Duties: Provide instruction on the childbirthing process to expectant women and their families; perform other duties as required

Alternate Title(s): Perinatal Educator

Salary Range: Unavailable

Employment Prospects: Good

Advancement Prospects: Poor

Prerequisites:

Education or Training—Completion of a certified Childbirth Educator training program

Experience—Previous experience in the childbirth process

Special Skills and Personality Traits—Communication, presentation, interpersonal, organizational, and management skills; small-business skills (if an independent instructor); be friendly, enthusiastic, caring, sympathetic, confident, and patient

Special Requirements—Professional certification may be required

CAREER LADDER

```
┌─────────────────────────────────┐
│    Lead Childbirth Educator or   │
│      Independent Instructor      │
└─────────────────────────────────┘

┌─────────────────────────────────┐
│        Childbirth Educator       │
└─────────────────────────────────┘

┌─────────────────────────────────┐
│             Trainee              │
└─────────────────────────────────┘
```

Position Description

In a series of classes, Childbirth Educators teach about the birthing process to expectant women and their families to help them prepare for the birth of their babies. Educators also present information about the different delivery methods so that women can make well-informed decisions for themselves.

Childbirth Educators teach classes as part of educational programs offered by hospitals, health departments, health centers, birthing centers, obstetricians' offices, and community centers. Many of these trained professionals are independent contractors; they work for organizations on a contractual basis. Some also offer private classes.

Childbirth Educators who are employed by hospitals, health departments, and other organizations generally follow the curriculum guidelines established by their employers. Independent instructors may develop their own curriculum or follow the guidelines of the childbirth-educator organization, such as the International Association of Childbirth Educators, under which they were trained. All

Childbirth Educators bring their own philosophy and teaching style into the classroom.

In general, childbirth instruction is taught in a series of four to 12 classes that are held once a week for two hours. Classes are small; they usually range from six to 10 couples who are made up of pregnant women and their labor coaches. (Coaches are husbands or other loved ones who will be in the delivery room to provide the women support as they give birth.)

These educators cover basic topics that include the conditions of pregnancy; signs of labor; labor management; delivery and anesthesia options; hospital and delivery room procedures; and parenting of newborn babies. They also teach coping and relaxation skills (such as breathing exercises) that can help women through the pain and discomfort of labor and the delivery.

Childbirth Educators use a variety of teaching strategies—short lectures, slides, videos, guest speakers, and, if possible, a tour through a hospital labor room. They arrange their classrooms so that the students feel comfortable and secure to ask questions and discuss their concerns, as well as to socialize and provide emotional support for each other.

Many Childbirth Educators hold the last class of the series several months later when all the mothers have given birth. Often known as the reunion class, mothers and coaches, with their newborn babies, return to share their experiences as well as to bring up questions and concerns about caring for their newborn babies.

Independent instructors are responsible for operating their businesses, which includes tasks such as collecting clients' fees, paying bills and taxes, bookkeeping, and finding classroom facilities. In addition, they continually look for ways to generate income through advertising, networking, and other means.

Many Childbirth Educators hold part-time or full-time jobs as nurses, health educators, or other professions. They usually teach classes in the evenings and on weekends to accommodate their students' schedules.

Salaries

Formal salary information for Childbirth Educators is unavailable. In general, most Childbirth Educators are paid hourly wages or for each series of classes they teach. According to Childbirth International (http://www.childbirthinternational.com), in 2005, educators generally charged $50 to $350 per series.

Employment Prospects

Childbirth education continues to be a growing and evolving field. Job opportunities in hospitals, childbirth centers, health centers, and medical offices are dependent on the availability of funds as well as the demand for childbirth education within communities. Most staff positions become available as Childbirth Educators retire, resign, or transfer to other positions.

Advancement Prospects

Staff Childbirth Educators are limited to few supervisory and management positions. For many Childbirth Educators, the ultimate goal is to become successful independent instructors.

Education and Training

Education requirements vary from employer to employer. In some work settings, Childbirth Educators must be registered nurses or other types of health care professionals, thus needing an associate's, bachelor's, or higher degree. In some settings, Childbirth Educators may need only a high school diploma if they have the appropriate training.

Many Childbirth Educators are initially trained in a specific methodology by a childbirth educator organization. Training programs combine instruction and practical experi-

ence. They cover topics such as anatomy, methodology, pedagogy, exercises for the pregnant woman, alternative birthing methods, and care of the newborn.

Special Requirements

Many employers require that Childbirth Educators possess professional certification that is granted by a recognized childbirth educator organization, such as Lamaze International. Obtaining professional certification is voluntary.

Some hospitals prefer to hire Childbirth Educators who are also registered nurses.

Experience, Skills, and Personality Traits

Employers typically choose candidates whose childbirth philosophy is in tune with theirs. Although candidates may not have previous childbirth teaching experience, they often have experience with childbirth that may include the birth of their own babies.

For their work, Childbirth Educators need effective communication, presentation, and interpersonal skills. Having adequate organizational and management skills is also useful. Independent instructors should have adequate small-business skills. Successful Childbirth Educators share several personality traits such as being friendly, enthusiastic, caring, sympathetic, confident, and patient.

Unions and Associations

Childbirth Educators may join professional associations to take advantage of networking opportunities, certification programs, and other professional resources and services. Some organizations at the national level include Lazmaze International, Birthworks, Inc., International Childbirth Education Association, Association of Labor Assistants and Childbirth Educators, American Academy of Husband-Coached Childbirth, and Childbirth and Postpartum Professional Association. For contact information, see Appendix IV.

Tips for Entry

1. Contact employers for whom you would like to work. Be sure your philosophies are similar to those of an employer before taking a position.
2. Many Childbirth Educators get new students through personal recommendations. Stay in contact with former students and be in touch with obstetricians, midwives, and other childbirth professionals and health care personnel.
3. You can learn more about the Childbirth Educator profession on the Internet. To get a list of relevant Web sites, enter these keywords in a search engine: *childbirth education* or *childbirth educator.*

CPR/FIRST AID INSTRUCTOR

CAREER PROFILE

Duties: Provide instruction of standard first aid and cardiopulmonary resuscitation (CPR) procedures; perform other duties as required

Alternate Title(s): None

Salary Range: Unavailable

Employment Prospects: Poor for full-time positions

Advancement Prospects: Poor

Prerequisites:

Education or Training—Certified training program

Experience—Knowledge of CPR and first aid techniques

Special Skills and Personality Traits—Communication, interpersonal, and presentation skills; small-business skills (if an independent instructor or a business owner); be friendly, enthusiastic confident, patient, flexible, and organized

Special Requirements—Standard first aid and CPR certificates; instructor certificate

CAREER LADDER

```
┌─────────────────────────────────┐
│   Lead Instructor, Independent   │
│   Instructor, or Business Owner  │
└─────────────────────────────────┘

┌─────────────────────────────────┐
│   First Aid and CPR Instructor   │
└─────────────────────────────────┘

┌─────────────────────────────────┐
│            Student               │
└─────────────────────────────────┘
```

Position Description

CPR/First Aid Instructors teach standard first aid and cardiopulmonary resuscitation (CPR) procedures to individuals of all ages so that they can respond to emergency situations. Instructors also teach them basic knowledge for assessing an emergency situation, calling for immediate emergency medical services, and applying lifesaving techniques that are appropriate for the baby, child, or adult. With these skills, individuals can attend to injuries, burns, wounds, hypothermia, poisoning, choking, drowning, heart attacks, and seizures until emergency medical service professionals arrive on the scene.

Many CPR/First Aid Instructors are volunteer teachers for the American Red Cross, the American Heart Association, or other organizations. Some instructors are employed by protective services training centers, medical facilities, or private safety training companies. Others are independent (or self-employed) instructors.

CPR/First Aid Instructors teach courses that are designed to meet the needs of different audiences, such as schoolchildren or the general public. Many instructors train medical and other health care professionals, and protective service professionals (such as firefighters, search and rescue technicians, emergency medical technicians, and police officers). Many CPR/First Aid Instructors specialize in training personnel in business, industry, and the government. They teach courses that meet OSHA requirements. (OSHA stands for Occupational Safety and Health Administration, which is a regulatory agency at both the federal and state levels.)

Some CPR/First Aid Instructors teach first aid and CPR courses that include the use of an automated external defibrillator (AED). The AED is a device used to administer an electric shock through the chest wall to the heart.

Classes are two to eight hours long, depending on the type of course. Instructors follow course outlines that are specifically developed by their employers or the organization from which they received their certified training. CPR/First Aid Instructors bring their own teaching style to the classroom. As part of their teaching role, instructors build students' confidence so that they can successfully learn the class material and be able to respond to emergency situations when they actually occur.

CPR/First Aid Instructors use a variety of teaching techniques that include lectures and demonstrations, as well as supplement their instructions with films and other media. They also give students mock emergency scenarios in which to practice the various skills. In addition, instructors provide students with pamphlets and other handouts to take with them when the class ends.

CPR/First Aid Instructors perform other tasks that include:

- gathering all equipment and instructional materials and setting them up properly before classes begin
- performing administrative tasks such as collecting class fees, keeping attendance records, and completing all required paperwork
- maintaining equipment, such as cleaning mannequins according to approved standards
- attending instructor meetings
- keeping instructor certification up to date

Most CPR/First Aid Instructors teach classes on a part time or voluntary basis while pursuing careers in teaching, medicine, protective services, and other fields.

Salaries

Formal salary information for CPR/First Aid Instructors is unavailable. Many instructors teach courses on a voluntary basis, and therefore receive no pay. Independent contractors are compensated through class fees or paid hourly wages.

Employment Prospects

CPR/First Aid Instructors are generally in demand to train (and retrain) employees in business, industry, and government. They are also needed to train protective services and health care professionals as well as the general public. However, most opportunities are for voluntary or part-time positions.

Advancement Prospects

There are no direct advancement opportunities for CPR/First Aid Instructors. Some may become independent instructors or business owners that offer CPR/First Aid instruction to companies, agencies, or other organizations.

Education and Training

Prospective CPR/First Aid Instructors must successfully complete a certified instructor training program. Training programs are usually short, but comprehensive and intense, providing for both academic instruction and hands-on teaching practice.

Training programs are offered through local offices of the organizations that certify CPR and first aid instructors.

They are also available through such other outlets as safety training companies and community colleges.

Special Requirements

CPR/First Aid Instructors must possess proper certification granted by one of the following nationally recognized organizations: American Red Cross, American Heart Association, National Safety Council, or American Safety and Health Institute. Each organization has its own requirements and selection process for obtaining certification. For more information, contact the local office of a national organization. (See Appendix IV for contact information for the national headquarters of these organizations.)

Depending on the organizations, instructors must renew first aid instructor certification every two or three years and CPR instruction certification every one to two years.

Experience, Skills, and Personality Traits

New CPR/First Aid Instructors must be knowledgeable of CPR and first aid techniques. They should also have the ability to teach others. In addition, they need good communication, interpersonal, and presentation skills. Independent instructors should have adequate small-business skills.

Successful CPR/First Aid Instructors share personality traits such as being friendly, enthusiastic, confident, patient, flexible, and organized.

Unions and Associations

CPR/First Aid Instructors join professional associations to take advantage of education programs, networking opportunities, and other professional services and resources. Many become members of the organizations (listed above) from which they earned their certification.

Tips for Entry

1. Learn basic CPR/First Aid skills from a local chapter of the American Red Cross, American Heart Association, or other organization.
2. Part-time and voluntary positions for CPR/First Aid Instructors are generally available in any community. Some places to contact are: community centers, community agencies, continuing education programs, and the local chapters of the organizations that certify instructors.
3. Learn more about CPR/First Aid Instructors on the Internet. To get a list of pertinent Web sites, enter the keywords *first aid and CPR* in a search engine.

FITNESS, RECREATION, AND SPORTS PROFESSIONALS

AEROBICS INSTRUCTOR

CAREER PROFILE

Duties: Teach group exercise classes; design exercise routines set to music; perform other duties as required

Alternate Title(s): Group Exercise Instructor, Fitness Instructor, Dance Exercise Instructor, Aqua Aerobics Instructor

Salary Range: $15,000 to $55,000

Employment Prospects: Good

Advancement Prospects: Fair

Prerequisites:

    Education or Training—Bachelor's degree is desirable

    Experience—One or more years taking aerobics classes; aerobic instructor internship or apprenticeship

    Special Skills and Personality Traits—Leadership, communication, interpersonal, motivational, public speaking, organizational, management, and customer service skills; be friendly, caring, enthusiastic, observant, confident, energetic, and creative

    Special Requirements—Professional certification

CAREER LADDER

```
┌─────────────────────────────────┐
│        Program Director          │
└─────────────────────────────────┘

┌─────────────────────────────────┐
│       Aerobics Instructor        │
└─────────────────────────────────┘

┌─────────────────────────────────┐
│   Intern or Assistant Instructor │
└─────────────────────────────────┘
```

Position Description

Aerobics Instructors are fitness professionals who lead groups of men and women through exercise routines that help them maintain or improve their fitness and health. The exercises are set to music. Some exercises are especially designed to increase the cardiovascular system's ability to deliver oxygen more quickly and efficiently to the body. Other exercises help tone and build up large muscle groups such as those of the stomach and legs.

Aerobics Instructors teach different types of group exercise classes. The most familiar is the aerobics class, which includes common exercises and dance movements. Many instructors also teach classes that include the use of step platforms with the exercises. Some Aerobics Instructors incorporate boxing or martial arts movements into exercise routines. Some instructors teach classes that involve a different type of aerobic exercise such as yoga. Others may lead group exercise classes in swimming pools.

Designing exercise classes is usually the responsibility of individual Aerobics Instructors. They make sure the classes are fun and safe, as well as interesting and challenging.

They create exercise routines that students of different abilities can perform and easily follow. Additionally, they choose different kinds of music that match the movements or steps of the different exercises, and that motivate students to perform the exercises. Some Aerobics Instructors specialize in developing aerobics classes for special groups such as pregnant women, elderly persons, or physically disabled individuals.

Aerobic classes are normally 30 to 90 minutes long, depending on the class level—beginning, intermediate, or advanced. The format is generally the same for all classes. Instructors begin with warm-up exercises, and then proceed to aerobic exercises. They follow with muscle toning and strength exercises for the large muscle groups, and finally end with cool-down exercises.

Aerobics Instructors monitor students' progress to make sure they are doing techniques safely and properly. During the aerobics segment, instructors have students monitor their heart rates to ensure that they are not overworking their hearts. In addition, Aerobics Instructors give out constant encouragement and positive feedback to their students to motivate them onward to finish one more repetition, one more exercise, and finally one more class.

Many Aerobics Instructors are self-employed. They might work for one or more organizations on a contractual basis. As independent contractors, Aerobics Instructors perform various administrative tasks such as collecting student fees, sending out invoices, paying bills and taxes, keeping accurate business records, and doing bookkeeping.

Aerobics Instructors work flexible hours. They may teach classes in the early mornings, evenings, as well as on the weekends.

Salaries
Salaries for Aerobic Instructors vary, depending on factors such as their employer and geographic location. According to the November 2004 *Occupational Employment Statistics* survey by the U.S. Bureau of Labor Statistics (BLS), the estimated annual salary for most Aerobics Instructors ranged between $14,550 and $55,110.

Employment Prospects
Aerobics Instructors work for various employers, such as health clubs, aerobic exercise companies, resorts, and community centers. Some instructors work for large residential complexes or corporations that have fitness facilities.

Job opportunities are favorable for qualified instructors. The BLS reports that Aerobics Instructors are expected to be among the fastest growing occupations in the U.S. through 2012. The federal agency predicts a 44 percent growth for Aerobics Instructors during this period.

Advancement Prospects
Advancement opportunities are limited to program managers and directors.

Aerobics Instructors can also pursue other fitness careers by becoming exercise physiologists, physical therapists, physical education teachers, athletic trainers, or fitness consultants.

Education and Training
More employers are preferring to hire instructors who have bachelor's degrees in exercise science, physical education, or other related fields.

To become certified professionals, Aerobics Instructors must successfully complete all training programs that lead to certification. Training workshops cover theoretical knowledge and practical skills that instructors need to teach a particular form of aerobic instruction. Anatomy, physiol-

ogy, injury prevention, sequencing, and cueing are some topics that are covered within training programs.

Special Requirements
Aerobics Instructors usually possess professional certification for each type of aerobics that they teach. They are either certified by their employer or by a recognized physical fitness organization such as the American Council on Exercise.

Experience, Skills, and Personality Traits
In general, Aerobics Instructors should have at least one year of experience taking aerobics classes, dance, or related fitness activities. They should also have completed an internship or apprenticeship under experienced, certified Aerobics Instructors.

In order to work well with their students, Aerobics Instructors need excellent leadership, communication, interpersonal, motivational, and public speaking skills. They should also have strong organizational, management, and customer service skills. Successful Aerobics Instructors share several personality traits such as being friendly, caring, enthusiastic, observant, confident, energetic, and creative.

Unions and Associations
Many Aerobics Instructors belong to professional associations to take advantage of certification programs, networking opportunities, and other professional resources and services. Some national societies are Aerobics and Fitness Association of America, American Council on Exercise, IDEA Health and Fitness Association, American Fitness Professionals and Associates, Aquatic Exercise Association, and National Exercise Trainers Association. For contact information, see Appendix IV.

Tips for Entry
1. Broaden your experiences to stay competitive in your field. Learn yoga, kickboxing, or other types of aerobic activities that interest you. Also take dance classes to pick up new dance steps and choreography skills. In addition, improve your teaching skills through self-study, networking, or classes.
2. There are different certification programs available. Be sure to choose one that best fits your needs. Talk with different Aerobics Instructors for their opinions about the different programs.
3. Use the Internet to learn more about aerobics instruction. To get a list of relevant Web sites to read, enter the keyword *aerobics* in a search engine.

PERSONAL TRAINER

CAREER PROFILE

Duties: Design personal fitness programs; provide personalized training and support to clients; perform other duties as required

Alternate Title(s): None

Salary Range: $15,000 to $55,000

Employment Prospects: Good

Advancement Prospects: Limited

Prerequisites:

Education or Training—Bachelor's degree is preferred

Experience—An internship or apprenticeship; experience designing personal exercise plans and providing one-on-one training

Special Skills and Personality Traits—Leadership, communication, interpersonal, motivational, organizational, management, and public speaking skills; (if independent consultants) public relations and small-business skills; be patient, friendly, caring, diplomatic, enthusiastic, observant, flexible, and trustworthy

Special Requirements—Professional certification

CAREER LADDER

```
┌─────────────────────────────────────┐
│ Training Director or Business Owner  │
└─────────────────────────────────────┘

┌─────────────────────────────────────┐
│          Personal Trainer            │
└─────────────────────────────────────┘

┌─────────────────────────────────────┐
│          Intern or Trainee           │
└─────────────────────────────────────┘
```

Position Description

Personal Trainers are fitness professionals who help clients develop safe exercise programs that meet their individual goals for health and fitness; they also help clients stay motivated to reach their goals. Their clients may include professionals, athletes, senior citizens, or pregnant women.

Personal Trainers start their working relationship with their clients by conducting an assessment interview. They discuss fitness goals, exercise history, and their clients' favorite fitness activities. They also discuss any health problems and health conditions—such as diabetes or heart disease—for which their clients may be at risk. Trainers also evaluate their clients' body composition and test their flexibility, strength, and endurance.

Individualized fitness programs are then designed with their clients' health, personal interests, abilities, and goals in mind. Programs may include training with free weights and resistance machines, as well as one or more forms of aerobics instruction (such as kickboxing, yoga, aerobic dance, low impact aerobics, or aqua aerobics).

To help their clients integrate fitness activity into their lifestyle, many Personal Trainers incorporate their clients' favorite fitness activities into their exercise programs. These activities may include hiking, rollerblading, skiing, mountain climbing, cycling, kayaking, swimming, and so on. Some trainers provide nutritional counseling and design nutrition programs that fit their clients' goals. Usually these Personal Trainers are nutritionists or dietitians.

Personal Trainers schedule hour-long training sessions with their clients, at least once or twice a week. They may work with clients in small groups or on an individual basis. Some clients prefer to schedule training sessions in the privacy of their homes.

In training sessions, Personal Trainers demonstrate correct exercise techniques to avoid injury. They show their clients how to use free weights and equipment safely and properly. In addition, they answer general questions about exercise, fitness, health, and nutrition. For specific medical information, Personal Trainers refer their clients to the appropriate health professionals. Furthermore, Personal

Trainers provide the right motivation to keep their various clients interested so that they come to their training sessions, complete their workouts, and successfully meet their fitness goals.

Most Personal Trainers are independent consultants, and so perform various duties to successfully run their small businesses. They develop policies regarding payments, cancellations, and other important matters. They perform administrative duties such as collecting payments, paying bills and taxes, obtaining liability insurance, doing bookkeeping, and maintaining accurate business records. Furthermore, they continue to look for ways to bring in new clients.

Personal Trainers work flexible hours to accommodate their clients' schedules. Thus, they may hold training sessions during early mornings, late evenings, and weekends.

Salaries

Salaries for Personal Trainers vary, depending on such factors as their experience, employer, and geographical location. The U.S. Bureau of Labor Statistics (BLS) reported in its November 2004 *Occupational Employment Statistics* survey that the estimated annual salary for most fitness trainers ranged between $14,550 and $55,110.

Employment Prospects

Personal Trainers work for health clubs, cruise lines, resorts, community centers, residential complexes, corporations, and other employers as salaried employees or on a contractual basis. Many trainers have their own training facilities or work from their homes or clients' homes.

Job opportunities are favorable for qualified trainers. The BLS reports that fitness trainers are expected to be one of the fastest-growing occupations in the United States through 2012, predicting a 44 percent growth for trainers.

Advancement Prospects

As employees, Personal Trainers can advance to supervisory and management positions. The ultimate goal for many Personal Trainers is to become high-salaried independent contractors or have their own fitness facilities.

Education and Training

More employers are preferring that Personal Trainers have a bachelor's degree in exercise physiology, exercise science, physical education, or another related field. Also some professional associations require that applicants for certification have college degrees.

To become certified professionals. Personal Trainers must complete a training program, which generally covers topics such as anatomy, exercise physiology, kinesiology, fitness assessments, exercise technique, nutrition, and injury prevention.

Special Requirements

Most employers require that Personal Trainers be certified by a recognized professional fitness organization, such as the American College of Sports Medicine. Completion of continuing education units is usually required to renew certifications. In some states, Personal Trainers who provide nutritional counseling may be required to obtain state licensure, certification, or registration. For specific information, contact your state licensing board for nutritionists and dietitians.

Experience, Skills, and Personality Traits

Personal Trainers generally complete an apprenticeship or internship under the tutelage of experienced trainers. Novice trainers should have experience in designing safe exercise programs that meet individuals' needs, abilities, and interests. In addition, they should have experience providing one-on-one training, including the safe and proper use of free weights and resistance equipment.

To work well with their clients. Personal Trainers need excellent leadership, communication, interpersonal, motivational, organizational, management, and public speaking skills. Independent trainers need strong public relations and small-business skills to run a successful business. Successful Personal Trainers share several personality traits such as being patient, friendly, caring, diplomatic, enthusiastic, observant, flexible, and trustworthy.

Unions and Associations

Personal Trainers can join professional associations to take advantage of networking opportunities, certification programs, and other professional resources and services. Some national societies that serve the interests of Personal Trainers include Aerobics and Fitness Association of America, IDEA Health and Fitness Association, American College of Sports Medicine, and National Strength and Conditioning Association. For contact information, see Appendix IV.

Tips for Entry

1. Do your research about a gym before taking a job. Spend some time there to see what the facilities are like. Also be sure to find out if the gym would be covering you under its liability insurance plan.
2. Call prospective employers directly and ask about job openings and application procedures.
3. Use the Internet to learn more about the personal trainer profession. To find relevant Web sites, enter the keywords *personal training fitness* or *personal trainer* in a search engine.

RECREATION LEADER

CAREER PROFILE

Duties: Plan, organize, and conduct recreational activities and programs; work with program patrons; perform other duties as required

Alternate Title(s): None

Salary Range: $13,000 to $35,000

Employment Prospects: Fair

Advancement Prospects: Fair

Prerequisites:

Education or Training—Associate's or bachelor's degree

Experience—Prior experience in the recreation field

Special Skills and Personality Traits—Writing, communication, interpersonal, teamwork, critical-thinking, leadership, and self-management skills; be outgoing, enthusiastic, energetic, organized, patient, tactful, creative, and inspirational

Special Requirements—CPR, first aid, or other certification or license may be required

CAREER LADDER

```
┌─────────────────────────────────┐
│   Senior Recreation Leader or    │
│      Recreation Supervisor       │
└─────────────────────────────────┘

┌─────────────────────────────────┐
│        Recreation Leader         │
└─────────────────────────────────┘

┌─────────────────────────────────┐
│         Recreation Aide          │
└─────────────────────────────────┘
```

Position Description

Recreation Leaders plan, organize, and conduct an assortment of leisure activities—such as crafts and art workshops, exercise classes, and field trips—for the patrons of their recreation centers. These professionals also coordinate sports programs as well as organize special events, such as Fourth of July picnics.

Many Recreation Leaders work at recreation centers that serve people of varying ages, from preschoolers to seniors. Some work at recreational facilities that serve a specific clientele, such as teenagers, senior citizens, developmentally disabled adults, corporate employees, or prison inmates.

Recreation Leaders fulfill different roles, depending on the needs and organizational structure of their employers. Some Recreation Leaders are assigned to be the leaders of one or more recreation centers. In this role, they are responsible for overseeing all the programs and activities at their assigned facilities. Other Recreation Leaders have the responsibility to oversee specific programs (such as an afterschool program) at their assigned recreation center. Some Recreation Leaders are specialists in particular activity areas (such as art, computers, or exercise) and provide leadership and teaching in their specialties to other recreation workers.

Recreation Leaders work directly with their patrons. For example, they might teach a crafts class, coach a basketball team, keep score at a volleyball game, or judge a costume contest. In addition, Recreation Leaders encourage new, as well as regular, patrons to participate in the various activities, sports, programs, and special events that are offered by their centers.

Recreation Leaders work under the general supervision of either a recreation center coordinator or, in a larger organization, a recreation supervisor. They perform a variety of general duties, such as:

- train and supervise recreation workers and volunteers
- evaluate recreational activities and programs
- inspect their facility for safety hazards
- maintain inventory of equipment and supplies
- keep attendance records of participants at different activities
- write and submit required reports on a regular basis

Recreation Leaders work part time or full time. They may work evenings and weekends. Some jobs are seasonal.

Salaries

Salaries for Recreation Leaders vary, depending on such factors such as their education, experience, job duties, employer, and geographical location. According to the November 2004 *Occupational Employment Statistics* survey by the U.S. Bureau of Labor Statistics (BLS), the estimated annual salary for most recreation workers ranged between $13,480 and $34,870.

Employment Prospects

Employers of Recreation Leaders include park and recreation departments, community centers, day care programs, youth service clubs, camps, nursing homes, rehabilitation facilities, resorts, and correctional facilities. Large corporations and residential complexes that have employee recreational facilities may also hire Recreation Leaders.

The BLS reports that employment for recreation workers is expected to experience average growth through 2012. In addition to job growth, replacements will be needed for employees who advance to higher positions, transfer to other jobs, or leave the workforce. However, the ability of employers, particularly local government and nonprofit organizations, to hire additional Recreation Leaders or maintain current staff is dependent on funding.

Competition for jobs, especially full-time positions, is high. Job opportunities are more favorable for part-time and seasonal positions than for full-time positions.

Advancement Prospects

Recreation Leaders can pursue supervisory and management positions such as program supervisors and directors. A bachelor's or master's degree is usually required to advance to high-level administrative positions.

This position is a stepping-stone to other recreation or related careers. For example, Recreation Leaders can become recreational therapists, park planners, personal trainers, coaches, park rangers, physical education teachers, or university professors.

Education and Training

To enter the recreational field at a professional level, Recreation Leaders generally need an associate's or bachelor's degree in recreational studies, leisure services, parks and recreation, or another related field.

Many employers hire applicants with a high school or general equivalency diploma for part-time and summer jobs. They may hire applicants for full-time positions if they have qualifying work experience, along with completing some college courses in recreation or other related fields.

New employees typically receive on-the-job training.

Special Requirements

Recreation Leaders may need CPR, first aid, lifeguard, or other certification that is pertinent to their job responsibilities. For some positions, Recreation Leaders need to possess a valid state driver's license.

Experience, Skills, and Personality Traits

Applicants should have several years of experience working in the recreational field, which may have been gained through part-time and summer employment, volunteer work, or internships. Employers prefer that applicants have work experience in the setting in which they would be working. In addition, applicants should have experience planning and organizing recreational programs, as well as supervising staff and participants in various recreational activities.

To do their jobs effectively, Recreation Leaders need strong writing, communication, interpersonal, teamwork, critical-thinking, and leadership skills. They should also have excellent self-management skills—such as the ability to follow directions, get to work on time, take initiative, work safely, and stay calm under pressure. Being outgoing, enthusiastic, energetic, organized, patient, tactful, creative, and inspirational are some personality traits that successful Recreation Leaders have in common.

Unions and Associations

Many Recreation Leaders join professional associations to take advantage of networking opportunities and other professional services and resources. One national society that serves the recreational field is the National Recreation and Park Association. For contact information, see Appendix IV.

Some Recreation Leaders belong to an employee union that represents them in contract negotiations with their employers.

Tips for Entry

1. As a high school student, you can start gaining valuable experience by participating in local recreational programs. Also, volunteer or apply for part-time recreational aide positions when they become available.
2. During your job search, contact people in the field. Also, network with family members, friends, teachers, and others who may know about job openings.
3. If you are placed on an employer's register of eligible candidates, find out how long the register is kept current. For example, an employer might use its register for six months before seeking new applicants.
4. Use the Internet to learn more about prospective employers. If an organization has a Web site, you can usually find it by entering its name in a search engine.

GUIDE

CAREER PROFILE

Duties: Conduct tours of an establishment or area; may oversee arrangement for meals, lodging, and transportation; perform other duties as required

Alternate Title(s): Tour Guide, Establishment Guide, Sightseeing Guide, Travel Guide, Travel Manager, Outdoors Guide, Adventure Guide, Fishing Guide

Salary Range: $13,000 to $60,000+

Employment Prospects: Good

Advancement Prospects: Fair

Prerequisites:

Education or Training—High school diploma or college degree

Experience—Knowledgeable in the subject matter or locations where tours are led; have experience planning, managing, and supervising tour programs and activities

Special Skills and Personality Traits—Leadership, interpersonal, conflict resolution, presentation, public speaking, organizational, and management skills; be friendly, enthusiastic, patient, calm, tactful, diplomatic, reliable, energetic, resourceful, flexible, and confident

CAREER LADDER

```
┌─────────────────────────────────┐
│  Senior Guide or Business Owner  │
└─────────────────────────────────┘

┌─────────────────────────────────┐
│              Guide               │
└─────────────────────────────────┘

┌─────────────────────────────────┐
│             Trainee              │
└─────────────────────────────────┘
```

Position Description

Guides conduct tours of a specific place for individuals and groups who are interested in learning more about it. Tours may be of a particular establishment, such as a candy factory, or of a specific area, such as a city or wilderness area. Guides follow specific routes, or itineraries, and stop at interesting points to tell participants facts and anecdotes about people, places, things, and events that are related to the establishment or locale.

Different Guides lead different types of tours. *Establishment guides* lead short indoor or outdoor tours. They guide tourists through museums, zoos, gardens, parks, underground caves, historical houses, manufacturing plants, and other places of interest. At the end of their tours, they may recommend other interesting places to visit or special events that are happening in the area.

Sightseeing guides conduct walking, limousine, or bus tours of a city or region, showing points of interest to tourists. For example, a Guide may lead a walking tour through his or her city's Chinatown, describing its history and pointing out important local landmarks.

Travel guides (also known as *tour managers*) manage tours that cover several cities or countries over several days or weeks. For example, a Guide may supervise a group of tourists on a 10-day bus tour through northern Italy. Trips sometimes include a combination of cruise and land tours. In foreign tours, Guides may work with local guides.

Outdoor guides conduct various types of day, overnight, and longer tours to parks, recreational areas, and the wilderness. Tours usually involve one or more outdoor activities such as bicycling, fishing, hunting, camping, backpacking, mountain climbing, kayaking, or rafting. For example, a Guide may be part of a week-long rafting trip down the Rio Grande. Outdoor Guides teach inexperienced members how to use equipment. They are also responsible for explaining relevant local hunting, fishing, and environmental laws and regulations to their tour groups. If they are camping in the wilderness, outdoor Guides take care of all necessities such as preparing meals and disposing of waste.

Tour Guides make sure that all group members are comfortable, safe, and enjoying themselves. They handle any unexpected situations that may arise such as injuries, discourteous group members, bad weather, or long lines. For overnight and long tours, Guides oversee all necessary arrangements and details for meals, lodging, and transportation.

Guides perform other duties, as required by their employers. For example, they might assist in planning new tours. They might help organize tours by making hotel reservations, contacting group members, or gathering information about special events. Guides might also create written materials about the various tours that are offered.

Many Guides are independent contractors, and usually provide their services to several tour operators and establishments at a time. Being self-employed, they are responsible for such business tasks as collecting fees, paying taxes and bills, and keeping accurate business records. They also set aside time to find future work.

As employees or contractors, Guides have flexible work schedules.

Salaries

Salaries for Guides vary, depending on such factors as their job status, type of tour, and employer. The U.S. Bureau of Labor Statistics (BLS) reports in its November 2004 *Occupational Employment Statistics* that the estimated annual salary for most tour guides ranged between $12,930 and $31,320, and for most travel guides, between $16,840 and $46,510.

Independent contractors usually receive a per diem rate, which generally ranges between $50 and $200 per day. Some experts report that highly experienced and popular Guides can earn up to $60,000 or more a year.

Guides usually receive free meals and lodging during tours. They may also receive gratuities from their customers at the end of their tours.

Employment Prospects

Tour operators, adventure tour companies, travel agencies, hotels, resorts, cruise lines, tour bus companies, museums, parks, and industrial establishments are some organizations that hire Guides for staff or contractual positions.

Competition is strong for both staff and contractual positions. According to the BLS, the job growth for tour guides is expected to increase by 10 to 20 percent through 2012. Guides will also be needed to replace those who have retired, advanced to higher positions, or transferred to other occupations.

Advancement Prospects

In major tour operations, Guides can advance to supervisory and management positions. For some Guides, the ultimate goal is to become freelancers or to have their own tour companies.

Guides might also pursue other career paths in the travel industry by becoming travel agents, travel writers, or public relations officers with visitor and convention bureaus.

Education and Training

Requirements vary from employer to employer. Some employers require only a high school diploma or high school equivalency diploma. Many employers prefer that Guides have bachelor's degrees in any field.

Employers provide Guides with training for their particular jobs.

Experience, Skills, and Personality Traits

Guides generally have broad life experiences that enrich their abilities to provide participants with enjoyable and memorable tours. They are knowledgeable in the subject matter or locations for which they would be leading tours. In addition, they have experience in planning, managing, and supervising tour programs and activities.

Because they work with people extensively, Guides need strong leadership, interpersonal, conflict resolution, presentation, public speaking, organizational, and management skills. Successful Guides share several personality traits, such as being friendly, enthusiastic, patient, calm, tactful, diplomatic, reliable, energetic, resourceful, flexible, and confident.

Unions and Associations

Various professional associations are available for Guides, such as the International Association of Tour Managers, the International Ecotourism Society, and the Outdoor Guides Association. (For contact information, see Appendix IV.) Professional associations offer their members various professional services and resources, such as networking opportunities, training programs, and job listings.

Tips for Entry

1. Having a broad knowledge in art, history, geography, and literature is an advantage for obtaining work.
2. To gain work experience, you might volunteer as a Guide with local museums or historical sites, or obtain internships with tour operators.
3. Contact prospective employers directly for staff or contractual positions. Be ready to talk about yourself and how you would be a valuable asset to a company.
4. Use the Internet to learn about various tour operators. To get a list of relevant Web sites, enter any of these keywords in a search engine: *tour guides, outdoor guides,* or *ecotours.*

COACH

Duties: Teach athletes the fundamentals of their sport; prepare athletes for competitions; manage sports programs; perform other duties as required

Alternate Title(s): A title that reflects a particular sport, such as Football Coach, or a position, such as Assistant Coach or Pitching Coach

Salary Range: $13,000 to $57,000+

Employment Prospects: Fair

Advancement Prospects: Fair

Prerequisites:

Education or Training—Bachelor's or advanced degree for high school and college positions

Experience—Extensive knowledge and practical experience in sport

Special Skills and Personality Traits—Leadership, organizational, teamwork, communication, and self-management skills; be patient, fair, trustworthy, passionate, dedicated, enthusiastic, quick-thinking, inspirational

Special Requirements—Teaching credential for school coaches; professional certification may be required for youth coaches

Athletic Director or General Manager

Head Coach

Assistant Coach

Position Description

Coaches provide instruction and guidance to athletes to help them excel and succeed in playing sports, whether they be novices or professionals, youths or adults, or females or males. Professional Coaches typically have years of experience and training in the sports they instruct, and many of these men and women have played as amateur or professional athletes.

Baseball, golf, football, soccer, basketball, handball, hockey, lacrosse, swimming, skiing, tennis, badminton, volleyball, bowling, boxing, wrestling, gymnastics, figure skating, tae kwon do, cheerleading, rowing, and sailing are only some of the sports in which Coaches are engaged. They may work with individual athletes or with teams that play at the recreational, amateur, or professional level of sports competition. Coaches may be employees or independent contractors, and work in such settings as community recreational centers, schools, colleges, amateur sports clubs, semiprofes-

sional sports organizations, or professional sports. Some Coaches are hired by independent athletes such as golfers, skiers, boxers, and figure skaters.

Coaches in youth sports work with different age levels, from young children to teenagers. Many Coaches who instruct middle school, junior high, or high school teams hold teaching positions in physical education, social studies, or other subjects at their schools. Some of them are assigned to coach more than one sport.

Regardless of the competition and age levels at which they work, Coaches have a similar goal: to help athletes learn and improve their skills so that they can have fun and perform to the best of their ability in sports competitions.

Coaches at all levels fulfill the same general roles and responsibilities. As teachers, Coaches instruct athletes in the basic skills, rules, and strategies for playing a sport. Coaches use various teaching methods, such as lecture and demonstration, to instruct athletes. To reinforce their teachings, Coaches design exercises and activities that allow athletes to practice their skills individually, in small groups, and in teams. Coaches also develop physical training programs for athletes to build up their strength, endurance, flexibility, agility, power, and speed. Coaches teach athletes a variety of training routines and supervise them during workouts. Furthermore, Coaches prepare athletes mentally for competition by teaching skills that help them stay relaxed, energized, and focused.

Coaches also play the role of leader. They develop realistic goals for individual athletes and teams and help them reach those goals. They continually strive to motivate athletes to perform to the best of their abilities in competitions. Before games or performances, Coaches go over strategies and tactics with their athletes, and they advise and encourage the athletes throughout the competition.

Part of their job involves evaluating the performance of athletes at practice and in competition. They identify the strengths and weaknesses of each of their athletes, and provide each with positive feedback about how to improve their skills. In addition, Coaches help athletes develop self-confidence and self-respect as well as learn the values of sportsmanship, work ethics, and personal responsibility.

Most Coaches are managers as well. They are responsible for the planning and coordination of their sports program, from preseason training to postseason evaluations. Their duties include developing and maintaining schedules for workouts, practices, and competitions; organizing and supervising all practices; designing drills that are suitable to the age, skill level, and physical abilities of the athletes; and supervising the athletes at competitions held at home and away. In addition, Coaches make sure that their athletes and sports programs are in compliance with the policies and rules that govern the sports leagues in which they compete. Coaches also seek to minimize the risk of injury to their athletes; for example, Coaches survey grounds before practices, games, and competitions for potential hazards.

Many Coaches are responsible for recruiting prospective players for their teams, which involves meeting with athletes and watching them perform in practices and competitions. In addition, Coaches are responsible for selecting players and informing all candidates if they have been chosen or not.

Coaches perform many administrative tasks on a daily basis, such as preparing correspondence, completing required paperwork, managing budgets, scheduling the use of sports facilities, ordering sports equipment, coordinating travel arrangements for away games, and attending meetings. Many Coaches also assist with the promotion of and publicity for their athletes' sports events, as well as participate in fund-raising for their teams.

Many sports teams have a coaching staff of two or more Coaches. The head coach is the one who is in charge. The other Coaches, sometimes called assistant coaches, help the head coach plan and run the sports program. The assistant coaches are usually assigned to coordinate or oversee one or more areas of the sports program. For example, an assistant coach on a college baseball team might be assigned to be the pitching coach, while another is responsible for coordinating the recruitment of new players. Head coaches supervise, train, and provide direction to their staff.

Coaches are constantly under pressure by their employers, fans, and, in the case of youth sports, the players' parents, for their teams to win competitions. Coaches, even popular Coaches, are often fired because of the failure of their teams or the weak performances of their athletes.

Coaches may be employed full time or part time. Many are hired on a temporary basis, usually for the length of a sports season. Their work hours are irregular, and they typically put in additional hours during the sports season. Many of them work evenings, weekends, and holidays. Coaches travel with their teams and athletes to sports events in other cities and states, and sometimes other countries.

Salaries

Salaries for Coaches vary, depending on such factors as their experience, education, sport, competition level, employer, and geographical location. At the recreational and amateur levels, many Coaches are volunteers, providing their services for free. Youth coaches with recreational programs may earn a salary based on their employment as recreation leaders. School coaches who are also teachers may receive additional compensation for coaching duties. At the semiprofessional level, Coaches may receive a stipend or wage, while highly successful Coaches at the professional level may be able to command high annual salaries up to $1 million or more.

According to the November 2004 *Occupational Employment Statistics survey,* by the U.S. Bureau of Labor Statistics (BLS), the estimated annual salary for most Coaches ranged between $13,270 and $56,740.

Employment Prospects

The BLS reports that employment for Coaches is expected to increase by 10 to 20 percent through 2012. In addition to job growth, Coaches will be needed to replace individuals who retire, advance to higher positions, or transfer to other occupations.

Most coaching positions in youth sports and recreational sports are for volunteers. The competition for paid positions is strong at all sports levels.

As school and college programs expand their athletic programs, additional coaching positions will become available. However, coaching staffs may be cut back when schools and colleges face tight budgets. Schools usually prefer to hire teachers who are also willing to hold coaching jobs.

Advancement Prospects

Coaches can advance in any number of ways, depending on their interests and ambitions. Some work their way up through the high school and college levels to the professional level of their sport. Other Coaches choose to work at a particular level, and seek advancement by becoming a head coach or by working with a particular team. To obtain higher positions, higher wages, and greater job satisfaction, Coaches typically need to move to other jobs which may involve relocating within the United States or to other countries.

Education and Training

Many Coaches have a bachelor's or advanced degree in physical education, exercise and sports science, physiology, sports medicine, or another related field. However, specific educational requirements for positions vary with the different employers. For example, applicants for school and college coaching positions are required to possess a bachelor's or master's degree.

Assistant coaches typically learn on the job. Volunteer coaches in youth sports usually complete required training programs provided by the organizations that sponsor the sports.

Throughout their careers, Coaches enroll in workshops, seminars, and courses to learn new knowledge and skills in the areas of coaching, physical conditioning, sports medicine, and so on. They also complete independent study and attend professional conferences.

Special Requirements

Teachers in public schools who also perform coaching jobs must possess a valid teaching credential. They may also be required to possess a coaching endorsement for each sport that they coach. Licensure requirements vary from state to state. For specific information, contact the state board of education in the state where you plan to work. See Appendix III for a list of state boards.

Youth coaches may be required to possess professional certification granted by recognized organizations in their sport. Professional certification is voluntary and is earned upon completion of an organization's professional coach education program.

Experience, Skills, and Personality Traits

In general, employers hire applicants who have extensive experience and knowledge about their sport and about phys-ical training. Employers typically select applicants who have prior coaching experience, especially with the sport level in which they would be working.

To be effective at their job, professional Coaches must have excellent leadership, organizational, teamwork, and communication skills. They must also have superior self-management skills, including the ability to work independently, meet deadlines, handle stressful situations, and to prioritize multiple tasks. Successful Coaches share several personality traits, such as being patient, fair, trustworthy, passionate, dedicated, enthusiastic, quick-thinking, and inspirational. In addition, they have a strong work ethic, can handle criticism, and are able to keep tempers and strong emotions in check.

Unions and Associations

Many Coaches join one or more professional associations to take advantage of networking opportunities and other professional resources and services. Some of the national societies that serve Coaches are the American Football Coaches Association, the American Swimming Coaches Association, the National Association for Sport and Physical Education, the National High School Athletic Coaches Association, the National Soccer Coaches Association of America, and the Women's Basketball Coaches Association. For contact information for these organizations, see Appendix IV.

Tips for Entry

1. As a high school student, participate in different sports in school or recreational centers. Gain experience playing in competitions. Also learn as much as you can about the sports that interest you.
2. Many coaches begin their careers as volunteer coaches in youth or recreational sports.
3. Find mentors whose coaching styles earn your respect and inspire you.
4. Jobs sometimes are found through referrals from people whom you know. Hence, build a network of contacts in and out of the sports world, and keep them up to date with your coaching career.
5. Use the Internet to learn more about a particular sport, sports level, or sports coach. Use terms such as *cheerleading, amateur sports, high school coaches,* or *volleyball coaches* for keywords to get a list of relevant Web sites.

ENVIRONMENTAL EDUCATORS AND ANIMAL TRAINERS

ENVIRONMENTAL EDUCATOR (NONSCHOOL SETTINGS)

CAREER PROFILE

Duties: Plan and conduct workshops, classes, presentations, tours, and nature walks; perform other duties as required

Alternate Title(s): Environmental Education Specialist, Naturalist, Park Interpreter

Salary Range: $18,000 to $45,000

Employment Prospects: Fair

Advancement Prospects: Fair

Prerequisites:

Education or Training—Bachelor's degree

Experience—An environmental education background

Special Skills and Personality Traits—Organizational, time-management, writing, teamwork, communication, interpersonal, leadership, presentation, and computer skills; be friendly, enthusiastic, responsible, reliable, flexible, self-motivated, and creative

CAREER LADDER

```
┌─────────────────────────────────────┐
│        Program Coordinator           │
└─────────────────────────────────────┘

┌─────────────────────────────────────┐
│       Environmental Educator         │
└─────────────────────────────────────┘

┌─────────────────────────────────────┐
│  Assistant Environmental Educator or │
│              Intern                  │
└─────────────────────────────────────┘
```

Position Description

Environmental Educators teach the general public about nature and environmental issues. Many of these professionals work in nonschool settings. Some work for environmental centers or organizations. Others are part of educational programs in zoos, aquariums, natural history museums, botanical gardens, parks, science centers, and other establishments. Still others work in environmental education programs sponsored by government agencies (such as the U.S. Environmental Protection Agency), academic institutions, and private companies.

Environmental Educators make presentations at their facilities as well as at schools, civic organizations, and community events. They conduct workshops and classes, and guide tours through their facilities. Some lead nature walks in natural settings such as forests, deserts, wetlands, shorelines, and mountains.

Environmental Educators are responsible for planning their classes, workshops, and presentations. They use various multimedia tools, such as films, slide shows, and videos, to bring the world of nature alive to their lectures. They sometimes bring in rocks, fossils, plants, and animals

for their audiences to experience. In addition, these educators plan hands-on activities that are age-appropriate and meet the interests and skill levels of their audiences.

Some environmental education programs offer curriculum and instruction support to schools, colleges, youth service groups, and community organizations. Public schools for example, are required to provide students with instruction about the environment. Thus, some Environmental Educators conduct workshops for schoolteachers, demonstrating methods for enhancing their lessons about the environment.

Some Environmental Educators provide instruction to schoolchildren in week-long day camps or residential camps during the spring, summer, or fall. These camps may be based on land as well as on ships at sea. Environmental Educators teach about ecology, natural history, conservation, and other environmental topics. They lead students on hikes and nature walks as well as conduct recreational activities such as art, nature crafts, games, drama, and songs. Many Environmental Educators also provide instruction in outdoor living skills—such as reading a compass and map, building a fire, setting up a tent, and using emergency procedures.

Along with teaching, Environmental Educators perform many other tasks which vary from one educator to the next. For example, educators might be responsible for setting up and maintaining educational exhibits, booking tours of their facilities, caring for animals, assisting in the development and evaluation of programs, or preparing grant proposals. Some educators may also have the additional duty of supervising and training volunteers, interns, and new staff members.

Environmental Educators work part time or full time. Depending on the type of facilities where they work, they may be assigned to work evenings, weekends, or holidays.

Salaries

Salaries for Environmental Educators vary, depending on such factors as their education, experience, job duties, employer, and geographical location. Many Environmental Educators are volunteers, and therefore earn no pay. According to the online version of *The Complete Guide to Environmental Careers in the 21st Century* by the Environmental Careers Organization (http://www.eco.org), the average salaries for entry-level educators range between $18,000 and $25,000, and for experienced educators, between $28,000 and $45,000.

Employment Prospects

Environmental education is a growing and evolving field. The competition is strong for paying positions. In general, opportunities become available as educators advance to higher positions, transfer to other jobs, or retire. Employers may create additional positions if funding is available.

Advancement Prospects

Environmental Educators can advance to supervisory and administrative positions, such as program coordinators and directors. Depending on their interests and ambitions, educators can pursue other environmental careers by becoming forest rangers, environmental engineers, researchers, regulatory specialists, or environmental lawyers.

Education and Training

Most employers require that applicants hold a bachelor's degree in biology, animal sciences, natural resources, environmental science, education, outdoor education, or another related field. Some employers prefer to hire candidates with a master's degree.

Environmental Educators are trained on the job. They are also expected to continue their professional growth through self-study, enrollment in continuing education programs and training programs, networking with colleagues, and so on.

Experience, Skills, and Personality Traits

In general, employers look for candidates who have a background in environmental education. Having teaching experience or training is highly desirable. Candidates should also have experience working with the target audience of the educational programs.

To do their work effectively, Environmental Educators need strong organizational, time-management, writing, and teamwork skills. They also need excellent communication, interpersonal, leadership, and presentation skills to work well with the various people they meet. In addition, they should have computer skills, including the use of databases, spreadsheets, word processing, and desktop publishing.

Successful Environmental Educators share several personality traits, such as being friendly, enthusiastic, responsible, reliable, flexible, self-motivated, and creative.

Unions and Associations

Many Environmental Educators join professional associations to take advantage of training programs, networking opportunities, and other professional resources and services. Some national societies that serve these educators' interests include the National Association for Interpretation, the National Association for Humane and Environmental Education, the National Association of Environmental Professionals, and the North American Association for Environmental Education. (See Appendix IV for contact information.)

Tips for Entry

1. In high school or college, get involved in environmental projects to gain experience.
2. Start looking for summer positions in early spring. This is also the best time to search for post-graduation jobs when you are a college senior.
3. Contact environmental organizations and professional associations in your area for job listings. Also check with college job placement centers and state employment agencies.
4. Learn more about environmental education on the Internet. To get a list of relevant Web sites, enter any of these keywords in a search engine: *environment education* or *environment educator*.

PARK NATURALIST

CAREER PROFILE

Duties: Plan, implement, and evaluate various interpretive programs, activities, exhibits, and materials; perform other duties as required

Alternate Title(s): Park Interpretive Naturalist

Salary Range: $20,000 to $49,000

Employment Prospects: Fair

Advancement Prospects: Fair

Prerequisites:

Education or Training—Bachelor's degree

Experience—One or more years providing naturalist interpretive work

Special Skills and Personality Traits—Teaching, organizational, project management, interpersonal, teamwork, writing, communication, presentation, public speaking, and leadership skills; be outgoing, enthusiastic, calm, tolerant, flexible, observant, curious, creative, and self-motivated

CAREER LADDER

```
┌─────────────────────────────────┐
│        Senior Naturalist        │
└─────────────────────────────────┘

┌─────────────────────────────────┐
│         Park Naturalist         │
└─────────────────────────────────┘

┌─────────────────────────────────┐
│   Seasonal Park Naturalist or   │
│    Naturalist Aide or Intern    │
└─────────────────────────────────┘
```

Position Description

Park Naturalists are park rangers who specialize in teaching the public about the natural resources in local, state, and national parks. As interpretive specialists, they use lectures, storytelling, exhibits, and audiovisual media to describe the geology, flora, fauna, and other natural wonders in their individual parks.

Park Naturalists plan, implement, and evaluate various interpretive programs and activities for park visitors, such as nature walks, trail hikes, nature crafts programs, campfire presentations, and exhibits. These naturalists also develop, create, and produce brochures, pamphlets, and other materials about their park's natural resources. To create accurate interpretations as well as educationally sound programs, Park Naturalists diligently conduct research on background materials.

Park Naturalists are also responsible for planning and conducting group presentations. Many give scheduled presentations at their park's visitor center or nature center. In addition, many Park Naturalists make guest presentations at schools, children's organizations, community clubs, senior citizen centers, and other groups.

Park Naturalists also assist with park resource management. For example, they help develop plans for new trails, additional campsites, and landscaping at their individual parks. Some Park Naturalists serve as technical advisers for area park agencies, which sometimes involves reviewing development and landscape plans for new and existing parks.

In addition, Park Naturalists perform a variety of administrative tasks. For example, they might maintain records and statistics about program participants and write required reports. Many Park Naturalists perform public relations duties to publicize park programs, activities, and special events. Some Park Naturalists hold supervisory positions, and thus provide training and guidance to other staff members, including park aides and volunteers.

Many Park Naturalists perform some of the duties of general park rangers. For example, they might:

- collect park entrance and camping fees
- provide visitors with general park information
- conduct research projects, such as studying wildlife behavior or monitoring air quality in the park
- patrol a designated area, including the back country

- perform maintenance of trails and park grounds
- assist in emergency situations, such as firefighting and search and rescue missions

Park Naturalists may hold seasonal or permanent, part-time or full-time positions. They work flexible hours that may include evenings, weekends, and holidays.

Salaries

Salaries for Park Naturalists vary, depending on their job status, experience, education, employer, and geographical location. According to the Career Prospects in Virginia Web site, park rangers generally earn between $20,000 and $40,000. In the U.S. National Park Service, permanent park rangers start at a salary based on the GS-5 to GS-9 levels of the general schedule (GS), the pay schedule for many federal employees. In 2005, the annual basic pay for GS-5 to GS-9 levels ranged from $24,677 to $48,604.

Employment Prospects

Park Naturalists work for federal, state, regional, county, and municipal park systems throughout the United States.

The turnover rate for Park Naturalists is low and the competition for available positions (seasonal or permanent, or part-time or full-time) is high. Opportunities usually become available when Park Rangers retire, advance to higher positions, or transfer to other locations.

To work for some parks, Park Naturalists may be required to be U.S. citizens or obtain naturalization within a specific time after being hired.

Advancement Prospects

With appropriate training and education, Park Naturalists can advance to supervisory and administrative positions or pursue law enforcement ranger positions. Many Park Naturalists realize advancement in the form of job satisfaction, higher pay, and park assignments to locations of their choice.

Education and Training

In general, employers prefer to hire applicants who have a bachelor's degree in botany, zoology, outdoor education, environmental interpretation, natural resource management, or another related field. Some employers accept candidates with associate degrees or some college work if they have qualifying work experience.

Experience, Skills, and Personality Traits

In general, candidates should have at least one year of experience providing naturalist interpretive work. It may have been gained as a seasonal Park Naturalist, naturalist aide, science teacher, naturalist intern, or nature program volunteer. (To get a full-time position with the National Park Service usually requires two to five years' experience as a seasonal ranger.) Candidates should be knowledgeable about principles and methods pertaining to science education and environmental interpretation. They should also be familiar with the flora and fauna of the parks where they would be working.

Park Naturalists need various skills to do their work effectively. They should have strong teaching, organizational, project management, interpersonal, teamwork, and writing skills. Additionally, having excellent communication, presentation, public speaking, and leadership skills is important as they work with colleagues, administrators, park patrons, and others on a daily basis. Being outgoing, enthusiastic, calm, tolerant, flexible, observant, curious, creative, and self-motivated and energetic are some personality traits that successful Park Naturalists share.

Unions and Associations

Many Park Naturalists belong to professional associations to take advantage of networking opportunities, job listings, and other professional services and resources. Some national societies that serve the interests of Park Naturalists include the National Recreation and Park Association, the National Association for Interpretation, and the Association of National Park Rangers. See Appendix IV for contact information.

Tips for Entry

1. In high school you can begin preparing for a naturalist career by taking courses in science, mathematics, social studies, English, public speaking, and journalism.
2. Internships and volunteer positions with park systems are available for individuals to obtain hands-on training.
3. To enhance your employability, you might obtain certification as an emergency medical technician (EMT), first responder, or paramedic.
4. Contact parks early in the year to find out when they are accepting applications for seasonal positions. For information about the U.S. National Park Service's seasonal employment program, call (877) 554-4550, or visit its Web site at http://www.sep.nps.gov.
5. Use the Internet to learn more about Park Naturalists and the field of park interpretation. To get a list of relevant Web sites, enter either of these keywords in a search engine: *park naturalists* or *park interpretation*.

HUMANE EDUCATOR

Duties: Provide humane education programs and activities that promote public awareness of compassionate and respectful treatment of animals; perform other duties as required

Alternate Title(s): Humane Education Specialist

Salary Range: $20,000 to $30,000

Employment Prospects: Poor

Advancement Prospects: Fair

Prerequisites:

Education or Training—A high school diploma or bachelor's degree

Experience—Previous experience working with animals; teaching experience desirable; experience working with people of all ages

Special Skills and Personality Traits—Writing, computer, organizational, project management, teaching, interpersonal, communication, classroom management, and public speaking skills; be friendly, approachable, flexible, reliable, dedicated, and energetic

```
┌─────────────────────────────────────┐
│   Humane Education Coordinator       │
└─────────────────────────────────────┘

┌─────────────────────────────────────┐
│        Humane Educator               │
└─────────────────────────────────────┘

┌─────────────────────────────────────┐
│  Intern, Shelter Technician, or Volunteer  │
└─────────────────────────────────────┘
```

Position Description

Humane Educators provide various educational programs and activities relating to the compassionate and respectful treatment and control of animals. Their primary responsibility is to educate children and adults so that they make wise decisions about how to interact with animals and the environment. In addition, Humane Educators promote responsible pet ownership by making people aware that their pets have the same needs of water, food, and shelter as humans and that pets should not be abused or neglected.

Working mostly for community animal shelters and humane societies, Humane Educators perform several duties. One major duty is developing effective humane education programs. Depending on the particular needs of their communities, Humane Educators plan programs that address topics such as animal control, pet overpopulation, animal ordinances, and basic animal care.

Humane Educators deliver education programs in various forms. They give presentations to schools and civic organizations, often bringing in animals from the pet shelter. They set up booths at local community events. Humane Educators might also sponsor public events in which they promote animal licensing, immunization shots for pets, pet care, spay/neuter clinics, and so on.

Humane Educators are also responsible for developing brochures, pamphlets, and written information on various topics for the public. Many educators gather appropriate materials from national humane organizations and other resources to distribute to the public. Some educators create materials or modify existing materials to meet their specific needs. In addition, many Humane Educators develop a library of humane education materials for the general public.

Humane Educators also perform other duties, as required. For example, they might:

- conduct tours of animal shelters
- provide training and supervision to staff and volunteers
- prepare grant proposals
- maintain accurate records, prepare reports, write correspondence, and complete required paperwork

Depending on the size of their facilities, Humane Educators may be in charge of all or some of a facility's humane education program. In some organizations, Humane Educators are in charge of coordinating presentations, developing materials, and managing the volunteer coordinator. In other organizations, the Humane Educator may also be the volunteer coordinator and the contact person for public information. In small facilities, the Humane Educator may also perform duties as executive director, animal adoption counselor, or other staff position.

Many Humane Educators work on a volunteer basis. Salaried Humane Educators typically work a 40-hour week.

Salaries

Salaries for Humane Educators vary, and depend on factors such as their experience, education, job responsibilities, employer, and geographical location. In general, most Humane Educators earn an annual salary in the $20,000 to $30,000 range.

Employment Prospects

The job market is limited for paid positions. They become available as Humane Educators resign, retire, advance to higher positions, or transfer to other jobs.

Advancement Prospects

Humane Educators can advance to administrative positions, such as program coordinators, education managers, and education directors. They can also become animal shelter directors. Some Humane Educators become consultants, providing educational services to schools and other facilities.

Depending on their interests and ambitions, Humane Educators can also seek paths to related careers. For example, they might become environmental educators, schoolteachers, animal researchers, veterinarians, and zookeepers.

Education and Training

Some employers require that Humane Educators have a high school diploma or general equivalency diploma with qualifying work experience. Other employers require or prefer that Humane Educators have a bachelor's degree in animal sciences, natural resources, wildlife ecology, education, environmental education, or other related field. In addition, most employers require or prefer that Humane Educators have completed internships with animal shelters, nature centers, zoos, or similar institutions.

Experience, Skills, and Personality Traits

In general, Humane Educators should have previous experience working with animals and be knowledgeable about animal welfare issues. Some employers require that Humane Educators have at least one year of experience working with animal shelters, which may include volunteer work, if they do not meet educational requirements. In addition, Humane Educators should have teaching experience or appropriate training, as well as experience working with a variety of people in a variety of settings.

Humane Educators need strong writing, computer, organizational, project management, and teaching skills. Having strong interpersonal, communication, classroom management, and public speaking skills is also needed to provide effective presentations. Successful Humane Educators share several personality traits, such as being friendly, approachable, flexible, reliable, dedicated, and energetic.

Unions and Associations

Many Humane Educators belong to professional associations to take advantage of professional resources, training workshops, networking opportunities, and other professional services. Some national organizations that many Humane Educators join are:

- American Society for the Prevention of Cruelty to Animals (ASPCA)
- American Humane Association
- Humane Society of the United States
- National Association for Humane and Environmental Education
- Association of Professional Humane Educators

For contact information, see Appendix IV.

Tips for Entry

1. In high school, start gaining experience by working with animals. You might volunteer at your local animal shelter, zoo, nature center, museum, or other similar institution.
2. Keep current with developments and issues in humane education.
3. Maintain a portfolio of the educational materials and presentations that you have developed, and bring it along to your job interviews.
4. Enhance your employability by learning how to write grant proposals.
5. Learn more about humane education on the Internet. To get a list of relevant Web sites, enter these keywords in a search engine: *humane education* or *humane educator*.

DOG TRAINER

CAREER PROFILE

Duties: Train dogs to obey commands, perform specific tasks or tricks, or behave a particular way; perform other duties as required

Alternate Title(s): Apprentice Trainer, Assistant Trainer, Master Trainer; a title that reflects a speciality such as Police Dog Trainer

Salary Range: $15,000 to $45,000

Employment Prospects: Fair

Advancement Prospects: Fair

Prerequisites:

Education or Training—A combination of apprenticeship, independent study, workshops, seminars, and classes

Experience—Several years of experience of training and handling various dog breeds

Special Skills and Personality Traits—Leadership, teamwork, interpersonal, communication, organizational, and self-management skills; (as business owners) customer service, public relations, and small-business skills; be ethical, methodical, fair, kind, enthusiastic, patient, confident, and motivated

Special Requirements—Professional licensure or certification may be required; business licenses required for business owners

CAREER LADDER

```
┌─────────────────────────────┐
│     Master Dog Trainer      │
└─────────────────────────────┘

┌─────────────────────────────┐
│        Dog Trainer          │
└─────────────────────────────┘

┌─────────────────────────────┐
│ Apprentice or Assistant Trainer │
└─────────────────────────────┘
```

Position Description

As experts in dogs and dog behavior, Dog Trainers are able to teach dogs to obey particular commands, perform certain skills, or to exhibit certain behaviors. These professionals provide services to customers who want their dogs trained for specific purposes. Dog Trainers typically specialize in offering one or more types of training programs, such as:

- pet dog obedience training
- show dog training
- service (or assistance) dog training, which is training dogs to help people with disabilities so that they may live independent lives
- guard dog training
- police dog training for law enforcement agencies that use canine teams (dogs and their handlers) for patrol duty, tac-

tical support, tracking, bomb detection, narcotics detection, explosives detection, or other purposes
- film animal training, which is teaching dogs to perform required behaviors for a movie, television show, commercial, or other filmed venue, as well as to accustom them to work on film sets and with actors

Dog Trainers design dog training plans with their customers. The trainers define details such as training goals and objectives, the length of the training, and the training schedule. Depending on the type of training and training plan, dogs may live with the trainers for the duration of the initial training, which may last several weeks or months.

Training is slow, repetitive, meticulous, and intense. Dog Trainers teach dogs to respond to voice and hand-signal obedience commands. Dogs are taught one skill or behavior at a time. Trainers use a variety of training methods, such as rewarding a dog with praise or food after performing a skill or behavior. They also create real-life scenarios in which dogs can practice their new skills or behavior.

Dog Trainers also work with dog handlers, and teach them how to handle their dogs so that they know the handlers are in control. In addition, the trainers instruct the handlers about how to maintain their dogs' training so that they will continue to respond appropriately to commands. Dog Trainers may provide instruction to handlers on such topics as animal behavior, dog grooming, and dog care. Some Trainers are also responsible for teaching handlers topics and skills that are specific to their purposes. For example, police dog trainers instruct handlers on proper tactical measures, as well as review current law enforcement practices and laws regarding the use of police canines.

Dog Trainers perform other duties, such as providing daily care for dogs, maintaining kennels, and keeping accurate records of training progress. They also have tasks that are specific to their training specialty; for example, police dog trainers are responsible for keeping up with developments in law enforcement canine training, current court cases regarding police canines, and relevant topics in their field.

Many Dog Trainers are self-employed. Some do freelance or independent contract work, and train dogs from their homes, within their clients' homes, or in rented facilities. Other self-employed trainers own businesses, such as dog obedience schools, law enforcement canine training facilities, or film animal training companies. Some business owners offer other services besides training. For example, they might offer boarding or breeding services.

As small business owners, Dog Trainers are responsible for performing various administrative duties, such as developing policies and rules, collecting client fees, bookkeeping, paying bills and taxes, and maintaining facilities. If they have employees, Dog Trainers are responsible for paying salaries, as well as providing training and supervision. In addition, Dog Trainers continually look for new ways to bring in new clients.

Dog Trainers work part time or full time. Some trainers hold other animal-related jobs, such as dog groomer, dog breeder, or veterinary technician, to supplement their income.

Salaries

Salaries for Dog Trainers vary, depending on such factors as their experience, employer, specialty, and geographical location. According to the November 2004 *Occupational Employment Statistics* survey by the U.S. Bureau of Labor Statistics, the estimated annual salary for most animal trainers, a category that includes Dog Trainers, ranged between $15,190 and $45,230.

Law enforcement officers normally earn salaries according to their rank and level; they may receive additional compensation for their dog training duties.

Employment Prospects

The job market varies for the different areas of dog training. Job opportunities for dog obedience training is favorable, as dog owners continually need help with training their dogs; whereas opportunities for service dog trainers are limited due to the small population they serve.

Some police dog trainers are law enforcement officers who provide in-service training or initial training to canines and their handlers. They perform training duties in addition to their regular duty as officers, who are also canine handlers. In-house openings are usually limited and based on the need of individual agencies as well as the size of the canine units. Opportunities are more favorable in law enforcement agencies that have in-house canine training facilities.

In general, most opportunities for salaried positions become available as Dog Trainers resign or transfer to other positions. Employers may create additional positions as their businesses grow. Competition is strong for Dog Trainers in all areas.

Advancement Prospects

Advancement opportunities are defined by an individual's own interests and ambition. Salaried Dog Trainers in large organizations may advance to supervisory or management positions. For most Dog Trainers, the ultimate goal is to have their own businesses. Many Dog Trainers realize advancement by way of job satisfaction, professional recognition, and higher earnings.

Education and Training

Dog Trainers develop their own training program, which they continue throughout their careers. Their training may include one or more apprenticeships under experienced Dog Trainers. It also includes independent study; enrollment in professional training and animal behavior workshops, seminars, and classes; participation in professional conferences; and networking with colleagues. Dog Trainers study animal behavior, dog handling skills, training methods, canine anatomy, dog care, and other topics relevant to their field.

Law enforcement canine trainers are usually required to complete certified training programs within their departments, in other law enforcement agencies, or at civilian canine academies.

Special Requirements

Depending on their area of training or their employer's requirements, Dog Trainers may be required to possess some type of licensure or professional certification. For example:

- Guide dog trainers in California must possess state licensure.
- Most law enforcement agencies require internal canine trainers to be certified by a nationally recognized profes-

sional organization, such as the United States Police Canine Association.

- Film animal trainers who own or supply dogs for performance must have an exhibitor license granted by the U.S. Department of Agriculture.

All business owners must possess all required state and local business licenses.

Experience, Skills, and Personality Traits

Employers generally hire Dog Trainers who have several years of practical experience training or handling dogs, which may have been gained through volunteer work or an apprenticeship. Applicants should have a broad background of training and handling various dog breeds, as well as be knowledgeable about animal behavior. In addition, they should have a repertoire of training methods to accommodate the various learning styles of dogs, and if appropriate, dog handlers or owners.

To be effective at their job, Dog Trainers must have excellent leadership, teamwork, interpersonal, and communication skills. Having strong organizational and self-management skills is also essential. As business owners, Dog Trainers also need adequate customer service, public relations, and small-business skills. Successful Dog Trainers have several personality traits in common, such as being ethical, methodical, fair, kind, enthusiastic, patient, confident, and motivated. They have a genuine love for and devotion to dogs.

Unions and Associations

Many Dog Trainers belong to professional associations that serve their particular interests in order to take advantage of various professional resources and services. For example, at the national level, dog obedience trainers might join the Association of Pet Dog Trainers or the National Association of Dog Obedience Instructors; law enforcement canine trainers might join the United States Police Canine Association or the North American Police Work Dog Association; and guide dog trainers might join the Guide Dog Users, Inc.

Some national societies that all Dog Trainers are eligible to join are the International Association to Canine Professionals, the Animal Behavior Society, and the American Society for the Prevention of Cruelty to Animals (ASPCA).

Film animal trainers may be required to join a labor union in order to obtain work.

For contact information for the above organizations, see Appendix IV.

Tips for Entry

1. As a high school student, you can start gaining experience working with dogs. For example, you might volunteer at an animal shelter, "pet-sit" for dog owners, or get a part-time job at a dog kennel.

2. To obtain an apprenticeship or internship, contact Dog Trainers under whom you would like to learn. Be ready to show a resume or to describe relevant experience and training that you have.

3. Many experts in the field say that one way to get started in the film animal training business is to work as a volunteer or assistant.

4. Use the Internet to learn more about the dog training field. To find a list of Web sites for a particular type of dog training, enter those words as keywords in a search engine. Examples: *dog obedience trainers, police dog trainers,* or *film animal trainers.*

GUIDE DOG INSTRUCTOR

CAREER PROFILE

Duties: Train guide dogs for the blind and visually impaired individuals; teach guide dog handlers; perform other duties as required

Alternate Title(s): Apprentice Trainer, Assistant Trainer, Guide Dog Trainer

Salary Range: $15,000 to $45,000

Employment Prospects: Poor

Advancement Prospects: Poor

Prerequisites:

    Education or Training—Associate's or bachelor's degree; complete an apprenticeship

    Experience—Extensive background in animal training and handling

    Special Skills and Personality Traits—Leadership, interpersonal, communication, writing, public speaking, problem-solving, and self-management skills; be patient, tactful, honest, reliable, responsible, dedicated, and compassionate

    Special Requirements—State license required in California; certified by employer

CAREER LADDER

```
+-----------------------------------+
|       Guide Dog Instructor        |
+-----------------------------------+

+-----------------------------------+
|         Guide Dog Trainer         |
+-----------------------------------+

+-----------------------------------+
|  Apprentice or Assistant Trainer  |
+-----------------------------------+
```

Position Description

Many blind and visually impaired individuals use guide dogs to help them walk independently down crowded sidewalks, across busy streets, up and down stairs, into buildings, onto buses, and so forth. Guide dogs and their owners receive special training from Guide Dog Instructors, who work in guide dog schools.

Guide Dog Instructors participate in every aspect of a guide dog's training. The training process begins several weeks after dogs are born. Guide dog schools place puppies with volunteers who can raise the puppies with lots of love, care, and attention. Instructors encourage volunteers to expose the puppies to new experiences—such as riding in cars, walking into unfamiliar buildings, and being in crowded places.

When dogs return to the guide dog schools, Guide Dog Instructors screen the dogs critically to see if they would make good guide dogs. Instructors look for such things in a dog as excellent health, an even temperament, and a willingness to learn. Dogs who pass the evaluation are then placed in formal training for four to six months.

Guide Dog Instructors work with dogs on a daily basis. Dogs learn to respond to basic commands. For example, a guide dog should stop completely when its handler commands, "Halt."

With patience and diligence, Guide Dog Instructors train dogs to stop at street curbs, move around obstacles, board escalators, and so forth. Instructors also train dogs to behave properly in any environment or situation. In addition, they train dogs to perform "intelligent disobedience" responses that keep the dogs and their handlers from dangerous situations. For example, a handler and a guide dog are stopped at an intersection. The handler commands the dog to go forward. But the guide dog does not move because it sees a car coming toward them.

When the dogs have completed their training, Guide Dog Instructors assist with matching dogs to new owners.

Instructors then teach the new owners how to handle their guide dogs in a wide variety of situations and environments.

Guide Dog Instructors provide students with both the theory and practice of handling their guide dogs. Each day, students practice working with their dogs in various simulated and real situations (such as crowded sidewalks, bus travel, and obstacles in the path). Instructors also work with students individually on any special problems or particular needs. In addition, they teach students how to care for their dogs. After students go home, Guide Dog Instructors follow up on how they are doing. When needed, instructors provide refresher training.

Guide Dog Instructors perform many other tasks. For example, they:

- supervise and train apprentices and trainers
- assist the school's veterinary staff
- clean dog kennels
- transport puppies to volunteer homes, or drive students and their dogs to various places for training purposes
- give presentations at civic organizations or conventions to promote their schools
- assist in fundraising activities

The work of Guide Dog Instructors is physically demanding, as they spend long periods of time walking, standing, stooping, kneeling, and bending. On occasion, they must handle difficult dogs or people. They work long hours and often travel to perform their various duties.

Salaries
Salaries for Guide Dog Instructors vary, depending on such factors as their experience, education, and employer. Formal salary information for Guide Dog Instructors is unavailable. Most animal trainers, in general, earn an estimated annual salary that ranged between $15,190 and $45,230, according to the November 2004 *Occupational Employment Statistics* survey by the U.S. Bureau of Labor Statistics.

Employment Prospects
The job market for Guide Dog Instructors is rather limited due to the small population that is served. Most job opportunities become available as instructors retire, resign, or transfer to other positions. However, competition for available positions is high.

Advancement Prospects
Guide Dog Instructors who wish to perform supervisory and administrative work can advance to such positions as field supervisors, training managers, and directors of training. Many Guide Dog Instructors realize advancement by way of job satisfaction, professional recognition, and higher wages.

Education and Training
Most employers prefer or require that trainers have associate's or bachelor's degrees. The degree may be in any field, but having a degree or course work in animal behavior, psychology, orientation and mobility, or rehabilitation counseling helpful for this profession.

Guide Dog Instructors must first serve an apprenticeship at a licensed guide dog school for two to four years, depending on the school program. Apprenticeships include self-study, supervised instruction, and practical experience working with guide dogs and blind students.

Special Requirements
As of 2005, California is the only state that requires licensure of Guide Dog Instructors. (For more information, visit the Board of Guide Dogs for the Blind Web site at http://www.dca.ca.gov/guidedogboard.

Experience, Skills, and Personality Traits
To become an apprentice, individuals should have an extensive background in animal training and handling, as well as the ability to teach or coach others. Apprentices must have good health, be physically fit, and have the stamina to work a physically demanding job.

Some skills that Guide Dog Instructors need to do their work effectively are leadership, interpersonal, communication, writing, and public speaking skills. They also need good problem-solving and self-management skills.

Successful Guide Dog Instructors share several personality traits such as being patient, tactful, honest, reliable, responsible, dedicated, and compassionate. They are able to work well with both animals and people.

Unions and Associations
Many Guide Dog Instructors belong to professional associations to take advantage of networking opportunities, and other professional resources, and services. One national organization that many trainers join is the Guide Dog Users Inc. For contact information, see Appendix IV.

Tips for Entry
1. Get as much experience as you can training dogs. For example, you might learn to become a pet dog obedience trainer.
2. Volunteer at organizations working with the visually impaired to gain valuable experience.
3. Schools often hire apprentice trainers from current staff members and volunteers.
4. Learn more about the guide dog field on the Internet. Use the keywords *guide dog* or *guide dog instructors* to get a list of relevant Web sites.

HORSE TRAINER

CAREER PROFILE

Duties: Train horses for a specific type of riding activity such as pleasure riding or jumping; teach owners how to handle their horses; perform other duties as required

Alternate Title(s): Assistant Horse Trainer, Master Horse Trainer

Salary Range: $15,000 to $45,000

Employment Prospects: Good

Advancement Prospects: Poor

Prerequisites:

Education or Training—Apprenticeship

Experience—An extensive background in training and handling horses; a strong foundation in horsemanship and horse behavior

Special Skills and Personality Traits—Leadership, communication, interpersonal, organizational, and management skills; (as independent trainers) customer service, writing, public relations, and small-business skills; be methodical, patient, dedicated, open-minded, calm, kind, and gentle

CAREER LADDER

```
┌─────────────────────────────┐
│      Business Owner          │
└─────────────────────────────┘

┌─────────────────────────────┐
│      Horse Trainer           │
└─────────────────────────────┘

┌─────────────────────────────┐
│   Assistant Horse Trainer    │
└─────────────────────────────┘
```

Position Description

Professional Horse Trainers offer horse training services to horse owners who do not have the time or expertise to do their own training. Owners usually want their horses trained for recreational purposes or horse competitions. Most Horse Trainers specialize in providing horse training for one or more types of riding activities, such as:

- pleasure riding—English style or Western style
- dressage competitions
- jumping competitions, such as cross-country jumping
- eventing, which is a competition involving dressage, cross-country jumping, and show jumping
- long distance or endurance riding
- barrel racing
- carriage driving
- horse racing

Horse Trainers work for horse training facilities, equestrian centers, horse farms, horse stables, dude ranches, and other horse-related businesses. Some Horse Trainers are self-employed, and may train horses at their customers' facilities. They sometimes live at their customers' facilities for the duration of the training. Many independent Horse Trainers have their own training facilities.

Before training any horse, Horse Trainers work with owners to determine what goals they wish their horses to achieve as well as to create a workout schedule. Horse Trainers then begin their training by first gaining the horse's trust and forming a bond that is the basis of their working relationship. They determine what horses are capable of doing and develop the horses according to their abilities. Like people, horses learn in different ways and at different paces, thus most Horse Trainers use various techniques to match the learning styles and abilities of the horses. Horse Trainers work patiently with horses, building up their skills slowly.

Horse Trainers maintain accurate training records of horses and keep owners up-to-date with the progress of their horses. When training is complete, Horse Trainers then teach the riders (who may or may not be the owners) how to handle their horses. The Horse Trainers also instruct the riders on how to continue training the horses on a daily basis so that they maintain their skills.

Independent Horse Trainers perform necessary administrative tasks. For example, they determine client fees, arrange working schedules, collect fees, pay bills, buy supplies and equipment, do bookkeeping, and promote their businesses. If they have employees, they are responsible for paying their salaries and providing them with proper training and supervision. Many facility owners also provide other services such as boarding for horses, horse breeding, or riding lessons.

After years of experience, some Horse Trainers become well-known for their training methods. They begin to supervise apprentice Horse Trainers as well as offer horse training clinics on topics such as problem horses, training techniques, and horse care.

Salaried Horse Trainers work part time or full time.

Salaries

Salaries for Horse Trainers vary, depending on such factors as their experience, employer, and geographical location. According to the November 2004 *Occupational Employment Statistics* survey, by the U.S. Bureau of Labor Statistics, the estimated annual salary for most animal trainers, which include Horse Trainers, ranged between $15,190 and $45,230.

Employment Prospects

The horse industry is a healthy and growing field, and the job outlook, in general, is favorable.

Job opportunities for most staff positions become available as individuals retire, resign, or advance to other positions. Employers may create additional positions as their businesses grow.

The success rate for independent trainers depends on such factors as how well the individual trainers run their businesses and the level of competition for their services in their area.

Advancement Prospects

Most Horse Trainers realize advancement with job satisfaction, professional recognition, and higher wages. The ultimate goal for most Horse Trainers is to become self-employed or to have their own training facilities.

Education and Training

There is no minimum educational requirement to become a Horse Trainer. Some Horse Trainers obtain associate's or bachelor's degrees in equine science or a related field as part of their overall training toward becoming Horse Trainers. All trainers serve several years as an apprentice under one or more experienced (or master) Horse Trainers in which they receive hands-on training.

All Horse Trainers are responsible for developing their own training program, which they continue throughout their careers. It typically includes a combination of independent study and networking with colleagues. They also attend professional conferences and enroll in horse clinics taught by master Horse Trainers in the United States and Europe.

Experience, Skills, and Personality Traits

Horse Trainers have an extensive background in the handling and training of various breeds. Additionally, they have a strong foundation in horse behavior and horsemanship.

Horse Trainers need good leadership, communication, interpersonal, organizational, and management skills. As independent trainers, they also need strong customer service, writing, public relations, and small business skills.

Being methodical, patient, dedicated, open-minded, calm, kind, and gentle are some personality traits that successful Horse Trainers share.

Unions and Associations

Horse Trainers might join professional associations that serve particular horse breeds or riding activities, such as dressage or training a specific breed. They might also join organizations such as the American Horse Council that serve the general horse industry. (For contact information, see Appendix IV.) By joining professional organizations they can take advantage of professional resources, networking opportunities, job listings, and other professional services.

Tips for Entry

1. Many Horse Trainers started off by working on horse farms or in stables in exchange for training lessons.
2. If you plan on becoming an independent trainer, learn basic skills in running a small business.
3. To broaden your chances for apprenticeships or jobs of your choice, be willing to relocate or live temporarily in another location.
4. Many professionals in the horse industry use the Internet as a means to network with colleagues, as well as to advertise their services to potential customers. To begin a general search of relevant Web sites, use any of these keywords in a search engine: *horse trainer, horse stables,* or *horse farm.*

EMPLOYEE TRAINING SPECIALISTS

TRAINING SPECIALIST

CAREER PROFILE

Duties: Provide instruction for employee training programs; prepare classes and workshops; perform other duties as required

Alternate Title(s): Technical Trainer

Salary Range: $26,000 to $75,000

Employment Prospects: Good

Advancement Prospects: Good

Prerequisites:

Education or Training—Bachelor's degree

Experience—Hands-on experience required; teaching experience desirable

Special Skills and Personality Traits—Communication, interpersonal, motivational, presentation, public speaking, organizational, teamwork, writing, computer skills; be patient, enthusiastic, energetic, flexible, and creative

CAREER LADDER

```
┌─────────────────────────────────┐
│   Senior Training Specialist     │
└─────────────────────────────────┘

┌─────────────────────────────────┐
│      Training Specialist          │
└─────────────────────────────────┘

┌─────────────────────────────────┐
│           Trainer                 │
└─────────────────────────────────┘
```

Position Description

Employee Training Specialists are responsible for providing instruction for in-house training programs that employers give their workers for various purposes. The following are some of the different types of programs for which trainers conduct individual or group training sessions:

- orientation training for new employees, in which trainers explain employers' mission and policies, organizational structure and services, compensation plans and benefits, and work requirements and rules
- technical training programs for different computer hardware, software, networks, and systems
- professional skills workshops, in which Training Specialists teach job-specific technical skills that are specific to a particular department (such as the accounting department) or to a particular type of employee within the organization (such as department supervisors)
- safety training workshops, which includes training that meets government-mandated health and safety training
- informational workshops on employer policies and practices, such as workplace diversity, sexual harassment, and health issues

- basic skills classes, in which trainers provide remedial instruction in reading, writing, and math

Training Specialists are assigned to provide instruction for one or more training programs, according to their expertise. Depending on the size of their training departments, trainers may be also responsible for managing individual training programs.

When teaching a course, Training Specialists follow a prescribed curriculum and use established instructional materials. However, they bring their own teaching styles to the training sessions. Like all teachers, those specialists plan for the most effective means of delivering instruction based on the topic, learning objectives, number of participants, length of training, and other factors. Often a combination of teaching methods is used, such as lectures, videotapes, computer-based instruction, and Web-based instruction. In preparation for their training sessions, they gather all materials, equipment, and supplies needed for instruction, and set up the classrooms appropriately.

Training Specialists manage the learning environment so that employees can learn successfully. They provide learners with various activities and exercises to reinforce learning; they also answer questions and provide employees with positive feedback on their learning progress. After the completion of a training session, they evaluate the participants' performances and the effectiveness of their instruction, then present the information to their superiors.

In addition to conducting training sessions, Training Specialists perform other duties. They assist with assessing the training needs within an organization, planning new training programs, and updating courses. They also develop instructional materials, as well as maintain training equipment.

In-house Training Specialists work part time or full time. Some specialists are contractual employees, working for a designated length of time which can be several weeks, months, or years.

Salaries
Salaries for Training Specialists vary, depending on such factors as their education, experience, employer, and geographical location. According to the U.S. Bureau of Labor Statistics (BLS), in its November 2004 *Occupational Employment Statistics* survey, the estimated annual salary for most training and development specialists ranged between $26,180 and $75,410.

Employment Prospects
In-house Training Specialists work for financial institutions, retail corporations, computer companies, manufacturing firms, transportation companies, government agencies, health care organizations, educational institutions, nonprofit organizations, and many other public and private sector organizations. They are also employed by training organizations that provide services to employers on a contractual basis.

In general, trainer positions are available nationwide, but job competition is strong. The BLS reports that employment for training specialists should increase by 21 to 35 percent through 2012. In addition to job growth, new employees will be needed to replace specialists who retire, advance to higher positions, or transfer to other jobs.

Advancement Prospects
Training Specialists can advance to supervisory and management positions within an organization as well as advance by seeking positions in other organizations. They can also become self-employed consultants or training company owners that provide training and development services to companies and organizations. Additionally, they can pursue other related careers such as by becoming schoolteachers, community college instructors, curriculum developers, or instructional technologists.

Education and Training
Most employers require that Training Specialists have bachelor's degrees in instructional technology, human resources, education, or another related field. Many employers will accept candidates with high school diplomas or associate degrees if they have qualifying work experience.

Experience, Skills, and Personality Traits
Previous teaching experience is usually preferred; but many employers waive the teaching requirement if candidates have the necessary hands-on technical experience, and have the ability to teach the necessary content and skills to adult learners. For technical training positions, candidates should have the appropriate technical experience.

To facilitate classes and seminars effectively, Training Specialists should have communication, interpersonal, motivational, presentation, and public speaking skills. They also need strong organizational, teamwork, and writing skills. In addition, they should have appropriate computer skills. Being patient, enthusiastic, energetic, flexible, and creative are some personality traits that successful Training Specialists share.

Unions and Associations
Many Training Specialists belong to professional associations to take advantage of networking opportunities, job listings, and other professional resources and services. The International Society for Performance Improvement and the American Society for Training and Development are national societies that trainers might join. Technical Trainers are also eligible to join the Information Technology Association of America. For contact information, see Appendix IV.

Tips for Entry
1. Keep up with developments in the training field. Also maintain your computer skills as technology is continually changing.
2. Post your resume at strategic Web sites for employers to read. Check with different professional associations to see if they offer that service.
3. Use the Internet to learn more about the field of employee training and development. To get a list of Web sites, enter either of these keywords in a search engine: *employee training* or *training and development.*

TRAINING DEVELOPER

CAREER PROFILE

Duties: Develop and design employee training programs and instructional materials; manage projects; perform other duties as required

Alternate Title(s): Instructional Designer, Training Specialist

Salary Range: $26,000 to $75,000

Employment Prospects: Good

Advancement Prospects: Fair

Prerequisites:

Education or Training—Bachelor's degree

Experience—Previous experience developing training programs and materials

Special Skills and Personality Traits—Communication, interpersonal, teamwork, organizational, management, writing, presentation, and computer skills; be patient, tactful, energetic, enthusiastic, creative, flexible

CAREER LADDER

```
┌─────────────────────────┐
│    Training Manager     │
└─────────────────────────┘

┌─────────────────────────┐
│   Training Developer    │
└─────────────────────────┘

┌─────────────────────────┐
│    Trainer or Intern    │
└─────────────────────────┘
```

Position Description

Training Developers are specialists in the training and development departments of hospitals, department stores, computer companies, banks, colleges, bus companies, distribution centers, government agencies, nonprofit organizations, and other private and public sector organizations. As experts in instructional design, they develop and design effective training programs for their employers, such as:

- new employee orientation training
- employee safety training
- technical training
- professional skills training for specific departments (such as customer service, sales, or warehouse) or specific employee positions (such as department supervisors, division managers, or sales representatives)
- basic skills training (remediation of literacy and math skills)
- informational workshops on work-related topics, such as sexual harassment in the workplace

Training Developers usually act as project managers in the development of training programs. They are responsible for defining the project and coordinating it from start to fin-

ish. They also ensure that a project is completed on time and within a given budget.

When starting a project, Training Developers first conduct a needs assessment. They gather information such as relevant characteristics of trainees, and different job procedures, by talking with appropriate personnel, observing workers, and reviewing work materials.

Training Developers work closely with subject matter experts—department managers, supervisors, and other personnel—as they design specific instructional programs. Together, they determine the content of the program—information to be taught, learning objectives, sequence of teaching, types of activities and exercises, and so on. They also discuss evaluation strategies for measuring employee performance upon completion of training, In addition, they determine the most effective way to deliver the instruction—such as classroom training, conferences, individual coaching, on-the-job training, interactive video training, or intranet instruction.

Depending on the complexity of a project, Training Developers may work alone or as part of a team. Training Developers design training programs that integrate adult learning principles, as well as take into account the different abilities and learning styles of the program participants.

Many Training Developers also develop and produce print, visual, and/or technology-based instructional materials that include both trainer and participant guides.

Training Developers are responsible for maintaining training programs. On a regular basis, they review and evaluate the effectiveness of current programs. When necessary, they update current courses and instructional materials.

Some Training Developers are responsible for managing the development of all training programs within their organization. This includes coordinating and administering contracts with outside vendors who provide specific training programs.

Training Developers are expected to update and improve their skills as well as keep up with current training and development research. They might join professional associations and network with colleagues. They might also enroll in training seminars and continuing education courses, read professional books and journals, and participate in professional conferences.

Training Developers are either in-house staff members or consultants working on a contractual basis. They generally work 40 hours a week, sometimes working additional hours to meet deadlines.

Salaries

Salaries for Training Developers vary, depending on such factors as their education, experience, employer, and geographical location. According to the November 2004 *Occupational Employment Statistics* survey by the U.S. Bureau of Labor Statistics (BLS), the estimated annual salary for most training and development specialists ranged between $26,180 and $75,410.

Employment Prospects

The BLS reports that employment for training specialists should increase by 21 to 35 percent through 2012. In addition to job growth, new employees will be needed to replace Training Developers who retire, advance to higher positions, or transfer to other jobs. Keep in mind that the job competition in this field is strong.

Advancement Prospects

Training Developers can advance to senior, supervisory, and management positions within an organization as well as by seeking positions in other organizations. They can also become training consultants or training company owners who provide training and development services to companies and organizations.

Training Developers can pursue other related careers in such positions as college professors, software developers, and desktop publishing specialists.

Education and Training

The minimum requirement for most Training Developer positions is a bachelor's degree in instructional technology, education, organizational development, or other related field. For some positions, employers require or prefer candidates with master's degrees, but will often waive the requirement if candidates have qualifying work experience.

Experience, Skills, and Personality Traits

In general, Training Developers have previous experience developing training programs and materials. They are also knowledgeable about adult learning principles, course development methodology, and creating learning materials that are computer-based or technology-based.

Training Developers need excellent communication, interpersonal, and teamwork skills to work well with training staff and other employees within their organizations. They also need strong organizational, management, writing, and presentation skills. In addition, they have appropriate computer skills needed to perform their work.

Successful Training Developers share several personality traits such as being patient, tactful, energetic, enthusiastic, creative, and flexible.

Unions and Associations

Many Training Developers join professional associations to take advantage of education programs, networking opportunities, and other professional resources and services. Two societies that they might join are the American Society for Training and Development and the International Society for Performance Improvement. For contact information, see Appendix IV.

Tips for Entry

1. Build up strong writing and public speaking skills.
2. Get experience teaching adult learners. For example, you might participate in an adult literacy program.
3. Many entry-level candidates have gained work experience through college internships.
4. In college, begin building a network of contacts whom you can call when you conduct a job hunt.
5. Learn more about the field of instructional technology on the Internet. To get a list of pertinent Web sites, enter either of these keywords in a search engine: *instructional technology* or *instructional designer.*

TRAINING MANAGER

CAREER PROFILE

Duties: Manage and administer employee training programs; perform other duties as required

Alternate Title(s): Training Director, Training and Development Manager

Salary Range: $39,000 to $124,000

Employment Prospects: Good

Advancement Prospects: Fair

Prerequisites:

Education or Training—Bachelor's degree

Experience—Several years of training and development experience in appropriate work settings; have supervisory and management experience

Special Skills and Personality Traits—Leadership, project management, writing, communication, interpersonal, team-building, teamwork, presentation, public speaking, and computer skills; be organized, flexible, adaptable, analytical, creative, and self-motivated

CAREER LADDER

```
┌─────────────────────────────┐
│    Training Director or      │
│    Training Consultant       │
└─────────────────────────────┘

┌─────────────────────────────┐
│      Training Manager        │
└─────────────────────────────┘

┌─────────────────────────────┐
│      Training Specialist     │
└─────────────────────────────┘
```

Position Description

Training Managers are in charge of administering the training departments of public and private sector employers. (The training department may be also known as the *training and development department,* and is usually part of a human resources department.) Training Managers oversee and coordinate all training programs that employers provide to their employees so that they can perform their jobs effectively and efficiently. Some of the various types of programs that Training Managers oversee are:

- new employee orientation training
- safety training
- workshops on employer's policies and practices regarding work-related topics such as equal employment opportunities
- technical training on computer software applications, such as word processors, spreadsheets, graphics, and databases
- specific job skills training for particular departments (such as the marketing department) or for particular employees (such as department supervisors)
- basic skills classes, or remedial instruction in reading, writing, and math
- training programs for clients, customers, or users of products and services

Training Managers work closely with human resource and departmental managers to determine the training needs for the overall organization as well as for the various departments. Training Managers then plan training strategies, and oversee the development and implementation of appropriate training programs.

Depending on the size of their staff, Training Managers may conduct needs assessments for new training projects. They may develop and design instructional programs, and may assist in the development of print, visual, and/or technology-based materials. Some Training Managers teach classes or workshops and provide individual coaching of employees.

Training Managers are also responsible for identifying and evaluating external, or outside, resources that may offer training programs. These sources include vendors, independent consultants, training companies, higher education institutions, professional associations, and trade unions. Training Managers assist human resource managers and various departmental managers in choosing appropriate external training programs that meet their specific needs. In addition, Training Managers make contracts with vendors, consultants, and training companies and coordinate the logistics of providing instruction. Managers may also form partnerships with community colleges, technical colleges, and university and college continuing education programs to develop specialized training programs.

Training Managers monitor all training programs to ensure that they meet employer standards as well as comply with any government requirements. They also evaluate the curriculum, instructional materials, and instructors' presentations, and make recommendations for changes and improvements.

In addition, Training Managers are responsible for performing various administrative tasks. For example, they develop and manage budgets, train and supervise staff, oversee contracts for consultants, schedule courses, locate facilities for training sessions, and complete required paperwork.

Training Managers work 40 hours a week, and sometimes work additional hours to complete their various tasks.

Salaries

Salaries for Training Managers vary, depending on such factors as their education, experience, responsibilities, employer, and geographical location. According to the November 2004 *Occupational Employment Statistics* survey by the U.S. Bureau of Labor Statistics (BLS), the estimated annual salary for most training and development managers ranged between $38,640 and $123,720.

Employment Prospects

Training Managers are employed by financial institutions, business services companies, retail companies, manufacturing firms, transportation corporations, government agencies, utilities companies, hospitals, health care organizations, educational institutions, nonprofit organizations, and many other corporations and organizations.

Most job opportunities become available as managers retire, resign, or advance to higher positions. Employers may create new training management positions to meet additional training needs.

Advancement Prospects

In small and mid-size organizations, Training Managers are usually the top administrative positions for the training departments. In larger organizations, they can usually pursue executive positions such as training directors and vice presidents of training and development.

Many Training Managers pursue higher pay and more complex responsibilities by seeking positions with other employers. They can also become consultants or owners of

businesses that provide training and development services to companies and organizations on a contractual basis.

Education and Training

A bachelor's degree is the minimum requirement for most Training Manager positions. Many employers, however, prefer candidates with master's degrees. College degrees should be in business administration, education, organizational development, instructional technology, or other related fields.

Experience, Skills, and Personality Traits

In general, candidates should have several years of experience providing instruction and developing training programs in appropriate work settings. Additionally, they should have supervisory and management experience.

To do their jobs effectively, Training Managers need leadership, project management, and writing skills. They also need communication, interpersonal, team-building, and teamwork skills as they work daily with various people within their organizations. In addition, they should have strong presentation, public speaking and computer skills.

Successful Training Managers share several personality traits such as being organized, flexible, adaptable, analytical, creative, and self-motivated.

Unions and Associations

Many Training Managers belong to professional associations to take advantage of networking opportunities, education programs, and other professional resources and services. Two national societies that these professionals might join are the American Society for Training and Development and the International Society for Performance Improvement. For contact information, see Appendix IV.

Tips for Entry

1. Before going to a job interview, learn all that you can about the employer and its training department. Think of a few things you could do to strengthen or improve the department.
2. Network with colleagues and employers (including former employers) to learn about current and upcoming job vacancies.
3. You can use the Internet to learn about job vacancies throughout the United States. To find specific information about an employer, enter the employer's name in a search engine to see if it has a Web site. On an employer's Web site, look for a link such as "employment opportunities" or "human resources department."

APPENDIXES

APPENDIX I
EDUCATIONAL AND TRAINING RESOURCES

In this appendix, you will learn about Internet resources for education and training programs for some of the occupations in this book. To learn about programs for occupations not listed here, talk with professionals as well as with school, career, or job counselors. You can also refer to college directories produced by Peterson's or other publishers, which may be found in your school or public library.

Note: All Web site addresses were current when this book was being written. If a URL does not work, you may be able to find a new address by entering the name of the organization, individual, or Web site into a search engine.

GENERAL RESOURCES
The following Web sites provide links to various academic or training programs at postsecondary institutions throughout the United States.

- Education Online Search, http://www.education-online-search.com
- Trade Schools Guide, http://www.trade-schools.net
- Web U.S. Higher Education, a listing of colleges and universities (maintained by the University of Texas at Austin), http://www.utexas.edu/world/univ
- The Princeton Review, http://www.princetonreview.com
- GradSchools.com, http://www.gradschools.com

ART THERAPY
The American Art Therapy Association provides a listing of graduate programs in art therapy at its Web site, http://www.arttherapy.org.

CAREER COUNSELING
A directory of listings in master's degree programs is available at the Council for Accreditation of Counseling and Related Educational Programs Web site, http://www.cacrep.org/directory.html.

CRIMINAL JUSTICE, CRIMINOLOGY, AND RELATED FIELDS
Listings of undergraduate and graduate programs are available at the American Society of Criminology Web site.

- For a list of undergraduate programs, go to http://www.asc41.com/UNDERGRAD.html
- For a list of graduate programs, go to http://www.asc41.com/GRADLINKS.html

CULINARY ARTS
A listing of schools that offer culinary degree or certificate programs can be found at the Culinary-Careers.org Web site, http://www.culinary-careers.org.

DANCE EDUCATION
A listing of colleges, universities, dance academies, and other schools that offer dance education programs can be found at the Voice of Dance Web site, http://www.voiceofdance.com.

EARLY CHILDHOOD TEACHER PREPARATION PROGRAMS
The Council for Professional Recognition provides a national database of programs at its Web site, http://www.cdacouncil.org.

EDUCATION LEADERSHIP (INDEPENDENT SCHOOLS)
The Klingenstein Center, at Columbia University in New York, offers master of arts and master of education degree programs in education leadership for independent schools. For more information, visit the center's Web site, http://www.klingenstein.org.

ENVIRONMENTAL STUDIES, NATURAL RESOURCE MANAGEMENT, OUTDOOR STUDIES, AND ENVIRONMENTAL-RELATED AREAS
A database of college programs can be found at EnviroEducation.com: The Environmental Education Directory at http://www.enviroeducation.com.

FLIGHT INSTRUCTION
For a listing of flight schools, go to either of these Web sites:

- National Association of Flight Instructors, http://www.nafinet.org
- Student Pilot Network, http://www.studentpilot.net

LIBRARY AND INFORMATION SCIENCE
A listing of accredited master's programs in library and information science is available at the American Library Association Web site. Go to http://www.ala.org/ala/education/accredprograms/accreditedprograms.htm.

LIBRARY TECHNICIAN
A listing of associate's, bachelor's, and certificate programs is available at the Council of Library/Media Technicians Web site, http://colt.ucr.edu/ltprograms.htm.

MUSIC EDUCATION
The College Music Society provides a database of institutions that offer music programs at its Web site. (These programs are listed in its *Directory of Music Faculties in College and Universities, U.S. and Canada.*) The URL is http://www.music.org.

NURSING

A listing of nursing programs can be found at either of the following Web sites:

- All Nursing Schools http://www.allnursingschools.com
- American Association of Colleges of Nursing, http://www.aacn.nche.edu

NUTRITIONAL SCIENCE

A directory of graduate programs is available at the American Society for Nutrition Web site, at http://www.asns.org.

OCCUPATIONAL THERAPY

A listing of accredited occupational therapy programs can be found at the following Web sites:

- American Occupational Therapy Association, http://www.aota.org
- Occupational Therapist.com, http://www.occupationaltherapist.com

PARKS AND RECREATION, LEISURE STUDIES, OR TOURISM

A listing of academic programs is available at the National Recreation and Park Association Web site. Go to http://www.nrpa.org, click on the link *Education and Conferences,* then click on the link *Higher Education.*

POLICE ACADEMIES

A listing of some police academies in the United States is available at the Acrecona–LEO Links Directory Web site at http://www.sover.net/~tmartin/Academy.htm.

PUBLISHING

A listing of publishing certificate and education programs can be found at Book Jobs.com: http://www.bookjobs.com/listprograms.php.

REHABILITATION COUNSELING

A listing of master's degree programs is available at the Council on Rehabilitation Education Web site at http://www.core-rehab.org/states/index.html.

SCHOOL COUNSELING

A directory of listings in master's degree programs is available at the Council for Accreditation of Counseling and Related Educational Programs Web site at http://www.cacrep.org/directory.html.

SCHOOL LIBRARY MEDIA EDUCATION

A listing of school library media education programs is available at the American Library Association Web site. Go to http://www.ala.org/ala/education/accredprograms/accreditedprograms.htm.

SCHOOL PSYCHOLOGY

A listing of graduate programs is available at the National Association of School Psychologists Web site at http://www.nasponline.org/certification/gradschools.html.

SOCIAL WORK

The Council on Social Work Education provides a database of undergraduate and graduate social work programs at its Web site, http://www.cswe.org.

SPECIAL EDUCATION

The National Clearinghouse for Professions in Special Education provides a directory of preparation programs for special education teachers, educational diagnosticians, assistive technologists, early childhood special education educators, and other professions. The URL is http://www.special-ed-careers.org/career_choices/preparation.html.

SPEECH-LANGUAGE PATHOLOGY

A listing of master's and doctoral programs is available at the American Speech-Language-Hearing Association Web site at http://www.asha.org/students/academic.

STUDENT AFFAIRS ADMINISTRATION

The National Association of Student Personnel Administrators provides a directory of graduate programs in student affairs administration at http://www.naspa.org/gradprep/index.cfm.

TEACHER EDUCATION

A listing of teacher education programs can be found at the following Web sites:

- National Council for Accreditation of Teacher Education, http://www.ncate.org
- Teacher Education Accreditation Council, http://www.teac.org

TEACHER EDUCATION—TESOL

TESOL, Inc., provides a listing of teacher education programs, as well as degree and certificate programs. Go to http://www.tesol.org, then click on the link *Professional Development.*

TECHNOLOGY EDUCATION

A listing of colleges and universities with technology education programs is available at the International Technology Education Association Web site. Go to http://www.iteaconnect.org.

PAYING FOR YOUR EDUCATION

Scholarships, grants, student loans, and other financial aid programs are available to help you pay for your postsecondary education. These programs are sponsored by government agencies, professional and trade associations, private foundations, businesses, and other organizations. (Contact information for many professional societies is available in Appendix IV.)

The federal government as well as many states have a loan forgiveness program for students who become public school teachers in high poverty areas. Applicants must be willing to commit to teach for a certain number of years. Qualifications for the programs vary.

To learn more about available financial assistance programs, talk with your high school guidance counselor or college career counselor. You might also consult college catalogs, as they usually include financial aid information. In addition, you might visit or contact the financial aid office at the college where you plan to attend or are attending now. Lastly, check out these Web sites for financial aid information:

- Information for Parents and Students by the National Association of Student Financial Aid Administrators, http://www.studentaid.org
- Student Aid on the Web (U.S. Department of Education Federal Student Aid), http://www.studentaid.ed.gov

APPENDIX II
HOW TO BECOME A PUBLIC SCHOOL TEACHER

In this appendix, you will learn about the basic requirements for teacher licensure as well as learn about the types of teacher programs that are available.

TEACHER LICENSURE

All teachers, from preschool to high school, in the U.S. public school system must have the proper teaching licensure for the grade level and subject matter that they teach. The licensure is granted by the state department of education in the state where they work. Possessing a teaching credential demonstrates that an individual has met the high level of competence required by a state to teach a particular subject area.

Each of the 50 states (and the District of Columbia) establishes its own requirements for teacher licensure. The licensure requirements are revised from time to time, so it is important to contact the appropriate state education agency for up-to-date information. For a listing of state teacher licensing offices, see Appendix III.

Depending on the state, new teachers may be required to first obtain initial licensure. Then, after a few years of teaching, along with completion of continuing education credits or a master's degree, they apply for full licensure.

BASIC LICENSURE REQUIREMENTS

The basic requirements for teacher licensure are similar throughout the United States.

First, teacher candidates must possess a college degree. In most states, the minimum educational requirement is a bachelor's degree in the field that candidates will be teaching. Some states require that candidates have a master's degree.

Second, candidates must have successfully completed an approved, accredited teacher preparation program.

Third, candidates must pass a standardized state test or a recognized exam, such as PRAXIS, to demonstrate their competency in basic skills and the subject matter they will be teaching, as well as their teaching skills.

THE NCLB REQUIREMENTS FOR HIGHLY QUALIFIED TEACHERS

In 2001, the Elementary and Secondary Education Act (of 1965) was reauthorized, amended, and renamed the No Child Left Behind (NCLB) Act. This federal legislation is intended to assist disadvantaged children in impoverished areas.

All public school teachers in core academic areas who teach in programs or schools funded with Title I (Improving the Academic Achievement of the Disadvantaged) grants must meet the NCLB's requirements for highly qualified teachers. The core academic subjects include English, reading, language arts, math, science, history, civics, government, geography, economics, foreign languages, and the arts. (Note: By 2005–06, all public school teachers in core academic areas must be highly qualified in every state that receives Title I funds.)

NCLB defines a highly qualified teacher as meeting these minimum requirements:

- possession of a bachelor's degree
- possession of full state licensure
- being able to demonstrate competency in the content knowledge of each core academic subject being taught

All states and the District of Columbia have the responsibility to define the licensure and competency elements according to their individual state's needs.

TRADITIONAL PATH TO LICENSURE

Enrolling in an accredited teacher preparation (or teacher education) program at a four-year college or university is the most familiar route to becoming licensed as a public school teacher. Relevant teacher education programs are available for early education, elementary education, middle-grades education, and secondary education. Teacher education programs typically vary from state to state, as well as from institution to institution.

Two types of teacher preparation programs are generally available. One is a four- or five-year teacher education degree program that also grants teaching certification upon completion of the program. The other is a post-baccalaureate teacher education program, in which students enroll upon earning their bachelor's degree in the field of their choice.

Institutions design their teacher education programs to meet the teacher licensure guidelines established by their state department of education. The programs cover general education courses such as the foundations of education, educational psychology, evaluation of learning, instructional planning, teaching methods, and classroom management. Students also take coursework in their teaching specialty as well as complete an internship or practicum (which is also known as student teaching).

In addition to being approved by its state, an institution's teacher education programs is accredited nationally by the National Council for Accreditation of Teacher Education (NCATE) or the Teacher Education Accreditation Council (TEAC). For information about accredited programs, visit either of the following Web sites: NCATE, http://www.ncate.org, or TEAC, http://www.teac.org.

ALTERNATIVE TEACHER PREPARATION PROGRAMS

Most states have alternative teacher preparation programs that place candidates full time in the classroom. The candidates are responsible for teaching classes while under the supervision of mentor or master teachers. They complete professional education coursework before receiving a teaching assignment and while teaching. Upon satisfying the requirements of their programs, candidates are granted professional certification.

To qualify for alternative teacher preparation programs, individuals must have a bachelor's degree and pass an intense screening process that may involve interviews, tests, and a demonstration of their mastery of the subject area in which they wish to teach.

Participants are often older and experienced mid-career individuals who want to enter the education field. Most states have one or more types of alternative teacher preparation programs. Some programs are designed to specifically recruit, select, and train candidates to teach subject areas or grade levels in which there is a shortage of qualified teachers.

States may also have programs that grant temporary credentials to allow individuals to teach while completing the necessary courses to fulfill licensure requirements.

Alternative teacher preparation programs and their requirements change from time to time. To get up-to-date information, contact your local school district office or your state's teacher licensing agency. (See Appendix III for a listing of state agencies.)

OTHER PROGRAMS

The U.S. Department of Education and state and local education agencies sponsor various programs to recruit individuals interested in becoming teachers in the public school system.

One such program is Teach for America, a national teacher corps that recruits college seniors and recent graduates to teach in public schools in urban and rural areas where teachers are needed the most. Participants make a two-year commitment and earn a salary comparable to a beginning teacher's salary in the location where they teach. Local school districts usually hire Teach for America teachers through state-approved alternative certification programs. Upon completion of their two-year commitment, participants may be granted full teacher licensure or provisional licensure while they complete additional coursework. For more information about this program, visit the Teach for America Web site at http://www.teachforamerica.org.

Another program is the Troops to Teachers Program, which was developed to recruit, prepare, and support former members of the military services. Participants must have a bachelor's degree and commit to teaching in schools in impoverished areas upon earning their teacher licensure. For more information, visit the Troops to Teachers Program webpage at http://www.ed.gov/programs/troops.

Teaching fellowship programs are among other available programs. These programs are established by academic institutions or state or local educational agencies to recruit a specific audience, such as college seniors, college graduates, or mid-career professionals. In exchange for scholarships and loans to fund their teacher preparation program, the participants agree to teach for a minimum number of years in a particular state or in a low-performing school. For information about available programs in your area, contact the local school district office or a teacher education program at an academic institution.

APPENDIX III
STATE TEACHER LICENSING AGENCIES

The following is a list of the 50 state education offices that oversee licensure for public school teachers. Some of the offices also provide licensure information for school administrators, specialists, and paraeducators.

Note: All contact information and Web site addresses were current when this book was being written. For more current information, you might contact a local school district office or a teacher preparation program at a college or university. If a URL no longer works, you may be able to find the agency's new address by entering its name in a search engine.

Alabama State Department of Education
Teacher Education and Certification Section
50 North Ripley Street
P.O. Box 302101
Montgomery, AL 36104
Phone: (334) 242-9977
http://www.alsde.edu

Alaska Department of Education and Early Development
Teacher Certification
801 West 10th Street, Suite 200
Juneau, AK 99801
Phone: (907) 465-2831
Fax: (907) 465-2441
http://www.educ.state.ak.us/TeacherCertification

Arizona Department of Education
Certification Unit
P.O. Box 6490
Phoenix, AZ 85005-6490
Phone: (602) 542-4367
http://www.ade.state.az.us/certification

Arkansas Department of Education
Office of Professional Licensure
4 Capitol Mall
Little Rock, AR 72201
Phone: (501) 682-4342
Fax: (501) 682-4898
http://arkedu.state.ar.us/teachers/teachers_licensure.html

California Department of Education
Commission on Teacher Credentialing
P.O. Box 944270
Sacramento, CA 94244-2700
Phone: (888) 921-2682 or (916) 445-7254

Fax: (916) 327-3166
http://www.ctc.ca.gov

Colorado Department of Education
Educator Licensing
201 East Colfax Avenue, Room 105
Denver, CO 80203
Phone: (303) 866-6628
Fax: (303) 866-6866
http://www.cde.state.co.us/index_license.htm

Connecticut Department of Education
Bureau of Educator Preparation, Certification, Support and Assessment
P.O. Box 150471, Room 243
Hartford, CT 06115-0471
Phone: (860) 713-6969
Fax: (860) 713-7017
http://www.state.ct.us/sde/dtl/cert/index.htm

Delaware Department of Education
Licensure/Certification Office
401 Federal Street, Suite 2
Dover, DE 19901
Phone: (302) 739-4686 or (888) 759-9133
http://deeds.doe.K12.de.us

District of Columbia Public Schools
Office of Academic Credentials
825 North Capitol Street NE, Sixth Floor
Washington, DC 20002
Phone: (202) 442-5377
http://www.teachdc.org

Florida Department of Education
Bureau of Educator Certification
325 West Gaines Street, Suite 201
Tallahassee, FL 32399-0400
Phone: (800) 445-6739 or (850) 245-5049
http://www.fldoe.org/edcert

Georgia Department of Education
Professional Standards Commission
2 Peachtree Street, Suite 6000
Atlanta, GA 30303
Phone: (800) 869-7775 or (404) 232-2500
http://www.gapsc.com

Hawaii Department of Education
Hawaii Teacher Standards Board
650 Iwilei Road, Suite 201
Honolulu, HI 96817
Phone: (808) 586-2600
Fax: (808) 586-2606
http://www.htsb.org

Idaho Department of Education
Bureau of Certification and Professional Standards
P.O. Box 83720
Boise, ID 83720-0027
Phone: (208) 332-6800
http://www.sde.state.id.us/certification/default.asp

Illinois State Board of Education
Division of Teacher Certification and Professional Development
100 North First Street
Springfield, IL 62777
Phone: (866) 262-6663
http://www.isbe.net/certification/default.htm

Indiana Department of Education
Division of Professional Standards
101 West Ohio Street, Suite 300
Indianapolis, IN 46204
Phone: (866) 542-3672 or (317) 232-9010
Fax: (317) 232-9023
http://www.doe.state.in.us/dps

Iowa Department of Education
Board of Educational Examiners
Grimes State Office Building
Des Moines, IA 50319
Phone: (515) 281-3245
Fax: (515) 281-7669
http://www.state.ia.us/boee

Kansas State Department of Education
Teacher Education and Licensure Team
120 Southeast 10th Avenue
Topeka, KS 66612-1182
Phone: (785) 291-3678
http://www.ksbe.state.ks.us/cert/cert.html

Kentucky Department of Education
Education Professional Standards Board
100 Airport Road, Third Floor
Frankfort, KY 40601
Phone: (502) 564-4606
Fax: (502) 564-7092
http://www.kyepsb.net

Louisiana Department of Education
Division of Teacher Certification and
    Higher Education
P.O. Box 94064
Baton Rouge, LA 70804-9064
Phone: (225) 342-3490
Fax: (225) 342-3499
http://www.doe.state.la.us/lde/tsac/home.
    html

Maine Department of Education
Certification Office
23 State House Station
Augusta, ME 04333-0023
Phone: (207) 624-6603
Fax: (207) 624-6604
http://www.state.me.us/education/cert/
    cert.htm

**Maryland State Department of
    Education**
Certification Branch
200 West Baltimore Street
Baltimore, MD 21201
Phone: (410) 767-0406
http://www.marylandpublicschools.org/
    MSDE/divisions/certification/
    certification_branch

**Massachusetts Department of
    Education**
Office of Educator Licensure
350 Main Street
Malden, MA 02148
Phone: (781) 338-6600
Fax: (781) 338-3391
http://www.doe.mass.edu/educators

Michigan Department of Education
Office of Professional Preparation and
    Services
608 West Allegan Street
P.O. Box 30008
Lansing, MI 48909
Phone: (517) 241-4410 (receptionist)
Fax: (517) 373-0542
http://www.michigan.gov/mde

Minnesota Department of Education
Educator Licensing and Teacher Quality
1500 Highway 36 West
Roseville, MN 55113-4266
Phone: (651) 582-8691
TTY: (651) 582-8201
Fax: (651) 582-8809
http://education.state.mn.us

**Mississippi Department of
    Education**
Office of Educator Licensure
P.O. Box 771
Jackson, MS 39205-0771
Phone: (601) 359-3483
http://www.mde.k12.ms.us/ed_licensure/
    index.html

**Missouri State Department of
    Elementary and Secondary
    Education**
Educator Certification
P.O. Box 480
Jefferson City, MO 65102
Phone: (573) 751-0051 or (573) 751-3847
Fax: (573) 522-8314
http://www.dese.state.mo.us/divteachqual
    /teachcert

Montana Office of Public Instruction
Educator Licensure
P.O. Box 202501
Helena, MT 59620-2501
Phone: (406) 444-3150
http://www.opi.state.mt.us/cert./index.html

Nebraska Department of Education
Teacher Certification
301 Centennial Mall South
P.O. Box 94987
Lincoln, NE 68509
Phone: (402) 471-0739
http://www.nde.state.ne.us/TCERT/index.
    html

Nevada Department of Education
Las Vegas Office:
Teacher Licensing Office
1850 East Sahara Avenue, Suite 205
Las Vegas, NV 89104

Phone: (702) 486-6458
Fax: (702) 486-6450
Carson City Office:
Teacher Licensing Office
700 East Fifth Street
Carson City, NV 89701
Phone: (775) 687-9115
Fax: (775) 687-9101
http://www.doe.nv.gov/licensing.html

**New Hampshire Department of
    Education**
Bureau of Credentialing
101 Pleasant Street
Concord, NH 03301
Phone: (603) 271-2408
http://www.ed.state.nh.us/education/doe/
    organization/programsupport/boc.htm

New Jersey Department of Education
Office of Licensure and Credentials
P.O. Box 500
Trenton, NJ 08625
Phone: (609) 292-2070
http://www.state.nj.us/njded/educators/
    credentials.htm

New Mexico Department of Education
Professional Licensure Bureau
300 Don Gaspar
Santa Fe, NM 87501-2786
Phone: (505) 827-6587
Fax: (505) 827-4148
http://www.ped.state.nm.us/div/ais/lic/
    index.html

New York State Education Department
Office of Teaching Initiatives
5N Education Building
Albany, NY 12234
Phone: (518) 474-3901
TTY: (800) 855-2880 or
    (800) 421-1220 (in NY)
http://www.nysed.gov

**North Carolina Department of Public
    Instruction**
Licensure Section
301 North Wilmington Street
Raleigh, NC 27601
Phone: (800) 577-7994 or (919) 807-3310
http://www.ncpublicschools.org/
    employment

**North Dakota Department of Public
    Instruction**
Education Standards and Practices Board
2718 Gateway Avenue, Suite 303
Bismarck, ND 58503
Phone: (701) 328-9641

Fax: (701) 328-9647
http://www.nd.gov/espb

Ohio Department of Education
Office of Certification/Licensure
25 South Front Street, Mail Stop 105
Columbus, OH 43215-4183
Phone: (614) 466-3593
http://www.ode.state.oh.us/teaching-
profession/Teacher/Certification_
Licensure/default.asp

Oklahoma State Department of Education
Professional Standards Section
2500 North Lincoln Boulevard, Room 212
Oklahoma City, OK 73105-4599
Phone: (405) 521-3337
http://sde.state.ok.us

Oregon Department of Education
Teacher Standards and Practices
Commission
465 Commercial Street NE
Salem, OR 97301
Phone: (503) 378-3586
TDD: (503) 378-6961
Fax: (503) 378-4448
http://www.tspc.state.or.us

Pennsylvania Department of Education
Bureau of Teacher Certification and
Preparation
333 Market Street
Harrisburg, PA 17126-0333
Phone: (717) 787-3356
TDD: (717) 772-2864
Fax: (717) 783-6736
http://www.teaching.state.pa.us

Rhode Island Department of Elementary and Secondary Education
Teacher Certification, Preparation and
Professional Development
255 Westminster Street
Providence, RI 02903

Phone: (401) 222-4600
http://www.ridoe.net/Certification_PD

South Carolina Department of Education
Division of Educator Quality and
Leadership
Landmark II Office Building
3700 Forest Drive, Suite 500
Columbia, SC 29204
Phone: (877) 885-5280 or (803) 734-8466
http://www.scteachers.org

South Dakota Department of Education
Office of Accreditation and Teacher
Quality
700 Governors Drive
Pierre, SD 57501-2291
Phone: (605) 773-3553
http://doe.sd.gov/oatq

Tennessee Department of Education
Office of Teacher Licensing
Fourth Floor, Andrew Johnson Tower
710 James Robertson Parkway
Nashville, TN 37243-0377
Phone: (615) 532-4885
Fax: (615) 532-1448
http://www.state.tn.us/education/lic/index.
php

Texas Education Agency
State Board for Educator Certification
Capitol Station
P.O. Box 12728
Austin, TX 78711
Phone: (888) 863-5880 or (512) 936-8400
http://www.sbec.state.tx.us/SBECOnline

Utah State Office of Education
Educator Licensing
250 East 500 South
P.O. Box 144200
Salt Lake City, UT 84114
Phone: (801) 538-7740
Fax: (801) 538-7973
http://www.usoe.k12.ut.us/cert

Vermont Department of Education
Educator Licensing Office

120 State Street
Montpelier, VT 05620-2501
Phone: (802) 828-2445
http://www.state.vt.us/educ

Virginia Department of Education
Division of Teacher Education and
Licensure
P.O. Box 2120
Richmond, VA 23218
Phone: (800) 292-3820 or (804) 225-2022
http://www.pen.k12.va.us/VDOE/
newvdoe/teached.html

Washington Office of Superintendent of Public Instruction
Professional Education and Certification
Old Capitol Building
P.O. Box 47200
Olympia, WA 98504-7200
Phone: (360) 725-6400
http://www.k12.wa.us/certification

West Virginia Department of Education
1900 Kanawha Boulevard East
Charleston, WV 25305
Phone: (800) 982-2378
http://wvde.state.wv.us/certification

Wisconsin Department of Public Instruction
Teacher Education, Professional
Development and Licensing
P.O. Box 7841
Madison, WI 53707-7841
Phone: (608) 266-1027
Fax: (608) 264-9558 or (608) 267-2920
http://dpi.state.wi.us/tepdl

Wyoming Department of Education
Professional Teaching Standards Board
1920 Thomas Avenue, Suite 400
Cheyenne, WY 82001
Phone: (800) 675-6893 or (307) 777-7291
Fax: (307) 777-6234
http://www.k12.wy.us/ptsb/index.html

APPENDIX IV
PROFESSIONAL UNIONS AND
ASSOCIATIONS

Listed below are the main offices for the professional organizations that are mentioned in this book. You can contact these groups or visit their Web sites to learn about careers, job opportunities, training programs, continuing education programs, professional certification programs, and so on. Many of these organizations have branch offices, as well as student chapters.

Other local, state, regional, and national professional organizations are also available. To learn about other relevant professional associations and unions, contact local professionals.

Note: All contact information and Web site addresses were current when this book was being written. If a URL no longer works, you may be able to find an organization's new Web site by entering its name in a search engine.

PRE-K–12 TEACHERS

**American Council on the Teaching of
  Foreign Languages**
700 South Washington Street, Suite 210
Alexandria, VA 22314
Phone: (703) 894-2900
Fax: (703) 894-2905
http://www.actfl.org

American Federation of Teachers
555 New Jersey Avenue NW
Washington, DC 20001
Phone: (202) 879-4400
http://www.aft.org

Council for Exceptional Children
1110 North Glebe Road, Suite 300
Arlington, VA 22201
Phone: (800) 224-6830, (888) 232-7733,
  or (703) 620-3660
TTY: (866) 915-5000
Fax: (703) 264-9494
http://www.cec.sped.org

International Reading Association
800 Barksdale Road
P.O. Box 8139
Newark, DE 19714-8139
Phone: (800) 336-7323 or (302) 731-1600
Fax: (302) 731-1057
http://www.reading.org

National Art Education Association
1916 Association Drive
Reston, VA 20191-1590

Phone: (703) 860-8000
Fax: (703) 860-2960
http://www.naea-reston.org

**National Association for the Education
  of Young Children**
1509 Sixteenth Street NW
Washington, DC 20036
Phone: (800) 424-2460 or (202) 232-8777
Fax: (202) 328-1846
http://www.naeyc.org

National Child Care Association
2025 M Street NW, Suite 800
Washington, DC 20036-3309
Phone: (800) 543-7161 or (202) 367-1133
Fax: (202) 367-2133
http://www.nccanet.org

National Council for the Social Studies
8555 Sixteenth Street, Suite 500
Silver Spring, MD 20910
Phone: (301) 588-1800
Fax: (301) 588-2049
http://www.ncss.org

National Council of Teachers of English
1111 West Kenyon Road
Urbana, IL 61801-1096
Phone: (877) 369-6283 or (217) 328-3870
http://www.ncte.org

**National Council of Teachers of
  Mathematics**
1906 Association Drive
Reston, Virginia 20191

Phone: (703) 620-9840
Fax: (703) 476-2970
http://www.nctm.org

National Education Association
1201 Sixteenth Street NW
Washington, DC 20036
Phone: (202) 833-4000
http://www.nea.org

National Head Start Association
1651 Prince Street
Alexandria, VA 22314
Phone: (703) 739-0875
Fax: (703) 739-0878
http://www.nhsa.org

National Middle School Association
4151 Executive Parkway, Suite 300
Westerville, OH 43081
Phone: (800) 528-6672 or (614) 895-4730
Fax: (614) 895-4750
http://www.nmsa.org

National Science Teachers Association
1840 Wilson Boulevard
Arlington, VA 22201
Phone: (703) 243-7100
http://www.nsta.org

National Substitute Teachers Alliance
802 East Sixth Street
Apopka, FL 32703
Phone: (888) 304-4001
http://www.nstasubs.org

PRE-K–12 TEACHING SPECIALISTS

American Federation of Teachers
555 New Jersey Avenue NW
Washington, DC 20001
Phone: (202) 879-4400
http://www.aft.org

American String Teachers Association
4153 Chain Bridge Road
Fairfax, VA 22030
Phone: (703) 279-2113
Fax: (703) 279-2114
http://www.astaweb.com

Council for Exceptional Children
1110 North Glebe Road, Suite 300
Arlington, VA 22201
Phone: (800) 224-6830, (888) 232-7733,
  or (703) 620-3660
TTY: (866) 915-5000
Fax: (703) 264-9494
http://www.cec.sped.org

International Reading Association
800 Barksdale Road
P.O. Box 8139
Newark, DE 19714-8139
Phone: (800) 336-7323 or (302) 731-1600
Fax: (302) 731-1057
http://www.reading.org

Learning Disabilities Association of America
4156 Library Road
Pittsburgh, PA 15234-1349
Phone: (412) 341-1515
Fax: (412) 344-0224
http://www.1danat1.org

MENC: The National Association for Music Education
1806 Robert Fulton Drive
Reston, VA 20191
Phone: (800) 336-3768 or (703) 860-4000
Fax: (703) 860-1531
http://www.menc.org

National Association for Bilingual Education
1030 Fifteenth Street NW, Suite 470
Washington, DC 20005
Phone: (202) 898-1829
Fax: (202) 789-2866
http://www.nabe.org

National Association for Sport and Physical Education
1900 Association Drive
Reston, VA 20191
Phone: (800) 213-7193 or (703) 476-3400
http://www.aahperd.org/naspe

National Education Association
1201 Sixteenth Street NW
Washington, DC 20036
Phone: (202) 833-4000
http://www.nea.org

TESOL, Inc.
700 South Washington Street, Suite 200
Alexandria, VA 22314
Phone: (888) 547-3369 or (703) 836-0774
Fax: (703) 836-7864 or (703) 836-6447
http://www.tesol.org

POSTSECONDARY EDUCATORS

American Association for Adult and Continuing Education
10111 Martin Luther King, Jr. Highway
Suite 200C
Bowie, MD 20720
Phone: (301) 459-6261
Fax: (301) 459-6241
http://www.aaace.org

American Association of Family and Consumer Sciences
400 North Columbus Street, Suite 202
Alexandria, VA 22314
Phone: (703) 706-4600 or (800) 424-8080
Fax: (703) 706-4663
http://www.aafcs.org

American Association of University Professors
1012 Fourteenth Street NW, Suite 500
Washington, DC 20005
Phone: (202) 737-5900
Fax: (202) 737-5526
http://www.aaup.org

American Correctional Association
4380 Forbes Boulevard
Lanham, MD 20706-4322
Phone: (800) 222-5646 or (301) 918-1800
http://www.aca.org

American Dairy Science Association
1111 North Dunlap Avenue
Savoy, IL 61874
Phone: (217) 356-5146
Fax: (217) 398-4119
http://www.adsa.org

American Farm Bureau
600 Maryland Avenue SW, Suite 500
Washington, DC 20024
Phone: (202) 406-3600

Fax: (202) 406-3604
http://www.fb.org

American Federation of Teachers— Higher Education Division
555 New Jersey Avenue NW
Washington, DC 20001
Phone: (202) 879-4400
http://www.aft.org/higher_ed

American Jail Association
1135 Professional Court
Hagerstown, MD 21740-5853
Phone: (301) 790-3930
http://www.corrections.com/aja

American Society for Training and Development
1640 King Street, Box 1443
Alexandria, VA 22313-2043
Phone: (800) 628-2783 or (703) 683-8100
Fax: (703) 683-8103
http://www.astd.org

Association for Career and Technical Education
1410 King Street
Alexandria, VA 22314
Phone: (800) 826-9972 or (703) 683-3111
Fax: (703) 683-7424
http://www.acteonline.org

Correctional Education Association
8182 Lark Brown Road, Suite 202
Elkridse, MD 21075
Phone: (800) 783-1232
Fax: (443) 459-3088
http://www.ceanational.org

Council for Learning Disabilities
P.O. Box 4014
Leesburg, VA 20177
Phone: (571) 258-1010
Fax: (571) 258-1011
http://www.cldinternational.org

International Reading Association
800 Barksdale Road
P.O. Box 8139
Newark, DE 19714-8139
Phone: (800) 336-7323 or (302) 731-1600
Fax: (302) 731-1057
http://www.reading.org

National Association of Scholars
221 Witherspoon Street, Second Floor
Princeton, NJ 08542-3215
Phone: (609) 683-7878
Fax: (609) 683-0316
http://www.nas.org

**National Association of County
    Agricultural Agents**
252 North Park Street
Decatur, IL 62523
Phone: (217) 876-1220
Fax: (217) 877-5382
http://www.nacaa.com

**National Association of Extension 4-H
    Agents**
1235-E East Boulevard, Suite 213
Charlotte, NC 28203
Phone: (704) 333-3234
http://www.nae4ha.org

**National Association of Industrial and
    Technical Teacher Educators**
http://www.coe.uga.edu/naitte

**National Education Association—
    Higher Education Division**
1201 Sixteenth Street NW
Washington, DC 20036
Phone: (202) 833-4000
http://www.nea.org/he

National Epsilon Sigma Phi
http://espnational.org

**National Extension Association of
    Family and Consumer Sciences**
P.O. Box 849
Winchester, VA 22604-0849
Phone: (800) 808-9133 or (540) 678-9955
Fax: (540) 678-9940
http://www.neafcs.org

Skills USA-VICA
P.O. Box 3000
Leesburg, VA 20177-0300
Phone: (703) 777-8810
Fax: (703) 777-8999
http://www.skillsusa.org

TESOL, Inc.
700 South Washington Street, Suite 200
Alexandria, VA 22314
Phone: (888) 547-3369 or (703) 836-0774
Fax: (703) 836-7864 or (703) 836-6447
http://www.tesol.org

OVERSEAS TEACHERS

**Association for the Advancement of
    International Education**
http://www.aaie.org

**International Association of Teachers
    of English as a Foreign Language**
http://www.iatefl.org

International Reading Association
800 Barksdale Road

P.O. Box 8139
Newark, DE 19714-8139
Phone: (800) 336-7323 or (302) 731-1600
Fax: (302) 731-1057
http://www.reading.org

**National Council of Teachers of
    Mathematics**
1906 Association Drive
Reston, VA 20191-1593
Phone: (703) 620-9840
Fax: (703) 476-2970
http://www.nctm.org

TESOL, Inc.
700 South Washington Street, Suite 200
Alexandria, VA 22314
Phone: (888) 547-3369 or (703) 836-0774
Fax: (703) 836-7864 or (703) 836-6447
http://www.tesol.org

SCHOOL ADMINISTRATORS

**American Association of School
    Administrators**
801 North Quincy Street, Suite 700
Arlington, VA 22203-1730
Phone: (703) 528-0700
Fax: (703) 841-1543
http://www.aasa.org

**American Association of School
    Personnel Administrators**
533-B North Mur-Len
Olathe, KS 66062
Phone: (913) 829-2007
Fax: (913) 829-2041
http://www.aaspa.org

**American Federation of School
    Administrators, AFL-CIO**
1101 Seventeenth Street NW, Suite 408
Washington, DC 20036
Phone: (202) 986-4209
Fax: (202) 986-4211
http://www.admin.org

**Association for Supervision and
    Curriculum Development**
1703 North Beauregard Street
Alexandria, VA 22311-1714
Phone: (800) 933-2723 or (703) 578-9600
Fax: (703) 575-5400
http://www.ascd.org

**Association of School Business Officials
    International**
11401 North Shore Drive
Reston, VA 20190-4200
Phone: (703) 478-0405 or (866) 682-2729

Fax: (703) 478-0205
http://asbointl.org

Council for Exceptional Children
1110 North Glebe Road, Suite 300
Arlington, VA 22201
Phone: (800) 224-6830, (888) 232-7733,
    or (703) 620-3660
TTY: (866) 915-5000
Fax: (703) 264-9494
http://www.cec.sped.org

International Reading Association
800 Barksdale Road
P.O. Box 8139
Newark, DE 19714-8139
Phone: (800) 336-7323 or (302) 731-1600
Fax: (302) 731-1057
http://www.reading.org

**National Association for the Education
    of Young Children**
1509 Sixteenth Street NW
Washington, DC 20036
Phone: (800) 424-2460 or (202) 232-8777
Fax: (202) 328-1846
http://www.naeyc.org

**National Association of Elementary
    School Principals**
1615 Duke Street
Alexandria, VA 22314
Phone: (800) 386-2377 or (703) 684-3345
Fax: (800) 396-2377
http://www.naesp.org

**National Association of Secondary
    School Principals**
1904 Association Drive
Reston, VA 20191-1537
Phone: (800) 253-7746 or (703) 860-0200
http://www.principals.org

**National Business Education
    Association**
1914 Association Drive
Reston, VA 20191-1596
Phone: (703) 860-8300
Fax: (703) 620-4483
http://www.nbea.org

National Child Care Association
1016 Rosser Street
Conyers, GA 30012
Phone: (800) 543-7161
Fax: (770) 388-7772
http://www.nccanet.org

National Council for the Social Studies
8555 Sixteenth Street, Suite 500
Silver Spring, MD 20910
Phone: (301) 588-1800

Fax: (301) 588-2049
http://www.ncss.org

National Middle School Association
4151 Executive Parkway, Suite 300
Westerville, OH 43081
Phone: (800) 528-6672 or (614) 895-4730
Fax: (614) 895-4750
http://www.nmsa.org

Phi Delta Kappa
408 North Union Street
P.O. Box 789
Bloomington, IN 47402-0789
Phone: (800) 766-1156 or (812) 339-1156
Fax: (812) 339-0018
http://www.pdkintl.org

School Nutrition Association
700 South Washington Street, Suite 300
Alexandria, VA 22314
Phone: (703) 739-3900
Fax: (703) 739-3915
http://www.schoolnutrition.org

Urban Superintendents Association of America
P.O. Box 1248
Chesapeake, VA 23327-1248
Phone: (757) 436-1032
http://www.usaa.org

HIGHER EDUCATION ADMINISTRATORS

American Association of Collegiate Registrars and Admissions Officers
1 Dupont Circle NW, Suite 520
Washington, DC 20036
Phone: (202) 293-9161
Fax: (202) 872-8857
http://www.aacrao.org

American Association of University Administrators
Roberts Hall 407
Rhode Island College
Providence, RI 02908-1991
Phone: (401) 456-2808
Fax: (401) 456-8287
http://www.aaua.org

ACPA: College Student Educators International
1 Dupont Circle, Suite 300
Washington, DC 20036-1188
Phone: (202) 835-2272
Fax: (202) 296-3286
http://www.myacpa.org

American Conference of Academic Deans
1818 R Street NW
Washington, DC 20009
Phone: (202) 884-7419
Fax: (202) 265-9532
http://www.acad-edu.org

ASIS International
1625 Prince Street
Alexandria, VA 22314-2818
Phone: (703) 519-6200
Fax: (703) 519-6299
http://www.asisonline.org

Association of College Administration Professionals
P.O. Box 1389
Staunton, VA 24402
Phone: (540) 885-1873
Fax: (540) 885-6133
http://www.acap.org

Association of Fundraising Professionals
1101 King Street, Suite 700
Alexandria, VA 22314
Phone: (703) 684-0410
Fax: (703) 684-0540
http://www.afpnet.org

College and University Professional Association for Human Resources
Tyson Place
2607 Kingston Pike, Suite 250
Knoxville, TN 37919
Phone: (865) 637-7673
Fax: (865) 637-7674
http://www.cupahr.org

International Association of Campus Law Enforcement Administrators
342 North Main Street
West Hartford, CT 06117-2507
Phone: (860) 586-7517
Fax: (860) 586-7550
http://www.iaclea.org

International Association of Chiefs of Police
515 North Washington Street
Alexandria, VA 22314
Phone: (800) THE-IACP or
(703) 836-6767
Fax: (703) 836-4543
http://www.theiacp.org

National Association of Collegiate Directors of Athletics
P.O. Box 16428
Cleveland, OH 44116
Phone: (440) 892-4000

Fax: (440) 892-4007
http://www.nacda.collegesports.com

National Association of Collegiate Women Athletics Administrators
4701 Wrightsville Avenue
Oak Park D-1
Wilmington, NC 28403
Phone: (910) 793-8244
Fax: (910) 793-8246
http://www.nacwaa.org

National Association of Scholars
221 Witherspoon Street, Second Floor
Princeton, NJ 08542-3215
Phone: (609) 683-7878
Fax: (609) 683-0316
http://www.nas.org

National Association of Student Personnel Administrators
1875 Connecticut Avenue NW, Suite 418
Washington, DC 20009
Phone: (202) 265-7500
Fax: (202) 797-1157
http://www.naspa.org

EDUCATIONAL ASSISTANTS

American Chemical Society
1155 16th Street NW
Washington, DC 20036
Phone: (800) 227-5558 or (202) 872-4600
Fax: (202) 872-4615
http://www.chemistry.org

American Federation of Teachers— Paraprofessionals and School-Related Personnel
555 New Jersey Avenue NW
Washington, DC 20001
Phone: (202) 879-4400
http://www.aft.org/psrp

American Institute of Biological Sciences
1444 I Street, Suite 200
Washington, DC 20005
Phone: (202) 628-1500
Fax: (202) 628-1509
http://www.aibs.org

American Society for Microbiology
1752 N Street NW
Washington, DC 20036
Phone: (202) 737-3600
http://www.asm.org

Council for Exceptional Children
1110 North Glebe Road, Suite 300
Arlington, VA 22201

Phone: (800) 224-6830, (888) 232-7733,
　or (703) 620-3660
TTY: (866) 915-5000
Fax: (703) 264-9494
http://www.cec.sped.org

National Association for Bilingual
　Education
1030 Fifteenth Street NW, Suite 470
Washington, DC 20005
Phone: (202) 898-1829
Fax: (202) 789-2866
http://www.nabe.org

National Association for the Education
　of Young Children
1509 Sixteenth Street NW
Washington, DC 20036
Phone: (800) 424-2460 or (202) 232-8777
Fax: (202) 328-1846
http://www.naeyc.org

National Career Development
　Association
305 North Beech Circle
Broken Arrow, OK 74012
Phone: (866) FOR-NCDA or
　(916) 663-7060
http://www.ncda.org

National Education Association—
　Education Support Professionals
1201 Sixteenth Street NW
Washington, DC 20036
Phone: (202) 833-4000
http://www.nea.org/esphome

SCHOOL CLASSIFIED STAFF

American Federation of Police and
　Concerned Citizens
6350 Horizon Drive
Titusville, FL 32780
Phone: (321) 264-0911
http://www.aphf.org/afp_cc.html

American Federation of Teachers—
　Paraprofessionals and School-
　Related Personnel
555 New Jersey Avenue NW
Washington, DC 20001
Phone: (202) 879-4400
http://www.aft.org/psrp

Fraternal Order of Police
Grand Lodge
1410 Donelson Pike, Suite A17
Nashville, TN 37217
Phone: (615) 399-0900

Fax: (615) 399-0400
http://www.grandlodgefop.org

International Association of
　Administrative Professionals
10502 Northwest Ambassador Drive
P.O. Box 20404
Kansas City, MO 64195
Phone: (816) 891-6600
Fax: (816) 891-9118
http://www.iaap-hq.org

International Association of Women
　Police
1417 Derby County Crescent
Oakville, Ontario L6M3N8
http://www.iawp.org

International Foundation for
　Protection Officers
P.O. Box 771329
Naples, FL 34107
Phone: (239) 430-0534
Fax: (239) 430-0533
http://www.ifpo.org

National Association of Educational
　Office Professionals
P.O. Box 12619
Wichita, KS 67277
Phone: (316) 942-4822
Fax: (316) 942-7100
http://www.naeop.org

National Association of School
　Resource Officers
14031 FM 315N
Chandler, TX 75758
Phone: (888) 31-NASRO
http://www.nasro.org

National Association of School Safety
　and Law Enforcement Officers
P.O. Box 3147
Oswego, NY 13126
Phone: (315) 529-4858
http://www.nassleo.org

National Education Association—
　Education Support Professionals
1201 Sixteenth Street NW
Washington, DC 20036
Phone: (202) 833-4000
http://www.nea.org/esphome

National Police and Security Officers
　Association of America
P.O. Box 663
South Plainfield, NJ 07080
http://npoaa.tripod.com

School Nutrition Association
700 South Washington Street, Suite 300
Alexandria, VA 22314
Phone: (703) 739-3900
Fax: (703) 739-3915
http://www.schoolnutrition.org

Service Employees International Union
1313 L Street NW
Washington, DC 20005
Phone: (202) 898-3200
TDD: (202) 898-3481
http://www.seiu.org

CLASSIFIED STAFF IN HIGHER EDUCATION

American Culinary Federation
180 Center Place Way
St. Augustine, FL 32095
Phone: (800) 624-9458 or (904) 824-4468
Fax: (904) 825-4758
http://www.acfchefs.org

American Federation of Police and
　Concerned Citizens
6350 Horizon Drive
Titusville, FL 32780
Phone: (321) 264-0911
http://www.aphf.org/afp_cc.html

Fraternal Order of Police
Grand Lodge
1410 Donelson Pike, Suite A17
Nashville, TN 37217
Phone: (615) 399-0900
Fax: (615) 399-0400
http://www.grandlodgefop.org

International Association of Campus
　Law Enforcement Administrators
342 North Main Street
West Hartford, CT 06117-2507
Phone: (860) 586-7517
Fax: (860) 586-7550
http://www.iaclea.org

International Association of Women
　Police
1417 Derby County Crescent
Oakville, Ontario L6M3N8
http://www.iawp.org

International Foundation for
　Protection Officers
P.O. Box 771329
Naples, FL 34103
Phone: (239) 430-0534
Fax: (239) 430-0533
http://www.ifpo.org

National Association of Educational
Office Professionals
P.O. Box 12619
Wichita, KS 67277
Phone: (316) 942-4822
Fax: (316) 942-7100
http://www.naeop.org

National Association of Executive
Secretaries and Administrative
Assistants
900 South Washington Street,
Suite G-13
Falls Church, VA 22046
Phone: (703) 237-8616
Fax: (703) 533-1153
http://www.naesaa.com

National Education Association
1201 Sixteenth Street NW
Washington, DC 20036
Phone: (202) 833-4000
http://www.nea.org

National Police and Security Officers
Association of America
P.O. Box 663
South Plainfield, NJ 07080
http://npoaa.tripod.com

Professional Grounds Management
Society
720 Light Street
Baltimore, MD 21230
Phone: (800) 609-7467
Fax: (410) 752-8295
http://www.pgms.org

SCHOOL SPECIALISTS IN STUDENT SERVICES AND SPECIAL EDUCATION–RELATED SERVICES

American Art Therapy Association
1202 Allanson Road
Mundelein, IL 60060-3808
Phone: (888) 290-0878
   or (847) 949-6064
Fax: (847) 566-4580
http://www.arttherapy.org

American Nurses Association
8515 Georgia Avenue, Suite 400
Silver Spring, MD 20910
Phone: (800) 274-4ANA or
   (301) 628-5000
Fax: (301) 628-5001
http://www.nursingworld.org

American Occupational Therapy
Association
4720 Montgomery Lane
P.O. Box 31220
Bethesda, MD 20824-1220
Phone: (301) 652-2682
TDD: (800) 377-8555
Fax: (301) 652-7711
http://www.aota.org

American Psychological Association
750 First Street NE
Washington, DC 20002-4242
Phone: (800) 374-2721 or (202) 336-5500
TTD/TTY: (202) 336-6123
http://www.apa.org

American School Health Association
7263 State Route 43
P.O. Box 708
Kent, OH 44240
Phone: (330) 678-1601
Fax: (330) 678-4526
http://www.ashaweb.org

American Speech-Language-Hearing
Association
10801 Rockville Pike
Rockville, MD 20852
Phone: (800) 498-2071
TTY: (301) 897-5700
Fax: (301) 571-0457
http://www.asha.org

Council for Educational Diagnostic
Services
Council for Exceptional Children
1110 North Glebe Road, Suite 300
Arlington, VA 22201
Phone: (800) 224-6830, (888) 232-7733,
   or (703) 620-3660
TTY: (866) 915-5000
Fax: (703) 264-9494
http://www.unr.edu/educ/ceds

Council for Exceptional Children
1110 North Glebe Road, Suite 300
Arlington, VA 22201
Phone: (800) 224-6830, (888) 232-7733,
   or (703) 620-3660
TTY: (866) 915-5000
Fax: (703) 264-9494
http://www.cec.sped.org

Learning Disabilities Association of
America
4156 Library Road
Pittsburgh, PA 15234-1349

Phone: (412) 341-1515
Fax: (412) 344-0224
http://www.ldanatl.org

National Association of School Nurses
Western Office:
1416 Park Street, Suite A
Castle Rock, CO 80109
Phone: (866) 627-6767 or
   (303) 663-2329
Fax: (303) 663-0403
Eastern Office:
P.O. Box 1300
163 U.S. Route 1
Scarborough, ME 04070
Phone: (877) 627-6476 or
   (207) 883-2117
Fax: (207) 883-2683
http://www.nasn.org

National Association of School
Psychologists
4340 East West Highway, Suite 402
Bethesda, MD 20814
Phone: (301) 657-0270
TTY: (301) 657-4155
Fax: (301) 657-0275
http://www.nasponline.org

National Association of Social Workers
750 First Street NE, Suite 700
Washington, DC 20002-4241
Phone: (202) 408-8600
http://www.naswdc.org

National Coalition of Creative Arts
Therapies Associations
8455 Colesville Road, Suite 1000
Silver Spring, MD 20910
http://www.nccata.org

National Education Association
1201 Sixteenth Street NW
Washington, DC 20036
Phone: (202) 833-4000
http://www.nea.org

School Social Work Association of
America
P.O. Box 2072
Northlake, IL 60164
Phone: (847) 289-4527
http://www.sswaa.org

COUNSELORS

American Counseling Association
5999 Stevenson Avenue

Alexandria, VA 22304
Phone: (800) 347-6647
TDD: (703) 823-6862
Fax: (800) 473-2329 or (703) 823-0252
http://www.counseling.org

American Federation of Teachers
555 New Jersey Avenue NW
Washington, DC 20001
Phone: (202) 879-4400
http://www.aft.org

American Rehabilitation Counseling Association
5999 Stevenson Avenue
Alexandria, VA 22304
Phone: (800) 347-6647
TDD: (703) 823-6862
Fax: (800) 473-2329 or (703) 823-0252
http://www.arcaweb.org

American School Counselor Association
1101 King Street, Suite 625
Alexandria, VA 22314
Phone: (800) 306-4722 or
    (703) 683-ASCA
Fax: (703) 683-1619
http://www.schoolcounselor.org

Council for Exceptional Children
1110 North Glebe Road, Suite 300
Arlington, VA 22201
Phone: (800) 224-6830, (888) 232-7733,
    or (703) 620-3660
TTY: (866) 915-5000
Fax: (703) 264-9494
http://www.cec.sped.org

International Association of Rehabilitation Professionals
3540 Soquel Avenue, Suite A
Santa Cruz, CA 95062
Phone: (800) 240-9059 or (831) 464-4892
Fax: (831) 576-1417
http://www.rehabpro.org

National Association for the Education of Young Children
1509 Sixteenth Street NW
Washington, DC 20036
Phone: (800) 424-2460 or (202) 232-8777
Fax: (202) 328-1846
http://www.naeyc.org

National Association of Social Workers
750 First Street NE, Suite 700
Washington, DC 20002-4241
http://www.naswdc.org

National Career Development Association
305 North Beech Circle
Broken Arrow, OK 74012
Phone: (866) FOR-NCDA
http://www.ncda.org

National Education Association
1201 Sixteenth Street NW
Washington, DC 20036
Phone: (202) 833-4000
http://www.nea.org

National Employment Counseling Association
5999 Stevenson Avenue
Alexandria, VA 22304
Phone: (800) 347-6647, extension 222
http://www.geocities.com/Athens/
    Acropolis/6491/neca.html

National Middle School Association
4151 Executive Parkway, Suite 300
Westerville, OH 43081
Phone: (800) 528-6672 or (614) 895-4730
Fax: (614) 895-4750
http://www.nmsa.org

National Rehabilitation Counseling Association
P.O. Box 4480
Manassas, VA 20108
Phone: (703) 361-2077
Fax: (703) 361-2489
http://nrca-net.org

CURRICULUM AND INSTRUCTIONAL DEVELOPERS

American Association for Adult and Continuing Education
10111 Martin Luther King, Jr. Highway
    Suite 200C
Bowie, MD 20720
Phone: (301) 459-6261
Fax: (301) 459-6241
http://www.aaace.org

American Association of School Administrators
801 North Quincy Street, Suite 700
Arlington, VA 22203-1730
Phone: (703) 528-0700
Fax: (703) 841-1543
http://www.aasa.org

American Chemical Society
1155 16th Street NW
Washington, DC 20036
Phone: (800) 227-5558 or (202) 872-4600
Fax: (202) 872-4615
http://www.chemistry.org

American Society for Training and Development
1640 King Street, Box 1443
Alexandria, VA 22313-2043
Phone: (800) 628-2783 or (703) 683-8100
Fax: (703) 683-8103
http://www.astd.org

Association for Computing Machinery
1515 Broadway, 17th Floor
New York, NY 10036
Phone: (800) 342-6626 or (212) 869-7440
http://www.acm.org

Association for Educational Communications and Technology
1800 North Stonelake Drive, Suite 2
Bloomington, IN 47404
Phone: (877) 677-AECT or
    (812) 335-7675
http://www.aect.org

Association for Supervision and Curriculum Development
1703 North Beauregard Street
Alexandria, VA 22311-1714
Phone: (800) 933-2723 or (703) 578-9600
http://www.ascd.org

Association for the Advancement of Computing in Education
P.O. Box 3728
Norfolk, VA 23514
Phone: (757) 623-7588
Fax: (703) 997-8760
http://www.aace.org

Association of Educational Publishers
501 Heron Drive, Suite 201
Logan Township, NJ 08085
Phone: (856) 241-7772
Fax: (856) 241-0709
http://www.edpress.org

Association of Shareware Professionals
P.O. Box 1522
Martinsville, IN 46151
Phone: (765) 349-4740
Fax: (765) 349-4744
http://www.asp-shareware.org

Computer Society
Institute of Electrical and Electronics
    Engineers
1730 Massachusetts Avenue NW
Washington, DC 20036-1992
Phone: (202) 371-0101
Fax: (202) 728-9614
http://www.computer.org

Council for Exceptional Children
1110 North Glebe Road, Suite 300
Arlington, VA 22201

Phone: (800) 224-6830, (888) 232-7733, or (703) 620-3660
TTY: (866) 915-5000
Fax: (703) 264-9494
http://www.cec.sped.org

Educational Software Cooperative
127 The Ranch Road
Del Valle, TX 78617
http://www.edu-soft.org

International Reading Association
800 Barksdale Road
P.O. Box 8139
Newark, DE 19714-8139
Phone: (800) 336-7323 or (302) 731-1600
Fax: (302) 731-1057
http://www.reading.org

International Society for Performance Improvement
1400 Spring Street, Suite 260
Silver Spring, MD 20910
Phone: (301) 587-5870
Fax: (301) 587-8573
http://www.ispi.org

MENC: The National Association for Music Education
1806 Robert Fulton Drive
Reston, VA 20191
Phone: (800) 336-3768 or (703) 860-4000
Fax: (703) 860-1531
http://www.menc.org

National Association of Elementary School Principals
1615 Duke Street
Alexandria, VA 22314
Phone: (800) 386-2377 or (703) 684-3345
Fax: (800) 396-2377
http://www.naesp.org

National Association of Secondary School Principals
1904 Association Drive
Reston, VA 20191-1537
Phone: (800) 253-7746 or (703) 860-0200
http://www.principals.org

National Council for the Social Studies
8555 Sixteenth Street, Suite 500
Silver Spring, MD 20910
Phone: (301) 588-1800
Fax: (301) 588-2049
http://www.ncss.org

National Council of Teachers of English
1111 West Kenyon Road
Urbana,IL 61801-1096
Phone: (877) 369-6283 or (217) 328-3870
http://www.ncte.org

TESOL, Inc.
700 South Washington Street, Suite 200
Alexandria, VA 22314
Phone: (888) 547-3369 or (703) 836-0774
Fax: (703) 836-7864 or (703) 836-6447
http://www.tesol.org

EDUCATIONAL AND INSTRUCTIONAL TECHNOLOGY SPECIALISTS

Alliance for Technology Access
1304 Southpoint Boulevard, Suite 240
Petaluma, CA 94954
Phone: (707) 778-3011
TTY: (707) 778-3015
Fax: (707) 765-2080
http://www.ataccess.org

American Association of School Administrators
801 North Quincy Street, Suite 700
Arlington, VA 22203-1730
Phone: (703) 528-0700
Fax: (703) 841-1543
http://www.aasa.org

American Society for Training and Development
1640 King Street, Box 1443
Alexandria, VA 22313-2043
Phone: (800) 628-2783 or (703) 683-8100
Fax: (703) 683-8103
http://www.astd.org

Association for Educational Communications and Technology
1800 North Stonelake Drive, Suite 2
Bloomington, IN 47404
Phone: (812) 335-7675
Fax: (812) 335-7678
http://www.aect.org

Association for the Advancement of Computing in Education
P.O. Box 3728
Norfolk, VA 23514
Phone: (757) 623-7588
Fax: (703) 997-8760
http://www.aace.org

Computer Assisted Language Instruction Consortium
Texas State University
214 Centennial Hall
San Marcos, TX 78666
Phone: (512) 245-1417
Fax: (512) 245-9089
http://calico.org

Computer-Assisted Language Learning Interest Section
TESOL, Inc.
700 South Washington Street, Suite 200

Alexandria, VA 22314
Phone: (703) 836-0774
Fax: (703) 836-7864
http://darkwing.uoregon.edu/~call

International Association for Language Learning Technology
http://iallt.org

International Society for Performance Improvement
1400 Spring Street, Suite 260
Silver Spring, MD 20910
Phone: (301) 587-5870
Fax: (301) 587-8573
http://www.ispi.org

International Society for Technology in Education
Washington DC office
1710 Rhode Island Avenue NW, Suite 900
Washington, DC 20036
Phone: (866) 654-4777 or (202) 861-7777
Fax: (202) 861-0888
Oregon office
480 Charnelton Street
Eugene, OR 97401-2626
Phone: (800) 336-5191 or (541) 302-3777
Fax: (541) 302-3778
http://www.iste.org

International Technology Education Association
1914 Association Drive, Suite 201
Reston, VA 20191-1539
Phone: (703) 860-2100
Fax: (703) 860-0353
http://www.iteaconnect.org

Rehabilitation Engineering and Assistive Technology of North America
1700 North Moore Street, Suite 1540
Arlington, VA 22209-1903
Phone: (703) 524-6686
TTY: (703) 524-6639
Fax: (703) 524-6630
http://www.resna.org

Technology and Media Division
The Council for Exceptional Children
1110 North Glebe Road, Suite 300
Arlington, VA 22201
Phone: (703) 620-3660
http://www.tamcec.org

LIBRARIANS

American Association of School Librarians
50 East Huron Street
Chicago, IL 60611
Phone: (800) 545-2433, extension 4382 or (312) 280-4382

Fax: (312) 664-7459
http://www.ala.org/aasl

American Federation of Teachers
555 New Jersey Avenue NW
Washington, DC 20001
Phone: (202) 879-4400
http://www.aft.org

American Library Association
50 East Huron Street
Chicago, IL 60611
Phone: (800) 545-2433
TDD: (888) 814-7692
http://www.ala.org

**American Society for Information
    Science and Technology**
1320 Fenwick Lane, Suite 510
Silver Spring, MD 20910
Phone: (301) 495-0900
Fax: (301) 495-0810
http://www.asis.org

**Association for Educational
    Communications and Technology**
1800 North Stonelake Drive, Suite 2
Bloomington, IN 47404
Phone: (877) 677-AECT or
    (812) 335-7675
http://www.aect.org

**Association for Library Services to
    Children**
50 East Huron Street
Chicago, IL 60611-2795
Phone: (800) 545-2433, extension 2163
http://www.ala.org/alsc

**Association of College and Research
    Libraries**
50 East Huron Street
Chicago, IL 60611-2795
Phone: (800) 545-2433, extension 2523
    or (312) 280-2523
Fax: (312) 280-2520
http://www.ala.org/acrl

Council of Library/Media Technicians
http://colt.ucr.edu

National Education Association
1201 Sixteenth Street NW
Washington, DC 20036
Phone: (202) 833-4000
http://www.nea.org

Public Library Association
50 East Huron Street
Chicago, IL 60611
Phone: (800) 545-2433, extension 5752
Fax: (312) 280-5029
http://www.pla.org

INDEPENDENT INSTRUCTORS

Aircraft Owners and Pilots Association
421 Aviation Way
Frederick, MD 21701
Phone: (301) 695-2000
Fax: (301) 695-2375
http://www.aopa.org

American Association of Riding Schools
8375 Coldwater Road
Davison, MI 48423-8966
Phone: (810) 496-0360
Fax: (810) 658-9733
http://www.ucanride.com

American Dance Guild
P.O. Box 2006
Lenox Hill Station
New York, NY 10021
Phone: (212) 932-2789
http://www.americandanceguild.org

**American Riding Instructors
    Association**
28801 Trenton Court
Bonita Springs, FL 34134
Phone: (239) 948-3232
Fax: (239) 948-5053
http://www.riding-instructor.com

Certified Horsemanship Association
5318 Old Bullard Road
Tyler, TX 75703
Phone: (800) 399-0138
http://www.cha-ahse.org

Dance Educators of America
P.O. Box 607
Pelham, NY 10803
Phone: (800) 229-3868 or (914) 636-3200
Fax: (914) 636-5895
http://www.deadance.com

**International Rescue Instructors
    Association**
http://www.iria.org

**MENC: The National Association for
    Music Education**
1806 Robert Fulton Drive
Reston, VA 20191
Phone: (800) 336-3768 or (703) 860-4000
Fax: (703) 860-1531
http://www.menc.org

Music Teachers National Association
441 Vine Street, Suite 505
Cincinnati, OH 45202
Phone: (888) 512-5278 or (513) 421-1420
Fax: (513) 421-2503
http://www.mtna.org

**National Association of Dog Obedience
    Instructors**
PMB 369
729 Grapevine Highway
Hurst, TX 76054-2085
http://www.nadoi.org

**National Association of Flight
    Instructors**
EAA Aviation Center
P.O. Box 3086
Oshkosh, WI 54903-3086
Phone: (920) 426-6801
Fax: (920) 426-6865
http://www.nafinet.org

National Dance Association
1900 Association Drive
Reston, VA 20191
Phone: (800) 213-7193, extension 464
http://www.aahperd.org/nda

Professional Ski Instructors of America
133 South Van Gordon Street, Suite 101
Lakewood, CO 80228
http://www.psia.org

HEALTH EDUCATORS

**American Academy of Husband-
    Coached Childbirth**
P.O. Box 5224
Sherman Oaks, CA 91413-5224
Phone: (800) 4-A-BIRTH
http://www.bradleybirth.com

**American Association for Health
    Education**
1900 Association Drive
Reston, VA 20191
Phone: (800) 213-7193, extension 437
http://www.aahperd.org/aahe

American College Health Association
P.O. Box 28937
Baltimore, MD 21240
Phone: (410) 859-1500
Fax: (410) 859-1510
http://www.acha.org

American Dietetic Association
120 South Riverside Plaza, Suite 2000
Chicago, IL 60606
Phone: (800) 877-1600
http://www.eatright.org

American Heart Association
National Center
7272 Greenville Avenue
Dallas, TX 75231
Phone: (800) 242-8721
http://www.americanheart.org

American Public Health Association
800 I Street NW
Washington, DC 20001
Phone: (202) 777-2742
Fax: (202) 777-2534
http://www.apha.org

American Red Cross
National Headquarters
2025 E Street NW
Washington, DC 20006
Phone: (202) 303-4498
http://www.redcross.org

American Safety and Health Institute
4148 Louis Avenue
Holiday, FL 34691
Phone: (800) 682-5067
Fax: (727) 943-7460
http://www.ashinstitute.com

American School Health Association
7263 State Route 43
P.O. Box 708
Kent, OH 44240
Phone: (330) 678-1601
Fax: (330) 678-4526
http://www.ashaweb.org

American Society for Nutrition
9650 Rockville Pike, Suite 4500
Bethesda, MD 20814
Phone: (301) 634-7050
Fax: (301) 634-7892
http://www.asns.org

Association of Labor Assistants and Childbirth Educators
P.O. Box 390436
Cambridge, MA 02139
Phone: (888) 222-5223
   or (617) 441-2500
Fax: (617) 441-3167
http://www.alace.org

Birthworks, Inc.
P.O. Box 2045
Medford, NJ 08055
Phone: (888) TO-BIRTH
http://www.birthworks.org

Childbirth and Postpartum Professional Association
P.O. Box 491448
Lawrenceville, GA 30049
Phone: (888) MY-CAPPA
Fax: (777) 932-7281
http://cappa.net

International and American Associations of Clinical Nutritionists
15280 Addison Road, Suite 130
Addison, TX 75001
Phone: (972) 407-9089
Fax: (972) 250-0233
http://www.iaacn.org

International Childbirth Education Association
P.O. Box 20048
Minneapolis, MN 55420
Phone: (952) 854-8660
Fax: (952) 854-8772
http://www.icea.org

Lamaze International
2025 M Street, Suite 800
Washington, DC 20036
Phone: (800) 368-4404 or (202) 367-1128
Fax: (202) 367-2128
http://www.lamaze.org

National Safety Council
1121 Spring Lake Drive
Itasca, IL 60143-3201
Phone: (630) 285-1121
Fax: (630) 285-1315
http://www.nsc.org

Society for Public Health Education
750 First Street NE, Suite 910
Washington, DC 20002
Phone: (202) 408-9804
Fax: (202) 408-9815
http://www.sophe.org

FITNESS, RECREATION, AND SPORTS PROFESSIONALS

Aerobics and Fitness Association of America
15250 Ventura Boulevard, Suite 200
Ventura, CA 91403
Phone: (877) 968-7263
http://www.afaa.com

American College of Sports Medicine
Mailing address:
P.O. Box 1440
Indianapolis, IN 46206-1440
Street address:
401 West Michigan Street
Indianapolis, IN 46202-3233
Phone: (317) 637-9200
Fax: (317) 634-7817
http://www.acsm.org

American Council on Exercise
4851 Paramount Drive
San Diego, CA 92123
Phone: (800) 825-3636 or (858) 279-8227
Fax: (858) 279-8064
http://www.acefitness.org

American Fitness Professionals and Associates
P.O. Box 214
Ship Bottom, NJ 08008
Phone: (609) 978-7583
http://www.afpafitness.com

American Football Coaches Association
100 Legends Lane
Waco, TX 76706
Phone: (254) 754-9900
http://www.afca.com

American Swimming Coaches Association
2101 North Andrew Avenue, Suite 107
Fort Lauderdale, FL 33311
Phone: (800) 356-2722 or (954) 563-4930
Fax: (954) 563-9813
http://www.swimmingcoach.org

Aquatic Exercise Association
201 Tamiami Trail, South Suite 3
Nokomis, FL 34275
Phone: (888) AEA-WAVE or
   (941) 486-8600
Fax: (941) 486-8820
http://www.aeawave.com

IDEA Health and Fitness Association
10455 Pacific Center Court
San Diego, CA 92121
Phone: (800) 999-4332, extension 7 or
   (858) 535-8979, extension 7
Fax: (858) 535-8234
http://www.ideafit.com

International Association of Tour Managers, North America
9500 Rainier Avenue South, #603
Seattle, WA 98118
Phone: (206) 725-7108
Fax: (206) 725-4020
http://www.tourmanager.org

International Ecotourism Society
733 Fifteenth Street NW, Suite 1000
Washington, DC 20005
Phone: (202) 347-9203
Fax: (202) 387-7915
http://www.ecotourism.org

National Association for Sport and Physical Education
1900 Association Drive
Reston, VA 20191
Phone: (703) 476-3410
Fax: (703) 476-8316
http://www.naspeinfo.org

National Exercise Trainers Association
5955 Golden Valley Road, Suite 240
Minneapolis, MN 55422
Phone: (800) AEROBIC or
   (763) 545-2505
Fax: (763) 545-2524
http://www.ndeita.com

National High School Coaches Association
3276 Nazareth Road
Easton, PA 18045

Phone: (610) 923-0900
Fax: (610) 923-0800
http://www.nhsca.com

National Recreation and Park Association
22377 Belmont Ridge Road
Ashburn, VA 20148-4501
Phone: (703) 858-0784
Fax: (703) 858-0794
http://www.nrpa.org

National Soccer Coaches Association of America
6700 Squibb Road, Suite 215
Mission, KS 66202
Phone: (800) 458-0678 or (913) 362-1747
Fax: (913) 362-3439
http://www.nscaa.com

National Strength and Conditioning Association
1885 Bob Johnson Drive
Colorado Springs, CO 80906
Phone: (800) 815-6826 or (719) 632-6722
Fax: (719) 632-6367
http://www.nsca-lift.org

Outdoor Guides Association
P.O. Box 12996
Tallahassee, Florida 32317
Phone: (850) 671-4409
Fax: (425) 485-3458
http://www.outdoorguidesassociation.com

Women's Basketball Coaches Association
4646 Lawrenceville Highway
Lilburn, GA 30047
Phone: (770) 279-8027
Fax: (770) 279-8473
http://www.wbca.org

ENVIRONMENTAL EDUCATORS AND ANIMAL TRAINERS

American Horse Council
1616 H Street NW, Seventh Floor
Washington, DC 20006
Phone: (202) 296-4031
Fax: (202) 296-1970
http://www.horsecouncil.org

American Humane Association
63 Inverness Drive East
Englewood, CO 80112
Phone: (303) 792-9900
Fax: (303) 792-5333
http://www.americanhumane.org

American Society for the Prevention of Cruelty to Animals
424 East 92nd Street
New York, NY 10128

Phone: (212) 876-7700
http://www.aspca.org

Animal Behavior Society
Indiana University
2611 East 10th Street, #170
Bloomington, IN 47408-2603
Phone: (812) 856-5541
Fax: (812) 856-5542
http://www.animalbehavior.org

Association of National Park Rangers
P.O. Box 108
Larned, KS 67550-0108
http://www.anpr.org

Association of Pet Dog Trainers
150 Executive Center Drive, Box 35
Greenville, SC 29615
Phone: (800) 738-3647
Fax: (864) 331-0767
http://www.apdt.com

Association of Professional Humane Educators
E-mail: aphe@aphe.org
http://aphe.org

Guide Dog Users, Inc.
14311 Astrodome Drive
Silver Spring, Maryland 20906
Phone: (888) 858-1008 or (301) 598-5771
Fax: (301) 871-7591
http://www.gdui.org

Humane Society of the United States
2100 L Street NW
Washington, DC 20037
Phone: (202) 452-1100
http://www.hsus.org

International Association of Canine Professionals
P.O. Box 560156
Montverde, FL 34756-0156
Phone: (407) 469-2008
http://www.dogpro.org

National Association for Humane and Environmental Education
67 Norwich Essex Turnpike
East Haddam, CT 06423
Phone: (860) 434-8666
http://www.nahee.org

National Association for Interpretation
P.O. Box 2246
Fort Collins, CO 80522
Phone: (888) 900-8283 or (970) 484-8283
Fax: (970) 484-8179
http://www.interpnet.com

National Association of Dog Obedience Instructors
PMB 369
729 Grapevine Highway

Hurst, TX 76054-2085
http://www.nadoi.org

National Association of Environmental Professionals
P.O. Box 2086
Bowie, MD 20718
Phone: (888) 251-9902 or (301) 860-1140
Fax: (301) 860-1141
http://naep.org

National Recreation and Park Association
22377 Belmont Ridge Road
Ashburn, VA 20148
Phone: (703) 858-0784
Fax: (703) 858-0794
http://www.nrpa.org

North American Association for Environmental Education
2000 P Street NW, Suite 540
Washington, DC 20036
Phone: (202) 419-0412
Fax: (202) 419-0415
http://www.naaee.org

North American Police Work Dog Association
4222 Manchester Avenue
Perry, OH 44081
Phone: (888) 4CANINE
http://www.napwda.com

United States Police Canine Association
P.O. Box 80
Springboro, OH 45066
Phone: (800) 531-1614
http://www.uspcak9.com

EMPLOYEE TRAINING SPECIALISTS

American Society for Training and Development
1640 King Street, Box 1443
Alexandria, VA 22313-2043
Phone: (800) 628-2783 or (703) 683-8100
Fax: (703) 683-8103
http://www.astd.org

Information Technology Association of America
1401 Wilson Boulevard, Suite 1100
Arlington, VA 22209
Phone: (703) 522-5055
Fax: (703) 525-2279
http://www.itaa.org

International Society for Performance Improvement
1400 Spring Street, Suite 260
Silver Spring, MD 20910
Phone: (301) 587-5870
Fax: (301) 587-8573
http://www.ispi.org

APPENDIX V
RESOURCES ON THE WORLD WIDE WEB

Listed in this appendix are some Web sites that can help you learn more about many of the professions that are discussed in this book. You will also find some resources that provide information about careers and employment.

Note: All Web site addresses were current when this book was being written. If you come across an address that no *longer works, you may be able find the new URL by entering the name of the organization, or individual, or Web site in a search engine.*

GENERAL INFORMATION

Open Directory Project
http://dmoz.org

Wikipedia
http://www.wikipedia.org

World Book Online Reference Center
http://www.aolsvc.worldbook.aol.com/
    wb/Home

GENERAL EDUCATION RESOURCES

Education Resources Information Center (ERIC)
http://www.eric.ed.gov

The Educator's Reference Desk
http://www.eduref.org

National Center for Education Statistics
U.S. Department of Education
http://nces.ed.gov

U.S. Department of Education
http://www.ed.gov

CAREER AND EMPLOYMENT RESOURCES

Academic Employment Network
http://www.academploy.com

America's Job Bank
http://www.ajb.dni.us or
    http://www.jobsearch.org

California Occupational Guides
California Employment Development
    Department

http://www.labormarketinfo.edd.ca.gov/
    cgi/career

CareerPlanner.com
http://www.careerplanner.com

Career Prospects in Virginia
University of Virginia
http://www.ccps.virginia.edu/career_
    prospects

Career Voyages
U.S. Department of Labor and U.S.
    Department of Education
http://www.careervoyages.gov

The High School Graduate.com
http://www.thehighschoolgraduate.com

eHow
(Click on the "Careers/Education" link)
http://www.ehow.com

ISEEK
Minnesota Internet System for Education
    and Employment Knowledge
http://www.iseek.org

Michigan Career Portal
State of Michigan
http://www.michigan.gov/careers

Monster
http://www.monster.com

Occupational Outlook Handbook
U.S. Bureau of Labor Statistics
http://stats.bls.gov/oco

O*NET OnLine
Occupational Information Network
http://online.onetcenter.org

Salary.com
http://www.salary.com

Teen Space: Career Paths
The Internet Public Library
http://www.ipl.org/div/teen/pathways

USA Jobs
U.S. Office of Personnel Management
http://www.usajobs.opm.gov

WetFeet.com
http://www.wetfeet.com

ADMINISTRATIVE SUPPORT PROFESSIONALS

Secretarialsite.com
http://www.secretarialsite.com

ADULT EDUCATION INSTRUCTORS

Division of Adult Education and Literacy
U.S. Office of Vocational and Adult
    Education
http://www.ed.gov/about/offices/list/ovae/
    pi/AdultEd

Education for Adults.com
http://www.educationforadults.com

Learnativity.com
http://www.learnativity.com

National Center for Family Literacy
http://www.famlit.org

National Institute for Literacy
http://nifl.gov

Office of Vocational and Adult Education
U.S. Department of Education
http://www.ed.gov/about/offices/list/ovae

AEROBICS INSTRUCTORS AND PERSONAL TRAINERS

FitMoves.com
http://www.fitmoves.com

Personal Training on the Net
http://www.ptonthenet.com

WebAerobics
http://www.webaerobics.com

ART THERAPISTS

Arts in Therapy Network
http://www.artsintherapy.com

Art Therapy Credentials Board, Inc.
http://www.atcb.org

Art Therapy on the Web
http://www.sofer.com/art-therapy

BILINGUAL TEACHERS

Bilingual Education
Center for Applied Linguistics
http://www.cal.org/topics/bilinged.html

California Association for Bilingual Education
http://www.bilingualeducation.org

BUILDING TRADES WORKERS

Office of Apprenticeship Training, Employer, and Labor Services
Employment and Training Administration
U.S. Department of Labor
http://www.doleta.gov/etainfo/Nt1Pgm/ATELS.cfm

Worldwide Masterlist of Physical Plants
Oklahoma State University
http://www.pp.okstate.edu/plants.php

CAFETERIA MANAGERS

The National Food Service Management Institute
http://www.nfsmi.org

School Meals Program
Food and Nutrition Service
U.S. Department of Agriculture
http://www.fns.usda.gov/cnd

CAREER AND EMPLOYMENT COUNSELORS

Career Planning and Adult Development Network
http://www.careernetwork.org

National Board for Certified Counselors, Inc. and Affiliates
http://www.nbcc.org

CHILDBIRTH EDUCATORS

Becoming a Childbirth Educator FAQ
http://www.childbirth.org/articles/cbefaq.html

BirthSource.com
Perinatal Education Associates, Inc.
http://www.birthsource.com

Childbirth Education Specialists
http://www.childbirtheducation.net

COACHES AND ATHLETIC DIRECTORS

Amateur Athletic Union
http://www.aausports.org

American Sport Education Program
http://www.asep.com

C.O.A.C.H.
Comprehensive Online Access to Coaching Help
http://www.coachhelp.com/index.php

Coaching Jobs.com
http://www.coachingjobs.com

The Market: Job Opportunities in College Athletics
National Collegiate Athletic Association
http://ncaa.thetask.com/market/ads/index.html

National Association for Kinesiology and Physical Education in Higher Education
http://www.csufresno.edu/kines/programs/opera

Sport Information Research Centre
http://www.sirc.ca

Sports Associations
http://www.50states.com/sports/associations.htm

CONTINUING EDUCATION INSTRUCTORS

Accrediting Council for Continuing Education and Training
http://www.accet.org

Ageless Learner
http://agelesslearner.com

University Continuing Education Association
http://www.ucea.edu

COOKS (HIGHER EDUCATION)

Culinary-Careers.org
http://www.culinary-careers.org

National Association of College and University Food Services
http://www.nacufs.org

Simmering Chefs
http://www.kitchenproject.com/SimmeringChefs/index.htm

CORRECTIONAL INSTRUCTORS

Compass1
http://www.voicenet.com/~compass1

The Corrections Connection
http://www.corrections.com

Federal Bureau of Prisons
http://www.bop.gov

National Institute for Correctional Education
http://www.iup.edu/nice

CURRICULUM SPECIALISTS AND INSTRUCTIONAL SUPERVISORS

Kathy Schrock's Guide for Educators
http://school.discovery.com/schrockguide

DANCE TEACHERS

Dance Education Web
http://danceeducationweb.org

National Dance Education Organization
http://www.ndeo.org

Voice of Dance
http://www.voiceofdance.com

DOG TRAINERS

American Dog Trainers Network
http://www.inch.com/~dogs

Canines.com
http://canines.com/index.shtml

Delta Society
http://www.deltasociety.org

Dr. P's Dog Training
http://www.uwsp.edu/psych/dog/dog.htm

K-911 Dog Training Resource Page
www.geocities.com/jetflair/index.html

K9 Search—The Dog Directory
http://k9search.k9nation.net

Leerburg Dog Training Articles
http://leerburg.com/articles.htm

**National Narcotic Detector Dog
    Association**
http://www.nndda.org

EARLY CHILDHOOD EDUCATORS

Child Care Bureau
Administration for Children, Youth, and
    Families
U.S. Department of Health and Human
    Services
http://www.acf.dhhs.gov/programs/ccb

Circle of Inclusion
http://www.circleofinclusion.org/index.
    html

Early Childhood.com
http://www.earlychildhood.com

**Early Childhood Education On Line
    LISTSERV**
University of Maine
http://www.umaine.edu/eceol

The ECE Web Guide
http://www.ecewebguide.com

**National Child Care Information
    Center**
Administration for Children, Youth, and
    Families
U.S. Department of Health and Human
    Services
http://www.nccic.org

Preschool Education.com
http://www.preschooleducation.com

**Standards for Early Childhood
    Teacher Preparation**
compiled by Tom Drummond
North Seattle Community College
http://northonline.sccd.ctc.edu/eceprog/
    standards.html

Zero to Three
http://www.zerotothree.org

EDUCATIONAL SOFTWARE DEVELOPERS

Dr. Dobb's Career Center
http://www.developercareers.com

Educational Software Directory.net
http://www.educational-software-directory.
    net

EFL TEACHERS

**The Center for Adult English
    Language Acquisition**
http://www.cal.org/caela

The Center for Applied Linguistics
http://www.cal.org

Dave's ESL Cafe
by Dave Sperling
http://www.eslcafe.com

eflweb
http://www.eflweb.com

English School Watch
http://www.englishschoolwatch.org

ESL Employment
http://www.eslemployment.com

The Linguistic Funland TESL Page
http://www.linguistic-funland.com/tesl.
    html

Mark's ESL World
http://marksesl.com

The TESOL EduFind Jobs Website
http://www.jobs.edufind.com

ENVIRONMENTAL EDUCATORS

EE Link
http://eelink.net

EnviroEducation.com
http://www.enviroeducation.com

**The Environmental Careers
    Organization**
http://www.eco.org

Green Teacher
http://www.greenteacher.com

National Audubon Society
http://www.audubon.org

National Wildlife Federation
http://www.nwf.org

Nature Conservancy
http://www.nature.org

Office of Environmental Education
U.S. Environmental Protection Agency
http://www.epa.gov/enviroed

Sierra Club
http://www.sierraclub.org

Ubiquity
http://www.geocities.com/RainForest/
    8974/homepage.htm

U.S. Environmental Protection Agency
http://www.epa.gov

ESL TEACHERS (K–12)

Boggle's World
http://bogglesworld.com

Everything ESL.net
by Judie Haynes
http://www.everythingesl.net

**National Clearinghouse for English
    Language Acquisition and Language
    Instruction Educational Programs**
http://www.ncela.gwu.edu

EXTENSION AGENTS

**Cooperative State Research, Education
    and Extension Service**
U.S. Department of Agriculture
http://www.csrees.usda.gov

Local Extension Offices
http://www.csrees.usda.gov/Extension

**National Association of State
    Universities and Land-Grant
    Colleges**
http://www.nasulgc.org

The National 4-H Web
http://www.4-h.org

U.S. Department of Agriculture
http://www.usda.gov

FLIGHT INSTRUCTORS

Aviation Career Guide.com
http://www.aviationcareerguide.com

The Student Pilot Network
http://www.ufly.com

Thirty Thousand Feet (Aviation Directory)
www.thirtythousandfeet.com

U.S. Federal Aviation Administration
http://www.faa.gov

GROUNDSKEEPERS

Professional Landcare Network
http://www.landcarenetwork.org

GUIDE DOG INSTRUCTORS

Guide Dog Foundation for the Blind, Inc.
http://www.guidedog.org

Guide Dogs.com
http://www.guidedogs.com

Guide Dogs of America
http://www.guidedogsofamerica.org

GUIDES

Chicago Tour-Guide Professionals Association
http://www.chicagotourguides.org

Travel Industry Association of America
http://www.tia.org

World Federation of Tourist Guide Associations
http://www.wftga.org

World Tourism Organization
http://www.world-tourism.org

HEALTH EDUCATORS

Health Education Assets Library
http://www.healcentral.org

Health Resources and Services Administration
U.S. Department of Health and Human Services
http://www.hrsa.gov

National Center for Health Education
http://www.nche.org

HIGHER EDUCATION

American Association for Women in Community Colleges
http://www.aims.edu/aawcc

American Association of State Colleges and Universities
http://www.aascu.org

American Association of University Women
http://www.aauw.org

Association of American Universities
http://www.aau.edu

CCollegeJobs.com
http://www.ccollegejobs.com

Chronicle Careers
The Chronicle of Higher Education
http://chronicle.com/jobs

HigherEdjobs.com
http://www.higheredjobs.com

Higher Education Resource Hub
http://www.higher-ed.org

National Association of Independent Colleges and Universities
http://www.naicu.edu

Office of Postsecondary Education
U.S. Department of Education
http://www.ed.gov/about/offices/list/ope

HIGHER EDUCATION ADMINISTRATORS

About Student Affairs
Jesuit Association of Student Personnel Administrators
http://jaspa.creighton.edu/about/student_affairs.htm

American Council on Education
http://www.acenet.edu

Association of College Unions International
http://www.acui.org

Council for Advancement and Support of Education
http://www.case.org

National Association of Student Affairs Professionals
http://www.nasap.net

National Association of Student Personnel Administrators
http://www.naspa.org

StudentAffairs.com
http://studentaffairs.com

HIGHER EDUCATION FACULTY

Academic Web Logs
Chronicle Careers
The Chronicle of Higher Education
http://chronicle.com/jobs/blogs.htm

AdjunctNation.com
http://www.adjunctnation.com

Postdoc Jobs.com
http://www.post-docs.com

Preparing Future Faculty Program
http://www.preparing-faculty.org

HORSE INSTRUCTORS AND HORSE TRAINERS

Equerry.com
http://www.equerry.com

Equine Info
http://www.equineinfo.com

EquuSite.com: The Ultimate Horse Resource
http://www.equusite.com

Shadowood Horse Pages
http://www.geocities.com/Heartland/Valley/1633/horse.html

HUMANE EDUCATORS

International Institute for Humane Education
http://www.iihed.org

The National Humane Education Society
http://www.nhes.org

World Animal Net
http://worldanimal.net

INDEPENDENT CONTRACTORS

Center for Self-Employment Excellence
http://www.self-employmentexcellence.com

Entrepreneur.com
http://www.entrepreneur.com

National Association for the Self-Employed
http://www.nase.org

INSTRUCTIONAL TECHNOLOGY SPECIALISTS (HIGHER EDUCATION)

The Consortium of College and University Media Centers
http://www.ccumc.org

Educational Technology WebRing
http://v.webring.com/hub?ring=edtech

EDUCAUSE
http://www.educause.edu

Instructional Technology Council
http://www.itcnetwork.org

The Teachnology & Webagogy Site
by Rick Ellis
University of Washington
http://staff.washington.edu/rells/teachnology/tandw.html

INSTRUCTIONAL TECHNOLOGY SPECIALISTS (SCHOOL LEVEL)

Hanau Model Schools Partnership
http://modelschools.terc.edu

National Educational Technology Standards Project
http://cnets.iste.org

Net Day Compass
http://www.netdaycompass.org

The Snorkel
http://www.thesnorkel.org

techLearning.com
http://www.techlearning.com

Technology Coordinator's Handbook
Office of Instructional Technology
Pinellas County School Board (Florida)
http://www.schools.pinellas.k12.fl.us/tchandbk/default.htm

Technology in the Classroom Center
Education World
http://www.education-world.com/a_tech/index.shtml

LANGUAGE TECHNOLOGY SPECIALIST (HIGHER EDUCATION)

CALL on the Web
by Claire Bradin Siskin
http://edvista.com/claire/call.html

iLoveLanguages
http://www.ilovelanguages.com

LAW ENFORCEMENT AND SECURITY PROFESSIONALS (HIGHER EDUCATION)

Campus Police and Security Web Sites
http://www.securityoncampus.org/schools/policesites.html

Campus Security
U.S. Department of Education
http://www.ed.gov/admins/lead/safety/campus.html

Police Employment.com
http://www.policeemployment.com

Security Jobs Network
http://securityjobs.net

Security on Campus, Inc.
http://www.securityoncampus.org

LAW ENFORCEMENT AND SECURITY PROFESSIONALS (SCHOOL LEVEL)

Hamilton Fish Institute
http://www.hamfish.org

National School Safety and Security Services
http://www.schoolsecurity.org

National School Safety Center
http://www.nssc1.org

LIBRARIANS

Association for Library and Information Science Education
http://www.alise.org

Become a Librarian.org
Central Jersey Regional Library Cooperative
http://www.becomealibrarian.org

Internet Library for Librarians
http://www.itcompany.com/inforetriever/index.html

Library of Congress
http://www.loc.gov

Libweb
Library Servers via WWW
by Thomas Dowling
http://lists.webjunction.org

LIScareer.com
The Library and Information Science Professional's Career Development Center
http://www.liscareer.com

Lisjobs.com
http://www.lisjobs.com

Progressive Librarians Guild
http://www.libr.org/PLG

Special Libraries Association
http://www.sla.org

LIBRARY MEDIA SPECIALISTS

School Libraries Online
International Association of School Librarianship
http://www.iasl-slo.org

School Libraries.Net
Peter Milbury's School Librarian Web Pages
http://www.school-libraries.net

LIBRARY TECHNICIANS

Library Support Staff.com
http://www.librarysupportstaff.com

MUSIC TEACHERS

American Music Conference
http://www.amc-music.com

College Music Society
http://www.music.org

Music Education Online
http://www.childrensmusicworkshop.com

MusicStaff.com
http://www.musicstaff.com

The Search Beat . . . Music Education Web Guide
Music Education Web Guide
http://www.searchbeat.com/learnmusic.htm

NUTRITIONISTS

Ask the Dietitian
by Joanne Larsen, M.S., R.D., L.D.
http://www.dietitian.com

Food and Nutrition Information Center
National Agricultural Library
U.S. Department of Agriculture
http://www.nal.usda.gov/fnic

OVERSEAS AMERICAN-SCHOOL TEACHERS

Council of International Schools
http://www.cois.org

International Schools Services
http://www.iss.edu

Office of Overseas Schools
U.S. State Department
http://www.state.gov/m/a/os

Overseas Placement Center for Educators
University of Northern Iowa
http://www.uni.edu/placement/overseas

U.S. Department of Defense Education Activity
http://www.dodea.edu

OVERSEAS TEACHERS (GENERAL)

Joy Jobs.com: Teaching Jobs Overseas
http://www.joyjobs.com

Overseas Digest
http://overseasdigest.com

Teach Abroad.com
http://www.teachabroad.com

Transitions Abroad
http://www.transitionsabroad.com

PARK NATURALISTS

The American Society of Naturalists
http://www.amnat.org

eNature.com
National Wildlife Federation
http://www.enature.com

National Park Service
http://www.nps.gov

National Parks Conservation Association
http://www.npca.org

Recreation.gov
http://www.recreation.gov

U.S. National Parks Net
http://www.us-national-parks.net

PEACE CORPS VOLUNTEERS

National Peace Corps Association
http://www.rpcv.org

Peace Corps
http://www.peacecorps.gov

The Peace Gallery
photographs by Peace Corps Volunteers
http://www.peacegallery.org

PHYSICAL EDUCATION TEACHERS

PE Links 4 U
Central Washington University
http://www.pelinks4u.org

Physical Education Web Resources and Links
Utah State Office of Education
http://www.schools.utah.gov/curr/pe_health/web_resources.html

PRIVATE AND INDEPENDENT SCHOOL EDUCATORS

American Montessori Society
http://www.amshq.org

The Association of Boarding Schools
http://www.schools.com

Council for American Private Education
http://www.capenet.org

National Association of Independent Schools
http://www.nais.org

National Private Schools Accreditation Alliance
http://www.npsag.com

REHABILITATION COUNSELORS

The National Clearinghouse of Rehabilitation Training Materials
Utah State University
http://ncrtm.ed.usu.edu

National Rehabilitation Association
http://www.nationalrehab.org

National Rehabilitation Information Center
http://www.naric.com

Rehabilitation Counseling Web Links
Department of Counseling, Human and Organizational Studies
George Washington University (Washington, D.C.)
http://www.gwu.edu/~chaos/rehab/Links4.htm

RehabJobs.org
http://www.rehabjobs.org

SCHOOL ADMINISTRATORS

Council of Chief State School Officers
http://www.ccsso.org

Council of the Great City Schools
http://www.cgcs.org

ERIC Clearinghouse on Educational Policy and Management
http://eric.uoregon.edu

K-12jobs.com
http://www.k12jobs.com

National Center for Education Information
http://www.ncei.com

National School Boards Association
http://www.nsba.org

School Administrators Center
Education World
http://www.education-world.com/a_admin

SCHOOL BUS DRIVERS

Ladydriver's Homepage
http://www.geocities.com/Heartland/Valley/2733

School Bus Fleet
http://www.schoolbusfleet.com

School Bus World
by Joe Metzler
http://hometown.aol.com/hamjoe/busmain.html

SCHOOL COUNSELORS

Adolescent Directory On-Line
Center for Adolescent and Family Studies
Indiana University
http://education.indiana.edu/cas/adol/counselor.html

The American Academy of Child and Adolescent Psychiatry
http://www.aacap.org

American Mental Health Counselors Association
http://www.amhca.org

Center for School Counseling Outcome Research
University of Massachusetts
http://www.umass.edu/schoolcounseling

SCHOOL CUSTODIANS

Custodial Staffing for School Facilities
National Clearinghouse for Educational Facilities
http://www.edfacilities.org/rl/custodial_staffing.cfm

Custodial Worker's Resource
http://custodian.info

SCHOOL NURSES

Division of Adolescent and School Health
Centers for Disease Control and Prevention
U.S. Department of Health and Human Services
http://www.cdc.gov/HealthyYouth/index.htm

National Board for Certification of School Nurses
http://www.nbcsn.com

SCHOOL OCCUPATIONAL THERAPISTS

American Occupational Therapy Foundation
http://www.aotf.org

National Board for Certification in Occupational Therapy, Inc.
http://www.nbcot.org

Occupational Therapist.com
http://www.occupationaltherapist.com

SCHOOL PSYCHOLOGISTS

Global School Psychology Network
http://www.dac.neu.edu/cp/consult

International School Psychology Association
http://www.ispaweb.org

The School Psychologists' Home Page
http://www.bartow.k12.ga.us/psych/psych.html

School Psychology Resources Online
Sandra Steingart, Ph.D.
http://www.schoolpsychology.net

UC Berkeley School Psychology
http://www-gse.berkeley.edu/program/sp/sp.html

SCHOOL SOCIAL WORKERS

Association of Social Work Boards
http://www.aswb.org

Council on Social Work Education
http://www.cswe.org

International Network for School Social Work
http://internationalnetwork-schoolsocialwork.htmlplanet.com

Office of Juvenile Justice and Delinquency Prevention
Office of Justice Programs,
    U.S. Department of Justice
http://ojjdp.ncjrs.org

SCHOOLTEACHERS

Awesome Library: K–12 Education Directory
http://www.awesomelibrary.org

Education World
http://www.education-world.com

Edutopia
http://www.edutopia.org

Future Educators Association
http://www.pdkintl.org/fea/feahome.htm

K-2jobs.com
http://www.k12jobs.com

Middle School.net
http://www.middleschool.net

MiddleWeb
http://www.middleweb.com

National Board for Professional Teaching Standards
http://www.nbpts.org

National Center for Alternative Certification
http://www.teach-now.org

National Dropout Prevention Centers
http://www.dropoutprevention.org

National Teacher Recruitment Clearinghouse
http://www.recruitingteachers.org

No Child Left Behind (NCLB) Act
U.S. Department of Education
http://www.ed.gov/nclb/landing.jhtml

Teachers Count
http://www.teacherscount.org

Teachers.net
http://teachers.net

Teachers Network.org
http://teachersnetwork.org

Teach for America
http://www.teachforamerica.org

Welcome to Kinder Korner!
http://www.kinderkorner.com

SPECIAL EDUCATION

Disabilities Studies and Services Center
Academy of Educational Development
http://www.dssc.org

EdGate: Special Education and Gifted Corner
http://www.edgateteam.net/sped_gifted/indexsped.htm

National Clearinghouse for Professions in Special Education
http://www.special-ed-careers.org

National Dissemination Center for Children with Disabilities
http://www.nichcy.org

SPECIAL EDUCATION TEACHERS

Marc Sheehan's Special Education/Exceptionality Page
http://www.halcyon.com/marcs/sped.html

Special Education Network
http://www.specialednet.com

Special Education Resources on the Internet
http://seriweb.com

Teacher's Corner
EdGate: Special Education and Gifted Corner
http://www.edgateteam.net/sped_gifted/teacher.htm

SPECIAL EDUCATION TECHNOLOGY SPECIALISTS

ABLEDATA
National Institute on Disability and Rehabilitation Research
http://www.abledata.com

National Center to Improve Practice
Educational Development Center, Inc.
Newton, Massachusetts
http://www.edc.org/NCIP

Washington Assistive Technology Alliance
http://wata.org

SPEECH-LANGUAGE PATHOLOGISTS

Caroline Bowen, Ph.D.
Speech-Language Pathologist
http://members.tripod.com/Caroline_Bowen/home.html

Speech-Language Pathologist.org
http://www.speechpathologist.org

Speech Language Pathology Web Sites
Sandy and Liz Herring
http://www.herring.org/speech.html

SUBSTITUTE TEACHERS

Substitute Teaching Institute
Utah State University
http://subed.usu.edu

Substitute Teaching—Tricks of the Trade
by Mr. Sturgeon, Substitute Teacher
http://www.av.qnet.com/~rsturgn/index.htm

TEACHER AIDES

National Clearinghouse for Paraeducators
Center for Multilingual, Multicultural Research
Rossier School of Education, University of Southern California
http://www.usc.edu/dept/education/CMMR/Clearinghouse.html

National Resource Center for Paraprofessionals
http://www.nrcpara.org

TEXTBOOK EDITORS

Association of American Publishers
http://www.publishers.org

Bookjobs.com
http://www.bookjobs.com

Editing Resources
Bay Area Editors' Forum
http://www.editorsforum.org/resources.html

Editorial Freelancers Association
http://www.the-efa.org

Society of Academic Authors
http://www.sa2.info

Text and Academic Authors Association
http://www.taaonline.net

TRAINING AND DEVELOPMENT SPECIALISTS

Learning and Training FAQs
http://www.learnativity.com/training_FAQs

Training and Development
Workforce Management
http://www.workforce.com/section/11

Training and Development Community Center
http://www.tcm.com/trdev

BIBLIOGRAPHY

A. PERIODICALS

Listed below are some publications that serve the different occupations described in this book. You may be able to find some of the print publications at a public, school, or academic library. Many of the print magazines also allow limited free access to their articles on the Web. Some of the Web-based publications are free, whereas others require a subscription to access certain issues and other resources.

Note: Web site addresses were current when this book was being written. If a URL no longer works, you may be able to find the new address by entering the name of the publication into a search engine.

ADULT EDUCATORS

Adult Basic Education: An Interdisciplinary Journal for Adult Literacy Educators
http://www.coabe.org/journal

Adult Education Quarterly
Phone: (800) 818-7243
http://aeq.sagepub.com

BILINGUAL, ESL, AND EFL TEACHERS

Bilingual Research Journal
http://brj.asu.edu

ESL Magazine
http://www.eslmag.com

The Internet TESL Journal
http://iteslj.org

TIE—The International Educator
P.O. Box 513
Cummaquid, MA 02637
(508) 362-1414; fax: (508) 362-1411
http://www.tieonline.com

CAREER AND EMPLOYMENT COUNSELORS

The Career Development Quarterly
National Career Development Association
P.O. Box 2513
Birmingham, AL 35201-2513
Phone: (800) 633-4931

Journal of Employment Counseling
National Employment Counseling Association
P.O. Box 2513
Birmingham, AL 35201-2513
Phone: (800) 633-4931

DIRECTORS OF PUBLIC SAFETY

The Police Chief
International Association of Chiefs of Police
Phone: (800) THE-IACP, ext. 218
http://policechiefmagazine.org

EDUCATIONAL SOFTWARE DEVELOPERS

Software Development
http://www.sdmagazine.com

INSTRUCTIONAL TECHNOLOGY SPECIALISTS (HIGHER EDUCATION)

Campus Technology
http://www.campus-technology.com

Journal of Technology Education
http://scholar.lib.vt.edu/ejournals/JTE

Language Learning & Technology
http://llt.msu.edu

INSTRUCTIONAL TECHNOLOGY SPECIALISTS (SCHOOL LEVEL)

Electronic School On-line
http://www.electronic-school.com

School CIO
http://techlearning.com/schoolcio

techlearning.com
http://techlearning.com

EMPLOYEE TRAINING SPECIALISTS

Trainingmag.com
http://www.trainingmag.com

EXTENSION AGENTS

Journal of Extension
http://www.joe.org

FLIGHT INSTRUCTORS

Avweb: Internet's Aviation Magazine and News Service
http://www.avweb.com

Landings
http://www.landings.com

Plane and Pilot Magazine
Phone: (800) 283-4330
http://www.planeandpilotmag.com

HIGHER EDUCATION ADMINISTRATORS AND FACULTY

Adjunct Advocate
http://www.adjunctnation.com/magazine

American School & University
http://www.asumag.com

The Chronicle of Higher Education
Circulation Department
1255 23rd Street NW
Washington, DC 20037
Phone: (800) 728-2803
http://chronicle.com

College Planning and Management
http://www.peterli.com/cpm

University Business
http://www.universitybusiness.com

Women in Higher Education
http://www.wihe.com

LIBRARIANS

Ex Libris
http://marylaine.com/exlibris

Library Journal
Phone: (800) 588-1030 or (515) 247-2984
http://www.libraryjournal.com

Library Trends
http://www.lis.uiuc.edu/puboff/catalog/
   trends

School Library Journal
Phone: (800) 595-1066 or (515) 247-2984
http://slj.com

SCHOOL ADMINISTRATORS

American School Board Journal
1680 Duke Street
Alexandria, VA 22314
http://www.asbj.com

Principal
National Association of Elementary
   School Principals
http://www.naesp.org

The School Administrator
American Association of School
   Administrators
Phone: (703) 875-0748
http://www.aasa.org/publications

School Planning and Management
2621 Dryden Road, Suite 300
Dayton, OH 45439
Phone: (800) 558-2292
Fax: (800) 370-4450
http://www.peterli.com/spm

Today's School
2621 Dryden Road, Suite 300
Dayton, OH 45439

Fax: (800) 370-4450
http://www.peterli.com/ts

SCHOOLTEACHERS

The Education Digest
Phone: (800) 530-9673
Fax: (734) 975-2787
http://www.eddigest.com

Education Week
http://www.edweek.org/ew

Edutopia Magazine
The George Lucas Educational Foundation
http://www.edutopia.org

edweek.org
http://www.edweek.org

Learners Online, Inc.
3616 Maple Avenue
Dallas, TX 75219
Phone: (800) 672-6988 or (214) 526-3700
Fax: (214) 521-1021
http://www.learnersonline.com

Phi Delta Kappan
Phone: (800) 766-1156
Fax: (812) 339-0018
http://www.pdkintl.org/kappan/kappan.htm

Physical Education
http://www.pedigest.com

Teacher Magazine
http://www.edweek.org/tm

Teaching Pre K–8 Magazine
http://www.teachingk-8.com

SCHOOL SPECIALISTS IN STUDENT SERVICES AND SPECIAL-EDUCATION RELATED SERVICES

AATA Journal
American Art Therapy Association, Inc.
1202 Allanson Road
Mundelein, IL 60060-3808
Phone: (888) 290-0878 or (847) 949-6064

Fax: (847) 566-4580
http://www.arttherapy.org

Counseling Today Online
American Counseling Association
http://www.counseling.org/Publications/
   CounselingToday.aspx

Journal of School Nursing
National Association of School Nurses
http://www.nasn.org/josn/journal.htm

*Journal of the American Academy of
   Child and Adolescent Psychiatry*
http://www.jaacap.com

The New Social Worker Online
http://www.socialworker.com

School Nurse
http://www.schoolnurse.com

HOW TO FIND MORE PUBLICATIONS

Here are some things you might do to find publications that are specific to a profession in which you are interested.

- Talk with librarians, educators, and professionals for recommendations of publications.
- Check out professional and trade associations. Many of them publish journals, newsletters, magazines, and other publications.
- Visit an online bookstore, such as Amazon.com, to view the listings of magazines it has to offer for sale. Use such keywords as *education, teachers, school administrators,* or *counselors.* If the Web site does not have a search engine for magazines, be sure to add the word *magazines* to your keyword (Example: *education magazines*).

B. BOOKS

Listed below are some book titles about general career information and about some of the different professions that are discussed in this book. To find other books, ask your school or public librarian for help. Also talk with different professionals, and ask them to recommend titles for you to read.

CAREER INFORMATION

Bolles, Richard N. *What Color Is Your Parachute?* Berkeley, Calif.: Ten Speed Press, 2005.

Camenson, Blythe. *Great Jobs for Liberal Arts Majors.* 2nd ed. Chicago: VGM Career Books, 2002.

Eikleberry, Carol. *The Career Guide for Creative and Unconventional People.* Berkeley, Calif.: Ten Speed Press, 1999.

Krannich, Ronald L., and Caryl Rae Krannich. *The Best Jobs for the 21st Century.* 3d ed. Manassas Park, Va.: Impact Publications, 1998.

Krantz, Les. *Job Rated Almanac.* New York: St. Martin's Press, 2002.

Likoff, Laurie, ed. *Encyclopedia of Careers and Vocational Guidance.* 12th ed. New York: Ferguson, 2005.

U.S. Bureau of Labor Statistics. *Career Guide to Industries, 2004–05 Edition (Bulletin 2571).* Washington, D.C.: Bureau of Labor Statistics, 2004. Available online. http://stats.bls.gov/oco/cg.

———. *Occupational Outlook Handbook 2004–05 Edition (Bulletin 2570).* Washington, D.C.: Bureau of Labor Statistics, 2004. Available online. http://stats.bls.gov/oco.

Yate, Martin. *Career Smarts: Jobs with a Future.* New York: Ballantine Books, 1997.

ADULT-EDUCATION INSTRUCTORS

Merriam, Sharon B., and Rosemary S. Caffarella. *Learning in Adulthood: A Comprehensive Guide.* 2d ed. San Francisco: Jossey-Bass Publishers, 1999.

Rios, Lorna. *Me . . . Teach Criminals? The True Adventures of a Prison Teacher.* New York: Vantage Press, 1996.

Vella, Jane. *Learning to Listen, Learning to Teach: The Power of Dialogue in Educating Adults.* Rev. ed. San Francisco: Jossey-Bass Publishers, 2002.

ANIMAL TRAINERS

American Kennel Club. *The Complete Dog Book, 19th Edition.* Foster City, Calif.: Howell Book House, 1998.

Bryson, Sandy. *Police Dog Tactics.* New York: McGraw-Hill, 1996.

Burns, Deborah. *Storey's Horse-Lover's Encyclopedia: An English and Western A-to-Z Guide.* North Adams, Mass.: Storey Publishing, 2001.

Coren, Stanley. *How Dogs Think: Understanding the Canine Mind.* New York: Free Press, 2004.

Eden, R. S. *K9 Officer's Manual.* Calgary: Detselig Enterprises, 1993.

Henderson, Kathy. *I Can Be a Horse Trainer.* Chicago: Childrens Press, 1990.

Lee, Price Mary, and Richard Lee. *Opportunities in Animal and Pet Care Careers.* Chicago: VGM Career Books, 2001.

Thomas, Heather Smith. *Storey's Guide to Training Horses.* North Adams, Mass.: Storey Publishing, 2003.

BILINGUAL AND ESL TEACHERS

Ashton-Warner, Sylvia. *Teacher.* New York: Simon and Schuster, 1986.

Bialystok, Ellen, ed. *Language Processing in Bilingual Children.* New York: Cambridge University Press, 1991.

Franklin, Elizabeth, ed. *Reading and Writing in More than One Language: Lessons for Teachers.* Alexandria, Va.: Teachers of English to Speakers of Other Languages, 1998.

Gehbard, Jerry G. *Teaching English as a Foreign or Second Language.* Ann Arbor: University of Michigan Press, 1996.

Genesee, Fred, ed. *Educating Second Language Children: The Whole Child, the Whole Curriculum, the Whole Community.* New York: Cambridge University Press, 1994.

Ovando, Carlos J., Virginia P. Collier, and Mary Carol Combs. *Bilingual and ESL Classrooms: Teaching in Multicultural Contexts.* 3d ed. Boston: McGraw-Hill, 2003.

COACHES

Chambers, Dave. *Coaching.* Buffalo, N.Y.: Firefly Books, 1997.

COUNSELORS

Baxter, Neale, and Philip A. Perry. *Opportunities in Counseling and Development Careers.* Lincolnwood, Ill.: VGM Career Horizons, NTC Publishing Group, 1997.

Figler, Howard, and Richard Nelson Bolles. *Career Counselor's Handbook.* Berkeley, Calif.: Ten Speed Press, 2000.

Kennedy, Eugene, and Sara Charles. *On Becoming a Counselor: A Basic Guide for Non-Professional Counselors.* 3d ed. New York: Crossroad Publishing Company, 2003.

Neukrug, Ed. *The World of the Counselor: An Introduction to the Counseling Profession.* 2d ed. Pacific Grove, Calif.: Thompson-Brooks/Cole Publishing 2003.

DANCE TEACHERS

Hanna, Judith Lynne. *Partnering Dance and Education: Intelligent Moves for Changing Times.* Champaign, Ill.: Human Kinetics, 1999.

H'Doubler, Margaret N. *Dance: A Creative Art Experience.* 3d ed. Madison: University of Wisconsin Press, 1998.

CHILDHOOD EDUCATORS

Dowd, Tom, et. al. *Effective Skills for Child-Care Workers: A Training Manual from Boys Town.* Boys Town, Neb.: Boys Town Press, 1994.

Fujawa, Judy. *(Almost) Everything You Need to Know about Early Childhood Education: A Book of Lists for Teachers and Parents.* Beltsville, Md.: Gryphon House, 1998.

Paley, Vivian Gussin. *The Girl with the Brown Crayon.* Cambridge, Mass.: Harvard University Press, 1998.

Tertell, E. A., S. M. Klein, and J. L. Jewett, eds. *When Teachers Reflect: Journeys Toward Effective, Inclusive Practice.* Washington, D.C.: National Association for the Education of Young Children, 1998.

EDUCATIONAL/INSTRUCTIONAL TECHNOLOGY SPECIALISTS

Connelly, Robert. *Opportunities in Technical Education Careers.* Lincolnwood, Ill.: VGM Career Horizons, NTC Publishing Group, 1997.

Druin, Allison, and Cynthia Solomon. *Designing Multimedia Environments for Children.* New York: John Wiley and Sons, 1996.

Heinich, Robert, et. al. *Instructional Media and Technologies for Learning.* 7th ed. Upper Saddle River, N.J.: Merrill, 2001.

Seels, Barbara, and Rita C. Richey. *Instructional Technology: The Definition and Domains of the Field.* Washington, D.C.: Association for Educational Communications and Technology, 1994.

Stair, Lila B., and Leslie Stair. *Careers in Computers.* Chicago: VGM Career Books, 2002.

EMPLOYEE TRAINING SPECIALISTS

Driscoll, Margaret. *Web-Based Training: Creating e-Learning Experiences.* San Francisco: Jossey-Bass Pfeiffer Publishers, 2002.

Gordon, Edward E., Catherine M. Petrini, and Ann P. Campagna. *Opportunities in Training and Development Careers.* Lincolnwood, Ill.: VGM Career Horizons, NTC/Contemporary Publishing Company, 1998.

Klatt, Bruce. *The Ultimate Training Workshop Handbook.* New York: McGraw-Hill, 1997.

Kruse, Kevin, Jason Keil, and Elliot Masie. *Technology-Based Training: The Art and Science of Design, Development, and Delivery.* San Francisco: Jossey-Bass Publishers, 1999.

Piskurich, George M., Peter Beckschi, and Brandon Hall, eds. *The ASTD Handbook of Training Design and Delivery.* New York: McGraw-Hill, 1999.

ENVIRONMENTAL EDUCATORS

Fasulo, Michael, and Paul Walker. *Careers in the Environment.* Lincolnwood, Ill.: VGM Career Horizons, 2000.

Lingelbach, Jenepher, and Lisa Purcell, eds. *Hands-on Nature: Information and Activities for Exploring the Environment with Children.* Hanover, Vt.: University Press of New England, 2000.

Orr, David W. *Earth in Mind: On Education, Environment, and the Human Prospect.* Washington, D.C.: Island Press, 2004.

Shenk, Ellen. *Outdoor Careers: Exploring Occupations in Outdoor Fields.* Mechanicsburg, Pa.: Stackpole Books, 2000.

FITNESS AND RECREATION PROFESSIONALS

Aerobics and Fitness Association of America. *Exercise Standards and Guidelines: A Reference Manual for Fitness Professionals.* Sherman Oaks, Calif.: Aerobics and Fitness Association of America, 1995.

Camenson, Blythe. *Careers for Health Nuts and Others Who Like to Stay Fit.* Chicago: VGM Career Books, 2004.

Cotton, Richard T, ed. *Personal Trainer Manual: The Resource for Fitness Professionals.* 2d ed. San Diego, Calif.: American Council on Exercise, 1996.

Gaut, Ed. *The Personal Trainer Business Handbook.* Gaithersburg, Md.: Willow Creek Publications, 1994.

Jordan, Peg, ed. *Fitness: Theory and Practice.* 2d ed. Sherman Oaks, Calif.: Aerobics and Fitness Association of America, 1997.

Miller, Mary. *Opportunities in Fitness Careers.* Lincolnwood, Ill.: VGM Career Horizons, 1997.

Taylor, Bill, and Christine Cochrane Yukevich. *Personal Training: Why Not You?* Allison Park, Pa.: Lion Press, 1996.

HEALTH EDUCATORS

American Heart Association. *Heartsaver Facts: First Aid, AED, CPR, Training System.* Boston: Jones and Bartlett Pub., 1998.

Korte, Diana, and Roberta Scaer. *A Good Birth, A Safe Birth.* 3d ed. Boston: Harvard Common Press, 1992.

National Safety Council. *CPR and AED.* 4th ed. Boston: Jones and Bartlett Pub., 2002.

———. *Essentials of First Aid and CPR.* Boston: Jones and Bartlett Pub., 1997.

Robotti, Suzanne B., and Margaret Ann Inman. *Childbirth Instructor Magazine's Guide to Careers in Birth.* New York: John Wiley and Sons, 1998.

HIGHER EDUCATION EDUCATORS

Altbach, Philip G., Robert O. Berdahl, and Patricia J. Gunport. *American Higher Education in the Twenty-first Century: Social, Political, and Economic Challenges.* 2d ed. Baltimore: Johns Hopkins University Press, 2005.

Boice, Robert. *Advice for New Faculty Members.* Boston: Allyn and Bacon, 2000.

Goldsmith, John A., John Komlos, and Penny Schine Gold. *The Chicago Guide to Your Academic Career: A Portable Mentor for Scholars from Graduate School through Tenure.* Chicago: University of Chicago Press, 2001.

Heiberger, Mary Morris, and Julia Miller Vick. *The Academic Job Search Handbook.* 3d ed. Philadelphia: University of Pennsylvania Press, 2001.

Lucas, Christopher J., and John W. Murry. *New Faculty: A Practical Guide for Academic Beginners.* New York: Palgrave Macmillan, 2002.

McKeachie, Wilbert J. *McKeachie's Teaching Tips: Strategies, Research, and Theory for College and University Teachers.* Boston: Houghton Mifflin, 2002.

Vesilind, P. Aarne. *So You Want to Be a Professor?: A Handbook for Graduate Students.* Thousand Oaks, Calif.: Sage Publications, 1999.

LIBRARIANS

McCook, Kathleen de la Peña, and Margaret Myers, revision by Blythe Camenson. *Opportunities in Library and Information Science Careers.* Chicago: VGM Career Books, 2002.

MUSIC TEACHERS

American Music Conference. *Exploring Careers in Music.* 2d ed. Reston, Va.: MENC: The Association for Music Education, 2000.

Hamann, Donald L., ed. *Creativity in the Music Classroom.* Reston, Va.: Music Educators National Conference, 1991.

OVERSEAS TEACHERS

Griffith Susan. *Teaching English Abroad: Talk Your Way around the World!* 6th ed. Oxford Vacation-Work, 2003.

Krannich, Ronald L., and Caryl Rae Krannich. *Travel Lovers: Opportunities at Home and Abroad.* 4th ed. Manassas Park, Va.: Impact Publications, 2003.

SCHOOL ADMINISTRATORS

Ackerman, Richard H., et. al. *Making Sense as a School Leader: Persisting Questions, Creative Opportunities.* San Francisco: Jossey-Bass Publishers, 1996.

Carter, Gene R., and William G. Cunningham. *The American School Superintendent: Leading in an Age of Pressure.* San Francisco: Jossey-Bass Publishers, 1997.

Connors, Nelia A. *If You Don't Feed the Teachers, They Eat the Students! Guide to Success for Administrators and Teachers.* Nashville, Tenn.: Incentive Publications, 2000.

Darling-Hammond, Linda. *The Right to Learn.* San Francisco: Jossey-Bass Publishers, 1997.

Monroe, Lorraine. *Nothing's Impossible: Leadership Lessons from Inside and Outside the Classroom.* New York: Public Affairs, 1999.

Robbins, Pam, and Harvey B. Alvy. *The Principal's Companion: Strategies and Hints to Make the Job Easier.* 2d ed. Thousand Oaks, Calif.: Corwin Press, 2002.

Thorpe, Ronald, ed. *The First Year as Principal: Real World Stories form America's Principals.* Portsmouth, N.H.: Heinemann, 1995.

Whitaker, Todd. *What Great Principals Do Differently: Fifteen Things That Matter Most.* Larchmont, N.Y.: Eye on Education, 2002.

SCHOOLTEACHERS

Bambino, Deborah. *Teaching Out Loud: A Middle Grades Diary.* Westerville, Ohio: National Middle School Association, 1999.

Boyles, Nancy S., and Darlene Contadino. *The Learning Differences Sourcebook.* Los Angeles: Lowell House, 1998.

Codell, Esmé Raji. *Educating Esmé: Diary of a Teacher's First Year.* Chapel Hill, N.C.: Algonquin Books, 1999.

Connelly, F. Michael, and D. Jean Clandinin, eds. *Shaping a Professional Identity: Stories of Educational Practice.* New York: Teachers College Press, 1999.

Connelly, Robert. *Opportunities in Special Education Careers.* Lincolnwood, Ill.: VGM Career Horizons, NTC Publishing Group, 1994.

Cramer, Eugene H., and Marietta Castle, eds. *Fostering the Love of Reading: The Affective Domain in Reading Education.* Newark, Del.: International Reading Association, 1994.

Culatta, Richard A., James R. Tompkins, and Margaret G. Werts. *Fundamentals of Special Education: What Every Teacher Needs to Know.* Upper Saddle River, N.J.: Merrill-Prentice Hall, 2003.

Cunningham, Patricia Marr (preface), and Richard L. Allington (preface). *Classrooms That Work: They Can All Read and Write.* 3d ed. Boston: Allyn and Bacon, 2003.

Edelfelt, Roy A., and Alan Reiman. *Careers in Education* Chicago: VGM Career Books, 2004.

Fine, Janet. *Opportunities in Teaching Careers.* New York: McGraw-Hill, 2005.

Gallas, Karen. *The Languages of Learning: How Children Talk, Write, Dance, Draw, and Sing Their Understanding of the World.* New York: Teachers College Press, 1994.

Glasser, William. *The Quality School Teacher.* 3d ed. New York: HarperPerennial, 1998.

Hancock, Joelie, ed. *The Explicit Teaching of Reading.* Newark, Del.: International Reading Association, 1999.

Haselkorn, David, and Andrew Calkins. *How to Become a Teacher: A Complete Guide.* Belmont, Mass.: Recruiting New Teachers, Inc., 2000.

Kane, Pearl Rock, ed. *Independent Schools, Independent Thinkers.* San Francisco: Jossey-Bass, 1992.

Kraut, Harvey. *Teaching and the Art of Successful Classroom Management: A How-to Guidebook for Teachers in Secondary Schools.* 3rd ed. Staten Island, N.Y.: AYSA Pub., 2000.

MacKenzie, Robert J. *Setting Limits in the Classroom: How to Move beyond the Classroom Dance of Discipline.* 2d ed. Roseville, Calif.: Prima Pub, 2003.

Pickering, Sam. *Letters to a Teacher.* New York: Atlantic Monthly Press, 2004.

Sell, Colleen, ed. *A Cup of Comfort for Teachers.* Avon, Mass.: Adams Media, 2004.

Siegel, Lawrence M., and Marcia Stewart, ed. *The Complete IEP Guide: How to Advocate Your Special Ed Child.* 3d ed. Berkeley, Calif.: Nolo Press, 2004.

Sizer, Theodore R., and Nancy Faust Sizer. *The Students Are Watching: Schools and the Moral Contract.* Boston: Beacon Press, 1999.

Stephenson, Frederick J., Jr., ed. *Extraordinary Teachers.* Kansas City, Mo.: Andrews McMeel Publishers, 2001.

Swope, Sam. *I Am a Pencil.* New York: Henry Holt and Company, 2004.

Thompson, Julia G. *First Year Teachers Survival Kit.* San Francisco: Jossey-Bass, 2002.

Wilhelm, Jeffrey D., and Michael W. Smith. *"You Gotta Be the Book": Teaching Engaged and Reflective Reading with Adolescents.* New York: Teachers College Press, 1996.

Winebrenner, Susan, and Pamela Espeland, ed. *Teaching Kids with Learning Disabilities in the Regular Classroom.* Minneapolis: Free Spirit Pub, 1996.

Wong, Harry K., and Rosemary T. Wong. *How to Be an Effective Teacher the First Day of School.* Mountain View, Calif.: Harry K. Wong Publications, 2001.

INDEX

Boldface page numbers denote main entries.